I0809151

BRIDLES AND BISCUITS

RED RIVER BOOKS,
Sponsored by Texas A&M University–Texarkana
Laura Sikes, General Editor

N S
L O N Y
the reserve
Line
Road
Clear Creek
Bay
Bolivar
Brasoria
Galveston
East Bay

BRIDLES AND BISCUITS

Contraband Culture in Spanish East Texas

GARY L. PINKERTON

in collaboration with

Tom H. Gann

TEXAS A&M UNIVERSITY PRESS

COLLEGE STATION

Copyright © 2025 Gary L. Pinkerton
All rights reserved
First edition

∞ This paper meets the requirements of ANSI/NISO Z39.48–1992 (Permanence of Paper).

Binding materials have been chosen for durability.

Frontis: A Map of Austin's Colony and adjacent Country in Texas drawn principally from actual survey by Stephen F. Austin, circa 1820–29. Courtesy Cumings Family Papers, 1824–1926, Col 8978, Daughters of the Republic of Texas Library Collection.

Library of Congress Cataloging-in-Publication Data

Names: Pinkerton, Gary L., 1954– author. | Gann, Tom H., author.
Title: Bridles and biscuits: the contraband culture of Spanish East Texas, 1770–1813 / Gary L. Pinkerton in collaboration with Tom H. Gann.
Description: First edition. | College Station: Texas A&M University Press, [2024] | Includes bibliographical references and index.
Identifiers: LCCN 2024039531 | ISBN 9781648432644 (hardcover) | ISBN 9781648432651 (ebook)
Subjects: LCSH: Spaniards—Texas, East—History. | Trade routes—Texas, East—History. | Texas, East—Commerce—History. | Texas—History—To 1846.
Classification: LCC F395.S7 P56 2024 | DDC 976.4/02—dc23/eng/20241214
LC record available at https://lccn.loc.gov/2024039531

Everything that you believe in this world that's important—
what's right, what's wrong, what's moral, what's immoral,
how should you live, vote, worship, raise your children—
everything you believe filters like coffee
through what you ever understood about history . . . or not.
—JAMES L. HALEY[i]

CONTENTS

ACKNOWLEDGMENTS

Gary L. Pinkerton

This book would not exist but for the tenacity of Tom H. Gann.

Tom and I began communicating about the old roads and trails of East Texas in 2017 not long after the publication of my first book, *Trammel's Trace, The First Road to Texas from the North.* As a member of the Angelina County Historical Commission and a seventh-generation Texan, Tom had already conducted research focused on the old roads of that county. To his advantage, he had also been involved in real estate for many years, so he knew the kind of riches that land records hold.

Tom noticed a pattern in reviewing land deeds south of Nacogdoches and at key crossings, like the former Gann Ferry on the Neches River. There were mentions of a "royal road" arcing to the southwest that was not part of the network now called El Camino Real de los Tejas. Pulling that historical thread led us toward a broader understanding of an ancient network of trails used for contraband trade. Although the trails are a part of this history, the people who used them and the events in which they played a role are far more significant. Their stories led us to this focus on a unique period of East Texas borderlands history.

In producing this work, I am keenly aware of coming to it as one without academic credentials. My interest in this slice of the Spanish colonial era in East Texas grew out of an innate curiosity and a desire to learn more about our region's rich history. In turning that curiosity into a work worthy of a reader's time, several individuals and organizations have helped with questions at crucial moments. Tom Gann's research has been pivotal and an anchor for the stories that evolved around it. Bob Skiles, an archaeologist and Renaissance man, supported the study with maps, documents, and his rigorous analysis. The two 16-gigabyte USB sticks I received in the mail from him were an honored gift of trust and support. Texas General Land Office staff members Brian Stauffer and Carlos Varela, as well as author Bruce Clavey, have patiently helped with questions regarding translations of Spanish archival documents. John Wheat, the translator for the Béxar Archives, has been supportive as well. Carolyn Spears at the Stone Fort Museum and Renee Benn Lee at the Texas Department of Transportation have weighed in with key components of information at just the right time.

The Béxar Archives at the Briscoe Center for American History at the University of Texas have been a critical primary source for documents from this period. Not only did the COVID-19 pandemic close many of our archives, but there were also other obstacles. In the middle of this research, the Briscoe had to move its repository to a completely different database and struggled to recover digital access. Working together to get past these difficulties has been critical. The Robert Bruce Blake Collection and Blake's translations of the Nacogdoches Archives were key sources for this research; both are available at the East Texas Research Center and in digital editions at the genealogical website Family Search. Advice and support from scholars such as Dr. David La Vere, Dr. Tim Perttula, Dr. Francis X. Galan, Dr. Light T. Cummins, and Dr. Frank de la Teja have been much appreciated. Their wisdom and knowledge kept me on the right track. Tim Seiter, an assistant professor at the University of Texas at Tyler, has been both knowledgeable and supportive as a trusted friend and colleague. If not for the gracious and generous involvement of Robert and Jere McCann of Huntsville, Texas, in allowing visits to their land on the Trinity River, there would be many more mysteries remaining about the Spanish settlement of Bucareli. My gratitude goes to David Hoffpauir and Sandra Rogers for that introduction and collegial support. Through it all my patient and tolerant wife, Mickey Hammond, has supported my seemingly unending work on this project. Her masterful tact always nudges me toward a better way to convey meaning. Readers owe her a nod of thanks for any simple clarity they may encounter.

Finally, my gratitude goes to you, the reader. I hope you will be engaged, informed, and inspired to acknowledge and respect the parts of East Texas history that are little known and underappreciated. East Texas was formed in a multicultural stew of people from many nations, and I pray it continues to honor that past.

Tom H. Gann

About forty-two years ago, Dean Leggett, a Lufkin surveyor who was in the same real estate office complex where I worked, crossed the hall and presented a legal description of a 129-acre tract. The words "King's Highway" were included as the west boundary line. This was the first time those words were identified in my mind with any property in Angelina County. As a young real estate broker, I did not recognize the historical importance of the King's Highway at that time. I remembered it years later, however, as I developed a taste for family history inspired by the Gann Historical Society and Library Inc. in Johnson City, Tennessee. My father, Woody Gann of Lufkin, was one of its founders in 1989.

Dean Leggett mentioned that Kenneth Johnson with the Angelina County Appraisal District had a folder with some information on the King's Highway. Although the real estate business causes you to constantly mix with attorneys, title companies, surveyors, appraisal districts, and banks, the contacts are about business and not historical research. In the last seven years, Kenneth Johnson became my contact for details about county maps, legal descriptions, flood maps, topographic maps, property owners (old and new), the discovery of locations from old city maps, old names in deeds on creeks and springs, and Lufkin city maps from 1882, 1888, 1914, 1925, and 1961. Most of all, I acknowledge Kenneth for the many hours I sat at his office and worked at the computer searching for the gems of history.

The late Abbott Hargraves was a surveyor who worked on numerous assignments of historical pleasure after he retired. He focused his expertise in deed research and his tireless attention to detail on Nacogdoches and Angelina counties as well as five other counties. His attention to historical detail on the 1836 map of Nacogdoches and the people who lived on Pilar Street was amazing. He loved what he was doing and worked with me until he was ninety-four years young.

Bob Skiles's generous sharing of information, including emails, texts, articles, and maps, was mentioned in Gary Pinkerton's remarks previously. Bob's assistance was also immeasurable for me even before Gary and I started this project. Emily Hyatt and Jonathan Gerland at The History Center in Diboll, Texas, have endured my many questions and requests with eagerly returned information. The Texas General Land Office staff members—Kevin Klaus, Mary Waite, and Brian Stauffer with the Spanish Collection—have always gone beyond the call of duty with each visit, call, or email. Here in the Lufkin and Nacogdoches area, Dr. Tom Middlebrook assisted with his patient leadership and took the time to encourage excellence by example. Special thanks to David Hoffpauir with Sam Houston State University for sharing an information diamond in a Texas Supreme Court Case from 1845. Renee Benn Lee with the Texas Department of Transportation supplied three early years of planning documents for Texas Highway 35, the first asphalt artery through Angelina County, which provided information about some older roads it was replacing.

Rob Tompkins, a friend and landman, has shared months of cumulative time at the Angelina County Courthouse's Deeds and Records section searching for any and everything. Heather Rhodes and Carol Donaldson with Gann Medford Real Estate Inc. have been inexhaustible with their years of support, time, and experience. The people at Skelton Slusher Barnhill Watkins Wells PLLC, in concert with Claudia Cook and Debbie Squires at Community Title, were indispensable in the discovery of information on old maps, surveys, old property owners, and legal descriptions in Angelina County. With their contributions, new maps can now be drawn of two early paths through Angelina County dating to 1691.

I would like to express my immense appreciation to Gary L. Pinkerton for agreeing to publish our research in addition to his added methods of computer-enhanced techniques in mapping, word searching, and sharing of information. His ability to gather a wide range of information and organize it by date, subject, and source—and then retrieve it with ease—has been nothing short of impressive.

BRIDLES AND BISCUITS

INTRODUCTION

Under Our Feet

The history of the place we know as Texas is not as simple as coonskin caps and cowboy boots. Many distinct, rich histories have converged over time. Those connected stories have formed a unique expression of Texas that has been multicultural and multilingual for centuries. With a closer look at both our perceptions and the facts, we find that the whole story is much richer and far more engaging than generally understood. Those stories are all around us . . . they are beneath our feet.

Ancient carvings scratched into the sandstone walls of a small East Texas cave tell stories using pictographs—word pictures we are unable to fully understand using a language long lost to time.[1] Excavations at a former farm outside of Austin, now known as the Gault Site, revealed over one million artifacts that are evidence of habitation and commerce dating back fifteen thousand years.[2] Centuries of habitation by indigenous people at Caddo Mounds State Historic Site near Alto, Texas, have been established through archaeological excavations, ground-penetrating radar, LiDAR sensing, and radiocarbon analysis. This Caddo site, with both ceremonial and burial mounds, began its earliest use about 800 AD and was actively used until about 1,200 AD. The cultural center represented by the mounds gave way to smaller settlements all along the watersheds of the Neches and Angelina rivers. The artifacts of their lives that survived centuries beneath the surface help us understand their daily existence, their relationships with other tribal groups, their culture, and their commerce.[3] The Kingdom of the Tejas, the ancestral home of the Caddo in East Texas, was the center of society and trade.

Then came Spain with its soldiers, priests, and pens. In 1519, Alonso Álvarez de Pineda of Spain mapped the Texas coast. In 1542, Luis de Moscoso Alvarado, a member of Hernando de Soto's expedition, roamed across eastern Texas. What began as a search for gold and riches simply became a trek to find their way home. Moscoso's path along Caddo trails in northeastern Texas followed footpaths that became known as Trammel's Trace.[4] After other

Pictographs from Monk's Cave Archaeological Site (41RK84), Rusk County, Texas, represent a language no longer understood. Photo by author.

Spanish soldiers and priests wandered across the terrain or established camps along the coast to explore, they were satisfied that the land had been claimed for the Spanish crown. It was not until 1685, when the Frenchman René-Robert Cavelier, Sieur de La Salle, began an active settlement along Matagorda Bay, that Spain became more aggressive in its efforts to remove the French and colonize inland from the upper coast of Texas. Expeditions by Alonso De León in 1690 and Domingo Terán de los Ríos in 1691 led to an extended period of Spanish occupation in East Texas through the Mexican Revolution in 1821. Though some know the general aspects of this period of history, few fully comprehend how it underpins the cultural foundations of Texas and of East Texas in particular.

We forget that the Caddo language was once the lingua franca of the region. We forget that for 294 years, Spanish was the primary non-indigenous language spoken in eastern Texas—currently over one hundred years longer than English.[5] In many ways, Texas and parts of the United States have never stopped being Spanish. As one author notes, it is impossible to ignore the ongoing impact of three states with Spanish origins on the history of the United States—California, Florida, and Texas. Their economies, their populations, and their cultural influences are undeniable. The family tree of the United States clearly shows its Spanish roots.[6]

Historians know a great deal about the early European presence in East Texas thanks to the Spanish administrative obsession with documentation and written records. Diaries, letters, reports, and royal edicts are stored in archives all over the world. There has been extensive academic work on Spanish colonial and borderlands history tracing back to two giants of the field, Herbert Eugene Bolton and Carlos E. Castañeda. With Spanish archival sources spread across centuries, continents, and languages, there is still much to be learned and much still to be discovered. The riches of these archives are beyond the reach of all but the most capable and committed historians.

What we know about the native people of eastern Texas during Spanish occupation is largely not what they said about themselves, but what others said about them. Parts of that indigenous history have been surmised through archaeological and anthropological research. The stories of their lives, from their point of view, are little told. Native Americans from many tribes made Texas home, living in the piney woods and the coastal prairies, across the plains, and along the river basins. In eastern Texas, the Nasoni, Nadaco, Nabedache, Hainai, Bidai, Nacodoche, Akokisa, Wichita, Tawakoni, Atakapa, Kichai, Ais, Tonkawa, Tejas, Taovaya, and others roamed and hunted, built villages, planted crops, raised families, and passed on the stories of their ancestors from long before any European presence.

Our Education, Our Perceptions

Notwithstanding the millennia of human history in Texas, the pivotal event for most Texans when it comes to the state's history is the Texas Revolution of 1836. Many know relatively little about the region's history before this significant event. This early Texas lore more generally known involves Sam Houston, Davy Crockett, the Alamo, San Jacinto, and other people and places around Texas' emergence as a republic. Those events were certainly a turning point in the history of Texas, but they do not define it. Student education on these matters began in earnest in 1912 with Eugene Barker's book *A School History of Texas*. In that work, Barker let all the little children know how to think about Indians.

> The Indians were the greatest annoyance and danger with which the colonists had to contend. The hostile ones murdered, and the friendly ones robbed them, and the worst of it was that nobody could tell when a friendly tribe might suddenly turn hostile and go on the warpath.[7]

Words like these set the tone for years and created a perception of native people as little more than heathens and savages. Those stuck in that mindset are sadly missing a rich, magnificent history.

H. W. Brands at the University of Texas is one of the country's most outstanding interpreters of history. He compared the teaching of Texas history in schools to Catholic confirmation by saying, "The kids are old enough to grasp the material but not so mature that they question the orthodoxy."[8] Historians like Brands, Randolph "Mike" Campbell, Light T. Cummins, James Crisp, Ty Cashion, and Andrew Torget have challenged prototypical historical narratives with careful research that has led to a more complete and accurate history. Stephen Harrigan's 2019 narrative history of Texas, *Big Wonderful Thing*, is authored by someone with enough historical perspective and journalistic chops to observe the facts of history while helping us understand how our feelings about the past can influence our current perceptions.[9] We may have learned some facts in school along the way, but much of what has been taught has left our historical viewpoints—in John Wayne's words as Davy Crockett—"dead as a beaver hat."[10]

An Instructive Moment

With Texas history occasionally suffering from misperception and myth, East Texas' important role in that broader history is even less fully appreciated and understood. Growing up in East Texas was no assurance that stories of one's localized past would become part of the curriculum. A real-life moment during the research for this book captured this disconnect. Early in this project, Tom Gann and I took most of the day to tour some of the river crossings and historic locations discussed. One of the stops was the Blanche K. Werner Library in Trinity, Texas, where an artifact called the Bucareli Rifle is displayed.[11]

Bucareli was an early Spanish settlement established on the Trinity River in 1774 by Antonio Gil Ibarvo and a focus of this work. Prisoners working in the fields of the Eastham Prison Farm found metal remnants of a flintlock weapon along the eastern bank of the Trinity River. Much like early East Texas at the end of the eighteenth century, the rifle included parts of mixed origins.

A Bucareli rifle on display at the Blanche K. Werner Public Library in Trinity, Texas. Photo by author.

English and French rifle parts that were discards or castoffs were often used to repair or piece together broken weapons. The rifle could have been used by American filibusters, Native Americans, French traders, or Spanish citizens from Mexico.

As Tom and I walked through the doors we noticed the glass display case topped by Christmas decorations. We told the person working there we came to see the Bucareli Rifle. We removed wrapping paper, a tiny Santa, and a cute fluffy reindeer to get a better look at the exhibit and expose the rifle for our viewing. The card inside read:

> The significance of this relic is that it serves as a reminder of our not so distant past when peoples of different customs and cultures mingled and settled in a wild frontier land that was to become Texas.[12]

The exhibit's description of the artifact got it right. East Texas itself was a multicultural mix of people with many origins and backgrounds.

This story is retold here not because of the rifle but because of what one of the onlookers said to us. As Tom and I examined the metal gun barrel we shared more of the story of Bucareli on the Trinity River and a bit about Spanish rule. Having never fully learned about Bucareli, both onlookers became interested and engaged. The patrons' response reflected a common reaction to tales of history. "Oh, I just love Texas history," said the woman listening to the conversation.

The woman really did love Texas history but had just never heard it explained or interpreted the way we had in only a few moments. History that had happened beneath her feet was unknown to her, tucked away in inaccessible books, occupying shelf space in a historical archive, or recorded in scholarly tomes undigestible by the public. On the day of our visit to see the rifle, a piece of history came to life for the onlookers when they learned about the relic beneath the snowman. That is what we hope to do with this book.

What Remained Is Now Gone

Part of the difficulty with interpreting our Spanish colonial history in East Texas for general consumption is the lack of physical remains related to that period. Evidence of the ancient cultures and inhabitants of the hills and creeks of East Texas endure in numerous collections of artifacts, but many of the sites from which they were collected have been looted or destroyed.[13]

In the case of Nacogdoches, the cost of progress has weighed heavily on any evidence of Caddo and Spanish history. There were once four Caddo mounds near downtown Nacogdoches built by an earlier people who drank from the same streams and hunted the same woods as those who came later from across the Atlantic Ocean. Dating from around 800 AD, the mounds were still ten feet high and one hundred feet across by 1888.[14]

If you had been at the Old Stone House, the outpost in Nacogdoches built by Antonio Gil Ibarvo, in 1835, you might have heard David Crockett swear an oath of allegiance to the Texian cause on his way to the Alamo. If you had been there in March 1902, you could have come away with a musket ball for one dollar or taken home a piece of heavy walnut timber to reinforce a crumbling doorway. You would have watched the Old Stone House, the one remaining physical connection to the late 1700s history of Spanish East Texas, topple to the ground.[15] There is little doubt it had become an eyesore, but a substantial and historic one.

A series of newspaper articles and editorials in 1890 compared the Old Stone House to the Alamo in its importance to Texas history. A visitor in 1896 described the structure as "the sorriest looking place" in a town about which he did not have too many good things to say.[16] All the effort came to naught. In a classified ad in the December 3, 1901, edition of the *Houston Post*, the Spanish history of East Texas was put up for sale and demolition. A year later in early March 1902, on the anniversary of the day that Texas won its independence from Mexico, relic hunters and curious onlookers stood among the ruins.[17]

The Old Stone House after demolition in 1902. Courtesy East Texas Digital Archives at the East Texas Research Center, R.W. Steen Library, Stephen F. Austin State University, Nacogdoches, Texas.

In 1910 the Nacogdoches town square—the former *plaza principal* where the Stone House was—was identified as a location for a new post office. By March of 1917 it was reported that "the work of excavating for the federal post office building is being finished and the work of construction will be begun within the next few days." Centuries of artifacts from Caddo, Spanish, Mexican, and Republic-era habitation were no doubt lost in the process.[18]

The demolition of the Stone House and the destruction of the *plaza principal* for a post office building were followed by further losses when a new county courthouse was built at the corner of North and Main streets in 1911. Newspaper accounts reported workmen were digging up grisly finds such as human bones and skulls. That was because the ground had been a cemetery used by Spanish, Mexican, and Native American residents for years. This left one newspaper to wonder "what the spirits of the dear departed think about such treatment."[19]

These facts of history are not recalled here to place blame or fault. Certainly, the efforts of local governments, universities, historical and genealogical groups, and local tourism organizations are more focused and informed today, making concerted efforts to honor, recognize, and preserve the region's true history. San Antonio has its missions to serve as physical reminders of centuries of Spanish occupation. East Texas is largely left with plaques and markers.

What This Book Hopes To Do

In 1773, the old Spanish capital of the Province of Texas at Los Adaes (near present-day Robeline, Louisiana) was emptied, and the residents were forced to move to the new capital of San Antonio de Béxar. Between that time and 1813—when American filibusters began threatening to take over Texas, and turmoil in Mexico was creating its own revolutionary pressures—there is a unique slice of East Texas history that has not been fully acknowledged. Historian William C. Foster called the years 1770–1820 "the last Spanish episode of the Texas drama."[20] During that period, the Spanish territory between the Trinity River and the Sabine River was a cultural ecotone. In ecology, an ecotone is a transition zone between two distinct and adjacent ecosystems where species from both grow together in a way they would not naturally occur. They are places where things that are different come together and coexist. It is a conglomeration, an aggregate, a transitional mix unique to the site where it exists.[21]

Spanish East Texas was a cultural ecotone in ways that did not exist before or after this unique period of history. It was a place of incredible human diversity and cultural difference. Yet, its inhabitants managed a relatively cohesive and cooperative existence even with the tensions that came along with life in the borderlands. The cross-cultural relationships and kinships between and among people of Spanish, French, Indian, and other European origin, facilitated by the trade-based economy, made Spanish East Texas a uniquely productive crossroads.

Bridles and Biscuits will focus on the events, people, and stories of that slice of Spanish colonial history in East Texas for people who may have only a limited understanding of this part of our heritage. Using primary sources, academic research, and on-the-ground study, we hope to connect readers to this history through facts, place, and emotion. In chapter one, "Seeing What the Land Remembers," we focus on the landscape of East Texas between the Trinity and the Sabine rivers that the earliest Spanish expeditions encountered. Using diaries and other firsthand accounts, it will establish the physical space where this history took place and places where it might still evoke a connection to the past.

Chapter two, "Before the Others," tells the story of the presence of two important tribes in East Texas, the Caddo and the Bidai. Though the Caddo will be familiar to many, the Bidai are little known and little understood. Their role in early contraband trade and their importance in establishing trade routes had an outsized impact on the future of the region.

Chapter three, "La Provincia de Tejas" provides a review of the earliest

Spanish colonial history of East Texas and the establishment of the missions and presidios. The cyclical nature of Spanish interest in the region, with missions being opened and closed and opened again, offers a backdrop to understanding the ups and downs of Spanish investment in and indifference toward East Texas. A highly regarded general survey of Spanish history is found in Donald Chipman's book *Spanish Texas:1519–1821*. This chapter will help connect the broader history of colonization to East Texas.

Chapter four, "Deep and Miry Places," is a review of the rivers and streams that crossed the terrain and that could present formidable challenges for crossing in difficult conditions. It will also make the case for the location of Paso Tomás, a key crossing of the Trinity River.

Chapter five, "By Way of Secret Roads," is a pivotal chapter. Roads and trails connect people and places. The primary roads of this period were used for contraband, commerce, and communication, and they predated Spanish entry to the region. A network of trails through Bidai territory between their villages along the Trinity River and their trading partners in French Natchitoches connected the Bidai all across the region. One of the trails led from Nacogdoches down to the Gulf Coast toward their allied tribal partners in trade, another to the crossing of Paso Tomás on the Trinity.

The first five chapters of the book summarize the conditions that preceded a continuously occupied East Texas, setting the stage for a truly unique period of Texas history. Beginning with Chapter six, "Their Tears Sprinkled the Road," the focus shifts to the fate of the people of Los Adaes who founded settlements that led to a lasting presence in East Texas and the beginning of Nacogdoches. The forced eviction of the Adeseños left them displaced and striving for a return as close to their former home as Spanish authorities would allow.

Chapter seven, "From Béxar to Bucareli," follows the life cycle of the village of Bucareli, built from nothing on the bank of the Trinity River. It was home to a few hundred Spanish subjects and a waystation for contraband trade, and it came to a disastrous end after only five years.

Chapter eight, "*Color Quebrado*, the Broken Color of Nacogdoches," establishes how the failure of one settlement led to the formation of another. The new home for the evicted Adeseños would become the most permanent and lasting reminder of Spanish Colonial Texas in the eastern region.

Chapter nine, "*La Mordida,* Contraband and Culture in Early Nacogdoches," discusses how cooperative trading partnerships and familial kinships led to a comfortable community and culture for the former Adeseños and others attracted to this provincial frontier along the borderlands.

Chapter ten, "The Arrest and Removal of Antonio Gil Ibarvo," chronicles the end of an era of contraband trade and how the removal of the man who was its overseer interrupted the diverse cultures involved in borderlands commerce.

Chapter eleven, "'It Is Just That He Suffer,' the Case Against Ibarvo," focuses on the years of back-and-forth accusations toward Ibarvo and their ultimate dismissal. The military officers appointed to fill the void in Nacogdoches were part of a transition in how commerce was carried out in the borderlands, and they became part of the problem they were sent to control.

Chapter twelve, "When Nations Intervene," describes how the threats to Spanish claims to the region, both real and imagined, led to a series of events resulting in Nacogdoches being virtually abandoned. The Louisiana Purchase, the Neutral Ground Agreement, filibustering by Americans, and internal unrest were the final events that led to both the Mexican and the Texas revolutions. An early nineteenth-century Spanish village and presidio on the Trinity, Trinidad de Salcedo, was ultimately burned to the ground as revolutionary forces from across the Sabine River and within Mexico challenged Spanish imperial authority.

Spellling and Naming Conventions

With a discussion of people and places from many cultures and backgrounds it is important to develop standards for naming conventions. A Spanish league will be calculated as 2.6 miles, and additional measures of distance, volume, and land will be addressed in the appendix. There is also an effort to identify current streams and rivers across the region with their earlier Spanish or Native American names. Bolton noted that the Spanish on various *entradas* tended to name their rivers "somewhat promiscuously," so this standardization will help the reader stay oriented to present-day maps. The names of Spanish viceroys, governors, and other key officials are also in the appendix.

One of the pivotal characters during this period of history was Antonio Gil Ibarvo. Born in Los Adaes, Ibarvo led the settlements at Bucareli and Nacogdoches. Rarely has there been a man whose name has taken on so many iterations. Y'Barbo, Ybarbo, Ebarb, Ybarvo, and dozens of other spellings have been used by the thousands who lay claim as his descendants. Ibarvo will be the historical spelling used in this work and matches that used by the Texas State Historical Association in *The Handbook of Texas*, the Dolph Briscoe Center for American History in the Bexar Archives, and the scholars Donald E. Chipman and Harriet Denise Joseph in *Notable Men & Women of Spanish Texas*.

The settlement of Bucareli on the Trinity River was named for Antonio María de Bucareli y Ursua, the viceroy of New Spain at the time it was established. For clarity, the settlement of Bucareli will be called simply that, and the viceroy's name will be spelled out as Bucareli y Ursua. The presidio of San Antonio de Béxar was established in 1718, named after a city in Spain. Béxar will be used most often to identify that important place in history.

The Bidai Indians are mentioned often in this work, and that spelling will be the standard use for their tribal name. The creek named for the tribe is commonly spelled Bedias Creek, and that convention will be used. If one wants to find the Bidai with an internet search, be prepared to search also for Badies, Beadeyes, Beddies, Bedees, Bedies, Bidaises, Biday, Bidayes, Bidias, Spring Creeks, Vidaes, Vidais, Vidays, Vivais, Bobida, Bibi, and Bibit. Just to keep things interesting, the name they reportedly had for themselves was Quasmigdo.[22]

The phrase "bridles and biscuits" used in the title of the book comes from the transcript of a contraband trial documented in the Béxar Archives. When a soldier who was caught smuggling goods was asked what he traded to a Native American to obtain the deerskin and woman's skirt he was caught with, he said that he traded the bridle off his horse and a morsel of his breakfast. This is the true nature of the contraband trade and an example of one of the reasons it was so pervasive and largely unstoppable. This poor soldier was willing to ride bridleless on horseback to Béxar and risk arrest so he could give his wife a gift.[23] No nation on earth could stop that kind of trade. The bolder smugglers dealt in arms and livestock, but for most, contraband trade was an activity carried out for convenience and economic survival more than riches.

A lengthy and enduring Texas history existed before any Anglo-American ever saw Texas. That history is beginning to be more fully appreciated and understood, and it is one of the goals of this work to contribute to that understanding. Broadening our perspectives on the importance and presence of Spanish influence on East Texas history will be a shared journey that can impact how we view and live our futures together.

1

Seeing What the Land Remembers

Once you have lived on the land, been a partner with its moods, secrets, and seasons, you cannot leave. The living land remembers, touching you in unguarded moments, saying, "I am here. You are a part of me."

—BEN LOGAN[1]

Before beginning a more focused history of the events and people engaged in the contraband culture of Spanish East Texas, it is important to provide context within the geographical region. It is important to understand the conditions, the terrain, the rivers, and the trails on which life took place.

A university-sponsored panel discussion about understanding a sense of place was titled with a phrase that is both poetic and expressive—"Seeing What the Land Remembers."[2] It is a lyrical phrase that resonates with both opportunities and challenges meaningful to this work. Seeing the landscape of East Texas in the context of its early Spanish history is a precursor to sensing it in a more current way. Seeing the present landscape through the lens of history makes it more accessible and present. This phrase also offers an ideal framework for understanding how to train our modern eyes to see historically, and by doing so, begin to think differently about the past. Being able to look at a current landscape, recognize how it may have come to be that way, and imagine earlier uses is a skill that once acquired never fades. Learning to see historically is part of what this book hopes to promote. To do so, one must get out in the field and begin to learn.

The most significant obstacle to establishing this kind of connection to the history of a place is the constant change in land use and development. Almost nothing in our landscape remains unchanged from those earlier historic periods. Even magnetic north has shifted over time. Plowing, terracing, flood control, road building, livestock raising, tree farming, and population growth make changes in ways that are irreversible. For instance, surface mining for lignite and the subsequent land reclamation have altered parts of East Texas terrain to the point that historic topographic maps no longer accurately portray the present-day landscape.

There are probably more than a few historians and archaeologists whose time travel bucket list would include seeing firsthand what the native forests of East Texas looked like before logging. We know with certainty that the pine plantations now seen across East Texas bear no resemblance to the native forests of Spanish East Texas. However, our common expectation that every tree was enormous and hundreds of years old was not the case. In 1907 a Yale professor of forestry got off the train with his students in Tyler County on the upper end of the Big Thicket. His goal for the students was to see virgin longleaf pine forests before they were logged. Professor Herman Haupt Chapman expected to find large stands of towering pines all about the same age. He based his assumption on the understanding that fires came through from time to time. Chapman assumed new trees would all grow back at about the same time and at the same rate. What he learned instead was that trees of all ages coexisted in proximity, from new seedlings to 350-year-old trees. One downed ancient tree meant there was new sunlight for hundreds of younger trees to grow.[3]

Changes to our historic landscapes have been wrought by what biology professor and naturalist Del Weniger called the "manipulative touch of man." He lamented our inability to look back in time by saying:

> An ever-increasing proportion of our people cannot, as they gaze across the fields and the cities, conceive of the original, natural Texas any more than one can, from opening a milk carton, imagine milking a cow or, from eating a package of potato chips, picture himself digging a hill of potatoes.[4]

It is easy to understand the attraction of having this visual perception of history. In teaching history to today's students, visual images are more easily communicated than written records. The technology that allows old photos and film to be colorized brings a different level of understanding and appreciation to the same images that were previously only available in black and white. Peter Jackson's 2018 film, *They Shall Not Grow Old*, slowed down the herky-jerky speed of film shot during World War I and colorized it, immediately making the subjects more real and present for modern viewers.[5] For events occurring before photography was invented, however, we have only the words of history to trigger our contemporary imagination.

We can better understand history if we can connect to a particular place named in a Spanish letter or journal. The names of places changed many times through the years but can still be a clue to locations where events of history occurred. If one can identify these places and stand on the same ground where a documented event in history took place, it makes the history much more real. Sometimes those locations are designated with historical markers, but many of them are not well known or identified. They are not breathtaking or awe-inspiring as a rule. But they are real, they are historic, and they connect us to our history.

Using firsthand descriptions and accounts, this chapter is an examination of the lay of the land as it was during that era. The focus area for this historical review of the terrain is the region between the Red River of Natchitoches and the Trinity River to the west of Nacogdoches. The current Texas counties of Nacogdoches, Cherokee, Houston, Trinity, and Angelina will get the primary attention. Surrounding areas that are now Walker, Shelby, Rusk, San Augustine, Madison, Sabine, Anderson, and Polk counties will be more briefly examined. The map of the Texas-Louisiana borderlands during this period will provide a reference point for the reader.[6]

Reimagining a Landscape

Reimagining a landscape from the late eighteenth century is an imperfect art. However, supported by firsthand accounts from multiple sources, there is sufficient detail to paint in broad strokes. Spanish *entradas* (expeditions) and inspection tours were tasked with keeping detailed accounts of their daily travels, noting rivers and other natural features. As one would expect, the chroniclers differed in their commitment to that task. Nevertheless, these are invaluable sources for looking back in history to understand the terrain across East Texas.

Four distinct types of terrain are found across East Texas: rivers and streams, floodplains, hills and slopes, and upland areas.[7] Rivers and streams were the tree-lined routes that provided water, and they were where most settlements and villages would be found. Different species of trees dominated the sandy waterways, including ash, sweet gum, and red oak. With the constant flooding along the wide floodplains, large trees might be covered with vines or bordered by several species of cane. Swamps, sloughs, and wetlands were places travelers sought to avoid.

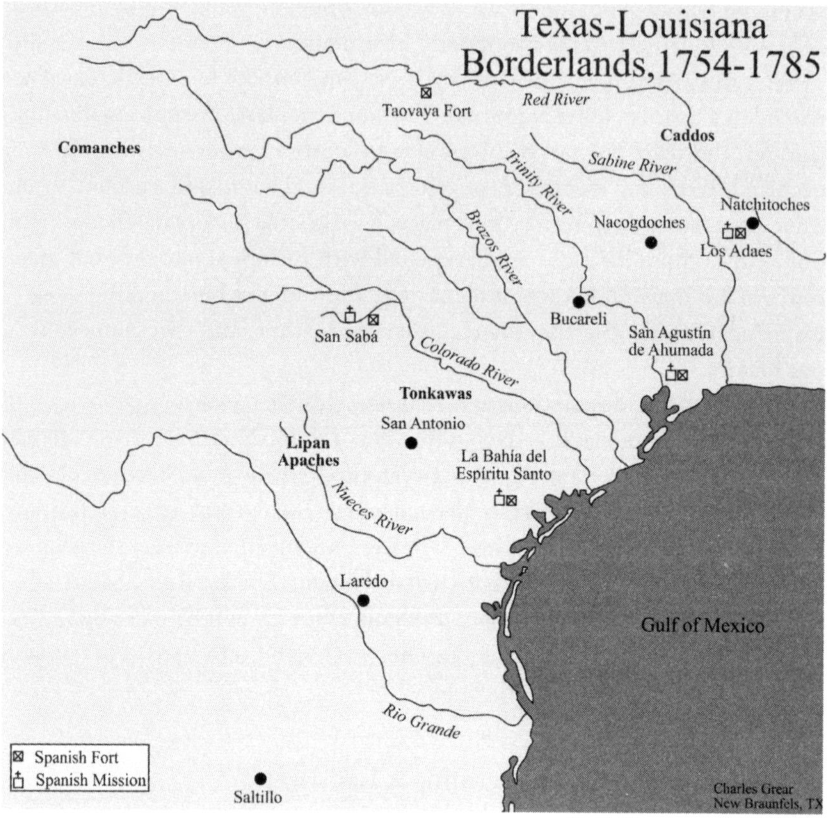

The Texas-Louisiana Borderlands, 1754–85. Image courtesy of Charles Grear.

Hillsides and slopes, particularly east of the Neches River, were generally obstacles to be circumvented. They held the most diverse tree growth with an abundance of hardwoods. Upland areas at the top of those slopes were typically less fertile, but prime ground for pine trees.

Native American Impact on the Landscape

Native Americans had a long-term impact on the landscape and ecology of East Texas. In and around the settlements scattered along the creeks and streams, these indigenous people established a "humanized [landscape] sustainable over a long period of time." Their lives were intertwined with the landscape in a way that ensured both their immediate survival and the long-term presence of their people.[8]

The Native American practice of burning prairies ensured the resurgence of fresh grasses and helped keep them from being subsumed by encroaching forests. As early as 1528, Álvar Núñez Cabeza de Vaca observed this use of fire firsthand.

> Those [Indians] from farther inland . . . go about with a firebrand, setting fire to the plants and timber so as to drive off the mosquitoes, and also to get lizards and other similar things which they eat, to come out of the soil. In the same manner they kill deer, encircling them with fires, and they do it also to deprive the animals of pasture, compelling them to go for food where the Indians want.[9]

Signs of grassland burning was noted in several journals of the early Spanish entradas. Not only was there evidence of blackened clumps of grasses left behind, but of the green, tender regrowth which soon took its place. The restorative power of fire is well known to forest managers, but the practice effectively ended with the settlement of Anglos, resulting in the loss of prairie acreage.

Historic Accounts

Unlike the locations of other Spanish settlements, East Texas was not chosen for favorable conditions in the terrain. Its forests were more of an obstacle than a blessing. Sources of water were plentiful enough but even a land full of creeks and bayous could be found "very short of water, and in dry seasons only a few small pools" were suitable for their use. In one forty-thousand-acre land grant, a surveyor found only enough arable land to grow less than five bushels of corn.[10]

A diarist for an expedition in the mid-1700s observed there "were so many fleas, ticks, horseflies, mites, and other insects that the Province of Texas was uninhabitable."[11] Though the region was experiencing unusually colder temperatures at the end of what is called the "Little Ice Age," this 1810 weather report from the Trinity River sounds familiar.

> I say that the climate is good but that it is cold and hot, although some years, by the nature of weather, some excess is experienced in winter, with abundant sleeting and snow, and some [excess] in summer due to the heat, which causes bilious fevers.[12]

Over time, trees have been felled and flood plains turned into farms and pastures, but the basic topography of East Texas remains. Though it is often difficult to pinpoint specific locations described in the notes of the Spanish diarists, today's historians and archaeologists can still attempt to compare those reports to known points on the ground. In this chapter, those accounts are gathered in a way that allows the reader to envision the East Texas of the eighteenth century.

From the Trinity to the Nacogdoches

This review of the late eighteenth-century landscape will be organized and presented as a journey from Mexico or Béxar following established routes to the northeast, across the Trinity River toward Nacogdoches, and then from Natchitoches across the Sabine.

West of the Trinity

The Trinity River is the longest river fully within the state of Texas. From just south of the Red River bordering Oklahoma all the way to Galveston Bay and the Gulf of Mexico, the Trinity has always marked a transition from west to east and a passage to a different terrain. The wide fertile floodplain was the result of repeated, extensive flooding. River bottoms in general are places where the trees grow larger and the canopy darker and thicker. A 1971 scientific review of the Trinity River basin found twenty-four species of trees that were either state or national champion big trees.[13] One account from an observer in 1828 thought the river had a "romantic pleasing gloom" due to the lofty surrounding timber.[14]

THE WOODS OF THE DEVIL

The earliest approaches to East Texas and the vast lands to the west of the Trinity were along a changing landscape of roads, some of which have now been identified as El Camino Real de los Tejas. Along that approach to the Trinity River was one of the most formidable obstacles along any journey—a dense and seemingly impenetrable band of trees.[15] Open prairie to the east of the Navasota River turned into a daunting, heavily wooded terrain the Spanish called *Monte Grande*. It was also called *Monte Sin Fin* (Woods Without End), and *Monte del Diablo* (the Woods of the Devil).[16] That is how it felt to those tasked with crossing it. Better known as the Cross Timbers after the Spanish period, the Monte Grande was a band of very dense forest that made travel extremely difficult. Where pine forests in East Texas grew so open in the understory that it could seem park-like, the *Monte Grande* was difficult, dangerous, and entangled.

> We crossed . . . a wood thick with shady trees of various kinds. In these woods there are many paths so narrow that we had to travel in single file and at times had to cut our way through the brushwood.[17]

Diary accounts regularly describe Spanish expeditions encountering these thick, almost impassable woods before arriving at the Trinity. At the Brazos crossing they found that "the whole forest was knocked down because the trees had been uprooted in some storm."[18] It took twelve soldiers and twelve mule drivers more than a day to clear a path wide enough to make only about four miles of progress. One description of a seventeen-league (forty-four-mile) travel itinerary said that a different path had to be cut for each subsequent passage.[19]

"A FOREST OF ENCUMBERED TREES"

The approach to the Trinity after leaving the Cross Timbers traversed a difficult, hilly terrain with woods of large oaks along its banks on the west (right) side and the clearings and prairies beyond to the east (left).[20] An account of one approach to the Trinity River mentioned a "plain with many large, sparse oak trees" and a prairie on the other side, but the crossing itself got no mention. The wandering trail that passed for a road in 1716 crossed many small streams and wove around large live oak and walnut trees, interlaced with grapevines yielding "grapes as large as pigeon eggs." Creeks and bayous were teeming with fish.

As one expedition approached the Trinity River from the west in 1721, they saw planted fields, indications of Indian settlement, but there were no huts immediately visible from their route.[21] About three miles before reaching the Trinity on a "very well used path," a large group of natives that included Bidai and Nacodoche came out to formally greet the Spaniards. A large group of 150 Indians met a 1716 expedition in a friendly encounter and exchanged green corn, watermelons, and cantaloupes for blankets, hats, and tobacco.[22]

A "light forest of encumbered trees"—a translation from the Spanish likely meaning the trees were covered in vines—shaded the edges of the route across three small prairies on the approach to the Trinity from the west. Only as groups approached the river did a scattering of pines begin to appear, a feature of the landscape that remains largely true today. A riverside forest of pecan and pine trees was a common *paraje* (campsite) for the night spent before making a difficult crossing. Campsites that were ill-chosen by those unfamiliar with the speed at which the river could rise risked the floodwaters quickly filling the low land where they slept.

The Banks of the Trinity

Later travelers at the end of the Republic era saw the fertile prairies along the Trinity for their commercial value. "The soil of these prairies is exceedingly rich and productive; of a deep, black, sandy loam, light and mellow," said one proponent of immigration.[23] Upon emerging from the woods near the later site of Robbins Ferry (the Texas State Highway 21 crossing of the Trinity), there were prominent hills completely barren of trees. One of these hills was a landmark known as Lomo del Toro, or Bull's Hill.

One diarist was so happy to be back out in the open that he wrote, "There is nothing that affords the traveler in these solitary regions greater joy than the sight of a plain [prairie] after coming out of the long, endless, thick woods."[24] Pasture grasses in the floodplains, however, could be so thick that horses had difficulty walking through them when the growth was vigorous and well-watered.[25] From the top of a hill near the Trinity one could see floodwaters spilling out across the prairie, but the river's course was defined only by the green band of trees along its banks.

Journeys across hundreds of miles in these conditions took a toll on men and stock. Many a traveler was plagued by fevers, floods, and muddy creek crossings.[26] Clouds of mosquitoes bit some to the point that their faces looked like they had been beaten. Starving mules with handkerchiefs covering their ears bled from the mosquitoes, gadflies, and gnats that swarmed them during the daylight hours. People waved tree branches waved over their heads to scatter the flying pests for some small relief.

A DARKENED SKY

In one account of travel across the prairie just east of where Bedias Creek entered the Trinity at a place known as Paso Tomás, the diarist noted that in the evening and morning hours "many thousands of wild Pidgeons [pigeons] flew over" their camp.[27] It is likely these were some of the three to five billion passenger pigeons that were once the most abundant bird on the continent. They were heavily hunted and lost to extinction around 1901. The pigeon's primary foods were nuts and berries. Their size allowed them to swallow small acorns whole. They returned to the same locations each fall and winter to forage and then moved on after decimating the acorn mast. They established a roost to which they returned each night, and some of those roosts were so significant they were mentioned in survey notes for land grants along the river. One such pigeon roost in nearby Leon County was almost four hundred acres in size.

The impact of their numbers left a smelly scar on the landscape, and their disappearance is a reminder that life is fragile.[28]

Ponds and pools of water left behind after floodwaters receded were home to "ducks, geese, swans, pelicans, and crows." One observation of a bird that "seemed as large as the ostrich" was likely a sighting of migratory sandhill cranes. With wingspans of over six feet, these large birds are impressive whether one sees a lone crane flying overhead or thousands gathered on a grassy plain.[29]

East of the Trinity River

Crossings of the Trinity could either be uneventful moments of scenic respite during a lengthy journey or a multiday life-threatening passage. It all depended on how much water flowed down the channel. In either case the river crossings were consequential and notable milestones.

A chronicler of Texas travels noticed there was a tendency for the eastern banks of Texas rivers, the left banks, to be lower and more likely to overflow than the right banks. That was certainly true of the stretch of the Trinity most used by these early Spanish entradas. The prairies on the left bank of the Trinity were immense. Unlike most of the other eastern Texas creeks and bayous bounded by hillier terrain, the Trinity River bottomland was very wide, often up to five miles of flat land bordering the river channel. With rainfall, any depression within the floodplain could turn into a lagoon, a small lake, or just a daunting mudhole. There were also intermittent high spots, or knobs, scattered among the flat land where travelers might find an island of escape even in a flood.

MUSTANG PRAIRIE

The area east of the Trinity was once described as a "continued series of rolling swells (swales), or gentle undulations overshadowed by one almost continuous forest."[30] That expanse was broken only by the prairies, and the most prominent of those was called Mustang Prairie, a roundish grassland reaching ten to twelve miles east of the Trinity. Smugglers gave the prairie its name because it was a place where wild horses could be found and captured.

The Neches/Angelina Watershed

The land between the Neches and Angelina rivers is unique to Texas geography and seminal to Texas history. To understand its importance to the development of the region over thousands of years, its centrality to this history, and why it was so prevalent a location for Caddo villages, one must understand the nature of watersheds. Watersheds are separated by the drainage divide—the ridge where water on one side flows to one set of tributaries and water on the opposite side of the hill to another set of tributaries. Along those slopes near the water sources feeding the Angelina and the Neches rivers, villages of Caddo Indians were spread over dozens of miles. The settlements were often only a few grass houses with associated granaries surrounded by agricultural activity in any nearby clearings. The Caddo were masters of their environment in a completely sustainable manner, and in the Neches-Angelina watershed they found favorable conditions for maintaining a stable lifestyle for thousands of years.[31]

The Nabadeche Caddo, members of the Hasinai confederacy, were the primary occupants of this vital watershed. A Spaniard who lived among them for fifteen months in 1691 wrote of nine tribes within a watershed thirty-five leagues long (ninety-one miles) in the terrain between the Neches and the Angelina rivers. Though the occupancy of East Texas by Spanish soldiers and priests was ostensibly to push back against the French, it was the Native American nations who proved to be of more consequence. It was Indian land, after all.

CROSSING THE SMALLER STREAMS

Between the Neches River and Nacogdoches, the roads were defined by the terrain and the waterways. Routes of El Camino Real and other roads avoiding Spanish presence each had to confront the same terrain. Heading east from the Trinity River, every traveler had to deal with crossings of Larrison Creek, Bean's Creek, the Angelina River, Caney Creek, Legg Creek, Bayou Loco, Alazán Bayou, Mill Creek, Moral Bayou, and finally Mill Branch and Bonita Creek.[32] The smaller creeks would often have steep banks but could also be more easily managed by building a temporary bridge. Archeological research has found a heavy concentration of Caddo sites along these creeks, some of them with indications of consistent trade with the French.[33]

A Frenchman, Monsieur Pierre Marie François de Pagès, wrote an account of a four-year journey that brought him through New Orleans and Natchitoches on his way through Texas to Mexico and points beyond. He left Nacogdoches headed west with a Spanish official and his party with twenty mules under load and another two hundred mules and horses in reserve.[34] They were stopped by heavy rainfall on the banks of a "large rivulet," likely the Angelina. One group described the storm that halted their travel toward the Angelina as coming from a storm where "the clouds seemed to come down to the ground."[35]

From Nacogdoches to the East

Nacogdoches in the early eighteenth century was little more than a tired mission and pueblo, but its location offered a respite for traders and travelers. De Pagès found the landscape between Los Adaes and Nacogdoches crisscrossed by small ridges and hills separated by lowland meadows and plains where the floodplains of the many creeks crossing the roads were found. The small prairies were covered with "a species of grass of a surprising height."[36] The better soils produced hardwood of many varieties, and the dryer areas were limited to large pines. Many of the pines were burned, some standing and some broken at the base, leaving large trunks fallen across his path. De Pagès encountered difficult stream crossings, and at one point his mule was overcome by a swarm of bees, prompting a hasty escape and a mud bath to tend to the stings.

When Stephen F. Austin traveled the road from the Sabine River to Nacogdoches in 1821, he found the character of the landscape familiar. The gently rolling hills and trees reminded him of the Barrens of Kentucky, a large and high plateau of land that was dry and somewhat sterile. Austin noted the timber west of the Sabine was larger with blackjack oak, black hickory, and mulberry predominant. The timber at that time was "all too low and scrubby for Rails, or building, except on the Creeks where the timber is very good and lofty."[37] The lushness of the grass is what impressed him the most, and it's what later made the area so important to ranchers. The red dirt was fertile and arable, interspersed with a lighter grey soil. One writer described "excellent land of a chocolate and sometimes a Vermillion color."[38]

Attoyac Bayou was the most significant stream between the Sabine River and Nacogdoches. Dense woods on either side hid a waterway lined by a variety of trees and vines and edged by "green and flowery hills and plains." Pine, cedar, sassafras, persimmon, hazelnut, and chestnut trees gave cover to strawberries, blackberries, and viperine. They also provided an environment for mosquitoes, gnats, ticks, and mites to lay in wait for any warm-blooded travelers.[39]

El Lobanillo, Ranch and Creek

In October 1788 when Father Francisco Xavier Fragoso passed through Nacogdoches, his diary of the journey reflected what he encountered along the way. Two leagues (five miles) after crossing the Sabine River headed west, the group passed El Lobanillo, a place he described as "a dwelling of Spaniards from the pueblo of Nacogdoches." El Lobanillo had been the home and ranch of Antonio Gil Ibarvo.[40]

The most repeated translation for *lobanillo* is tumor or wart. Another option to consider is that the ranch was named for the nearby Lobanillo Creek, sometimes referred to as Lobanella Creek or Boggy Creek. One of the alternate meanings for *lobanillo* is burl, or knot—a swelling. A burl or gall on a tree is a misshapen round mass, often quite large, that is caused by the larvae of the aptly named gall wasp when it lays eggs in the bark of an oak tree. Galls in the oak trees along the Arroyo de Lobanillo were so numerous they were mentioned by the surveyor for one of the land grants surrounding the ranch.[41]

In the document transferring El Lobanillo from Antonio Gil Ibarvo to Juan Ignacio Pifermo in 1794, there is mention of "*las mojoneras correspondientes por estos dos Rumbos*," or landmarks that correspond or converge at the two routes.[42] The landmark in that brief description exists today and is the most exceptional place on that historical terrain. There is no other site that can more dramatically communicate the concept of "seeing what the land remembers" than the ruts of ancient trails at Lobanillo Swales.

A swale is a low place between two ridges that is typically thought of as more sloped than what we might call a ditch. Deep swales near Ibarvo's ranch are remains of a road segment of El Camino Real de los Tejas, now a National Historic Trail managed by the National Park Service. Also called the Lobanillo Cuts, the location was purchased by El Camino Real de los Tejas National Historic Trail Association for acquisition as part of the National Park Service. It is about two miles west of Geneva, Texas, on Highway 21.[43] The incredible road scape that remains consists of eight braided, parallel ruts left behind by hundreds of years of use by people walking on foot, riding on horseback, and pulling wagons or carts. The largest of the cuts is about twelve feet deep and twenty feet wide. Archeological study indicates the ruts have remained largely unchanged. Within the boundaries of the site, artifacts dating from the Spanish colonial period through the Texas Republic and statehood and all the way to the nineteenth century were found.[44]

This historic trail site is one of those places on the ground that makes your senses tingle. The extraordinary size and depth of the ruts are like nothing else on the landscape in Texas. Visible swales exist all along El Camino Real, Trammel's Trace, and other notable trails, but they are commonly worn down from logging, plowing, or pasturage. The National Park Service application for National Register of Historic Place status for the site said it well:

> When one walks up and sees the monumental, undulating landmark and proceeds to walk in the deep, wide swales between the soaring, high ridges, one has a palpable sense of the Spanish Colonial experience of traveling on El Camino Real de los Tejas.[45]

These surviving ruts at Lobanillo Swales are not only spectacular in their scale but give a sense of the extreme volume of heavy traffic they have borne over the centuries. It is a place that must be seen to be fully appreciated and understood.

Nacogdoches Proper

In a long journey around the province in the late eighteenth century, Pedro Vial recorded places and people along the way.[46] Upon leaving Natchitoches and heading west on El Camino Real, Vial entered "woods and rolling country" on both sides of the Sabine. Familiar places were noted along the way—the campsite at Patrón (Patroon) Creek, Ayish Bayou, El Lobanillo, and another ranch called Atascoso.

After a night spent on the road east of Nacogdoches, the group of travelers entered the village early the next morning. The sun rising at their backs cast the surroundings in a beautiful glow. The quality of the light sharpened the contrast between the varying shades of green, reminding them that they were "in the midst of a forest of different kinds of trees." The outcroppings of bright red clay or stone of the "ferruginous hills" are features that can still be seen there now.

When Vial arrived in Nacogdoches in 1789 after it had been resettled for ten years, a decent-sized pueblo had grown up. Spanish, French, and Indian peoples made up the population. Nacogdoches was built between two small but well-supplied streams: La Nana (Bayou La Nana) to the east and El Bonito (Bonita Creek) to the west. A later writer during the period just before statehood described the location using florid language meant to stir up interest and immigration. He said it was "beautifully situated" in a location where it was "embosomed in a small valley, like a cup within a saucer."[47]

Karle Wilson Baker was a Pulitzer Prize-nominated poet and Nacogdoches resident who wrote one of the best definitions of the role of Nacogdoches in Texas history. She said, "Almost every foot that marked the soil of revolutionary Texas passed through the town; and almost every wayfaring head dreamed its restless dreams upon her pillows for at least one night."[48] Though Baker was correct about the role of early Nacogdoches, like many others she underestimated the time span of that importance. Caddo mound builders, French and Indian traders, Spanish priests, and enslaved runaways had all found a haven between the creeks.

2

Before the Others

What you are holding in your hand is about nine
—TOM MIDDLEBROOK, archaeological steward

It is difficult to imagine the emotions stirred by hearing those words unless you were Tom H. Gann, the collaborator on this work, holding a tangible piece of history in his palm. On a summer morning sometime around 2017, he and Tom Middlebrook, a Nacogdoches physician and notable member of the Archaeological Stewards Network of the Texas Historical Commission, relocated a Caddo site not examined since the 1930s. Middlebrook is one of only a handful of experts who intimately know this aspect of the history of East Texas and the people of the Caddo confederacies. Along with an assistant, the group found a likely spot to begin their investigation of the rediscovered site by conducting a shovel test. Shovel testing is a process that involves digging a measured hole, sifting the dirt through a screen, and examining any artifacts hidden in the soil. What the test turned up was a spectacular three-inch long spear point, a reminder of the people who called Texas home thousands of years before any Europeans even knew it existed.

Some Contextual Realignment

Before the arrival of the Spanish, the indigenous people of East Texas managed inter-tribal relationships, carried on commerce and trade, respected the lands of others, and had spiritual lives with long traditions. They survived and endured without Spanish arms, French cookware, or the Catholic religion for millennia before they knew any of that existed.

For the territory and time that is the focus of this work, one must acknowledge the culture, traditions, and stewardship of the Bidai and Caddo people. The Bidai were affiliated with tribes of the Atakapan in the southern half

The range of Eastern and coastal Indian tribes, 1778–89. Courtesy of Timothy Seiter.

of East Texas all the way to the coast, but they actively traded with others, including the French, before the arrival of the Spanish. There were twenty to thirty different other tribal groups on the eastern side of Texas from the Red River to the mouth of the Trinity during this period, including the Ais, Akokisa, Choctaw, Coushatta, Mayeyes, Karankawa, Osage, and Tonkawa.[1]

In the traditional understanding of the history of relations between Spanish officialdom and the first people of Texas, there has been a tendency to focus on the Spanish as the dominant power. Paintings of Spanish soldiers clad in armor sitting astride their magnificent mounts talking to a breechcloth-wearing tribal member armed only with a bow and arrow reinforce the impression that Spain came to Texas with superior military might. The earlier history of the Spanish conquistadores seeking wealth in the Indies and Central America included cruelty and torture. The scholarship on the borderlands fifty years ago tended to absolve the Spanish for their behavior. One author in a 1971 article said:

> For all the mistakes, for all the failures, for all the crimes committed . . . in its overall performance Spain, in relation to the American Indian, need offer no apology to any other people or nation.[2]

We are learning to overcome the bias that originates in an Anglocentric perspective. A respected scholar of the borderlands and former Texas State Historian, Light Cummins, tactfully explained that this quote "represents an older historiographical viewpoint which is no longer current in the scholarship of the Spanish Borderland."[3] What Cummins is saying is that our understanding of the facts and how we view them has evolved and been corrected since that time. But culturally biased and Anglocentric perspectives still persist. Current scholarship acknowledges that both the Spanish and French were more inclusive of native tribes than the English and Americans.[4] However, the Spanish still wished to "reduce" native populations to a religion and a lifestyle of subjugation that was foreign and unpalatable.

The ideological lenses that lead to cultural prejudices in viewing First People continue to be reexamined and questioned. An essay by historian Pekka Hämäläinen, as well as his larger body of work, presents an overview of this trend in what came to be called the New Texas Indian History beginning in the 1980s.[5] A monumental work along this line of scholarship began in earnest with Elizabeth A. H. John in 1975. Her book *Storms Brewed in Other Men's Worlds* is an incredible work that updates our perspectives on the interaction of Spanish, French, and native peoples from the earliest encounters in 1540 through the end of the eighteenth century.[6] A masterful book in 2008 by Hämäläinen, *The Comanche Empire*, made clear that the Comanche, not the Spanish or French, were the empire builders of this period.[7] A 2007 work by Juliana Barr, *Peace Came in the Form of a Woman*, more closely focuses on Native American and Spanish relations in the borderlands. Not only does she make the case for women playing a much larger role than generally acknowledged, but she also documents how indigenous nations were the dominant force and the feared conquerors in Texas.[8] These highly regarded and awarded works are among the most prominent which seek to correct the record and interpret the changing relationships that came with a growing Spanish presence.

History is about perspective. Much like the ancient perception that the earth was the center of the universe, once the point of view on what was being observed changed, so did an understanding of what was being seen. As Hämäläinen observes, it is important we remain "alive to the ever-present possibility that events could have turned out differently."[9] Spanish observers correctly understood that the native tribes had "little respect for the Spanish [who were] admitted only as friends, but without any authority."[10] Texas may have been a Spanish colony on paper, but on the ground, it was an indigenous nation.

Archaeology

Artifacts from archaeological sites are the primary means for learning about the early Caddo and other tribal groups in eastern Texas. The spaces and landscape where Caddo settlements are found tell us much about these people's daily lives and their manner of living. In Nacogdoches County alone, the Texas Historical Commission has identified and logged over 450 archaeological sites.[11] Most of those show evidence of hundreds of years of habitation by the Caddo people. Their culture and aspects of their history are partially established by the existence of pottery, copper or shell trade goods, arrow and spear points, and other artifacts that can be dated using the stratigraphy and composition of the soil where they are found.[12] Though there were many small tribal groups throughout East Texas from the Red River to the Gulf Coast during this time period, the focus here will be on the Caddo nation and the Bidai.

The Caddo are a well-researched group about whom much is known. Scholarly work continues to discover and interpret their central role at the time of the first Spanish expeditions and long before. The Bidai are a much smaller, little-known tribe. There are no distinctive artifacts from their material culture that allow archaeologists to know if a particular site belonged to the Bidai. However, they played an outsized role in the contraband economy of East Texas, and their trading trails were alternate routes for anyone wanting to avoid detection.

The Caddo

The Caddo perspective on the intrusion of Europeans into their lands is seen in some clarity by an encounter some two hundred years after the first entradas by the Spanish. In 1828, seven years after Texas became Mexican territory, there was an uneasy wariness by Mexico toward the United States just across the Sabine River. To the east of Béxar there was nothing but Nacogdoches fronting the United States. Mexican General Manuel de Mier y Terán was sent to the eastern reaches of the province on a border inspection tour to determine what actions Mexico should take to maintain its tenuous claim on the territory. When he arrived in Nacogdoches, tribal members from around the region recognized that Terán was an important man of stature and importance. Their efforts at diplomacy were directed toward someone who might help them secure their land and conduct trade.

While in Nacogdoches, Terán was visited continually by tribal leaders. A Caddo chief appeared before Terán with military-style epaulets on his shoulders and a large medallion around his neck bearing the image of King Carlos III of Spain, gifts from earlier Spanish visitors. He also bore evidence of a disease brought by Europeans. Smallpox had left the old chief's face disfigured, pock-marked, and wrinkled. The chief was not there to placate or beg Terán; from his perspective Terán was his peer as a leader of their respective tribes.

As a military man, Terán wanted to understand where the Caddo villages were found to assess where the chief's allegiance might lie in the event of conflict. It took some time for the chief to understand what Terán was asking. Once it became clear, his answer to Terán was unequivocal. Terán asked if his people were occupying land that was part of Mexico or in that of the United States. The nature of the words the chief spoke in answering were uttered by a man who had endured much during his many years with his people. Terán wrote:

> When he [the chief] fully understood what was being asked, he replied that he was not in Mexican territory nor in that of the North Americans, but in his own land, which was nothing else but his.[13]

It is likely that Terán's later recording of this event in his journal did not give full gravity to the seriousness of the Caddo chief's reply. Terán had not even considered that as one of the possible answers. He did not take into consideration that the land belonged to those who had occupied it for thousands of years. His failure to do so, indeed his inability to do so, represented a Eurocentric view still held by many.

Kingdom of the Tejas

Subjects of the Spanish crown had a better perspective than Terán. In 1690 they knew a kingdom when they saw it. When they came upon the Hasinai villages and ceremonial structures on San Pedro Creek at the Neches in 1690, they called it the "Kingdom of the Tejas." Tejas was the name given to the Hasinai, while the French called them the Cenis.[14]

In the Spanish paradigm, being a nation meant occupying it with missions, buildings, and boundaries. It meant religious and cultural institutions that exercised their hierarchical authority. It meant God and King. Though many of the indigenous nations were characterized as roaming bands of uncivilized people, the Caddo people were substantively different. The Caddo were an organized society of successful people with practices and customs that led to an enduring presence in the land they populated between southwestern Arkansas, northeastern Texas, and northwestern Louisiana. Barr called it their "territorial stability," based on advanced settlement practices.[15] Three major Caddo confederacies or tribal groupings were present in this region: the Kadohadacho near the Great Bend of the Red River, the Natchitoches in that southern region of the Red River, and the Hasinai in the Neches-Angelina watershed of East Texas. In the Hasinai confederacy there were eight distinct groups: Hainai (the leading group), Anadarko, Nabedache, Nacogdoche, Nacono, Namidish, Nasoni, and Neche.[16]

Caddo Communities

The Caddo did not roam or migrate like some tribes. Evidence indicates they occupied their villages year-round, operating them as sustainable, agricultural communities. Their villages were not concentrated but instead were spread over miles, often along a stream bank, with groups of seven to fifteen grass houses. Along the Neches-Angelina watershed, Caddo communities included small farms and homes separated by unoccupied land over miles of terrain. The farms were part of *rancherias* strung out over more than forty miles.[17] Even with the villages being dispersed there would be a central plaza where a chief might live and that included community temples or other shared structures. Fertile spots in natural clearings or prairies were used to grow maize, beans, corn, watermelons, squash, and nuts. The Caddo people's ability to store their food led one missionary priest to acknowledge that they perhaps had it better than did the tribes who agreed to live at the missions.

At the Angelina River in 1766, one Spanish expedition found several villages of Hasinai that were each separate and distinct. They admired the conical, grass and reed structures, comparing them to a similar style of construction used for shepherd's huts in Estremadura, a remote area of western Spain. On the interior of the grass houses were partitions built to separate sleeping areas and beds elevated high on the walls.[18]

"Good Will and Strange Behavior"

In 1767, a priest described the Caddo who lived near the mission at Nacogdoches as "peaceful Indians, gentle, jovial, except now and then some are bad and perverse." He saw in the Caddo indications of traits that cross cultures, such as a desire to "esteem the men who are handsome, brave, and strong" and to appoint them as leaders of the tribe.[19] A group of Caddos visiting one expedition near Alazán Bayou west of Nacogdoches showed "good will and strange behavior with their vermilion paint, adornment of beads, and hair combed French-style, smeared with mud, and whitened, of which they show the greatest vanity."[20] The men were observed to be naked except for a breechcloth but decorated themselves with bead and feathers. The women wore buckskins decorated with colored beads. Beneath their red, straight hair hung long bones from their ears as earrings.[21]

Behaviors one diarist saw as "wise and cunning" were sensible in a time when dangers could take them by surprise. He noticed that when crossing open spaces, the Caddo would stay along the edge of the woods until they could see the open ground was unoccupied. Even then, they might hold a tree branch on their side to disguise their human form from anyone observing them from a distance. When the roles were reversed and they wanted to observe others without their knowledge, the Caddo were seen climbing a tall tree to gain a better vantage point.

The Caddo were formidable in commerce, culture, and consistency. Their presence surpassed that of Spanish settlements and their nation prevailed . . . for a time.

The Bidai

Brushwood. That is one interpretation of what the Caddo word *bidai* meant. It is a loose translation of the name they had for themselves—Quasmigdo.[22] The name for the tribe could have referred to the forested land thick with understory which they inhabited along the Trinity River and south into the Big Thicket. The Bidai are associated with the Atakapan traditions and language. They intermarried with the Akokisa and the Patiris to their south. The Deadose to their north and west were a former branch of the Bidai. The Karankawa, Kickapoo, and Koasati, and later the Coushatta, were all in their sphere of relationships. The Orcoquisa, Bidai, Deadoses, and other smaller groups totaled around 3,500 in 1698 when first encountered by Spanish expeditions.[23] The Bidai were likely never more than five hundred in number, and by 1756 the tribe may have had only one hundred warriors. As with other tribes, epidemics in 1777 and 1778 tragically reduced their numbers.

The Bidai were noted in reports from the first Spanish attempts to found missions in 1691 and continued to turn up in virtually every report following.[24] The Marqués de Aguayo expedition in 1721 found them at their village just west of the Trinity at a creek the Spanish called Nuestra Señora del Buen

Suceso (Our Lady of Good Success), likely along Bedias Creek, which empties into the Trinity River. When Spanish subjects started a new settlement on the Trinity at Bedias Creek in 1774, a Bidai village was only five miles away. They were most often counted among the tribes friendly to the Spanish, and they did so without sacrificing a long trading history with the French.

A Bidai Homeland

With villages along the Trinity River, the Bidai were in a location where they could be alert to the passage of every Spanish expedition from Mexico into East Texas. During a Spanish visit to the newly formed East Texas missions in 1718, a chronicler wrote that the Bidai "nation is extremely numerous and extends for [a distance of] three days on the road from this pueblo of La Concepción de Agreda [Mission Concepción] to the coast where other nations are [living] who are friends of the Tejas [Caddo]."[25] In their physical location and their interactions with both native and European nations, the Bidai occupied a middle ground. Their territory was between Caddo groups to the north and Akokisa and Karankawa to the south. They traded hides for guns with the French, then traded guns for horses with the Apache, who stole the horses from the Spanish. It was a tidy arrangement for a tribe clearly skilled with salesmanship if nothing else. Spanish officials spent decades trying to interrupt that source of weapons to the Apache.

Bidai Settlements and Communities

Bidai villages snaked along the middle Trinity River and its tributaries to the east and west. One group of Bidai lived near the mouth of Bedias Creek and a set of shoals that came to be called Paso Tomás. Chief Tomás was the head of the Bidai, who had settled there as early as 1728.[26] Near a low waterfall on the Trinity where the shoals allowed an easier crossing, the Bidai lived near the primary entry point of Spanish expeditions over hundreds of years. They were at the gateway to the larger Caddo villages along the Neches and San Pedro Creek. Trails also wound north to the Caddo villages and south to the Atakapan and Orcoquisa people.

Bidai living structures were reportedly cone-shaped like those of the Caddo but used the material they had available in the form of poles and vines rather than straw from prairie grasses. In the winter, they covered their smaller shelters with bearskins for warmth. Their skill and use of materials available in the coastal and riverine forests allowed them to produce furnishings made of bamboo cane and palmetto fronds. Later documentation shows they made improvements to their products using new materials, producing chairs made of rattan and hickory for trade with Anglo settlers. Those products—as well as the cane baskets, daub pottery, and skin pouches—did not survive being buried to await discovery by modern archaeologists. [27]

Personal Traits

The Bidai were described as short, dark-skinned, and stoutly built. They also practiced head-flattening, or shaping the skull by binding. With animal skins barely covering themselves and dark tattoos on their skin, they looked imposing to Europeans. The Bidai and other less well-regarded tribes were often the object of derision.

Hasinai medicine men blamed the Bidai and other nearby tribes for diseases caused by their witchcraft.[28] In 1778 the French trader Athanase de Mézières said the Bidai had become "a vagrant, miserable, lazy people, who, having forsaken the chase as a means of subsistence, beg constantly for their living . . . and thus contribute not to the relief but to the hindrance of its own poverty-stricken and needy inhabitants."[29] In contrast, by 1805 Indian agent John Sibley said they had "an excellent character for honesty and punctuality."[30] His impressions were based on a somewhat limited exposure to the tribe, and he used terms that were a bit condescending.

Bidai Trade with Apache

The Bidai were also middlemen in the borderlands supply chain. They served as intermediaries in the trade between the French and tribal groups including the Apache, Karankawa, and Tonkawa. Spanish governors at Los Adaes, only a few miles from French traders at Natchitoches, were involved in illicit trade for many years. In the 1750s the Spanish governor based in Los Adaes was known to trade with the Bidai and the Akokisa along the Trinity. He obtained knives, scissors, tobacco, combs, beads, and weapons from the French in Natchitoches and then had his soldiers transport the goods to the Trinity to trade for corn, buckskins, buffalo hides, and horses. The corn and horses were sold in Los Adaes, and the skins went to Natchitoches to start the cycle all over again.[31]

What the Bidai did with the weapons they acquired in trade was an ongoing thorn in the side of Spanish authority. The trade relationship between the Bidai and the more hostile and aggressive Apache meant that Apache attacks were made using French weapons and stolen Spanish horses. De Mézières said in 1772:

> I have not included the Bidais tribe among our friends, because the peace which they have made with the Apache seems to be sufficient reason to consider them as quasi-enemies, and because it is notorious that they continue supplying these Apache with firearms and munitions in exchange for mules and horses, well known to be stolen.[32]

To try and stop the Bidai supplying weaponry to the more aggressive Lipan Apache, the Spanish temporarily cut off trade to the Bidai and their closely affiliated allies the Akokisas, Cocos, and Mayeyes. An even more effective deterrent for the Bidai to trade with the Apache was that by 1793 the Apache were stealing horses from the Bidai themselves.[33]

Epidemics of Disease

Before 2020 and the COVID-19 pandemic, few Americans understood what happens when a disease gets so out of control that it results in an inordinate number of deaths. At the time of this writing, almost 1.2 million Americans have died due to COVID-19, and many individual families have felt the impact of an unchecked illness. The history of our nation's response to the flu epidemic in 1918 appeared lost on those of us not prone to learn from the past. As a people we survive, but we know things will never be the same.

It must have been a similar situation when the indigenous people of the New World first met Europeans. Europeans brought their diseases to places and people who had no immunities. One month after Cabeza de Vaca landed in the New World, half of the tribe that rescued him from the beach died from what is suspected to have been cholera.[34] Trade relationships extended the opportunities for disease to spread. By the early 1700s, conditions were right for the transmission of disease across the entire Texas province. In addition to epidemic diseases like smallpox, chronic diseases such as dysentery, influenza, measles, and a gift from the Europeans in the form of syphilis, also had an impact.[35] In one mission 50 percent of the deaths were children younger than three years old.[36] Diseases did not discriminate based on age, but the old and the young were particularly susceptible.

A Spanish expedition in 1768 saw signs of illness among the Bidai and other Texas tribes. They noted that smallpox, measles, typhoid fever, and other diseases made the victims "horrible to the sight and filthy." In an image from the sixteenth-century *Florentine Codex*, one can see the personal impact of these illnesses.[37] Observers blamed the native people's diet as well, saying these ailments were caused by "drinking whiskey and sugar cane wine with the bear grease that

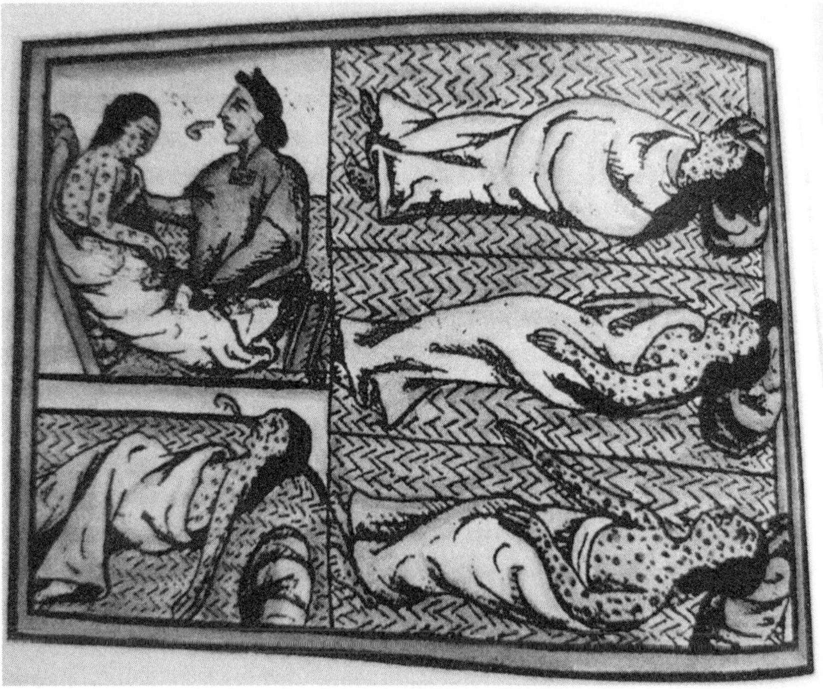

Indigenous people suffering from smallpox. From the Florentine Codex (Wikimedia Commons). With thanks to Dan Worrall.

is drunk as if it were water because it is drinkable and does not curdle."[38] If that was intended to be the cure, it may well have been worse than the illness. There may have been only seventy Bidai warriors remaining within ten years.[39]

Even after all the death and illness, the Bidai and other tribes knew little about where the diseases came from other than they were associated with their contact with Europeans. In 1785, Pedro (Pierre) Vial, a French trader and interpreter, met with a great assemblage of Comanche. He was able to reassure them of their safety by recognizing that since his party's arrival at the Comanche village, "the sun had not clouded and that it was always very clear and bright, which proved our coming healthy and well."[40]

Priests and Medicine Men

The relationships of mission priests to tribal medicine men came with inherent conflict. The priests saw the Caddo *xinesi* as tricksters at best, and devil worshippers and idolaters at worst.

> All of them [xinesi] are liars and guilty of a thousand deceptions, while some of them are enchanters. Once one of them by his tricks tried to prevent me from baptizing a woman. I hurled an exorcism against him, and all at once, he ran away as if I had tried to kill him.[41]

A description of an attempt the Bidai used to cure typhoid fever during an epidemic in the nineteenth century provides an indication of a cure that did not rely on spells and incantations. In one village, about thirty wooden scaffolds were seen with head-high platforms. Those suffering from the symptoms of chest congestion were lain on the platform above a smudge—a slow-burning fire—with the dense smoke enveloping them. There were no reports of the success of the treatment. A cure for dysentery, using sparkleberry roots and berries, was more likely to have had a positive effect.[42]

Emotional Impact

In most discussions of the impact of European-borne disease on native populations, the accounts are quantitative and somewhat generalized. One study suggests that in the first one hundred years of Spanish contact, 75 percent or more of the native population succumbed to foreign-borne disease.[43] What we do not hear much about is the emotional impact of that level of mortality on the natives. We do not know how they felt from their words, but we do from their humanness.

Athanase de Mézières was the most widely respected French trader and diplomat for tribal relations of the period. In a report on tribal epidemics in 1778, he implied that he personally felt differently about death among the Caddo and friendly tribes, He offered a glimpse into his perception of how the tribes managed the loss by saying they were responding with "civilized resignation."[44] Whether he was seeing the native version of having a stiff upper lip, or whether they were simply not exposing him to their emotions, one will never know. His opinion does seem to contrast with an observation by Cabeza de Vaca in 1528 when he among coastal Texas tribes, likely the Cocos and Atakapa.

> When someone's child happens to die, the parents and relatives and the whole village weep with him for a full year. The parents begin crying each morning before dawn, and then the whole village joins in. They do the same thing at mid-day and at sunset. At the end of a year, they honor the dead child and wash themselves clean of the soot on their bodies. They mourn all their dead in this manner except old people, whom they ignore, saying that their time is passed.[45]

In the present day, perhaps the Native American community better remembers the impact disease can have on a people, on a culture. One activist explained that native people should "act in honor of ancestors who fought to ensure their survival and elders who carry on their traditions and cultures."[46] They also appealed to a recognition of how their actions might impact the next seven generations. This seven-generations thinking predates the arrival of the Spanish in Texas and reminds Native Americans to look ahead. In general, it means that people should consider how the decisions they make today will have a ripple effect seven generations into the future. We are now seven generations past the epidemics of 1778–79. Perhaps the "civilized resignation" of the Caddo has evolved into a civilized resistance.[47]

It Is About Cultures

In the second half of the eighteenth century, after the parade of Spanish priests and soldiers abated, Texas was still very much a Native American nation. Their dominance was not only measured by their ability to fight, but also by their control of trade and commerce.[48] Eastern Texas indigenous groups were engaged in cooperative trade with English, Spanish, and French traders, Anglo immigrants, and tribes in all directions from the pueblo of Nacogdoches. At times it was unclear whether the Spanish or the Native Americans would ultimately dominate Texas, but the Spanish at every turn demonstrated an inability to control trade and a recognition that they were in no position to conquer any of the tribes. In 1689 when de León entered present-day Texas, it was Native American country; eighty years later when Marqués de Rubí completed his inspection, that was still true.[49]

The United States' Declaration of Independence proclaimed in 1776 that Indians were "merciless savages."[50] Over the centuries, this lack of perspective persisted. Former Senator Rick Santorum said in 2021, "We birthed a nation from nothing. I mean, there was nothing here. I mean, yes, we have Native Americans, but candidly there isn't much Native American culture in American culture." As the editorialist citing his quote observed, "Ignorance lives in close proximity to racism."[51]

At the same time the fledgling colonists were decrying the savages in their midst in 1776, Spain was learning to coexist as lesser partners in the tribal nations of Texas. Spanish officials learned their place and the best means for maintaining the peace.

> Both the Indians of these nations and the Comanches, when they enter here, are treated in the fashion that experience has taught me in dealing with Indians, which is: to speak the truth to them; make clear to them the offenses that they commit against us; and provide them with the gifts made possible by what is destined for this purpose and is currently on hand.[52]

Spain learned very quickly that the indigenous people of eastern Texas were the dominant power. If Spanish settlement was to survive in East Texas, the Spaniards would have to recognize and acknowledge that fact.

3

La Provincia de los Tejas

> If His Majesty (who God protects) does not take warning . . .
> the French will be masters of all this land.
>
> —DIEGO RAMÓN[1]

Imaginary Kingdom is the title of a noteworthy book written by Jack Jackson and William C. Foster. The title of the book refers to the condition of the Spanish presence in Texas reported by the Marqués de Rubí in 1767. Following his firsthand review of the missions and presidios scattered across East Texas, Rubí affirmed the perceptions of other military inspections in a way that only a man with a secure relationship with the crown could deliver.

Rubí's observation was that the Spanish ruled nothing in Texas. There was no Spanish conquest, or an empire extended as a buffer to Louisiana. The land was not theirs, it belonged to the tribal nations; Spanish maps said as much. The *tierra* of the Apache, Comanche, Wichita, Caddo, and others was well marked. Their boundaries were not proscribed by edict, but by the territorial consensus that ruled the land.

The power and dominance of the indigenous nations of Texas was the impetus for Spanish imperial policy. The Spanish presence at Béxar, La Bahía, and Los Adaes in the middle of the eighteenth century was only possible by the tacit consent of the indigenous people. Whatever military presence the Spanish were able to project was ineffective, under-resourced, and rife with corruption. The fact that it was an "imaginary kingdom" was not completely unexpected.

Spanish Ambivalence Toward Texas

When Spanish conquistadors found Incan gold in Central America, their focus became finding out how far those riches extended to the north. Francisco Vásquez de Coronado searched for the imaginary Seven Cities of Cibola through what is now the southwestern United States and North Texas in 1540. His mammoth effort included a "swarming mass of humans and livestock: thousands of cattle, sheep, and hogs to feed an expeditionary force made up of between three and four hundred Spanish soldiers, probably an equal number of slaves and servants, and an accompanying army of thousands of *indios amigos*, native allies from various Mexican tribes."[2] They returned empty-handed to Mexico City. Luis de Moscoso Alvarado's 1542 report to the king temporarily ended the costly search for nonexistent riches. When it was finally determined that the existence of gold and silver deposits ended well to the south of the Rio Grande, subsequent expeditions came to Texas with different goals in mind.[3]

The Spanish empire in the Americas was vast and feebly maintained. When it came to Texas and the northern provinces, it was also largely beyond the reach of any possible military defense.[4] Spain's interests conflicted with those of France, the tribal nations, and with the later ambitions of the United States. Maintaining the semblance of control was a never-ending exercise for an empire remotely ruled from Madrid and Mexico City. Texas was at the farthest edge of the land Spain claimed, hundreds of miles and weeks of travel away from Mexico City.

The interests of Spain in Texas were reduced to little more than their ability to hold the territory as a buffer to more valued land to the south. Herbert Bolton, an eminent historian focused on this period of history, described the ebb and flow of Spanish interests in Texas by saying:

> The activities of the Spanish government in Texas were from first to last inspired largely by fears of foreign aggression. When these fears slept, Texas was left pretty much to itself, so far as the government was concerned, but when serious rumors of encroaching strangers reached the official ears, there was likely to be vigorous proceedings for a time.[5]

Scott Sosebee, professor of history at Stephen F. Austin State University, described it more generally when he compared Spain's interest in Texas to an inattentive boyfriend who becomes jealous only when someone else becomes desirous of his girlfriend. Spain had little interest in occupying Texas until a Frenchman named La Salle showed up on the Texas coast.[6] Spain's ambivalence and on-and-off interest in Texas rose and fell over the decades but its impact on the history of the region continued across hundreds of years.

A Foundational History of the Region

For this work on East Texas history in the period between 1772 and 1813, it is important to understand what was happening in Spanish East Texas in the years leading up to that period. There are many excellent sources cited here and in the bibliography that offer a broader and deeper examination of Spanish colonial history in Texas. Two giants in the study of Spanish Texas borderlands whose works have been relied on for this book are Herbert Bolton and Carlos Castañeda. Herbert Bolton was a professor of history at the University of Texas from 1901 to 1909, leaving to join the faculty of the University of California at Berkeley. During his time in Texas, Bolton's interests in the early Spanish and native dominance of Texas and the Southwest led to his becoming the primary point of reference for borderlands historical research. Bolton's 1905 article, "Spanish Abandonment and Re-Occupation of East Texas, 1773–1779," and his 1915 book, *Texas in the Middle Eighteenth Century*, are a foundation for much of this research. Bolton's article is something that can be read and understood by anyone, but the book is a voluminous work covering decades of history and requires a bit more commitment. Light T. Cummins, former State Historian of Texas and Austin College professor emeritus, cautions today's readers against the inherent cultural biases of historical works from that time. Nevertheless, Bolton is still the foundation on which much subsequent work is built.

Carlos Castañeda's authoritative work, *Our Catholic Heritage in Texas, 1519–1936*, edited by Paul J. Foik, is seven volumes of detailed historical accounts covering hundreds of years of Spanish history in Texas. His masterpiece work is an essential part of any study of Texas history. It is not the kind of work you read for pleasure, but as a reference it is remarkable to explore and dissect.[7] The primary volumes in that series used for this work were Volume III, *The Mission Era: The Missions at Work 1731–1761*, Volume IV, *The Passing of the Missions 1762–1782*, and Volume V, *The End of Spanish Regime, 1780—1810*.[8]

For readers who want to build on their understanding of this period of Texas history there are two other highly readable books recommended for further study. One is written by an eminent professor of history and the other by a Washington attorney with Texas roots. *Spanish Texas 1519–1821*, by Donald E. Chipman (and with Harriet Denise Joseph for the revised edition), is an outstanding synopsis of three hundred years of Spanish governance over Texas.[9] Written by professors of history, the work is a good starting point for any reader who wants to dig more deeply into this era. Chipman was knighted by King Carlos I of Spain for the research he has conducted on Spanish Texas.

William C. Foster's *Spanish Expeditions into Texas 1889–1768* is the work of an independent researcher driven by the fires of curiosity who also happened to be a corporate attorney.[10] The core of Foster's book on Spanish exploration is an attempt to retrace the routes of Spanish expeditions using descriptions from Spanish source documents and expedition diaries. With his financial resources and determination, he used pickups, canoes, and helicopters to conduct his research. The result is a thoroughly researched work but one that was challenged by some for his geographical assumptions.[11]

Interested readers will also want to find works by Juliana Barr, Jack Jackson, Frank de la Teja, and Francis X. Galan. There are many other outstanding scholars who cover the broader aspect of Spanish colonialism, contraband trade, and related aspects of this history referenced in the bibliography. With these foundational works on a future reading list, this chapter reviews key events leading up to the focal years of this work.

Spanish Entradas to Eastern Texas

Spain's blueprint for extending its territory was a combination of the two major means at their disposal for the control of people and land—the establishment of Catholic missions for the "heathen" Indians, and the installation of presidios to project a semblance of military strength.

The earliest Spanish attempts to penetrate indigenous lands, particularly those of the Caddo east of the Trinity River, were intercepted and turned back well before entering territory the tribes controlled. An expedition in 1650 could only learn that a Hasinai settlement was "very large and contained many people" by being told about it by others. Alonso de León in 1689 was also prevented from making it all the way into the Hasinai kingdom. One of the native escorts monitoring Spanish movements would only describe for him how there were "ten towns fifteen leagues [forty miles] long and seven leagues [eighteen miles] wide" with homes, gardens, and a highly cultured social structure.[12] The Kingdom of the Tejas was impressive, but it was also initially inaccessible.

1690—De León Expedition

Spain's efforts to extend its presence in East Texas evolved in 1690 with the establishment of missions to the Hasinai Caddo on the Neches River at San Pedro Creek. A Nabadeche (Caddo) village thirty-five miles east of the Trinity River at San Pedro Creek was where an expeditionary group found itself in May of 1690. De León's arrival at the western Caddo village of the Nabadeche tribe, part of the Hasinai confederacy, was graciously acknowledged while still unwelcomed. The approach that the Caddo allowed was tentative and cautiously regimented. The Hasinai exercised full ceremonial control and made clear through their actions that they were not welcoming a conquering army or a superior race, but simply allowing a diplomatic outreach. The Spanish were there by permission, not by power.

This was a turning point in the history of Spanish occupation in East Texas. Missionaries and soldiers took up lasting residence among the forests and along the rivers occupied by the Caddo. During the period from 1690 through 1730, Spanish ambivalence toward Texas showed itself in a wavering pattern of commitment to missions and presidios at the eastern edge of the province. Religious and military sites were established and abandoned, only to be reestablished and abandoned again. As leaders came and went, their policies shifted between concern over losing the territory to Anglo interests and the cost to the crown for maintaining and supplying the distant placement of people. Like a Foucault pendulum, decisions about the missions swung back and forth as the world moved in a different direction beneath them.

After the Spanish communicated that they wished to build a place that would house a mission, the Caddo allowed only three priests and three soldiers to remain behind. The result was Misíon Nuestro Padre San Francisco de los Tejas, the oldest established presence of the Spanish Catholic Church in East Texas.[13] When another expedition returned with supplies the following year, it learned that an additional mission, Misíon Santísimo Nombre de María, had been established not far away but closer to the Neches River.

The mission period that began in 1690 was fraught with practical challenges, like the lack of supplies, and external pressures from outside the empire. The soldiers who returned to resupply Mission San Francisco de Tejas endured an ice storm that killed many of their horses and floods that forced them to cross fast-moving rivers and streams.[14] The same floods overwhelmed the second mission, washing it away.

1716—Ramón Expedition

In 1716 the pendulum swung once more toward reviving the Spanish presence in East Texas. When Domingo Ramón and Fray Isidro Félix de Espinosa returned to the lands of the Caddo, they did so when the rivalry between Spain and France was at a critical juncture. The resolve to again make an effort to occupy East Texas was the result of the cross-country journey of a French trader.

It is difficult to imagine today how much of a stir Louis Juchereau de St. Denis created when he suddenly appeared at the Spanish presidio of San Juan Bautista along the Rio Grande. The mission's Spanish captain was fearful and vigilant when St. Denis, who was born in Quebec, educated in France, and lived in Natchitoches, arrived unexpectedly in July 1714, having crossed the entire northern province from Louisiana with trade goods considered illegal.

Along the way, St. Denis had traded with the Hasinai of East Texas, so he knew eastern Texas well. Ramón wrote a letter reiterating the concern that the Spanish held regarding this part of the empire. If Spain did not consider St. Denis's crossing all of Texas and trading with the Native Americans to be a warning sufficient to take action to settle the region, he said, then "the French will be masters of all the land."[15]

Capt. Diego Ramón held St. Denis under light arrest while waiting for instructions from Mexico City on what to do with him. During his time in the mission, St. Denis's charm won over Ramón, and his ability to promote good will also gained him favor in Mexico City. St. Denis was hired to support a grand Spanish return to Texas in an expedition that created the first continuous European settlement of Texas. The decision was made in August 1715 to reestablish missions and presidios in East Texas to regain some semblance of presence within the vast territory, and they needed the help of a Frenchman to do it.

The Logistics of an Entrada

Domingo Ramón led the return to Texas with the support and participation of the Frenchman St. Denis along with priests from the missionary colleges of Querétaro and Zacatecas. Ramón and twenty-five mounted soldiers left Saltillo on February 17, 1716, with almost a dozen priests and lay clergy. They erected ten large crosses along their route and celebrated over three hundred masses during the trek. The priests and soldiers were accompanied by seventy-five additional men and women, some with families, who hoped to settle somewhere along the journey. These were the first Spanish women to establish homes within Texas.

In addition to the large numbers of people, herders managed the sixty-four oxen, 490 horses and mules, and one thousand head of goats and sheep, which they drove across Texas. Along the way there were storms and disasters, abandonments and injuries, deaths and weddings. Eighty-three horses drowned in a single unfortunate river crossing.[16] The logistics of such a caravan were chaotic and imposing. Though the diaries describing this expedition and others provide descriptive details, there is almost no mention of the practical difficulties of such a movement of people and animals. There was at least some inherent support for travelers in the way that the well-used Native American trails made their way across the landscape. One Spanish traveler noted that the roads passed springs and watering holes about a day's travel apart, in places where they could also find pastures, food sources, and wood for fires and shelter.[17]

Historian Light T. Cummins shed some light on the nature of the entrada in communication with the author.[18] His suggestion was to think of the progress of the entrada as a moving town rather than as simply travel. Daily routines for morning prayers, cooking, vespers, and bedding guided the day, but they were constantly adjusted depending on the terrain, weather, or other difficulties. Members of the entrada had assigned duties, and there were those who could repair guns and manage saddles and packs. Scouts went ahead, often with Native American guides or escorts, so that they might know what was to come. Small groups would also be sent out to hunt or fish. Cummins pointed out that the movement of the entrada would not necessarily have been in a single line, like a military march. When it could, the group moved in a long, lateral line facing forward, hundreds of feet wide from side to side. In places where that approach would not work, the group would tighten up the columns, but either way such massive numbers of feet and hooves left scars on the landscape.

The lack of details about mundane aspects of their journey leaves the curious unsatisfied. Diaries were official government documents detailing the excursion for the governor, viceroy, or the king; they could not be expected to include an update on the smell of the bodies, the nature of the food or lack of it, and exactly where and how 1,500 hooved animals left their waste. We are left to our own imaginations. Certainly, the native inhabitants would have no problem seeing them coming or following where they had been.

The Establishment of East Texas Missions

Domingo Ramón did not enter the land of the Caddo for exploration. His assignment was to reestablish a series of missions across the region to proselytize local tribes in the hope they would become allies and provide a buffer to entry by the French.

Misíon San Francisco de los Tejas

Upon reaching the fertile and well-populated Neches-Angelina watershed, Ramón encountered Nabadeche Caddo who welcomed him with great fanfare and celebration, apparently having forgotten their ill will toward the disease-bearing Spaniards who were there until 1693. On July 3, 1716, Ramón reestablished the mission to the Nabadeche, renamed as Misíon Nuestro Padre San Francisco de los Tejas. The new site was located on the east side of the Neches this time, eliminating a river crossing and perhaps to avoid the flooding that befell Mission Santísimo Nombre de María. It should have been clear from the beginning that the Caddo people had no interest in the Spanish religion, but the holy fathers and their escorts wasted little time in pushing farther into the province. Saving souls was also a way to save the soil.

Presidio Nuestra Señora de los Dolores de los Tejas

The east side of the Neches is also where the Spanish built their first East Texas presidio—Presidio Nuestra Señora de los Dolores de los Tejas, located about eight miles east of the mission. The history of the presidio would be uneventful, even following a relocation farther to the east. The location of the old fort has not been found.

Misíon Nuestra Señora de la Purísima Concepción de los Hainai

When the next mission site was selected at a principal village of the Hainai, Domingo Ramón described it in his 1716 diary as a location along one of the many trails to the east. This path led some of the entradas to a crossing of "the Angelina at a shallow bottom of the river and then crossing a subtle rise in the eastern floodplain," where the mission was constructed.[19]

Domingo Ramón depicted the site selected for the mission in a way that could have described any number of locations up and down the Angelina River watershed. Crossing land with plentiful water and large pines, Ramón's expedition found a village of Nabadeche Indians in a settlement large enough for him to call it a town. The bounty of the village was described as an "infinity of rancherias" with corn, watermelons, beans, cantaloupes, tobacco, and an unnamed edible flower, likely sunflowers.[20] The village's crops of maize and other plantings were so extensive that the soldiers altered their route to reduce any damage.

A work by Tom Middlebrook, Morris Jackson, and George Avery in 2012 included a translation by Matthew Babcock, a professor of history, of an unpublished document written by Ramón himself. In it, he described the site in more detail:

> A small area somewhat large from where it extends further is from south to north covered by sparse woodlands of diverse trees. The eastern part has an extended mesa where a trail crosses on whose slope has different springs and one especially big one and connected to it a small little marsh. To the west of this place at a distance of half a league is the river of this nation, which is very big.[21]

After possible locations for this mission were proposed by Bolton (1918), Robert Bruce Blake (1938), and Jim Corbin (prior to his death in 2004), the tenacity of local archaeologists finally led to an identification of the location of Mission Concepción. Through their patient efforts, Tom Middlebrook, Jeff Williams, Bo Nelson, Mark Walters, Connie Hodges, Morris Jackson, George Avery, and a host of other volunteers identified the site of the mission proper and three other associated archaeological sites—known as Gallant Falls site (41NA344)—in May 2010 on private land. The misplaced historical marker for Mission Concepción was also moved to the location later that year.

Archaeological field work at the site through 2019 recovered hundreds of Spanish, French, and Caddo artifacts.[22] This reflects the cross-cultural trading activity that was widespread in the region. Middlebrook, Jackson, and others on the project documented many indications that Mission Concepción was a key trading and cultural hub. Caddo from confederacies to the north and Bidai from the south would have made their way here along the ancient trails that were pathways for trade.[23]

Misíon Señora Guadalupe de los Nacogdoches

The mission of Nuestra Señora Guadalupe de los Nacogdoches, founded in July 1716, would become the cornerstone of all future Spanish settlement of East Texas. Log buildings for the chapel and a cabin for the priest were quickly erected, and the mission was appointed as the focal point for other Zacatecas missions headed by Father Antonio Margil de Jesús.

There is disagreement regarding the placement of the original mission.[24] One indicator that one of the earliest missions may have been south of Nacogdoches proper is a brief mention of an abandoned mission in a diary kept for an inspection by Marqués de Rubí in 1766.

> We traveled five leagues to the south [of Nacogdoches] along a middle course over ground like the preceding. At a quarter of a league from the mission we crossed the Nana arroyo. In the interval between it and the Angelina River, which runs southwest, we passed another nameless mission.[25]

The general location of this "nameless mission," clearly older and abandoned, was south of the later town as well, although the active mission was closer to the road from Natchitoches where they started. This nameless mission would have been well south of the confluence of the Bonita Creek and Bayou La Nana. These sparse details only leave questions.

Misíon San José de los Nazonis

Mission San José de los Nazonis was established north of Nacogdoches just across the present Rusk County line. The route there was part of the corridor of Native American trails that became Trammel's Trace from the Red River.

Bolton called it the "highway from the Nasoni to the Kadohadacho," the Caddo confederacy focused along the Red River to the north.[26] On the way to the location of the Nasoni village where the mission would be established some seven leagues to the north from Mission Concepción, Father Isidro Félix de Espinosa and St. Denis noted that "on the way there [were] many Indian ranches and arroyos with water with good stopping places for settling."[27] The location at the site of a Nasoni and Nacono village was "near a good-sized arroyo which runs to the north."[28]

That course is generally opposite the direction of the flow of other streams in the vicinity, and that detail provided a clue that helped Robert Bruce Blake, a Nacogdoches historian, find the site in the mid-1930s. Blake searched for the site using information from the diaries and the input of folks he called the old settlers. Along a path he called an Indian road, Blake found a stepping-stone ford across what is now called Dill Creek, leading to a small hill. He saw piles of native rock with burn marks and wondered if they might have been part of a chimney. Another mound of rock looked to him like a kitchen cairn.

In the 1980s, Bill Young, an archaeological steward of the Texas Historical Commission, identified artifacts after the site was cleared in a timber cut. Young laid out a site plan, did systematic metal detector work, and recovered a significant collection of both Caddo and European goods. Beginning in the late 1980s, James E. Corbin and Kathleen Gilmore were the first archaeologists to conduct excavations at the site. In 2006, Young turned over his artifacts for a more complete archaeological study, which revealed much more about the life of the mission.[29] Across the approximately six-acre site, archaeologists found over 8,500 sherds of Caddo pottery that were distinctively Nasoni. This indicates a high level of interaction between the missionaries and soldiers at the site and the Nasoni Caddo nearby. Also found were products of the Spanish occupation encompassing "gun parts (including butt plates, frizzens, and trigger guards), iron knives, lead bullets and shot, hand-wrought nails, horse trappings, iron awls, and a Spanish spur." There were also "gunflints, glass trade beads, bottle glass, and sherds from European ceramic vessels such as black luster ware, majolica, olive jars, and porcelain," as well as arrow points and other lithic parts and pieces. The dispersal of the goods indicated there were perhaps four or five mission structures.[30]

Misíon Nuestra Señora Dolores de los Ais and Misíon San Miguel de los Linares de Los Adaes (1717)

In the second year of Ramón's expedition to the more distant reaches of Spanish presence, the Spaniards built two more missions further to the east—

Misíon Nuestra Señora Dolores de los Ais near present San Augustine, Texas, and Misíon San Miguel de los Linares de Los Adaes near present Robeline, Louisiana. Los Adaes became the Spanish capital of the entire province, only a few miles from French Natchitoches. Mission Dolores sought to reach the Ais tribe, who were resistant to living at the mission but allowed the coexistence of the Spanish priests.

Both Mission Dolores and Los Adaes are state historic sites with interpretive exhibits of their own.[31] In addition, an outstanding book by Francis X. Galan on Los Adaes tells the complete history of the settlement.[32]

Early Mapping of the Province

Through the efforts of St. Denis and other French traders, maps showing the routes followed by explorers to the Spanish mines in what is now Mexico had already made their way to France by 1717. It was largely French maps, not Spanish ones, that showed the way across Spanish Texas.[33] Attempting to interpret these old maps is an exercise in generality and approximation. Though the accuracy of the maps at the macro level is surprising in their placement of landforms and rivers, the details leave much to be desired. Given the lack of instruments and engineering skills on the frontier, it is remarkable that the features they illustrate are as accurate as they are. What can be noted on the maps are the locations of tribes and villages in relation to the rivers, and the placement of Spanish presidios and missions. The general direction of roads and trails, and in particular their approximate location for crossing rivers, can also advise ideas about the possibility of any legitimate comparison to present terrain.

The 1717 *Mapa Geografico* is a superlative map of the early eighteenth century in which two items stand out. The first is the labeling of a large amount of territory to the east of the Trinity River (R. Trinidad) as Nacion de los Tejas, or the Tejas [Caddo] Nation. It was not the *tierra*, or land of the Tejas, or the *rancherias* of the Caddo. It was the nation—one of the many acknowledgments of the Caddo as an entity separate from Spain that it should relate to diplomatically. Other notable points are the placement of missions (with crosses) and the presidio Tejas (with flag) at the original location.

The *Carte de la Louisiane* is a finely detailed French map of the interior of Spanish Texas dated 1718. The full map includes the eastern half of what is now the United States. This map reveals the kind of detailed knowledge about Texas that caught the Spanish off guard when they learned of it after St. Denis found his way across Texas to the Rio Grande. In this map are details of roads and by whom they were used, villages for the Bidai along the Trinity, and the clearly marked village of other "wanderers" (*indiens errans*) along the coast. It is also crystal clear from the central intersection of the roads at the Hasinai villages at the Neches that it was the most important place on the map in eastern Texas at the time.

Alarcón Expedition, 1718

Martín de Alarcón, governor of the province of Texas, understood that the difficulty of establishing mission outposts distant from the source of supplies was not in building them but maintaining and resupplying them. The Spanish knew they were in the region only with the acquiescence of the Native Americans, and their unease was magnified when they saw how well supplied those tribes were with French guns, ammunition, and trade goods. Alarcón not only brought supplies to the missions, but distributed gifts among the tribes to gain their allegiance and counter the kinship that the French had already formed with the native people.

Alarcón crossed the Rio Grande on April 9, 1718, with "seventy-two persons, including three religious, six soldiers with their families, muleteers, and servants of the governor." There were also "six droves of mules laden with supplies, cattle, sheep, and goats, chickens, and more than 550 horses, more or less."[34] After establishing the mission and villa at Béxar, he continued to his inspection of La Bahía and any activity along the coast. Leaving La Bahía to head for the missions in northeast Texas put him on roads that were somewhat unexplored by the Spanish, not the well-known Native American paths normally taken. Alarcón's arrival at the Trinity River was through a "continuous lake" of flood waters that was twelve miles long. Their raft of logs almost sank when only half of the party was across, and eight horses drowned. At Mission Concepción, the governor was received in grand style, with Diego Ramón still present. The Caddo there welcomed him with their own ceremonial treatment and built the governor a grass house where he could stay.

Though the governor's trip to resupply the missions was completed, the remaining focus of the journey seemed to be more about pomp and accolades for Alarcón rather than the needs of a starving and desperate mission population. His efforts would not last long. The missions were about to be evacuated again.

Missions Abandoned, The Chicken War, 1719

Archie McDonald, the venerable professor of history at Stephen F. Austin State University, called a confrontation between French and Spanish interests at Los Adaes the borderlands version of "the sky is falling" fable starring Chicken Little. His humor was as spot-on as his historical knowledge in describing what came to be called the Chicken War.[35]

The Chicken War was a distant ripple in a real war taking place across the Atlantic Ocean. Spain went to war with France in 1718 to recover territory to which they once laid claim in a conflict called the War of the Quadruple Alliance. Their battles were not limited to European soil. In 1719 the French took command of Pensacola, a Spanish possession in current Florida. Spain won Pensacola back, then lost it again before the French burned and destroyed the town. What was unusual about these conflicts was that they took place during a period when Spain and France were allied against the British. Nowhere was that cooperative relationship clearer than in the proximity of French Natchitoches to Spanish Los Adaes and the supportive relationship the two settlements enjoyed. When the French lieutenant at Natchitoches got word of France's war with Spain and the sacking of Pensacola, some months after the conflict began, he felt duty-bound to do his part. In June 1719 he led a contingent of seven French soldiers in an "attack" of the mission at Los Adaes. They found Los Adaes occupied by only one lay religious official and one soldier.

Feeling the need to declare a conquest of something on behalf of France, the soldiers gathered up the only things of value, which were the sacred vestments of the mission and the occupants of the henhouse. To add to the comedy of the moment, when the lieutenant tried to tie several chickens bound by their feet to his saddle, they did what chickens do, cackling and flapping their wings wildly. The horse reared and dumped the lieutenant on the ground. The war was not going well.[36]

The lay brother who had been captured took advantage of the confusion, and possible giggling of the lieutenant's soldiers, to escape into the woods. Days later he arrived at Mission Dolores with breathless accounts of coming French attacks by one hundred French soldiers headed to East Texas. It is likely the brother exaggerated the dangers of French attack as he raced toward safety. Father Margil had no confidence in his native neighbors to protect them, and Spanish military resistance was nonexistent. Everyone at Mission Dolores evacuated westward to Mission Concepción.

Domingo Ramón remained at the presidio near Mission Concepción west of Nacogdoches with his military contingent. They knew that, if true, the French attack would easily overwhelm them. Soldiers, their families and livestock, the religious at the mission, and all the livestock withdrew even further to the west. The plan was for two priests and two soldiers to stay behind while most of the group went with Ramón for military reinforcements—which never came. On the basis of a rumored attack, the Spanish missions were swiftly abandoned in 1719. Perhaps in their desperation and hunger, the mission population was already looking for a reason to pull back from the distant frontier with its attendant difficulties. Almost since the missions began, the Spanish understood they were overextended. Clothing, food, and other supplies were far away and costly to deliver. Crop failures in 1717 and 1718 led to hunger. Their improbable inability to secure wild game made crow a meat course on their menus.[37]

Father Margil pled for help when Governor Alarcón visited in November 1718, but Alarcón gave no response. The governor had "appeared with great show" but had twice disappointed the mission population with inadequate supplies. In desperation Father Margil wrote to the viceroy, Marqués de Valero, from Mission Concepción in July 1719, looking for aid.[38] He told the viceroy that the weakness and inadequacy of the soldiers were but a "mockery to the local Indians, when they see that our soldiers are mere boys who are on foot and have no uniforms or arms." They were "rendered helpless by the breaking and loss of arms and the lack of fresh provisions." While watching the French give hundreds of arms to the Indians in their contraband trade, the Spanish had not a single gun.

As vehicles for Christianizing the local tribes, the missions offered little achievement if one was counting souls. In the competition for Native American alliances, the French won them over with "gifts and disinterestedness."[39] Record books of the Mission of Guadalupe de los Nacogdoches, lined in red sheepskin, began on August 6, 1716, and ended on February 12, 1773. During that entire time, there were only 340 entries of baptisms, from seven days old to one hundred years.[40] The missions were abandoned, but two years later the pendulum of settlement swung back to East Texas.

Missions Reestablished; Aguayo Expedition, 1721

Not long after the abandonment of the East Texas missions, a new, more capable governor for the provinces of Texas and Coahuila was appointed—the Marqués de San Miquel de Aguayo. Despite a subsequent truce with France and the reduction of tensions on the frontier, the viceroy made clear to Aguayo that "if the French make any movement in continuance of their designs [on Texas], you will have them thrust by force from the province of Texas."[41] Tough talk was cheap from a distant viceroy.

Spanish priests lobbied hard to reestablish their presence in East Texas. Father Espinosa's view was to send married soldiers with their families, along with craftsmen and mechanics, pay them in advance, and give them land to gain their long-term commitment. His appeal resulted in the return of only seven such families. The balance of those resettling the missions more frequently came from prisons and jails.[42]

Governor Aguayo's cross-country trek back into eastern Texas followed paths becoming well-worn by one Spanish insertion after another. When he arrived at the Trinity River on July 9, 1721, he was met by Bidai tribal members who lived near the crossing and Deadose who lived to the north.[43] It took sixteen days for the governor's entire procession to cross the Trinity and arrive at the villages of the Hasinai at San Pedro Creek. The governor counted 158 Caddo and gave them clothing, beads, knives, hoes, mirrors, and other gifts. Aguayo warned them that the French only wanted their chamois, buffalo, and horses, and would enslave their women and children.[44]

When Aguayo finally arrived at the former site of Mission Nuestra Señora de Guadalupe de los Nacogdoches, there were no traces of either the church or the living quarters for the priests. Everything had either rotted away or been destroyed by time and neglect. There was no permanence in the structures and no acceptance of the Catholic religion. During a four-week period in August 1721, Marqués de Aguayo reestablished the Mission San Francisco de los Neches (August 5), Mission Nuestra Señora de la Concepción (August 6), followed by Mission San José de los Nazonis and Mission Nuestra Señora de Guadalupe de los Nacogdoches (August 16). His resupply of the missions included cargoes of corn and flour, as well as four hundred sheep and three hundred cattle. The missions felt more established, more secure, and more supported than ever. Soldiers were in place, though their character was suspect. The costs of this effort were extreme, however. Due to weather and conditions on the road, out of five thousand horses and eight hundred mules engaged over the duration of the expedition, only fifty horses and one-hundred mules survived to return.[45]

Historians credit Aguayo for firmly establishing a military presence and putting families in place in distant settlements. Priests left behind in the flurry of mission rebuilding complained that the progress was "all show and no go," in a modern colloquialism. Spanish presence was secured for years to come no matter how tenuous. At least it would have been secured had the pendulum not swung again with a coming inspection of the missions and all the Spanish settlements across North America in 1727 by representative of the crown.

The Regulations of 1729

The extension of Spanish presence to the distant province of Texas led to a growth in people and expense that became intolerable and unsupportable. By

1727, the soldiers scattered around Texas in presidios and as members of the so called "flying companies" numbered 650 men and was costing 300,000 pesos a year.[46] Suspicions of corruption at the presidios, the poor locations of the presidios, and misuse of the soldier's payroll were among the practical concerns. One of the Spanish leaders clamoring for an investigation and a reassessment of Spain's approach to protecting itself from outside forces was Pedro de Rivera Villalón. His inquiries resulted in what was not a small assignment. He was asked to inspect Spanish placements all the way to the West Coast. Before returning to Mexico City in June 1728, Rivera had taken almost four years to travel eight thousand miles.[47]

Rivera took his time in preparing a sweeping report with recommendations for drastic changes. These were codified in a document known as the *Reglamento*, or *Regulations of 1729*. For Texas, it meant that the Presidio de los Tejas near the main Caddo villages on San Pedro Creek was shut down, and the presidio at Los Adaes was reduced by half its force. With the presidios in East Texas gone, the three Queréteran missions of San José de los Nasonis, Concepción, and San Francisco de los Tejas were also closed. The only missions left in place in East Texas were those of the Zacatecas missionaries at Los Adaes, Los Ais (Mission Dolores at San Augustine), and Nacogdoches.[48]

The *Regulations of 1729* essentially reversed Aguayo's approach from only six years earlier. One of the most bitter critics of Rivera's edicts was Father Juan Agustín de Morfi, a Catholic priest and historian.

> As a result of these measures [the *Regulations of 1729*] the province declined from day to day, so that though we still call ourselves its masters we do not exercise dominion over a foot of land beyond Béxar.[49]

The Spanish presence in Texas was forever altered by these changes in 1731. Missions in Nacogdoches, Los Adaes, and among the Ais were supported militarily only by the presidio at Los Adaes, which had also been declared the capital of the province. Yet they all were even further separated from their support and supply in Béxar. They were out on the frontier alone and did whatever was needed to survive.

Spanish Inspections

The periodic changes in the nature and level of Spanish presence within Caddo territory in East Texas had swung dramatically since 1690 until the methodical, strategic abandonment of all but three missions after the *Regulations of 1729*. Béxar, formed as a way station along the route from Mexico City to the East Texas missions, was hundreds of miles distant. As Béxar began to grow in stature, population, and resources, the East Texas missions languished as lonely outposts. From the perspective of faraway officials, the presence of the missions served only to satisfy the need to "defend" the province from the French. For the people who lived in East Texas, it was their home.

The missions had been directed not to engage in trade with Natchitoches, but their survival depended on it. By 1735 the conditions in Los Adaes were so difficult that the lieutenant governor had to beg for pants to clothe himself. The Adeseños were starving. The stockade walls had rotted away. Spanish "power" was not projecting well, its subjects were only trying to survive. By 1762, however, France ceded Louisiana to Spain and eased some of the international tensions. But Louisiana was still occupied by the same people with the same needs and the same trading relationships as before that change. There was no real integration, and Spain continued to manage territory on opposite sides of the Sabine River from two distant poles of imperial influence with little coordination of policy.

Within those conditions, in a span of two years between 1766 and 1768, there were two official inspections of Spanish East Texas. One was made by a priest hoping to ascertain whether Native American souls were being saved. The other was made by a titled baron from Spain and accompanied by a mapmaker and engineer.

Father Solís Visit, 1767

In 1767, Father Gaspar José de Solís was tasked with an inspection tour of all the missions in the province on behalf of the Zacatecas college of missionaries. His journey included La Bahía, Béxar, and the distant East Texas missions. East of the Neches, land along El Camino Real must have been lovely in early May 1767 when he visited. It had been a wet, harsh winter, so the unique palette of greens from the freshly leafing hardwoods was evident across the hills and along the series of small meadows across the watershed. Strawberries and blackberries were profuse, as were the ticks, mosquitos, and gnats. His diary includes not only the usual descriptions of road conditions, crossings, and stopovers, but it also focuses in much detail on the people of the missions, including the natives. Father Solís's visit to the mission at Nacogdoches provides a personal glimpse into life at the edges of Spanish settlement.[50]

Near the crossing of Bayou Loco, Solís was met by Father Francisco Voceta, along with Chief Bigotes of the Navidachos and Chief Gorgoritos of the Bidai on Durasno Creek. Upon the hill where the Mission of Our Lady of Guadalupe de Nacogdoches was found, Solís was greeted "with much love, appreciation and charity" by Father Joseph Calahorra y Sanchez. The small church was made of adobe and roofed with wooden shingles he called *taxamanil* (also known as *tejamanil*). A palisaded fence of logs staked vertically into the ground surrounded the mission and a few related buildings. The kitchen, a structure for storing grain, and simple quarters for the soldiers and the priest were "well-constructed" and within the stockade. Solís was somewhat forgiving of the signs of decay.

Even though Father Calahorra's efforts at the mission did not result in many conversions, they at least led to some form of respect for his dedication. The mission retained possession of eighty sheep, thirty oxen, fifty cows and bulls, twenty-five horses, and twenty mules that could have been an easy target for tribes not inclined to the priest's protection.[51] Father Calahorra had spent forty-three long years at the Nacogdoches mission, but not every visitor assessed that tenure as a measure of his dedication.

Rubí Inspection, 1767

During a visit to Nacogdoches in September 1767, only a few months after Solís, the Marqués de Rubí was less forgiving of the aged priest's life work. Though the setting for the mission and the creeks lined by large trees was attractive, Rubí's impression was that the tired buildings gave testament to the lack of energy that remained for the central purpose of the missions—to convert the native tribal members to the Spanish religion and lifestyle.

The mission was at the end of its existence and largely deserted. Only the priest, two soldiers with families, and a few servants occupied the mission. There were no Native Americans living in the pueblo, no cultivation, and no will for change. Rubí's biting criticism noted that for all his years at the distant mission, Father Calahorra "had little more to do than baptize a few of the dying, whose catechism, in that condition, has been somewhat difficult to practice."[52] The dead could hardly become good Catholics.

Rubí's response to his visit was captured by one word—*Dictamen*. That is the Spanish word that describes the report of the Marquez de Rubí after his inspection of the province's farthest settlements. The word translates as opinion or recommendation but has the harsh sound of a directive. Based on Rubí's stature and the political importance of this document to Spanish East Texas, it might as well have been an order by the king himself.

When France ceded Louisiana west of the Mississippi River to Spain in 1762 to keep it away from England, it was like when someone gives another a pet—the gift came with obligations, responsibilities, and expenses. Spain's treasury was depleted, and the gift was an unsettling burden. If Spain was going to use Texas as a buffer and future line of defense, Spain had to know how best to use its resources. Rubí recommended, since Louisiana no longer belonged to the French and the eastern missions were failures, that both the presidios and the missions of the frontier should be closed. Los Adaes, Mission Dolores, and Mission Guadalupe at Nacogdoches were to be shut down. Only Béxar and La Bahía would remain in operation, and Béxar would become the capital of the province.

It took four years for the crown to act on his recommendations. The royal order in 1771 known as *New Regulations for Presidios* changed history and represented a major transition period for East Texas.

"The Diversity of Their Origins"

One of the difficulties Spanish officials had in managing life in the province of Texas was that the people there were different than those in other parts of the empire. The settlers of eastern Texas were typically not Spaniards, but Spanish subjects from Mexico familiar with the methods of Spanish governance. It may have been an escape from tighter controls that led these people move to a distant province. Although the cession of French Louisiana to Spain in 1762 dramatically changed the nature of Spanish attempts to rule the region, the integration of the people on either side of the Sabine River continued on tenuous and adversarial ground.

Spain still feared its lack of control over foreigners from the east. Foreigners coming to Texas to live without authorization had always been prohibited, but the viceroy was especially concerned about "those suspicious of wanting to take the lands at intervals of places, ports, funds, and other similar, causing great suspicion of treason."[53] By 1769 new rules were established to limit Native American trade and illegal contraband and to promote the more domesticated commerce of agriculture and ranching. This meant immediate regulation for a group of traders who exchanged French-made goods with tribal members for fur, horses, cattle, and even native slaves. They were instructed to be licensed for their work. Instead, many simply left the territory and moved north of the Red River.

The Spanish never quite seemed to learn that regulations from distant seats of government meant little in the borderlands. Spanish East Texas was different . . . and not in a manner that was understood by anyone other than those who were part of it.

4

Deep and Miry Places

We arrived at the bank of the Trinity River which was rising greatly.
We crossed it on a raft with evident danger of life
from which God saved us. Blessed be his mercies.
—FATHER GASPAR JOSÉ DE SOLIS[1]

Rivers were always in the way. No traveler could avoid the watery impediments and the perils they presented. They were ever-present obstacles no matter what the conditions. To understand the region in which this period of history took place, it is critical to understand the rivers and the means used for crossing them. Historian Herbert Bolton said the rivers were named "profusely and promiscuously" by each successive Spanish entrada.[2] At various times the Spanish called the Neches River the San Pedro de Navidachos, San Pedro de los Nechas, Rio de Nechas, or the Rio Mexicano. The Caddo knew it as the Nachawi. The Angelina was once known as the Santa Barbara. La Salle called the Trinity River the River of the Canoes. Subsequent crossings of the Trinity by Spanish entradas led to different names: Encarnación de Verbo, San Fernando, and La Santisima Trinidad. The Rio Trinidad (Trinity River) ultimately became the name most used.[3] Though the names of the rivers and streams of eastern Texas changed often across the years of Spanish rule, the risks remained.

Rio Trinidad

The Trinity River winds almost six hundred miles from its headwaters where the river's three forks join near Dallas to its mouth at Galveston Bay. It divides east from west across Texas, separating unique ecosystems and landscapes. The river slashes a geologic line between the red soil, pine, and hardwood found to its east and the black soil and prairies to the west.[4]

The Rio Trinidad could not be avoided by early Spanish *entradas* and *visitas*. Its banks witnessed many attempts by Spanish soldiers and priests, and by natives of many tribes and origins, to manage a difficult crossing. The means and methods for crossing depended on the terrain and the water level at the time. Typical water depths along the stretch of the middle Trinity most often crossed by the Spanish were only a few inches over the rock shoals. Between the shoals and falls there could be river depths up to twelve feet interspersed with sections where the water was almost stagnant.

Crossings were made at natural shoals created by sandstone or lignite outcroppings, which created shelfs or small waterfalls across which travel could easily continue. Even if the crossings could be easily managed at normal water levels, there were still dangers going into and out of the rivers while on horseback. The banks of the smaller streams and bayous were often steep and slick. A worn path down the edge of a creek bank that proceeded directly up on the other side might appear to be a suitable ford but could instead be slippery and dangerous. A crossing that angled up the sides was safer.

Crossing flowing waters could be easy or impossible, routine or life-threatening, depending on the conditions. Flooded crossings were scenes of discomfort, delay, or death for both men and animals. Although the current was strongest in the river channel, it still flowed rapidly across the prairies that bordered the river. One traveler described the width of the floodplain at the Trinity River as being at least "two gun-shots in breadth," and others described it as more than five miles.[5] Even when floodwaters subsided enough to cross, the river left behind a swampy slog across flat floodplains that extended for miles on either side.

Crossings by Horseback, Bridges, and Rafts

Official Spanish reports and diary accounts often described riverside difficulties in detail, along with the various means used to attempt crossings. The stories of their crossings illustrate both the challenges of the moment and the gravitas of the various political and military men leading the entrada. In a crossing in 1605, ten soldiers built a log bridge only to find that the water had risen over their structure by the next morning. But they attempted to cross anyway, losing two horses and a pack mule to drowning. In an act of devotion bordering on foolhardiness, soldiers jumped into the flood waters to save the chapel vestments loaded on one of the mules.[6] Such was the power of the church.

When Mier y Terán and his large party arrived at the Trinity River hungry and exhausted on December 13, 1692, it was bitterly cold.[7] At the edge of the Trinity, they found flooding so extreme that those in the group who had crossed the river three times before could hardly believe what they were seeing. As one group began searching for another crossing, a second group began building a log raft. The problem with the raft was that someone had to get a rope to the other side of the swollen river so it could be pulled across. Mier y Terán's large contingent included seagoing soldiers who had once inspected the coast. Mier y Terán assumed they would be the better swimmers and that one of them should man the raft, but the current made it impossible to pull the log raft across. With the water still rising after ten days, carpenters worked for three days to turn a hollow tree trunk into a canoe. "We did more than seemed humanly possible," wrote Mier y Terán. It took three days to move everyone from the west side of the Trinity River to the east, only to face prairies that had become large lakes. Occasional small high spots above the water appeared as lonely islands, but they would soon be inundated as well.

In 1718, Spanish Governor Alarcón had a bad feeling one day. Twenty-four vultures had ominously circled him that morning, leaving him with a sense of dread. Despite the omen, he attempted to cross the swollen Trinity River on a strong horse with a sergeant of his military escort hanging on tightly behind him. They made it across safely, but on the slope up out of the river the horse slipped and fell back into the current with both riders still clinging to the saddle. Alarcón and his sergeant bobbed beneath the surface a couple of times before grabbing onto tree branches and being rescued with ropes.[8]

With one catastrophe averted, there was another one looming. The ordeal caused the buttons on the governor's pants to pop off, and the rapid current sucked his trousers down around his feet. There can be little doubt the soldiers rescuing the pair had to disguise their amusement beneath strained expressions as they hauled out the unfortunate officials. The priests found a positive way out of the situation by reminding everyone it was a miracle that not only was the pants-less governor saved, but the boxed rosary and prayerbook in his pocket somehow endured the soaking.[9]

On Governor Alarcón's return trip to Mexico the following year, he was determined not to lose his breeches in the floodwaters this time. He better prepared for a crossing of the Trinity by dismounting and crossing on a raft built by the soldiers. Whether it was the current, the construction of the raft, or simply the bad misfortune of the governor, his vessel capsized in the current. Perhaps the vultures were still circling him. Though he kept his pants up this time, he lost some of the luxuries that accompanied him. When the raft capsized, the governor and his cook survived, but a traveling kitchen and a silver service were lost in the river. The governor's misfortune may have contributed to the Spanish name for one of the nearby creeks—Quita Calzones—which literally means "remove pants."[10] Besides the contents of the pockets of the governor, there is indeed Spanish silver at the bottom of the Trinity River.

In 1721, Aguayo's soldiers decided to build a bridge from tree trunks they felled along the bank of the river, lashing them together with ropes. Typically, men and supplies would cross the rivers on bridges, and the livestock would swim. The bridge was remarkably large at eighty-three feet long and twelve feet wide. Whether to give thanks to God for the structure or to pray that it did not kill them, the bridge was blessed by their priest before anyone attempted to cross.[11] Upon Aguayo's return, the bridge was gone, a casualty of the rush of high water. His experience in crossings led him to order the construction of two rafts this time to get people, stock, and supplies across the Trinity River. The Spaniards and the Native Americans guiding them each built rafts over two days and took quite different approaches to the task. The natives' usual method was to make use of fallen trees or large limbs, dead but not decayed, which they lashed together with reeds for additional strength and flotation. The Spanish method created a vessel that seemed just short of the size of a galleon. Being constructed with "tree trunks and barrels," meant that it was substantial and heavy. It too failed to work. Not only was it almost impossible to control, but the party's supplies got wet in the crossing.[12]

Points of Crossing Along the Trinity River

The central point of reference on the Trinity River for this work is the mouth of Bedias Creek. At this point, Madison, Houston, and Walker counties connect and share a point of contact with the river. Even before the county boundaries aligned at this location, it was a historically significant landmark because of the natural crossings both upstream and downstream. It was also the location where Calhoun's Ferry was established in the late 1800s. Knowing the location where Bedias Creek enters the Trinity River will be an advantage in reviewing this history.

At the mouth of Bedias Creek, natural shoaling that takes place when a stream enters a river's flow creates shallower water that tends to block the flow and restrict access to the creek. The damming of the Trinity River to create Lake Livingston, begun in 1966 and completed in 1971, created an impoundment fifty-five miles long behind the dam. It also raised water levels and forever altered the natural flow of the Trinity and many of its tributaries.

The shoals, crossings, falls, and other features described by Spanish diarists are now submerged below the normal water level.

The Trinity River Above Bedias Creek

From Bedias Creek upstream to what is now the crossing of Texas State Highway 21 there was twenty-nine miles of water only three to four feet deep when observed in the late 1800s. Kickapoo Rapids and Hurricane Shoals were both used as upper crossings of El Camino Real de los Tejas, only a few miles north of the present Texas State Highway 7. The shoals were a natural crossing and may have been the location used by DeSoto in his 1690 entrada, as well as by subsequent expeditions.

In a seven-mile stretch of the river north of present Highway 21, there exists one of the most interesting geological features in the middle Trinity. Branch Creek and Youngs Creek carve a ravine that slices eighty feet into the banks and runs for almost a mile. On topographic maps, the cleft is labeled as "The Falls" and "The Canyon." In a 1972 survey there was a rock ledge forming a twenty-foot waterfall near the head of the canyon.[13] Shoals on Boggy Creek upstream from the canyon and Bozeman Shoals downstream were also later crossings. One source reported that at times, Bozeman's was the only passable ford in the area.[14]

Hyde's Crossing was nine and one-half miles downstream from Highway 21 on the left bank, and just upstream from the current Coleman's Boat Launch on the right bank of the river. It is thought to be near the location of the lost presidio of Trinidad de Salcedo.

The Trinity Below Bedias Creek

An engineering study in 1893 found an eight-mile stretch of river south of the mouth of Bedias Creek to average only about two-and-a-half feet in depth. Donahue (Donahoe) Shoals is 2.2 miles downstream from the mouth of Bedias Creek.[15] The crossing of the Trinity at Nelson Shoals was about a half-mile south of the mouth of Nelson Creek. A major geological report in 1918 noted that a rock shelf there showed evidence of lignite coal beneath the surface and created about a four-foot waterfall.[16]

In correspondence to Governor Salcedo in 1810, Nelson Shoals was referred to several times as El Salto, a generic Spanish term for a waterfall, in this case for water cascading across a shoal. There were multiple locations across East Texas associated with the name "El Salto" in documents of the period, and it was perhaps the height of this one that singled it out for specific naming.[17]

White Rock Shoals farther downstream had a substantial base of rock on which to build a structure to try and tame the Trinity for navigation. The Army Corps of Engineers liked the location so much that it chose the site for a lock and dam. Constructed in 1917, the locks were part of a failed plan to make the Trinity navigable. Any remaining structure is now beneath the waters of Lake Livingston.[18]

Although there are still visible outcroppings of stone, clay, or lignite on the banks of the Trinity and Bedias Creek, the shoals are forever altered by the rise in water levels due to the construction of Lake Livingston.[19] Boaters familiar with the underwater hazards of the Trinity River have learned they might still break a propeller on remains of the shoals just beneath the surface when the water is low.

Paso Tomás, A Historic Crossing

Paso Tomás plays a key role in the history of Spanish East Texas. The crossing was named for a Bidai chief who led villages established nearby along the confluence of the Trinity River and Bedias Creek and south of the Angelina River to the east.[20] The crossing was repeatedly named in Spanish documents of this period, and it was the focal point of several Bidai villages on both sides of the Trinity River.

The ford at Paso Tomás was not along the *caminos reales* customarily used by the Spanish entradas. Paso Tomás was a lesser used crossing of the river and a passageway for smugglers to move contraband between Natchitoches and La Bahía. The earliest Spanish entradas typically used crossings much farther upstream, near the present location of Kickapoo Shoals, on their way to the Caddo villages the Spanish called the Kingdom of the Tejas. Paso Tomás was farther south along the Bidai trading trails between Natchitoches and the Trinity, and south to the outpost of Orcoquisac.

The location of Paso Tomás is critical to an understanding of this period in history because it became the point of reference for the location of Bucareli, a Spanish colonial settlement formed in 1774. The locations of Paso Tomás and Bucareli were essentially the same. One Spanish official wrote that "the new settlement of Nuestra Senora del Pilar de Bucareli [was] established, at the insistence of Don Antonio Gil Ybarbo [Ibarvo], at the site named El Paso de Tomás."[21] These two early landmarks are inextricably linked.

A review of the literature, maps, and other sources, combined with studies on the ground, leaves researchers focused on this river crossing with a common dilemma. It is impossible to declare with certainty which one of the Trinity

Tom H. Gann in search of Paso Tomás at the end of Wilson Shoals Road. The mouth of Bedias Creek is to the right, and the Trinity River to the left. Photo by author.

River shoals upstream or downstream from the mouth of Bedias Creek is the Paso Tomás of Spanish historical accounts. However, that does not mean a strong case cannot be made, and it is the intent of this work to propose a likely location.[22]

Where Paso Tomás is NOT Located

Bob Skiles, in his research on Spanish colonial settlement on the Trinity, in particular Trinidad de Salcedo, learned that some of the greatest historians focused on this period made mistakes in their determination of the location of Paso Tomás. Bolton noted that Governor Ripperdá said Bucareli was near Paso Tomás on the right bank of the Trinity River at the place where the "lower Adaes road" crossed the river, also calling it "the road leading [from Béxar] to . . . [Los] Adaes and Orcoquisac."[23] Orcoquisac was a Spanish mission to the south near present-day Liberty, so there was also a north-south trail at this location.

The common error is assuming that there was only one place along the Trinity where the roads split going southwest to Béxar and more southerly to La Bahía.[24] The upper and lower roads crossed the Trinity at different locations at different times. In Herbert Bolton's early twentieth century writing, the only crossing well understood was the crossing near Robbins's Ferry and Highway 21. Since that time, much more has been learned about other crossings along the middle Trinity. Even though there is a historical marker for Bucareli and

Paso Tomás at the Highway 21 crossing of the Trinity River, this research shows that is not the location for either of those two historically significant landmarks. Both will be found near the shoals of Bedias Creek.

Two Shoals at Bedias Creek

The Marquès de Rubí, the Spanish inspector of presidios, described a ford in 1767 when crossing the Trinity "over a rock ledge that extends across the whole breadth of the stream, and over which there was hardly more than a span of water." His crossing seemed remarkably easy, but the diarist noted that the "approaches are very bad in time of rains, being steep and sharp because of the deep riverbed."[25] The current road nearest to that crossing is Wilson Shoals Road off Texas Farm to Market Road 247 in Madison County. It terminates at the Trinity River. To visit Wilson Shoals is to travel back in time—the dusty limestone road dead ends at the point where Houston, Walker, and Madison counties intersect. Although there was a crossing also named Wilson Shoals farther upstream during an 1873 survey, it is this crossing that has retained the identity.[26]

Before the rise in water level caused by the impoundment of Lake Livingston, Bedias Creek was noted as one of the "the larger class of creeks in Texas, though in low water but a little stream."[27] Both upstream and downstream from the mouth of Bedias Creek, the Trinity River contained wide, rocky shoals that made crossing the river easy much of the year. One of those distinctive shoals was the one just upstream from the mouth of Bedias Creek where it feeds the Trinity River.[28] A 1918 publication on the geology of eastern Texas presents an incredibly detailed description of the shoals. The rock formations that created the shoals and small waterfalls are the same as those visible along Farm to Market Road 247 just south of its crossing at Bedias Creek.

> At the corner of Madison, Houston, and Walker counties [are found] two large rapids, with an estimated combined fall of at least 6 feet. The rapids are formed by massive medium-grained, opaline-cemented light gray sandstone. Interbedded with this is the usual "shell," brown, clayey sandstone. The sandstone contains many carbonaceous leaf imprints. The lower fall has a 4 ft. drop over a ledge of sandstone at least 6 feet thick. Overlying the sandstone is a foot of lignite, overlain unconformably by blue-gray and brown mottled, sandy, alluvial clay. Just above the upper shoals, second bottom terraces are present on opposite banks of the river. Natural levees, sometimes 10 feet in height and forming very perfect embankments, are found along [the banks of] the Trinity.[29]

The same shoal was identified in a detailed travel narrative from 1839 in which it was noted "the river [the Trinity] near the Bedais [Bedias Creek] makes its passage over a bed of [red sandstone], which at low water is apparent at the bottom of the stream."[30] The names most often assigned to these shoals near the mouth of Bedias Creek by accounts in the early 1800s were Bedias Shoals or Bedias Falls. For this work, the name Wilson Shoals will refer to the current naming and placement on current maps.

The Shoals of Paso Tomás

Based on the research conducted by scholars, independent researchers, geographers, historians, and archaeologists, the shoals most likely to be those known as Paso Tomás crossed the Trinity River just downstream from the mouth of Bedias Creek.[31] Though there are logical reasons to focus on this crossing as the one noted in historical accounts, it is important to remember that roads forked, and crossings changed over time. That there would have been several crossings used by the Bidai tribe and their Spanish neighbors over time in the vicinity of Bedias Creek and the Trinity River is assumed and expected. As noted from an 1899 river survey map, there were two shoals near the mouth of Bedias Creek, one upstream and one downstream. Having those options for crossing facilitated travel in completely different directions. Both crossings would have been used at various times, but there are indications that the one downstream from the creek led toward Bidai villages and to a road that continued to La Bahía.

The Terrain Tells the Tale

At its juncture with the Trinity River, the downstream flow of Bedias Creek is almost directly due north, while the Trinity crosses it running west to east. They are virtually perpendicular to each other. The banks of Bedias Creek are very different in their topography than those of the Trinity. At the river level, both sides of Bedias Creek are clearly within the floodplain at an elevation of about 130 feet above mean sea level. However, approximately one mile upstream on the right (east) side of Bedias Creek, the terrain becomes quite hilly and is far more elevated than the flatter plains on the left (west) side. The elevation quickly rises to 180 feet at the leading edge of a bluff that curves to the southwest for over three and one-half miles along a former channel for Bedias Creek. Elevations along that ridge range from about 170 feet to slightly over two hundred feet.

On the left (west) side of Bedias Creek, the land is relatively flat and remains marshy in some spots. There are islands of elevation within that space, but the

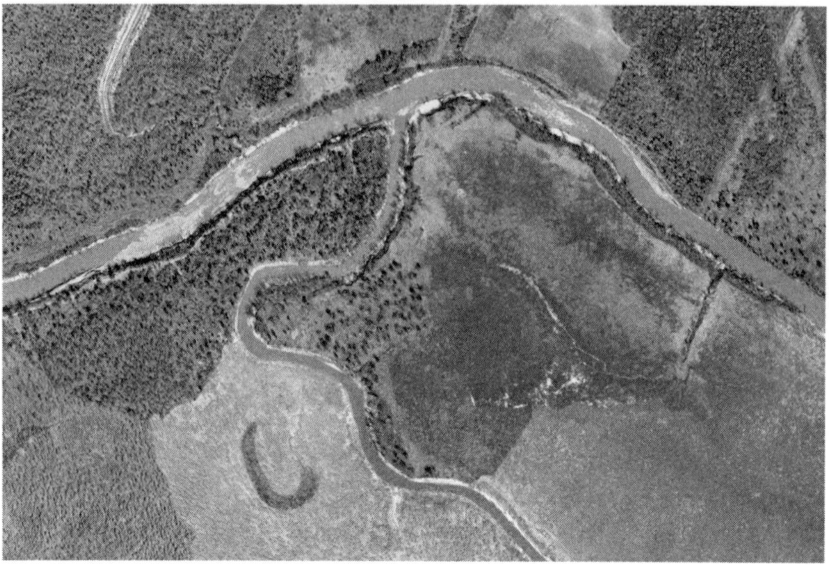

Wilson Shoals (Bedias Shoals) upstream and Paso Tomás downstream at the mouth of Bedias Creek on the Trinity River. The image is from 1960 before Lake Livingston was formed. Shoals were no longer visible in 1972 after Lake Livingston was impounded. Courtesy Historic Aerials.

elevation does not rise above 160 feet. To cross Bedias Creek from that side toward the southwest, toward La Bahía, a trek of about three and one-half miles was required before reaching shoals crossing Bedias Creek farther upstream.

Archaeological Sites

Another indicator for the crossing of Paso Tomás downstream from the mouth of Bedias Creek is the wealth of archaeological sites indicating early indigenous occupation on the right side of the creek. Within a three-and-a-half-mile segment along an elevated ridge southeast of Bedias Creek, there are seven archaeologically significant sites that have been surveyed. One of them was examined in the 1950s, and the others were lightly surveyed in the mid-1980s when the area was considered for strip mining of lignite. Sites with names like Lost Horizon, Wild Hare, and Spotted Tick revealed signs of habitation that included stone debitage, charcoal from fire pits, aboriginal ceramics and sherds, projectile points, and a hand ax. Since only shovel testing was done, the archaeologists recommended further study be considered, but the impetus and funding for that was never sought.

The Floodplain

The alignment of archaeological sites along the ridge is another indicator that the east side of Bedias Creek was likely more peopled and well-traveled. Each of the sites is found at elevations between 165 and 185 feet above sea level, above the height of normal flooding on the Trinity. A current one-hundred-year floodplain map shows the wide extent of periodic flooding. It also clearly shows that the upstream (left) side of Bedias Creek at the Trinity River was more prone to flooding over a much broader expanse.

Considered Altogether

The indications of Paso Tomás being downstream of the confluence of Bedias Creek with the Trinity River supports more favorable conditions for travel across the river and between Los Adaes or Nacogdoches, or toward La Bahía or Béxar. Making a best-guess proposition for that placement allows the consideration of other related historical landmarks like settlements and roads more focused. Other possibilities for the location of the historic crossing will always remain, but the strength of the facts allows attention to focus on a location for Paso Tomás that is far more accurate than what was indicated by earlier historians.

A Lost Indian Shows the Way

In the 1950s, Robert E. Samuels and his wife, Opal, were well known around Huntsville, Texas. Bob lettered in four sports in high school, operated the Plaza Hotel downtown, and was known as "Uncle Bob" to children who enjoyed his playful good humor. His wife painted, wrote poetry, and anchored the upbringing of her two children, Robert Jr. and Jerelyn, whom everyone called Jere. Opal's family, the McAdams, had owned land along the Trinity River at the mouth of Bedias Creek for many years. That land, 1,600 acres known as the Rafter-S Ranch, is still family-owned and is the likely location of Paso Tomás.

In 1956, Bob Samuels decided he wanted to open a summer camp at the ranch called Lost Indian Camp. There was a Lost Indian Lake not far to the east, and the lake had that name since the 1930s. Sessions of one or two weeks included horseback riding, swimming, archery, riflery, and other more traditional activities, but Samuels added his own unique flavor to the summer experience. Boys might learn how to play musical chairs on horseback and go home with a mohawk haircut. On Sundays, the campers' meal tickets were letters they wrote home to their parents. No letter, no lunch.

A view near Bedias Creek toward the Trinity River from Lost Indian Camp lodge, March 2021. Photo by author.

A view from the Trinity River, looking back to Lost Indian Camp lodge, 1957. Courtesy Jere (Samuels) McCann.

Unexpectedly, the name of the camp became even more relevant as they prepared to open for the first year. In June 1956 while excavating the hilltop where the bunkhouses were located to remodel a building, workers discovered a burial, likely a Bidai Indian. After work was stopped, Dr. T. N. Campbell of the University of Texas studied the remains and artifacts found at the site. Joseph L. Clark, a well-known historian of the time and a member of the faculty at Sam Houston State University, also spoke with Samuels and advised him of

Boys at the Lost Indian Camp in the 1960s. Note the shallowness of Bedias Creek before Lake Livingston was impounded and covered the shoals shown behind the riders. Bob Samuels is in the lead. Courtesy Jere (Samuels) McCann.

the history of the land. As a result, Samuels knew some of the history of Paso Tomás and of Bucareli, the later Spanish settlement, though he believed it had been a Spanish fort.

A camp brochure used as a marketing piece had a photo on the front page of Jere Samuels (McCann) and some of her classmates in bathing suits "enjoying historical El Paso Tomás." The girls were standing on the shoals on the Trinity River downstream from the mouth of Bedias Creek. Standing atop the shoal itself, the girls barely wet the bottom of their feet. Jere and one other girl stood below in water only mid-calf deep. Before the impoundment of Lake Livingston, this was the normal flow during the summer months.

It was Clark who informed Samuels his land was likely the location of Paso Tomás and Bucareli. That history inspired the artist and the poet of the family, Opal, to create sketch maps of the camp for some of the brochures. Two of the maps, from 1958 and 1959, are interesting in the story that they tell, and in their differences and similarities.

The maps have different names and placement of crossings and roads. At the time the research for this book was conducted, the author had not yet learned of these sketch maps. Though they are informal maps, Opal Samuels's placement of Paso Tomás is exactly where the author has determined through research.

One must keep in mind that these sketch maps are not historical documents. They were intended to entice boys and girls aged eight to fifteen, and

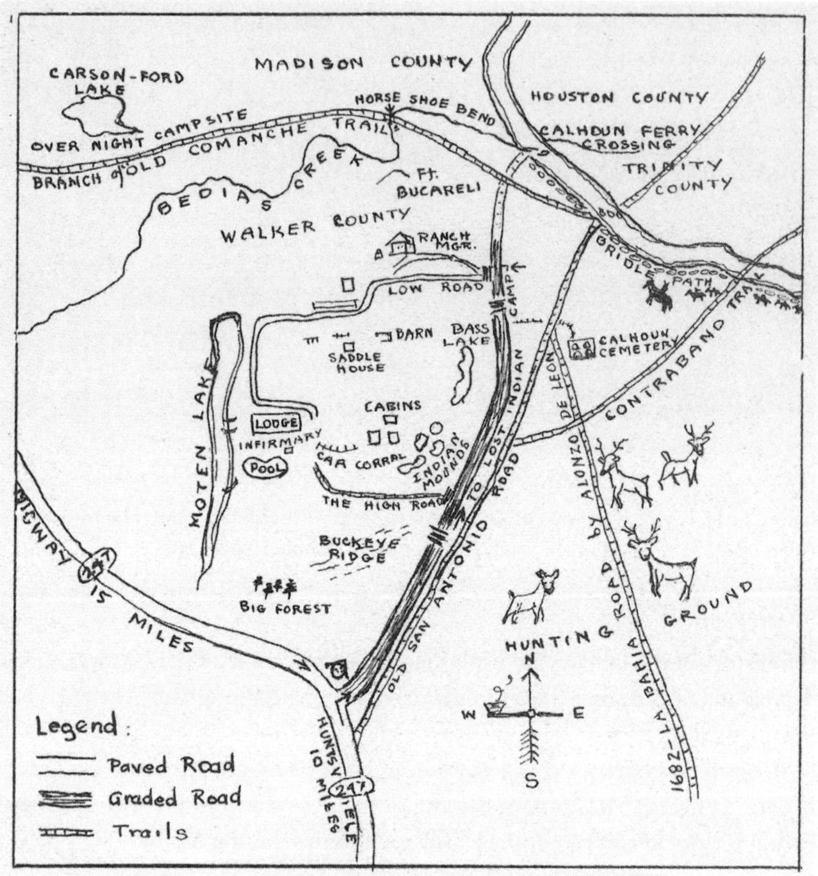

Sketch of Lost Indian Camp, circa 1958. Courtesy Jere (Samuels) McCann.

their parents, into a summer adventure. Insight into what Samuels learned from Clark and Campbell, two well-respected professionals in history and anthropology, respectively, is not extant. Nevertheless, local knowledge is still a factor in historical research of this nature. Even though much of it is folklore, there is often a thread of history that ties back to the broader facts.

The diligence of research has delivered a conclusion that is not far off from the tales Bob Samuels's campers heard around a campfire on the edge of Bedias Creek at Lost Indian Camp. The Trinity River crossing at Paso Tomás was a historic passage for native people and European traders for hundreds of years.

5

By Way of Secret Roads

> This country has roads and collateral paths which facilitate the introduction of clandestine, forbidden [goods] from the Province of Louisiana.
>
> —CAPT. PEDRO LÓPEZ PRIETO

Robert Moor's exceptional book, *On Trails: An Exploration*, takes a philosophical perspective on the existence of trails and their role in our lives. He observes that "a path is a way of making sense of the world." Moor helps bring focus to the complexities of early travel by defining the function of a path "to reduce this teeming chaos into an intelligible line."[1]

The use of the earliest pathways across eastern Texas was a practical demonstration of that observation. The native inhabitants made pathways to sources of water and food, to cultural gatherings and trade fairs, and to places where they found the spirit to be strong. Their destination and the terrain determined the route. Trails created and tested by others are the result of trial and error. There was little sacrifice in taking a longer route around a steep hill or across a river by going a bit farther to avoid changes in elevation or difficult conditions. For cross-country treks made with contraband goods, a little-used or a more distant path meant the difference between being discovered or avoiding scrutiny.

Our current understanding of the meaning of a trail or a road gets in the way of imagining what they were like during earlier periods of history. Preconceived ideas based on our own experience are insufficient to understand the travel networks that existed across East Texas in the late eighteenth century. Ancient trails followed the natural paths offered by the land, generally along ridges. One author described evolving tracks where "the free wilderness road may be recognized as a series of linear compromises" and a "latticed network of trails rather than a finite, linear feature."[2] Understanding the pathways of history is fundamental to knowing where events took place and how people moved across the landscape.

This chapter focuses on eastern Texas trails in existence prior to 1779. This discussion includes the evolution of Indian trails to *caminos reales*, as well as the use of lesser-known trails for smuggling. A road that Stephen F. Austin labeled as an "old road" in an 1822 map of his colony will be examined in detail. One of his maps reveals information that has been largely undocumented. It was the research of Tom H. Gann that brought these early roads to a closer examination. Gann's determined research on routes that crossed Angelina County led him to other ancient routes leading to Béxar, La Bahía, and beyond.

Long Distance Trade Routes

An international trade corridor for the movement of goods between the Upper Peninsula of Michigan to the Rio Grande and Mexico sliced north and south through East Texas and allowed long distance trade and commerce. The route extended over 2,500 miles in multiple segments between existing communities where unique products could be bought and sold. Along that corridor, over one thousand miles were along routes already in use, but over time more convenient or accessible tracks were added. That explanation sounds like a description of early Native American trade routes, but it is virtually verbatim for how the Interstate 69 corridor across Texas is being described.[3]

Although we tend to think of trails and roads as localized features, early pathways through Texas were part of a vast network of trade routes crisscrossing the continent. There is nothing new about the idea of trade corridors, or even about the routes they follow over extreme distances. Some of the earliest proof of this notion can be found in an extensive network of Native American trading trails that covered thousands of miles. Jason Barrett, an archaeologist formerly with the Texas Department of Transportation, researched an archaeological site northwest of Houston called Dimond Knoll. Evidence at the site showed that it had been a major hub for long-distance trade over centuries of human occupation.

Archaeological projects in all parts of Texas unearth trade goods with origins in distant locations.[4] Shell, turquoise, chert, or ceramics with material origins far from where they were found give evidence for the wide distribution of goods over hundreds of miles. Consistent evidence from as early as 600 AD

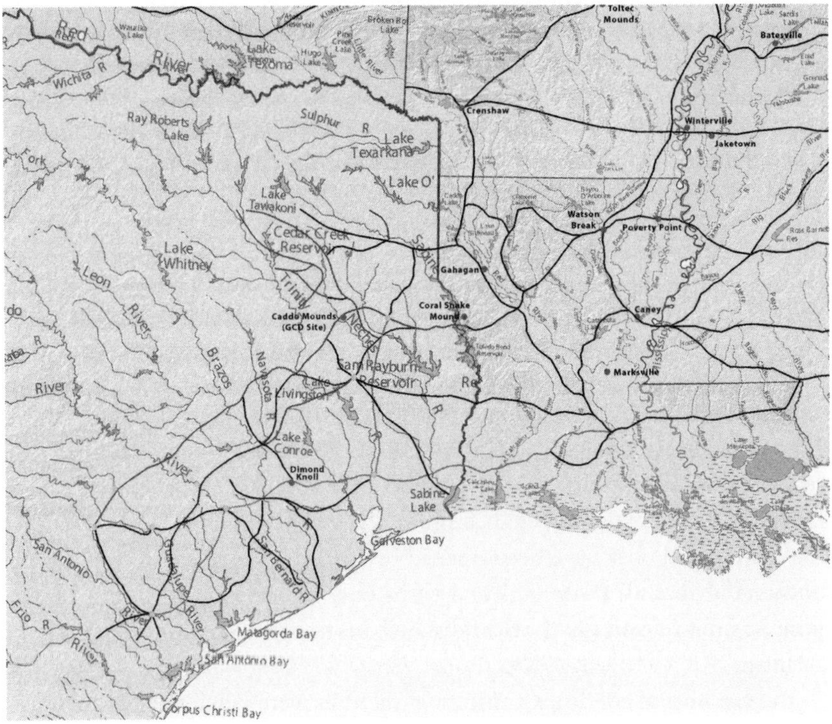

Native overland trading trails, compiled on a map by Jason Barrett, archaeologist formerly with the Texas Department of Transportation. Courtesy Jason Barrett.

indicates the Caddo of East Texas conducted trade over distances that are hard to envision taking place on foot.[5]

The museum at the Sam Houston Regional Library in Liberty displays artifacts that were found in nearby archeological sites with origins hundreds of miles away.[6] Artifacts made from a stone that can only be found at a particular location in Alabama indicate that distance and river crossings were little impediment when it came to trade. Artifacts containing hematite from Arkansas and galena from near the intersection of Kansas, Missouri, and Oklahoma could not have been produced locally. The copper used to create an awl and a metal projectile tip came from even further away. That material could only have come from copper-bearing rocks near the Great Lakes. Material and artifacts dated from thirteen thousand to five thousand years before the present, and from distances up to two thousand miles away, have found their way to the museum less than a mile from the archaeological site where they were found.[7]

Use of Existing Indian Trails by the Spanish

Alonso De León led four expeditions into Texas, but it was his fifth in 1690 that began to alter the nature of the existing trails he used. Native trails that had been used for hundreds of years were becoming Spanish *caminos* across Texas. Though there were certainly many paths crisscrossing East Texas, the Spanish were not predisposed to wander through the woods to see where a trail might lead. Soldiers of the 1557 expedition led by de Soto, and subsequently by Moscoso, were so afraid they might "get lost in some unpeopled region," that Moscoso killed a native guide who led them off the visible trail for two days.[8]

Domingo Terán's entrada into East Texas in 1692 was dependent on his Native American guides. Terán wrote in his journal that one section of road seemed to weave through all four points of the compass and take five leagues of trail to make one-and-a-half leagues of forward progress. Terán was sure the road "could only have been opened by a man in his sleep." Terán did not understand that all those cuts and turns only indicated that the trail's purpose was not to find the shortest distance between two points for use by the Spanish.[9]

The terrain and conditions of these early trails were a challenge to their use, no matter what the means of transportation. Changes in the elevation, soils, and rocks beneath the paths, as well as the forests, cane, and briars through which they passed, offered a unique set of difficulties to be overcome. The Native American trails the Spanish used may have been well trod, both by foot and by horseback, but their prior use was nothing like what the Spanish would bring. The sheer volume of people, supplies, and livestock is difficult to imagine, and no prior use of these existing trails would compare.[10]

Locating Old Roads

Trying to identify the present-day track for historic roads and trails is largely destined to be a "fool's errand," doomed to be wrong in one way or another.[11] In 1528, four survivors of the shipwrecked Narváez expedition, unfortunate men that historian Donald Chipman called the "Four Ragged Castaways," made a long-distance trek from just west of Galveston Island to a Spanish post on the western coast of Mexico, arriving eight years later. Three of the castaways later wrote accounts that described the land, topographical features, and plants they saw along the way. There has been much discussion among both academic and non-academic historians about how they managed their cross-country travel. One of the non-academic efforts suggested the four men could have built rock cairns along their route that might still be found five hundred years later. Chipman called that book "an incredible series of errors in geography, travel time and distance, Indian customs, [and] distribution of native plants and animals." As Chipman politely summarized, historians "are in substantial disagreement over the path followed."[12]

Erroneous conclusions can be drawn from maps, documents, and other indicators about where a particular road was located hundreds of years earlier. Maps with lines crudely drawn across hundreds of square miles with no instruments to determine latitude or longitude only suggest the placement of an actual route, they do not define it. For this project, in addition to diaries and other firsthand accounts, maps going back four hundred years have been examined for clues to the placement of the primary trail systems for this eighteenth century time frame. Efforts to establish the likely path of roads long gone is a disciplined exercise in understanding the nature of the terrain and a close examination of archival material, including old maps. Despite insufficient details to locate a road three hundred years old or more, the corridors of old trails can still be generally surmised and mapped along the current terrain using multiple sources.

Old Maps

Historical maps do not easily align with modern maps. Researchers and cartographers use techniques called warping, stretch-to-fit, and georeferencing to overlay historical maps on present-day landscapes. By aligning historical map overlays with common points like stream confluences, elevation changes, land survey corners, distinctive river curves, and other fixed points, historical maps can add data points to an assessment of old roads and trails.

These techniques are substantially less precise when it comes to maps from the Spanish colonial period of the 1700s. Paying careful attention to the features of the land that would make one route easier than another can help create a case for the selection of a track. This is inexact science, if science at all, but following such indicators for historical road corridors has legitimacy if they are accepted as guidance and doubted as proof.

Physical Remains (Ruts and Swales)

The possibility of ruts and swales remaining on the landscape of East Texas after three hundred years is one of the least likely methods available for locating old trails from the Spanish colonial period. Even the magnificent swales of El Lobanillo on El Camino Real east of San Augustine are under a quarter mile long and bounded by agricultural and highway improvements that have obliterated any signs of the road on either end. However, along the corridors of historic roads, remnants of ruts from the older routes may still be found running alongside the rights-of-way for current paved highways or county roads. An old trail will sometimes be off to one side, visible through the woods, and at other locations it will weave back and forth across a newer, straighter road. Though ruts from the more heavily used El Camino Real de los Tejas can still be seen from the existing roadway, no known swales have yet been identified for the roads examined for this work. More on-the-ground research and the engagement of private landholders may ultimately reveal more.

Known Markers

Land records from the Texas General Land Office (GLO) document the Original Texas Land Surveys (OTLS) in what are called headright surveys. These are official documentations of the grants of land by Spain, Mexico, the Republic of Texas, or the State of Texas.[13] The records contain field notes made by the surveyor expressed in a language and style that defines the boundaries of the grant. In some instances, the surveyors identify a measurable spot on a boundary with the name of a road or trail. Even with a limited number of markers, identifying the placement of later roads can help identify possible trail corridors that predated them. The linear uniformity, however, can lead to relatively precise placement of old roads existing at the time of the survey.

Road Corridors

The phrase "historic road corridor" is commonly used in preservation projects. Road corridors are general pathways across which roadways, both historical and current, made their way across a landscape. A corridor can be a strait of land as narrow as the gap between two hills or across a known ford, or it can be as wide as a flatland prairie or floodplain where the possible paths are spread across a wide area. A road corridor may contain one route or several that existed over time.

An example of a more recent road corridor that points toward early routes can be found south of Lufkin across land that has been owned by the McCall family for almost 150 years. The road between the family's former cabin and a family cemetery was the earliest route to the south from Lufkin during the lifetime of the present owner, Homer McCall.[14] That dirt road, still visible through the woods, was known to him as the road to Houston. To its west was the Old State Highway 35 with origins around 1917, and to the east is the current US Highway 59 which saw initial construction between 1935 and 1942.[15]

Property Boundaries

Existing property boundaries can often align with road corridors that existed in the past but are no longer currently maintained roadways. McCall's land and road are along a survey boundary identified as the King's Highway in early property deeds. That road corridor included the route that Spanish soldiers took to investigate French incursions to the south. New roads follow old roads and often do so in grand scale. Deed surveys into the 1950s indicate that the property boundaries were along "public roads."

Archaeological Sites

Archaeological sites can also be an indicator of the locations of settlements and travel between villages. The Texas Historical Commission documents the location of archaeological sites in the state of Texas. The locations of those sites, largely on private land, are not released publicly to protect the integrity of the sites for future generations. Ancient artifacts, some of them associated with burials, have been lost to decades of looting by "pot hunters" who have decimated sites in Northeast Texas. Their practice is no different than digging up graves in any known cemetery—the sacrilege of which is easily understood.[16]

The documentation of archaeological sites in East Texas has helped identify a pattern of precolonial settlement, which offers an additional set of data points to consider. Native American villages were often not on a main trail but nearby. While Caddo tended to maintain stable village locations, the Bidai and other tribes south of Nacogdoches moved their villages routinely. Even though there are not artifacts that can be uniquely tied to the Bidai, there are sites in an area south of the Angelina River and west of US Highway 59 which help establish a likely corridor for significant early trails of the Spanish colonial period.

A Focus on Two Historic Road Networks

Using each of the methods described, this work focuses on two major road networks that were central to the cross-cultural trade and relationships between the Spanish, French, and Native American populations of northeastern Texas in the late 1770s. The first is very well known, widely documented, and has been designated as a National Historic Trail. Consequently, it will not be addressed here in detail. It was the major road network of the time and has come to be called El Camino Real de los Tejas. These roads connected Los Adaes in the east, through Nacogdoches to Béxar and La Bahía to the west and south.

A second network of roads of that time is little known and has been only alluded to in historical works. As a result, it has not been well documented. Through the initial research efforts of Tom H. Gann, this work is the first effort to focus on the trails used by the Bidai tribe for its trade with the French, and by other tribal groups like the Caddo, Akokisa, and Atakapa.

Though mention of a so-named Bidai Trail can be found scattered in historical literature, its description is broad and not well defined. Rather than a single path, there were multiple trails within Bidai territory. The trading trails that originated with the Bidai created a network of roads for others. Traders who wanted to avoid passing through the sites of the East Texas missions and presidios had other options to the south. Over time, segments of the Bidai trails network were called smuggler's roads and even later named as a King's Highway, mistakenly assigning two sections of the old trail with the status of a *camino real*. This work intends to bring new focus to the origins of these trails, their paths, and their role in the history of East Texas.

El Camino Real to Béxar

As a result of historical research and a revival of interest, in 1915 the Texas legislature appropriated $5,000 to survey the route of El Camino Real across the state. A surveyor named V. N. Zivley was hired to do the on-the-ground research. Zivley's maps are the foundational work for mapping performed to this day. In 1918, the Daughters of the American Revolution (DAR) placed granite milestones every five miles along the route. Additional attention came to the trail in 1936 during the Texas centennial celebration. Over time, the many names for the route—including the Road to Béxar, San Antonio Road, and King's Highway—have been consolidated under that single name El Camino Real.

A landmark work in 1991 celebrated the tricentennial history of the *caminos reales*. It recalled comments by a Spanish governor in 1792 who attested to the nature of the roads across Texas one hundred years after the first missions were established. Governor Muñoz offered his opinion in a report to the viceroy.

> I make known to your Superiority that in this Province under my charge there is not a single inn, nor any hostelries other than those which the residents provide to the guests and acquaintances who visit them, owing to

> the small number of settlements as well as their poverty, and the region not being traversable by anyone not having been raised and resident there.[17]

These trails and routes had been laid out by others and in use for hundreds of years before the Spanish ever arrived. The Spanish designation of them as a king's highway or a royal road was an illustration of how the Spanish viewed their colonization of New Spain and the province of Texas. The Spanish did not create or improve these existing routes, and they certainly could not claim to have "discovered" them.

The National Historic Trail

El Camino Real took on even greater acknowledgement and support in 2004 when it was designated as El Camino Real de los Tejas National Historic Trail and became part of the National Park Service. A map of the trail segments that make up El Camino Real de los Texas National Historic Trail looks like veins and capillaries carrying blood down an arm or a leg.[18] The branches and routes used over time diverge at one point and then intertwine at another. There is complexity in the informality of their direction, but they are simple in their purpose.

Travelers headed east from Béxar toward eastern Texas during the earliest Spanish expeditions found two primary options for the route. In the early 1800s the lower route through modern day Bastrop gained some favor, and that is the route primarily described when speaking of the Old San Antonio Road.[19] The northern or upper route was more direct but was also closer to a territory where attacks by Apache were more frequent. Consequently, the lower trail found greater use over time.[20]

While the emphasis and attention to El Camino Real de los Tejas has led to extensive, multidisciplinary studies since the early twentieth century, the bright light shone on it has left some of the lesser-known roads of the same period in the shadows. A network of other trails passed through the ancestral homeland of the Bidai. To better understand the nature of this period of contraband and culture, it is vital that the reader learn more about the "alternate routes" of East Texas used during the Spanish colonial period—the trails of the Bidai people.[21]

Trails of the Bidai

Through the detailed diaries of the earliest Spanish entradas and *visitas*, historians have noteworthy accounts of the expeditioners' daily travels. Those accounts, however, can be irritatingly ill-defined when compared to the modern landscape. The same river might be named differently by each passing expedition. Distances and directions are difficult to decipher. The routes they describe have been a point of contention and often bitter disagreement among historians, archaeologists, and others trying to establish points of the ground described over three hundred years before. Since this work seeks to delve into those questions, the author has no doubt that passionate disagreements will continue but will hope for less vitriol than shown by archaeologists Joachim "Al" McGraw and James Corbin toward William C. Foster. Their review of Foster's book *Spanish Expeditions into Texas, 1689–1768,* and his rebuttal, is a case study in the perils of such efforts.[22]

The Bidai occupied a sort of middle ground in East Texas, literally and culturally. The tribe ranged from the Neches-Angelina watershed near Nacogdoches westward to land between the Trinity and the Brazos and south of El Camino Real and Nacogdoches. Their villages along the Trinity River were south of the Hasinai and other Caddo groups and north of the Atakapan coastal tribes that included the Akokisa and Karankawa. The physical locations of Bidai villages were not unlike their role in trade across the region. They moved their villages around within a space between the Spanish and French, and among their native trading partners.

Trails between Bidai villages were part of a network involving more than cultural interaction. The trails were paths for commerce and trade. *Contrabandistas* were the primary users of the routes after Nacogdoches was resettled in 1779. Smugglers had no interest in writing about their travels or describing their clandestine routes, and as a result, information about them is limited. The Bidai engagement with French traders from Natchitoches meant there was a path from their villages near the Trinity River toward the east to Natchitoches. Since the Spanish considered French goods to be contraband, the Bidai trails provided an option to avoid missions found along the middle and upper routes of El Camino Real. The Bidai also hunted and fished at the coast, then returned home to the middle Trinity. A network of regular routes associated with locations the Bidai visited would be expected. Unlike other major routes across East Texas, there are no surveyor field notes calling a "Bidai Trail" by that name in the Original Texas Land Surveys. A few scattered surveyors' references to a road "down river," "old trails," and "Indian traces" hint at possible locations.[23]

By the time the Original Texas Land Surveys were conducted, the Bidai had been largely eliminated as a unique tribal identity. Their numbers decreased by disease, and they joined other tribes with similar languages, intermarrying and blending traditions. Anglos and the Coushatta people adopted the trails into the Bidai homeland, resulting in earlier names for trails being abandoned. The Coushatta Trace was named after the Alabama and Coushatta tribes that immigrated to Texas. They did so along trail corridors into the former Bidai homeland. Traces of Native American footpaths and horse trails not used for wagon traffic were quickly obscured by forest growth after they fell into disuse. The Bidai were forgotten, and their earliest trails were as well. The trails of the Brushwood People were quickly overgrown.

Three Bidai Trails

Visualizing the Bidai trading trails and their subsequent role in the early Spanish history of East Texas is important in understanding the movement of contraband through the region. Although the most common reference to the Bidai trail by name is an individual route, study of historical documentation and maps suggests three distinct trail corridors through Bidai territory to the south and west of Nacogdoches. Though they were part of the same network, each had a unique identity and importance to early East Texas history and the region's role as a focal point for contraband trade.

- **Bidai Trail between Nacogdoches and Orcoquisac.** This is the earliest documented segment of a route which was named as a Bidai trail. It ran south from Nacogdoches to active villages in the mid-1700s and later to a Spanish settlement called Orcoquisac near present-day Liberty.
- **Contraband Trail from Natchitoches to the Bidai Homeland.** This segment of trails gave the Bidai and other tribes along the Trinity River direct access to French traders from Natchitoches while bypassing Nacogdoches. These trails south of Nacogdoches were later known as El Camino del Caballo and sometimes called the Contraband Trace.
- **Bidai Trail to Paso Tomás and La Bahía.** The most notable of the Bidai trails and the one most central to this work is the path between Nacogdoches and the Bidai villages on the Trinity River, continuing to La Bahía. This "old road" on one of Stephen F. Austin's earliest maps was the most direct route to Nacogdoches and Natchitoches used by the Spanish who later settled at Paso Tomás on the Trinity River.

It is important to remember that these trails did not come into existence for travel between Spanish pueblos and presidios. These ancient routes existed

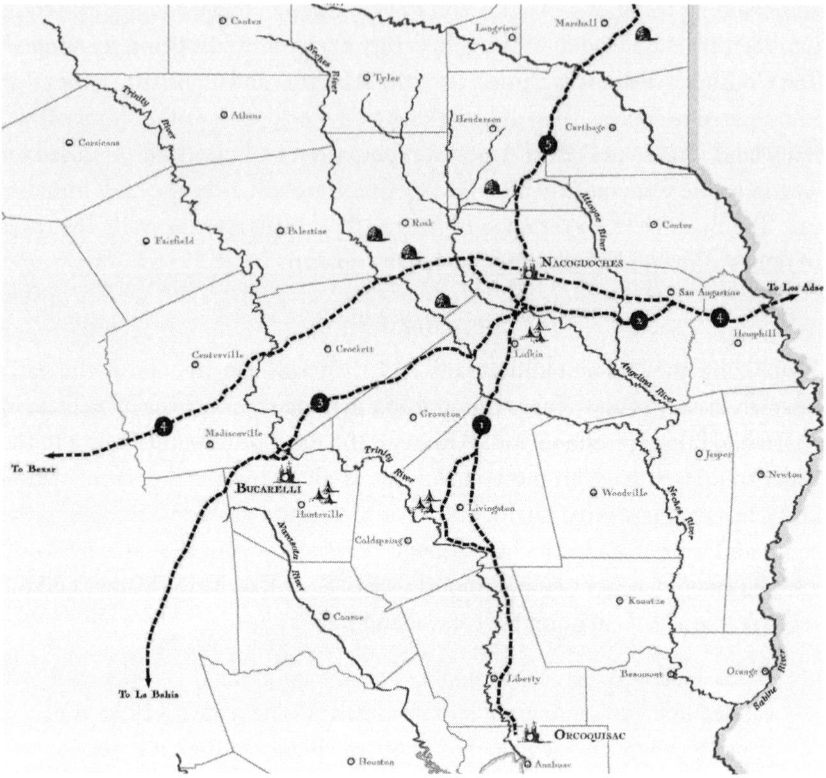

Trails and settlements of Spanish East Texas, 1770–79. Research by Gary Pinkerton and Tom Gann; map by Brian Wooten.

1. Bidai Trail to Orcoquisac;
2. Contraband Trail from Los Adaes;
3. "Old Road" to Bucareli;
4. El Camino Real de los Tejas (before 1806);
5. Caddo Trail (later Trammel's Trace.)

long before Columbus ever sailed. Travel for trade among Native American tribes in all directions was the reason for the existence of these ancient trail networks, not as routes created on behalf of the king of Spain, as the name *caminos reales* later implied. The Bidai used these three trails in the network of routes to travel between Bidai villages and their trading partners. The destinations of the trails mirror the reasons for their existence and the purposes for which they were used. Their interconnectivity is a testament to the mobility of the Bidai and their attention to trade.

Bidai Trail between Nacogdoches and Orcoquisac

The longest leg of the Bidai trail network and the one most often referred to when it is referenced in historical literature is the section between Nacogdoches and the mouth of the Trinity River at the upper end of Galveston Bay.[24]

"A PATH WHICH THE VIDIAS HAVE MADE" (1745)

The earliest documented reference to a Bidai trail was by a Spanish captain of the presidio at La Bahía, Don Joaquín de Orobio y Basterra. Acting on the viceroy's concern about French intrusions along the coast, Orobio was instructed to personally investigate and attempt to locate any possible settlement. It was a testament to how little the Spanish understood the coastal region east of La Bahía that Orobio was unsure how to get there. He found it too flooded to march from La Bahía along the coast. An effort to canoe down the Guadalupe River to the coast also failed due to high water and logjams. Historians report he experienced "discouragements and difficulties" in trying to comply with the orders.[25]

In 1745 there was no established Spanish route in the direction he needed to travel, because there had been no reason for the Spanish to go there. Instead, Orobio used the roads known to others and went up the road from La Bahía to the northeast toward Nacogdoches. Orobio arrived at the Trinity River on January 9, 1746. Accounts of his visit say he made "diligent inquiry among the Indians [there] but failed to obtain satisfactory information" about how to get back down to the area north of Galveston Bay at the mouth of the Trinity where the French intrusion was suspected.[26] Bidai Indians were known to have *rancherias* just south of the mouth of Bedias Creek, but Orobio said he could not get any information from the Bidai because "they remained in hiding in their homes." He did not explain why they might have done so, leaving us to wonder how the Bidai viewed his arrival. Perhaps they understood more than we know about his mission to disrupt commerce with their French trading partners [27]

Orobio continued to the Tejas villages on San Pedro Creek, twenty leagues (fifty miles) past the Trinity. There he found evidence of French trade goods everywhere he looked. French rifles, powder flasks, and bullet sacks were among the arms and ammunition Orobio saw. Some of the natives were wearing white shirts on top of "strips of fine scarlet cloth for decency" covering their genitals. Others wore what the natives called *naguizas*, a seven-foot-long piece of red cloth worn like a cape.

The Tejas traded chamois, buffalo hides, bear tallow, horses, and mules for the French goods.[28] The chief explained that the goods had come to his people from Natchitoches by way of the Hasinai to the east, not from French traders on the coast. The chief confirmed that he too had heard the rumors about the French creating more permanent settlements to the south. The French had been coming to the Texas coast for trade since 1722.

Orobio had inquired of the Tejas about how to get to the location of the rumored French settlement. From that village, following the Trinity River to its mouth would have been the most direct route. There are indications that the Caddo themselves traveled south along the Trinity toward the location of tribal villages and the later Spanish presidio of Orcoquisac. A governor's comment about Paso Tomás being at the intersection of roads east to Los Adaes and south to Orcoquisac hints toward the likelihood that a north-south road along the left side of the Trinity existed for years.[29]

Orobio asked the Caddo chief if he could get to the coast directly from their village using that route. It had been a particularly cold and rainy winter, so he was told it was not possible to go that way due to the conditions.[30] The reply to Orobio's question was essentially, "You can't get there from here." Instead, Orobio learned that the place where the French might be found could best be reached by traveling south from Nacogdoches. The route Orobio was told to take was "a path which the Vidias [Bidai] have formed in going to Nacogdoches."[31] The trail the Bidai made from the south to trade and receive gifts from the mission in Nacogdoches was apparently well known to the tribes of the region, but not to the Spanish—at least not to the captain of the La Bahía presidio.

On February 7, 1746, Orobio left Nacogdoches and headed toward the coast with four soldiers and limited supplies led by a Native American guide of unnamed tribal affiliation. Though Joaquín de Orobio y Basterra was not familiar with the trail, it is his name that has been attached to the crossing of the Angelina south of Nacogdoches. The Don Joaquín Crossing, just to the west of where US Highway 59 crosses the Angelina, remains a well-known landmark, and a historical marker referencing it stands nearby.[32]

Orobio arrived at a place he called Santa Rosa de Viterbo, where there were Bidai living near the Trinity.[33] At that location Orobio found seven Bidai rancherias, likely meaning seven separate villages scattered along the lower Trinity. It was an unusually severe winter in East Texas and the Bidai were using bearskin tents for shelter against the cold. Orobio had noted that the "repeated snows and rains" that had fallen that year prevented proper care of the horses and led to limited food supplies. A chief told Orobio that some of the Bidai had left the harsh conditions and had "gone to the hills to find refuge in bear caves." It is unclear to which hills the chief was referring.

Unsurprisingly, historians differ in their interpretations of Orobio's encounter with this group of Bidai. While Bolton implies the Bidai had not seen Spanish soldiers before, Castañeda says it was simply the first time Spaniards had been seen that far south. Given that this particular Bidai trail was formed by tribal members visiting Nacogdoches from the south, it seems unlikely they had never encountered Spanish people before. In fact, a different translation of Orobio's diary simply says that Spanish visits "did not happen customarily."[34]

A NAKED FRENCHMAN (1719)

Few would suspect that their curiosity into the history of Spanish East Texas would lead to learning about a naked Frenchman. An interesting firsthand account places a stranded French sailor along the Bidai trail that led from the coastal plains to Nacogdoches. Around twenty-five years before Orobio made his way south, a captive Frenchman found his escape along that route to the north.

Francois Simars de Bellisle was one of five French sailors who were left behind on the coast of Texas in 1719.[35] He alone survived the winter, only to be captured in 1720 by Akokisa Indians along the Texas coast. His story tells how they kept him enslaved and naked, and how they beat and abused him. Bellisle's captivity was believed to be in one of the villages near upper Galveston Bay at the mouth of the Trinity River.

Bellisle had no other options than simply staying alive, so he endured. When Bidai tribal members from the north visited the Akokisa camp where Bellisle was held, he managed to give them a letter, which he scratched out with charcoal, pleading for his life. He hoped the Bidai would deliver his appeal to someone who could read his crude call for help. After passing the letter among their own people and other tribes for their curiosity and amusement, the letter ultimately made it to Louis Juchereau de St. Denis, the masterful French trader who lived in Natchitoches but traded with tribes across the Sabine. St. Denis asked the Hasinai to rescue Bellisle and return him to safety among his countrymen.

Bellisle's difficulties at the coast are pertinent to this story because the path he described taking from the Akokisa camp where he was held north to Nacogdoches and Natchitoches trends in the same direction as those used by the Marqués de Rubí and Orobio, perhaps encountering the same villages.[36]

RUBÍ/LAFLORA DIARIES (1767)

The Marqués de Rubí, a titled Spanish baron who was an inspector of the Spanish presidios, took his assignment very seriously. Before submitting a report that was pivotal in the history of Spanish settlement on the continent, not just in Texas, he traveled 7,600 miles over twenty-three months and his report was issued as his *Dictamen*.[37] For the portion of Rubí's trip from Béxar to Los Adaes, he followed the existing routes of El Camino Real de los Tejas. Both Rubí and Nicolás Lafora kept detailed diaries of their journeys. Using accounts from their respective diaries, we know quite a bit about what they experienced on the trail from Nacogdoches toward the Gulf Coast and the Akokisa villages.[38]

The first thirteen miles between Nacogdoches and the Angelina River to the south were filled with pines, oaks, walnuts, and persimmon trees. In early October, they may have experienced a little fall color, and the vines and undergrowth would have begun releasing their hold on ground level travel. After fording an apparently shallow Angelina River at the Don Joaquín Crossing, they found an abandoned Bidai village. Indications were that it had not been emptied for long. The huts were still furnished with "furniture of woven cane and palm fiber constructed with excellent workmanship."[39]

After crossing the Angelina, the party camped on a small hillside which can still be identified based on their description. The hill looked out over a floodplain bisected by what is now Procella Creek. To the southeast on the other side of the creek was another hill which they correctly identified as a quarter of a league distant, about six-tenths of a mile.[40] From Nacogdoches south toward the coast, Rubí seemed to believe that he was following the same route used by Orobio twenty-two years earlier, but Rubí's route may have placed him farther to the east. Rubí's impressions of swampy travel through impenetrable forest match a picture of the Big Thicket in present Tyler County. His descriptions of the terrain indicate a route much farther to the east along a corridor that later became known as the Liberty to Nacogdoches Road. That path crossed the Neches at a location that became the site of a Mexican military post, Fort Terán, in 1831.[41] Theories differ about the precise route Rubí followed, but they agree on the destination. That there is a network of Bidai trails is well demonstrated.

INDICATIONS IN EARLY MAPPING

Dan Worrall, geologist and author of the outstanding book, *A Prehistory of Houston and Southeast Texas—Landscape and Culture*, suggests that "the Spanish were not known for their interior cartography." His polite description of maps of the Spanish colonial period notes the graphic challenges presented by trying to use them to locate modern features on the ground.[42] The location of the Bidai villages in proximity to the route of the coastal trail are imprecise

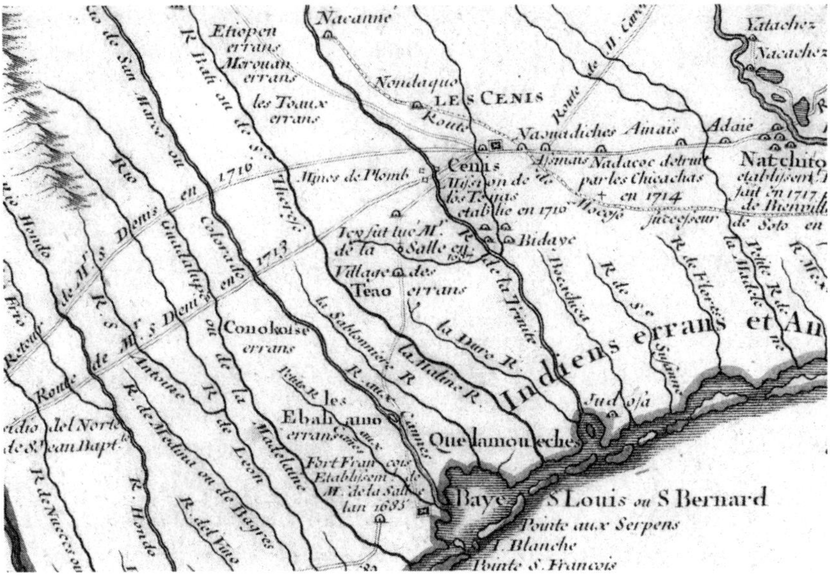

Louisiane, Cours du Mississipi, Guillame de L'Isle, 1718. Image courtesy of David Rumsey Map Collection, www.davidrumsey.com, image #4764098.

by modern standards, but several indicators are available that help determine the possible locations.

One of the most important and accurate maps of the mid-eighteenth century is a 1742 French map dubbed *Louisiane, Cours de Mississippi* [Louisiana and the course of the Mississippi].[43] The map's placement of Bidai villages along the middle Trinity River is done in a manner that allows a general comparison to a modern map. In the illustration of the map shown, the "Bidaye" villages are noted at the mouth of two streams into the Trinity River. The Bidai villages shown on Guillaume De l'Isle's map, gleaned from French traders, are about twenty to thirty miles downstream from known Bidai villages near Paso Tomás.

Whether the Bidai villages shown on this 1742 map are the same Bidai rancherias that Orobio encountered or not is hard to say. This route would have been oriented almost directly south to a point on the Trinity River where four later Coushatta villages, including Long King's Village, were found. The idea that the Coushatta villages of the early 1800s were in roughly the same locations as Orobio's Bidai rancherias is a reasonable conjecture.[44]

Another indication of the Bidai trail south from the Angelina River is the arrangement of land grants made along that road. Tom H. Gann made note of this in his research of the early East Texas landscape. Land grants made to former residents of Los Adaes who made their way to East Texas line the trails south. Given the opportunity to locate land along the road corridors headed south, these early grantees made their selections opportunistically and established themselves along a well-traveled route. These early settlers had highway frontage.

Contraband Trail from Natchitoches to the Bidai Homeland

The accounts of Bellisle and Orobio provide historical context to the general direction of the Bidai trail between Nacogdoches and Orcoquisac at the upper end of Galveston Bay. However, it was not the only travel corridor through the area where Bidai villages were predominant. One of the early east-west trails across Bidai territory had a role in promoting the commerce of the day—contraband goods prohibited by Spanish authorities. The Bidai were known to have traveled from their villages on the Trinity River to Los Adaes and as far as New Orleans in search of trade opportunities. Over time, the merchandise that traders moved along the trail changed, but their intent did not.[45]

In the first half of the eighteenth century, a contraband trail connected French traders from Natchitoches with Bidai villages along the Trinity River to the west. One intercepted smuggler explained his reason for following the route was not to avoid detection, but rather that he simply "deviated from the road [*camino real*]" to find a way to Natchitoches, an action that drew suspicion.[46] At various times this "bypass" to the south around Nacogdoches was called the Smuggler's Road, the Contraband Trail or Trace, and El Camino del Caballo (the Road of the Horse). Whether it was tobacco and guns, or cattle and mustangs, the purpose of this Bidai trail was to avoid detection.

INDICATIONS IN EARLY MAPPING

The existence of a trail around Nacogdoches to the south during the Spanish colonial period is indicated by multiple maps of the period. Though few precise points relevant to today's landscape are revealed, there are enough to establish a corridor that can then be followed along the topography.

Walker's Route des Contrabandieres

Juan Pedro Walker was a cartographer of the early nineteenth century who had as excellent an apprenticeship as one could have. Born in New Orleans, which was Spanish at the time, he started his surveying career by being a chain carrier under the tutelage of Andrew Ellicott, the most distinguished surveyor and cartographer of that era. After the Louisiana Purchase, Walker

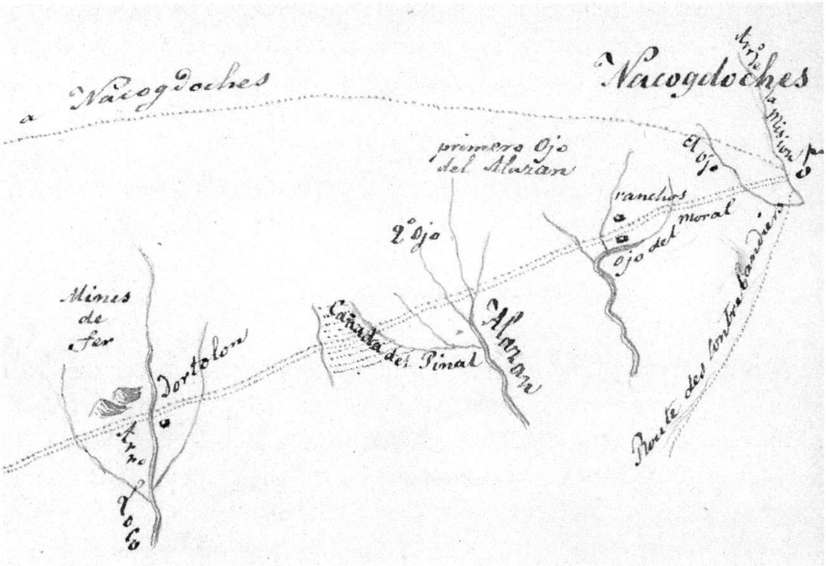

Route of the Smugglers, by Juan Pedro Walker, circa 1808. "Texas, Route de Nacogdoches au Rio Trinidad, J.P.W." Voyage au Mexique: Itineraires, ports, cotes, baies, etc. de la Republique Mexicaine. Courtesy Jean Louis Berlandier Papers. Yale Collection of Western Americana, Beinecke Rare Book and Manuscript Library.

moved to Spanish Texas, where he served governors and commandants with his superior skills.

Though Walker's maps were never published, fifteen of his detailed and remarkably accurate maps are in archives around the world.[47] One 1806 map by Walker was discovered mixed in with the papers of a Mexican inspection tour of Texas conducted in the 1820s. One of his broad and somewhat crude manuscript maps displays many details of El Camino Real and features along the road between Nacogdoches and the Neches, stopping short of the Trinity River. Walker's 1808 map contains an upper road angling to the north and west from Nacogdoches labeled "*Ancienne route de Béxar a Nacogdoches*," or the old route of Béxar to Nacogdoches. Walker's understanding of this upper route was that it was not the primary route at the time; it was instead "ancient" from his perspective.[48]

The information on Walker's map most pertinent to this work is the route branching to the southwest from Nacogdoches. Walker labeled this road as "*Route des Contrabandieres*," the route of the smugglers. This map also indicates the existence of a separate Bidai trail to Paso Tomás and Bucareli at the Trinity

River that will be discussed later in this chapter. Walker knew there was a way around for smugglers coming into the province from Louisiana who had gone there to acquire items that the Spanish crown considered contraband.

The Contraband Trace, El Camino del Caballo

There was an additional road known as a route for smuggling contraband that connected Walker's Road to Natchitoches. A 1940 article by a young Nacogdoches resident whose family lived along the route of this smuggler's road described it in some detail using Spanish surveys and on-the-ground knowledge.[49] Edward Blount, a junior historian at Nacogdoches High School in 1945, called it the Contraband Trace, while the Texas State Historical Association uses El Camino del Caballo to designate the trail.[50] Blount's illustration of the trail for an article in *The Junior Historian*, a journal published by the Texas State Historical Association, showed it curving to the south of Nacogdoches as if it were a modern loop laid out by the highway department. From the east he showed the trail leaving El Camino Real just south of Chireno at the Attoyac Bayou. As it tracks to the west, the trail was shown passing known points on the ground including Oil Springs, Shawnee Springs, and Palisada Springs on the east side of present US Highway 59.

The location of Shawnee Springs is just north of an existing boat ramp and fishing spot known as Shawnee Landing on the Angelina. The US Forest Service manages it as part of the Angelina National Forest at the upper end of Sam Rayburn Lake.[51] The extreme uplift to the north side of the river, a bluff of Cook Mountain sandstone, abruptly rises above the creek bottom fifty feet or more giving the impression of the "palisades" referred to historically. In 1978 an inspection by geologist Gunnar Brune for his *Springs of Texas* book found that a large beech tree near the springs had an 1887 date carved into it. Palisade Springs was noted to have a significant waterfall and was used as a campsite for those traveling along the road. Its location is just to the east of Highway 59. There are no longer falls or other features of the spring as noted in the past, but the water from the springs now fills a man-made lake.[52]

The historic Don Joaquín ford of the Angelina River is just to the south of where the smuggler's road crossed the coastal trail to the lower Trinity. On the west side of current Highway 59, the smuggler's road traversed Moral Bayou at a place that was called *El Paso Viejo*. Noted historian and avocational archeologist, Morris Jackson of Nacogdoches, has identified the location of that area.

> El Paso Viejo (The Old Pass) was an area of land where the Alazán Creek converged with the Moral Creek and was just southeast of a natural lake

> now called Blount Lake. This site was also the major lower east-west road north of the lowlands of the Angelina River and had the reputation of being a Contraband Trail which would bypass the authorities in the pueblo of Nacogdoches.[53]

Later land grants to major traders like William Barr, Samuel Davenport, Vicente Micheli, and Jose Lucobiche were aligned on the south side of the Angelina. These holdings were strategically placed away from Nacogdoches and along these roads making them an ideal place to avoid trade restrictions.[54]

The venerable Texas historian Henderson K. Yoakum understood the relationship of this trail to others in the region. In a map of Spanish Texas he published in 1856, he shows this contraband trail separating from El Camino Real miles to the east of Nacogdoches and trailing to the south.[55] Obvious errors detract from the blanket acceptance of many of the details of his map. His placement of a Vidaes [Bidai] village far up the Sabine is not supported by other accounts. The Cenis [Caddo] village he placed where Bedias Creek entered the Trinity was a known Bidai village.[56]

THE BIDAI AT EL DURÁZNO

Durasno [Durázno] Creek flows north to the Angelina River on the east side of Highway 59. *Durázno* is the Spanish word for peach. The current name for the creek is Paper Mill Creek, named for a paper mill at the mouth of the creek. Within a six-mile radius of the Don Joaquín Crossing of the Angelina, there are several archaeological sites along the corridors of the earliest Bidai trails. Though there are no remains of pottery, arrow points, or other lithic objects that can definitively identify a site as Bidai, the location of these villages is along the floodplain of Durasno Creek and near the route of the Bidai smuggling trail.

In 1767, when Father Gaspar José de Solís came to East Texas on an inspection tour of the missions, his diary recorded his interaction with the Bidai at El Durasno, a village named after the nearby stream. His diary was a daily log of the conditions, terrain, and people he encountered.[57] Solís complained about the ticks, mosquitos, gnats, and harvest mites at the Angelina River, but he was impressed by the size and number of the tribal nations who had "big towns."

Solís was also impressed enough with two native leaders who came out to greet him that he identified them by name. One of them was a chief of the Navidachos named Bigotes, who was accompanied by a Spanish priest. Bigotes, also known as Sauto, was the chief of the Hainai and head of the Hasinai Confederacy. The other chief who came to visit the priest was Gorgoritos.

Gorgoritos, also referred to as Melchor, was the Bidai chief and head of a Bidai-Akokisa Confederacy at the time,[58] Both Bigotes and Gorgoritos were referred to as "medal chiefs," designated as leaders by the Spanish and presented with medals and special gifts to gain their allegiance.[59] In naming Gorgoritos, Solís said he was from "Duráznos de Los Vidays," the same village along Durasno Creek near the Angelina where a Spanish priest was suspected of smuggling.

Father Zedano's Contraband at El Durázno, 1766

In November 1766, Sgt. Domingo Chirinos, an official of the presidio at Los Adaes, was patrolling roads to the west of the Sabine River, doing his duty for the crown. Just east of the Angelina River along the Bidai contraband trail, he encountered Father Domingo Zedano at the head of a mule train near a Bidai village.[60] The name of the village was apparently quite well known, and its name placed it in a general location. The Bidai village known as El Durázno was just to the south of the Angelina River along Durasno Creek.

The sergeant and four other soldiers confronted the priest and asked to search his cargo. The priest offered a gracious diversion when he "asked [Chirinos] to get off the horse so he could eat because lunch was ready." The sergeant replied "that he was very grateful for the offer, but it was already late, and he was only there to do his job." The priest asked if he had permission to search a man of the church. Sergeant Chirinos said the governor himself had given him the authority in the name of his majesty the king, implying that nothing more was needed.

The holy father finally complied, and the sergeant asked the priest to have his muleteers untie the cargo. Seven men accompanied Father Zedano and his mission mules. Zedano further tried to divert Chirinos and said the men were not muleteers but were *arrimados*, servants he hired for the trip. The priest's challenges to the sergeant's authority were polite but ineffective. The sergeant ordered the men to untie the loads, and Zedano's *arrimados* complied with the orders of the military man, who was armed and sitting astride his horse.

In testimony regarding his confiscation of the goods, Sergeant Chirinos explained how he found contraband in the possession of the father conductor of the missions of Texas. The priest's baggage included velvet, linen, gold braid, a barrel of *aguardiente* (alcohol that could be made from any number of ingredients), beads, red- and blue-stiped Indiana cloth, and 229 bundles of "good tobacco like the ones from Nachitos [Natchitoches]." Zedano carried all of this in ten trunks and two sacks on the backs of seven mules of the Aix brand, the mark of Mission Dolores at current San Augustine.

The goods were confiscated and sold at auction for 660 pesos, including 140 pesos for the seven mules. Some of the goods—bundles of tobacco, velvet, and a religious ornament—belonged to another priest and was only being transported by Zedano. Though charges were filed on the other members of the caravan, the priests escaped any legal consequences and later recovered some of the property that was legitimately intended for the Native Americans at the mission. The case indicates how broadly contraband trade existed, even with the participation of the clergy, despite it being a violation of the king's laws.

"KNEW NO OTHER ROAD"

Perhaps there is no more certain depiction of the Bidai contraband trail as a smuggler's route than an 1804 encounter between José Ugarte, the lieutenant at Nacogdoches, and a trader to the Comanche, Manuel de León.[61] In a brief letter to the governor, Ugarte explained that despite de León having a passport giving him permission to travel to the province, he was arrested with thirty-five horses and mules. De León's apparent failing was that he left the *camino real* to make his way around Nacogdoches to the south.

Simply based on de León's selection of the route used to avoid detection, Ugarte was convinced that he must certainly be engaged in contraband trade. Generally, that was a safe assumption. De León's defense was that "he did not know any other road than the one he took." The Bidai contraband trail around Nacogdoches to the south supported their trade with the French in Natchitoches and served as a secretive smuggling trail for many years. Walker's route of the *contrabandieres* also connected with another Bidai path toward the Trinity River at Paso Tomás.

Bidai Trail to Paso Tomás and La Bahía

The Bidai trail between Nacogdoches and the Trinity River at the mouth of Bedias Creek was one of the most important pathways in the history of Spanish East Texas and one about which little is known to historians. As one of the primary trails in the Bidai homeland south of El Camino Real de los Tejas, the trail from Nacogdoches to Paso Tomás had been used for many years before the first Spanish expeditions to establish missions in the early 1700s. To the northeast the trail connected with the contraband trail from Natchitoches, and to the southwest its forks connected to both La Bahía and Béxar.

Though it was the most direct route between the Trinity River and Nacogdoches, based on the diaries of Spanish entradas, it was not a route the entradas regularly used for travel. That would be true because Nacogdoches was not initially their primary destination. Spanish visitors in the eighteenth century generally took the upper route of El Camino Real de los Tejas, crossing at Hurricane/Kickapoo Shoals toward the principal villages of the Caddo at the Neches River and San Pedro Creek.

In 1721, Aguayo may have come closest to identifying this route. On his approach toward the Trinity River from the southwest, the governor stumbled upon a road that branched off to the south, in the direction opposite the road toward the Caddo villages.[62] The soldiers he dispatched to investigate, along with three of the priests, followed the road and came upon some cultivated fields about seven miles to the south down the Trinity River. The people who the soldiers and priests met were the Bidai. The path the Spanish took to find them was also part of a continuing means to travel down the Trinity to the coast, connecting the Caddo to the Atakapan tribal groups to the south. It was likely part of that deep and miry route Orobio was cautioned to avoid.

AUSTIN'S *MAPA TOPOGRÁFICO DE LA PROVINCIAL DE TEXAS*

Stephen Fuller Austin is best known as the leader of the Texas colonization movement in the early 1820s and "the father of Texas." Not everyone knows he was also an incredibly detail-oriented mapmaker. Two of his maps signal the existence of an "old road" between Nacogdoches and the Trinity River, a road now identified as the Bidai trail to Paso Tomás.

Austin's 1822 *Mapa Topográfico de la Provincial de Texas* is one of the most unique and expressive maps of the colonization period. Even though very general and containing errors of scale and orientation, it has several features significant to an understanding of the roads used by the Spanish in the late eighteenth century. Part of what makes it so distinctive is the coloring Austin added to indicate the vegetation and landscape. This map details Austin's understanding of the network of roads across East Texas. It also reflects what this research has found regarding the three trails that have Bidai origins.

On Austin's *Mapa Topográfico*, there is a single road running east-west through Nacogdoches labeled as Camino que va a Nachistoches (Road that goes to Natchitoches). There is no branch of the road going to the Tejas village on the Neches River, although substantial villages labeled Texas (Tejas) are shown north of the route. A darkened block on the Trinity River is labeled Salcedo, the location of the Spanish presidio at Trinidad de Salcedo, begun in 1806. It is notable that Austin shows roads both to the north and to the south of Trinidad de Salcedo, indicating that it was located at neither crossing. As this research shows, the road crossing the Trinity to the south of Trinidad de Salcedo was at or near Paso Tomás. As was documented on multiple occasions, there was a branch in this road west of the Trinity with separate routes toward Béxar and La Bahía.[63]

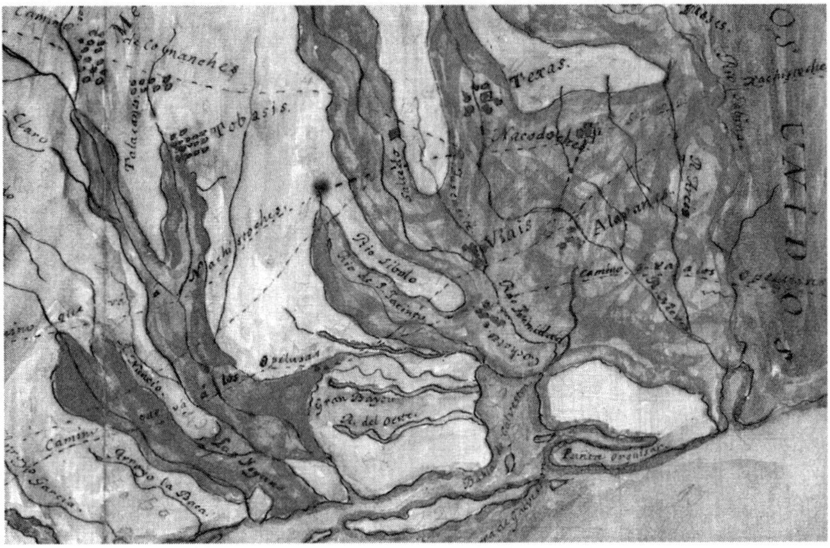

Stephen F. Austin's 1822 *Mapa topográfico de la provincial de Texas*. In his note at the bottom of the map, Austin explained the meaning of the different colors or shades. They represent forests, riverbanks, plains, and villages or ranches. Courtesy Library of Congress, https://lccn.loc.gov/98687158.

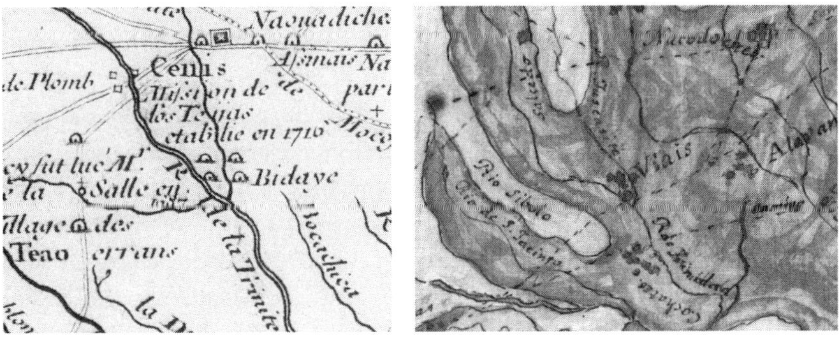

Bidai villages shown in same location over an 80-year span—the 1742 D'lisle map and 1822 Austin map.

Austin also illustrated a segment of the Bidai trail that led to the lower Trinity and the coast through Bidai villages, though he used the spelling "Viais." That road is shown connected with the *camino que va a los Opelusas*, the road to Opelousas, later known as the Atascosita Trail. For whatever reason, Austin did not often illustrate north-south routes with the same level of interest as those heading east-west. Austin's focus was farther to the west at the center of his colony, San Felipe de Austin.

As a broad view of the trails of eastern Texas in the early 1820s, this map is helpful in affirming some of the decisions made for this work in placing the Bidai trail corridor between Nacogdoches and the Trinity River. All these mapping judgments must, of course, consider the lack of any accurate scale or georeferencing which could make it easier to match early maps with current terrain. However, a consideration of the major landmarks and features Austin shows in comparison to other data delivers a strong sense of how the roads would have existed one hundred years prior to his mapping.

MAP OF AUSTIN'S COLONY AND ADJACENT COUNTRY

Another of Austin's earliest maps illustrates a key aspect of this placement of the Bidai trail to Paso Tomás—the *Map of Austin's Colony and adjacent Country in Texas drawn principally from actual Survey*. The map labeling is in English, rather than in Spanish, which Austin routinely used, indicating it was for a different audience. The date on this map is uncertain but was sometime during the early 1820s.[64] Given the level of detail in this map and some of the corrections he made, it is presumed this map is a few years after *Mapa Topográfico*.[65]

On this map, there is one road leading into Nacogdoches from Natchitoches to the east and four distinct routes continuing to the south and west. The two upper routes to the west are both part of El Camino Real, splitting and merging again at the Neches River and San Pedro Creek. The most southerly trail along Bayou La Nana is the approximate route of the Bidai coastal trail. This map shows it passing through some Alabama villages along the Trinity at what are three known archaeological and historical sites including Long King's Village.[66]

It is the second road from the bottom on Austin's map that depicts the road to Paso Tomás. The road shown that angles toward space between Bedias Creek and the crossing of the upper El Camino Real is the Bidai trail from Paso Tomás to Nacogdoches. Since it continued southwest from the Trinity, it had also been called the *camino de La Bahía*. What is significant about Austin's map is how he chose to label the crossing at the falls just above the mouth of Bedias Creek. His notation names it as the "old road," meaning that it was old when the map was created in the 1820s. That naming continued until the trail reached the Brazos River. Austin's "old road" is the Bidai trail to Paso Tomás at the Trinity.

Austin's old road on the map connected with the Trinity River at a point marked by falls created by sandstone or lignite outcroppings. He shows that crossing slightly upstream from the mouth of Bedias Creek and the crossing at Paso Tomás. It is important to note that the old road did not merge with or cross any of the segments of El Camino Real leaving Nacogdoches until it reached the Brazos River. The old road to the Trinity did not respond to the cultural gravity of the Kingdom of the Tejas, or veer south down the Trinity. Its primary destination was La Bahía to the southwest, crossing the Trinity at Paso Tomás.

ROADS AND COLLATERAL PATHS

Despite the old road shown crossing the Trinity upstream from Bedias Creek and Paso Tomás, research regarding the crossings used during the Spanish colonial period indicate that the falls mentioned on Austin's map were likely farther downriver. Support for that idea is found in research done by archaeologist Bob Skiles, on the later location of the Spanish presidio Trinidad de Salcedo.

South of Loma del Toro are two marked features on Austin's map—The Falls and Bedi (Bedias) Creek. It is significant that Hurricane Creek, above Lomo del Toro, and Bedias Creek are the only tributaries Austin labeled on this entire section of the Trinity River, over 150 miles. This distant separation of the two crossings is further supported by the 1810 observations of Capt. Pedro Lopez Prieto, a Spanish captain at Trinidad de Salcedo. Captain Prieto was commandant of the presidio at Trinidad. In a report to the governor, Prieto showed he had quickly learned the complications of Spanish life in the borderlands. In 1810, he reported that the area had "roads and collateral paths which facilitate the introduction of clandestine, forbidden [i.e., contraband goods] from the Province of Louisiana." He called the lower road as one of those, being "on this Trinity River at the second falls." The second falls was one of three between Trinidad and Atascosito (Liberty), the falls near Paso Tomás.[67]

There is also support for this designation of an old road by Austin within correspondence regarding the establishment of the location of the village of Bucareli in 1774. The new settlement was to be founded along the "shortest route from La Bahía to Los Adaes."[68] It is notable that while Los Adaes had just recently been abandoned at the time of the letter, it was still the end point mentioned. Naming it thus avoided any confusion with the upper road toward the Caddo villages at the Neches and San Pedro Creek. Austin's "old road" was clearly the shortest route toward the former Spanish capital if a side trip to the Tejas village was not part of the itinerary.

INDICATIONS ON THE GROUND

About one-and-a-half miles north of the Nacogdoches-Angelina County line at the Angelina River, the Bidai trail to Paso Tomás crossed the Bidai contraband trail heading east-west near Palisada Springs. To the east of US Highway

59, Old Ferry Road along the right-of-way of Old State Highway 35 passes the Procella Cemetery, where the earliest known burial is dated 1860 and many of the deceased have Hispanic surnames.

At the Angelina River, the road crossed near the former Highway 35 bridge to the west of Highway 59 at the Don Joaquin Crossing.[69] Deed research within the headright surveys reveals much about the precise path of the old road into Angelina County. By the time that land was surveyed, the boundary between Barr and Davenport land to the west and Vicente Micheli's land to the east was labeled as a king's highway.

Survey calls and deed records establish a path for the Bidai trail corridor tracking to the southwest from the Don Joaquín crossing. Just south of the Angelina River, in an area known to have had Bidai villages, the trail passed among three known archaeological sites.[70] South of the Angelina River there are many indications of a historic road corridor. Known Native American sites to the east and west of the road and the east of the Micheli survey have been identified by the Texas Historical Commission. Old GLO maps record a historic location for Las Lagunitas in the J. Magano survey.[71] Small lagoons at this location, probably nothing more than marshy low spots holding water, were mentioned in some of the earliest surveys. A survey for Pedro de Lara mentions a *placeta* (a plaza or perhaps a clearing), and *Las Castanas* prairie in the same general location. Survey calls to the west of the Bidai trail corridor indicate an unnamed "Indian trace" tracking from northwest to southeast, and there is also mention of the Duncan Trace in this segment, a later road from Nacogdoches to the Trinity River.

The most significant and personal point of contact for the Bidai trail is the John D. Gann house and the Gann Ferry on the Neches.[72] Though neither existed during the time frame of this history, ferries like this were placed at well-used road crossings where only a shoal might have existed before. The Rocky Crossing on the Neches was the natural ford near the later location of Gann Ferry. It led to the Bluff Prairie Saline.[73] On the west side of the Neches River and along the county line between Trinity and Houston counties, the possible route of the trail is difficult to ascertain. A twentieth century plat map indicates an "old road" along the possible path, tempting interpretation.[74] Later roads like the Cummins Trace, which appears in survey calls near the Trinity, are found to the southwest of Rayville.

The route also passed through the almost nine thousand-acre land grant of José Antonio Sepulveda. The survey was conducted in 1826 after Texas became part of Mexico. A description of the two tracts he desired provides insight into the isolation of the land, as well as a sense of how its ownership

A photo of the John D. Gann House in 1936, near Gann's Ferry and Rocky Ford. Courtesy The Portal to Texas History, University of North Texas Libraries.

was considered. In Sepulveda's petition to Governor José Antonio Saucedo, Sepulveda let the governor know that "these two have always been vacant [unclaimed] tracts." Ensuring there was no prior claim on land being requested was a critical starting point. In the same sentence in which Sepulveda said the land was vacant, he said it was a place where "for a very long time only the Indians have lived." That the land could be considered vacant yet identified as the home of indigenous people of East Texas demonstrates the cultural disconnect when it came to respecting the rights of the people who had lived there for centuries.[75]

Bending to the southwest, just inside the county line with Trinity County, the trail likely wove its way along the terrain passing just to the south of present-day Pennington, turning west into Houston County just north of the little community of Holly. The current roads of Farm to Market Road 1280 and Farm to Market Road 230 passing through Lovelady are probably close approximations of the Bidai trail corridor toward the Trinity River. This direction is supported by an early survey call of a road going "down river" along the course of Cedar Bayou.[76]

Farm to Market Road 230 heads to the south-southwest near Weldon and directly toward the location of Paso Tomás and Bucareli. To the west, upriver at the later site of Trinidad de Salcedo, there are multiple survey calls for a "contraband trace" in the direction of Spanish Bluff and Hyde's Ferry. Given the fluidity of the roads network and the five-mile-wide floodplain, there is little evidence that further on-the-ground points might better define the trail corridor.

The Stage Is Set

In the first five chapters, the stage has been set for "the last Spanish episode of the Texas drama" as it unfolded in East Texas. The period between 1773, when Spanish missions and presidios were closed to cut expenses, and 1813, when *filibusteros* began trying to take over parts of Texas, was a unique time in history. Not only was the Spanish colonial period beginning a decline, but there were also dramatic changes impacting Spanish subjects in Los Adaes, far to the east. They would soon become the lone European occupants of East Texas. A vast landscape where little Spanish control was felt would be their home, in a region where Caddo and other tribes were the dominant human presence. Relationships with the Caddo and other tribes were built through commerce and trade that the Spanish government considered unsanctioned and illegal. That contraband trade was carried out over a network of Native American trails, which allowed some measure of secrecy from Spanish authority, such as it was.

It is into this territory, this terrain, and this history that events led to the abandonment of the Spanish capital of the Province of Texas at Los Adaes and the establishment of a new way station for contraband trade on the banks of the Trinity River at Paso Tomás.

6

Their Tears Sprinkled the Road

> Los Adaes and its Missions were depopulated . . . at the cost of their grief, their homes, their ranches . . . their possessions scattered in the forests, and full of inexpressible miseries.
>
> —FATHER JOSEF FRANCISCO MARIANO DE LA GARZA[1]

In the first five chapters of this work, the places, landscapes, rivers, and trails of eastern Texas in the eighteenth century have been defined and described. The remainder of the work will focus on the people who found themselves living in East Texas and the contraband culture of which they were a part. For the period between 1773 and 1803, when the United States completed the Louisiana Purchase, people from many nations lived across eastern Texas in an ill-defined borderland. On the edges of Spanish authority, they were largely able to exist with minimal interference. Their distance from the Spanish seats of power allowed them room to maneuver around royal edicts and viceregal pronouncements. One thing some of them could never escape, however, was the sadness of being forced from their homes.

The Adaeseños

The place referred to as Los Adaes included a presidio, a mission, and a small settlement surrounding them. With both religious and military roots, Spanish settlements in the borderlands took on a character along a spectrum between those two cultures. There was little success in converting the native people to Catholicism in the mission, and the fort was falling apart. The character of Los Adaes was largely that of a Spanish post with little to offer.[2]

Since its founding in 1721, the interdependency of Los Adaes with French Natchitoches across the ill-defined border was one of its distinguishing characteristics. The common people conducted trade for their own personal survival.

Traders, merchants, and even Spanish governors engaged in trafficking and contraband trade on a scale well beyond personal needs. Despite the efforts of the priests, the illicit commerce included prostitution, alcohol, tobacco, and enslaved people and cut across all levels of the hierarchy.

Intermarriage across the border, particularly between Frenchmen with status and means and Spanish girls from Los Adaes, reinforced kinship ties that were intertwined with commercial and business relationships. As Francis X. Galan explains in his book *Los Adaes: The First Capital of Texas*, "French merchants used such marriages to strengthen commercial ties with *Adaeseños* who in turn took advantage of opportunities to relieve their own poverty by participation in markets beyond the control of the Spanish governor."[3] Given the methods used to recruit Spanish soldiers, Spanish mothers were wise to look elsewhere. The Marqués de Aguayo, who established Los Adaes, wanted men with families to follow him as soldiers to populate the presidios. Instead, his recruits were largely prisoners and other undesirables. Of 117 soldiers recruited from one location in Mexico, 107 were from the jail. The Adaeseños were also of diverse backgrounds and castes with forty-four *españoles*, thirty-one mulattoes, twenty-one *coyotes*, seventeen *mestizos*, two *castizos*, one *lobo*, one free *negro*, and one *indio* represented in the population.[4]

The people of Los Adaes had never known wealth. For all but a few, much of the trade they carried on with the French across the Red River at Natchitoches was for food and other basic needs, conducted largely to stay alive. If illicit goods came along in a trade all the better. The Spanish requirement that they obtain goods via Spain by way of Béxar was impractically onerous. Waiting for shipments of food and supplies from hundreds of miles away made no sense to them. Long supply missions from Mexico City delivered ruined flour and rancid grains. The edicts that prohibited trade with people less than twenty miles away were issued by a distant monarch with no understanding of the borderland realities. Trading for what they needed with the French did not require a second thought for those living on the edge of the province.

Life in the most distant settlement in Spanish Texas during the 1700s was tenuous at best. Though Los Adaes was the capital of the province of Texas, it was largely one in name only. Having a titled governor did not transform a sad village into a Spanish presence for securing an international border. Crumbling houses, rotting stockades, and a lack of firearms and ammunition made their military presence laughable.

Though the Adaeseños' very existence in the borderlands seemed constantly threatened, various efforts to end the Spanish presence at this distant post always seemed to wither. They did not worry much in 1743 when the governor,

Tomás Felipe Winthusyen, recommended that the mission and presidio at Los Adaes be closed.[5] When Governor Jacinto de Barrios y Jáuregui profited mightily from contraband trade during his tenure as governor from 1751–1759, they accepted his wealth because it lifted their own condition. When French Louisiana became Spanish Louisiana in 1762, little changed for them since their interaction and comingling with the French was already a common condition.

The years 1767 to 1770 must have increased their worries, however. The Marqués de Rubí's inspection in 1767 found conditions at the presidio to be deplorable. Scattered around the landscape nearby were families who lived in plank huts and raised only enough cattle and crops to survive. The presidio design was impressive, but its fortification was in shambles. The presidio was surrounded by a stockade made from 3,500 wooden pickets, but the condition of the badly built structure had deteriorated to the point of being useless for any defense. Within the walls there was a plaza, a well, seven barracks, the presidial church, and a guard room. Sixty soldiers had only two working muskets and seven swords—hardly the armaments of an empire.

In 1768, Father Gaspar José de Solís's visit to Los Adaes to inspect the fruits of the religious found no better. There were no Native American people in the mission, and even the church ornaments, normally carefully protected and looked after, were broken and worn. It is unclear if the Adaeseños knew that both Rubí and Solís would declare their settlement a failure and recommend the presidio and mission be closed, an act which would require the *extinción* of Los Adaes.[6]

It was not only military and religious shortcomings that led to those recommendations. There was also the official perception of contraband trade as an ever-present blight. Although some of the former governors personally benefitted from the illicit commerce, there were still distant officials who worked to eliminate it according to the king's command.

The presidio at Béxar and the accompanying villa of San Fernando were growing in status and importance far to the southwest. Concerns about French threats subsided somewhat with Spain's acquisition of French Louisiana. Rubí's recommendation to close the presidio seemed to be an idea whose time had come. The expense to the crown of maintaining distant posts was a constant concern. As one official wrote unsympathetically in summarizing events in the Texas province:

> If the clamors, the importunities, the representations, and the appeals which have been made without ceasing by the governors of the Provincias

> Internas, the captains of presidios, the reverend missionary fathers, and the citizens, had been listened to, each province would have an army and each commandant a mine of gold.[7]

Rubí's *Dictamen*, the *New Regulations for Presidios*, changed Spanish policy across the entirety of New Spain, from the Pacific to the Gulf of Mexico. Rubí believed there would be no downside to abandoning the "unpeopled territory" between Béxar and Los Adaes.[8] Rubí's rationale was hard to dispute. The presence of a governor was not needed at so distant a location. Having a large military presence seemed unnecessary as well. In peace, forty soldiers might be sufficient, but in war six hundred would not be enough because, the Spanish believed, the native people in the area would immediately ally with their French trading partners and overwhelm the Spanish. It was also pointed out that while Spain maintained a governor and a captain general in positions at Los Adaes, the highest-ranking French officer at Natchitoches was only a commandant. The French were not there to make war or take over territory. They were there for commerce.

The status of Los Adaes as a capital was officially ended in 1770. The governor had relocated to Béxar two years earlier, and all but ten of the soldiers were sent there as well. That was not enough for the Marqués de Rubí. He wanted an end to Los Adaes entirely.

The Orders to Abandon Los Adaes

Given all the signs of impending change, the Adaeseños had to have known their days were numbered. Perhaps they simply chose to believe they could be forgotten again and no longer receive the scrutiny of Spanish officials visiting from afar. Maybe they thought the end of Spanish support would allow them to be left alone to make their lives the way they always had, by being a part of a diverse community and economy involving their French and native neighbors and partners. It was not their lot in life to look at the broader forces at work. There was no reason for them to know or understand the policies of a distant Spanish ruler. The Adaeseños simply wanted to live their lives [9]

The day they learned they would be forced to leave their homes was chiseled in the hearts of those who heard the news firsthand. As early as February 1773, the viceroy in Mexico City told Governor Juan María, Baron de Ripperdá, that he was to carry out Rubí's *New Regulations for Presidios* and close the East Texas missions and presidios. By early April, Ripperdá began communicating that inevitability to Governor Unzaga of Spanish Louisiana and preparing contingencies to address any concerns by native people upset with the decision. When formal instructions from the viceroy were delivered to Ripperdá on April 15, the governor began the process of informing the presidios in Los Adaes and Orcoquisac on the lower Trinity River to begin preparing for closure.

This time the decision was final. The residents' homes, their place of birth, the place where they were married and raised children would soon have to be left behind. Even then their shock and disbelief led them to play it down to the point that Ripperdá had to send more detailed orders almost a month later. A May 10 letter told them they were to stop all planting and to roundup any cattle. They were to get their property in order and make plans to transport what they could to Béxar.[10]

Having spent time in Los Adaes during his service as governor, Ripperdá had the decency to make the difficult journey there to reinforce the decision. After a twelve-day trek across the province, Ripperdá arrived at the presidio on June 6, 1773. Upon arrival he gathered the *vecinos* to hear about their fate. No record of his words remains, but one can imagine the emotions that coursed among the residents. They learned their worst fears were indeed true. They were being forced to leave their homes and travel to a distant, strange, and unwelcoming villa at Béxar. Though there were promises of land, it was not <u>their</u> land. Many of them had never been to Béxar, but the ones who had described a landscape far different than the forested environs where they lived. Stories about the constant threats of Native American deception, thievery, and attacks led them to fear for their safety in advance of the move.

Once the realities of the decision sank in so did the practicalities. Ripperdá gave the Adaeseños only five days to prepare their departure. That was an impossible request, so he extended the deadline to June 25. When the governor left Los Adaes on June 14 after a week with the Adaeseños, he must have felt the personal weight of the decision and the impact on the poor villagers. He had been among them while the news sunk in. He had been among them long enough to know their anguish.

The Exit Begins, June 1773

Four hundred people lived in and around Los Adaes, strewn across the landscape; they were people of diverse origins, including Spanish, French, Native Americans, Blacks both free and enslaved, and all the various racial blending that came with intermarriage in the borderlands. The sheer volume of people, property, and supplies created a scene of chaos and disbelief.

Anger and resentment surely simmered just beneath the sadness and sense of loss. Although most complied with the order, some simply would not. Around thirty-five Adaeseños refused the eviction and fled into the forest. Others simply relocated to Natchitoches and tucked themselves away until the exodus was over. Ripperdá asked the Spanish governor of Natchitoches to watch for those stowaways and made clear that they were disobeying an order to be resettled in Béxar. It mattered little. Among the group remaining at Los Adaes were three Frenchmen who had Spanish wives.[11] Further evidence of their refusal to leave came years later during a border dispute with the United States. Spanish officials said there were ranches "belonging to these same citizens of Los Adaes; they owned them when the place was inhabited and, at the time of the removal [in 1773] to Béxar, they remained on them." In other words, they never left.[12]

The Trek to San Antonio

On June 25, 1773, the day of the Adaeseños' departure from Los Adaes, there were still attempts to hold out against the order. Ripperdá had left Lt. José Gonzalez, a soldier of the presidio for almost forty years, in charge of ensuring compliance with the governor's orders. Gonzalez took these orders seriously. He drew complaints for his aggressiveness in mounting a horse and going from house to house forcing people outside. The scene is almost unimaginable. Possessions had to be left behind due to the scarcity of transportation. Many were on foot due to the shortage of horses and mules. Women and children, some only infants, huddled together with their families so no one would be lost in the confusion. Slowly, tearfully, as they looked back on their former homes, all that remained were questions about what was to come.

Antonio Gil Ibarvo

Antonio Gil Ibarvo [Y'barbo] was a native of Los Adaes and a true offspring of the culture of the borderlands. His father, Mateo Ibarvo, and his mother, Juana Lugard Hernández, emigrated from Spain to Mexico. His father came to East Texas in 1721 with the Aguayo expedition when the presidio at Los Adaes was established. Mateo Ibarvo was one of 219 soldiers Aguayo quartered at the presidios established across Texas, one hundred of those at Los Adaes. Ten years later, that number was down to fifty-nine.

Antonio was born in Los Adaes in 1729 but lived briefly in Béxar when his father was posted there. Before his father died in 1744, the family had moved back to Los Adaes when Antonio was about fifteen years old.[13] There are few details of Antonio Gil Ibarvo's life before his relocation to the interior of the

Texas province. His trading skills allowed him to acquire a large ranch just to the west of the Sabine River. His ranch, El Lobanillo, was home base for his trade to the east in Natchitoches and New Orleans. During that period of Ibarvo's adulthood, the governor ad interim, Hugo Oconór, jailed Ibarvo in New Orleans for seven months for smuggling. Oconór had a lifelong antipathy toward Ibarvo. Oconór's replacement, Governor Ripperdá, secured Ibarvo's release and developed a trust in Ibarvo. Ripperdá appointed Ibarvo to manage the presidial funds and the purchase of supplies for the presidio in Los Adaes. In both of those roles, Ibarvo served in positions where trade and monies were a daily focus.

Though Ibarvo came to be recognized as a leader of the Adaeseños, he was not the one initially charged with leading the people out of Los Adaes. That assignment went to Lieutenant Gonzalez. Given that Ibarvo was a trusted aide to the governor, this omission leads one to wonder what the expectations were for Ibarvo. During the difficult journey, Ibarvo's leadership and resources became critical. His willingness to provide for the needs of the Adaeseños was most appreciated during the time the group rested and regrouped at El Lobanillo. As time went on, Antonio Gil Ibarvo would become their protector and the foundation of their hopes.

A Stop at El Lobanillo

The *rancho* of Antonio Gil Ibarvo, El Lobanillo, was approximately forty-five miles west along the *camino real* from Los Adaes, about halfway between the Sabine River and Mission Dolores. On the Adaeseños' sad journey to the west, Ibarvo's ranch was the first opportunity for them to stop and rest. El Lobanillo is marked on a crude map done in 1763 by a French soldier who deserted and joined Spanish forces. In his meanderings across Texas, he noted the location of the "*casas de Y'Barbo*" along his route. When Aguayo passed by El Lobanillo in 1767, he thought it was a ranch operated by the missionaries at Mission Dolores.[14]

Ibarvo's mother, a sister, and a sister-in-law had never left El Lobanillo—it was their home. His mother had been an invalid for ten years and was bedridden. Chronic ulcers covered a sister's body for nine months, so she was unable to leave as well. His brother's wife was also in poor health due to complications from an abortion. One of Ibarvo's sons and a few others remained behind at Lobanillo and did not join the forced eviction to Béxar. Altogether, there were twenty-four people who stayed behind at Lobanillo.[15]

Ibarvo later defended himself against questions from Cmdr. General Hugo Oconór about the decision to leave his family in place by telling Oconór that

Governor Ripperdá gave permission for them to remain. Ibarvo's behavior seemed to indicate his confidence he could simply return to his ranch at El Lobanillo after accompanying the Adaeseños to Béxar.[16] Even if Ripperdá gave permission for most of Ibarvo's family and others to stay behind, they most assuredly were not given permission to continue illicit trade in Natchitoches. Before the other Adaeseños even arrived in Béxar, the commander in Natchitoches reported that "many fugitives who escaped from the convoy going from Los Adaes have taken refuge at Lobanillo," and they were coming to Natchitoches to trade for liquor to sell to the Indians. Despite the edicts, East Texas was never fully abandoned.[17]

Arrival at the Nacogdoches Mission

Under typical conditions, it took about three weeks to travel from Los Adaes to Béxar, but conditions were rarely ideal. Fifty years earlier, the Marqués de Aguayo took two months, from November 1721 to January 1722, to return to Béxar from Los Adaes after founding the earliest missions in eastern Texas. Delays by rivers heavy with winter rainfall were just one of the logistical challenges that would hamper timely travel.[18]

For the unhappy exodus of the Adaeseños, it took an entire month just to reach Nacogdoches, forty-seven leagues (120 miles) from Los Adaes. It is likely the entire group lingered at Ibarvo's *rancheria* for quite some time as part of their three-month-long trek to Béxar. Lieutenant González, the aged Spanish military lifer charged with the leadership of the group, succumbed to an illness and died in Nacogdoches on July 30, as did two women who had become sick along the way. In their sourcing of primary documents, both Bolton and Castañeda indicate that with González's passing, it was a lesser-ranked sergeant with the remaining military contingent who took charge of the group.[19] Given his status, Ibarvo was a visible leader and decision maker rather than simply another person in the caravan.

To Béxar

The ensuing trek from Nacogdoches brought even more misery for the poor Adaeseños. The drought they encountered in the first month of the journey was followed by heavy floods the rest of the way. More sickness, hunger, and hopelessness rose among them. Few of their animals survived. Native people they encountered along the way provided food in exchange for rosaries and articles of clothing.

A contingent of Spanish soldiers sent by Ripperdá met the Adaeseños at the Brazos River and helped ease their hunger and weariness with food and horses but could do nothing to replenish their spirits. One hundred sixty-seven families made it that far, but some would no longer continue and simply stayed at the crossing of the Brazos.[20] Even more dropped out of the caravan when they reached Cibolo Creek near present New Braunfels. At every juncture, Adaeseños simply abandoned the journey and went back in the direction of their homes. Hope could not overcome uncertainty for them, and their loyalty to the crown diminished with every step they took farther from their homes.

The three-month-long journey from Los Adaes to Béxar did not lead to an arrival filled with optimism. When the depleted group arrived in Béxar on September 28, 1773, they were met with looks of suspicion and defensiveness. There was no welcome committee or receiving line. There were no offers of compensation for their forced relocation. All that accompanied their arrival was a temporary end to the suffering the Adaeseños endured along the way and the substitution of a different version of the dread they already knew too well. What awaited them was simply another command. Governor Ripperdá ordered them to begin immediately the difficult work of making something from nothing at the villa of San Fernando.

The proud Adaeseños were forced to beg for food, and some resorted to stealing from others. The already limited resources in Béxar meant there was little to share. Promises of land for a house and a garden out on the fringes of the villa—where they would not subject to assaults or thievery—were not fulfilled. Within only two days, a group of indigenous recognized their vulnerability and stole what few horses, mules, and cattle had survived the trip.[21]

Their numbers had dwindled not only with groups of people abandoning the caravan along the way, but due to the sadness of human loss. Ten children and two adults died from hunger, illness, or accident during the trip. Any journey where loved ones must be buried along the way is a sad one. The pain of losing a child only magnified the devastation caused by being uprooted from their homes. As one priest passionately explained years later, the Adaeseños were forced to give up their homes, their ranches, and their comforts in exchange for "inexpressible miseries." On their forced expulsion, the holy father lamented, the tears of wives and children had sprinkled the road to Béxar.[22]

An Appeal to Mexico City

When confronted with the kind of personal loss and despair faced by the Adaeseños, there are two typical human responses—give in or resist. The resilient Adaeseños decided to resist. On October 4, 1773, only eight days after their arrival in Béxar, they presented a written petition to the governor to allow them to return to East Texas. It is likely that the plan had been in their minds during their three-month journey.

A representative from each of the 127 families who had come to Béxar signed the petition.[23] The formal petition was written with the appropriate royal deference and was both well-crafted and emotional. They reminded the governor that upon their arrival in Béxar on September 26, they read the official decree from the viceroy in Mexico City which required their expulsion from Los Adaes. They reported "having examined well and generally the clauses and articles" in the act. What they read was that the Adaeseños were instructed to find "lands that may appear most profitable to us for our establishment, harvests, rearing of cattle, and the rest that may be profitable to our well-being." The act also required the Adaeseños to accept that offer in a way that would not damage or inconvenience the current residents of their new presidio and town.[24] They believed they had come up with the perfect way to do just that. The petition was their request to move back to the old mission site of Nuestra Señora de los Dolores de los Ais.

Although they had no money to build anew in Béxar, they offered to make the journey back toward their homes and ranches at their own expense. The only support they asked was that the viceroy provide them with a priest at no cost for ten years, something that would typically happen for any new settlement. Even though it was clear they would not be permitted to return to Los Adaes, moving to the old site of Mission Dolores would put them about fourteen miles west of El Lobanillo and about forty-five miles from their former homes in Los Adaes. At the old mission they would be nearer to their "abandoned dwelling-houses, [where] we hope to gain the restoration of all the goods that it is certain we left in them, scattered through the small opportunity that was given us for gathering them up."[25]

They reminded Ripperdá of their "blind obedience of all of us in whatever you have commanded." They also appealed to his sympathies by calling attention to their "lamentable miseries with which we traveled so long a road, experiencing on it thirst, very dry, lack of beasts of burden, death of some children and parents." They made sure the governor understood their pain. Despite all their misery, the wandering Adaeseños explained they were not resentful—at least not officially and in writing. Ripperdá's permission would be enough for them to end any questions about compensation for the damages, loss, and injury they endured.

Governor Ripperdá, who had ridden to Los Adaes to personally deliver the order to abandon their homes, understood their situation but was unable to act on their request on his own. He knew an appeal to sympathy alone would not suffice in Mexico City, particularly not with Hugo Oconór. In his own letter to the viceroy, Ripperdá bolstered their argument with the advantages to the government of returning the Adaeseños to eastern Texas. Ripperdá also covered his own political bases by directing them to continue looking for suitable homes and land near Béxar and Cibolo Creek, which was nearby and southeast of the main settlements. Ripperdá wrote to Viceroy Bucareli y Ursua to ask his indulgence "particularly for Don Antonio Gil Ibarvo, who, with a Ranch that already was a Village [pueblo] has lost more than all, remaining ruined."[26]

Second-guessing over the decision that Los Adaes was not needed as a bulwark against others moving into Spanish East Texas began shortly after the Adaeseños arrival in Béxar. Pulling back all the way into Béxar left too much open ground where things could go wrong. When the chief of a tribe friendly to the Spanish expressed his concern about the evacuation of eastern Texas, two families that included nine people agreed to stay behind in Nacogdoches "in order not to displease the principal Captain of the Texas [Indians], who wished . . . to ask that the Spaniards return."[27] No one wanted the Caddo, Bidai, or other tribes friendly to the Spanish to believe that the Spaniards had abandoned them to the more aggressive Comanche.

On December 10, 1773, two months after their petition, the group selected Ibarvo and Gil Flores to travel to Mexico City to represent them before the viceroy and the ruling council. By that time, thirty more Adaeseños had died due to illness or simply succumbed to their despair.[28]

A Difficult Journey

The current journey from Béxar to Mexico City by highway is 869 miles and a fifteen-hour drive. To compare that distance to something perhaps more familiar to Texans, at least visually, it is almost the same distance as the route from Orange on the Sabine River to El Paso. At twenty miles per day on horseback, the trek to Mexico City could have taken forty-four days with no time for rest.

Following the physical demands of a journey of hundreds of miles to Mexico City, Ibarvo and Flores found themselves in an unfamiliar city and culture. A Spanish priest later remarked that Ibarvo, like others making a plea to the crown, went to Mexico City "at the cost of the embarrassments, the deprivations, the slights, and the submission which the humble must undergo in the courts in order to present a brief and to gain admission to a higher tribunal."[29]

Ibarvo, Flores, and a Caddo chief, perhaps the medal chief, Bigotes, left

Béxar for Mexico City in late December 1773 or early January 1774. Bigotes wanted to make his own plea on behalf of the tribes that the petition be granted. By January 8, Ibarvo and Flores were in Santa Rosa María below the Rio Grande. Their petition was presented to the *junta de Guerra y hacienda* on February 28, 1774. In addition to their petition, they carried two letters from Governor Ripperdá—one for the viceroy and one for Hugo Oconór. The letter to Oconór had a different tone since Ripperdá knew all too well the strength of his opposition to a resettlement of eastern Texas. Ripperdá made clear in both letters that he did not understand the decision to evacuate the settlements and laid out his political and tactical arguments in full detail for reversing the decision.

The governor acknowledged there was still concern about illicit trade with the French who remained in Spanish Natchitoches, but vacating the region only meant that trade would continue between the French and the Native Americans, or with the more troubling English, to the detriment of Spain. Ripperdá made his case in support of the Adaeseños petition to return to Mission Dolores, but there was also a separate private appeal on Ibarvo's behalf. Ripperdá told Oconór that if the petition for the resettlement of the entire group was not allowed, "ultimately his [Ibarvo's] ranch, El Lobanillo, might come to form a pueblo of more than sixty persons," recommending support for a backup option for Ibarvo because he had suffered the greatest financial loss.

Not a No, Not a Yes

Following a series of political maneuverings, the viceroy's council of advisers granted the Adaeseño's petition over the known objections of an absent Hugo Oconór. Oconór was not only a literalist in interpreting the order to vacate eastern Texas, but he also despised and mistrusted Ibarvo. Oconór wrote to the viceroy with a powerful objection to any resettlement in eastern Texas, demanding that the governor bring to Béxar all the ammunition and people left behind at the abandoned presidios and missions. Oconór wanted everyone and everything out of eastern Texas as ordered. In his own exaggerated state of caution, Oconór even objected to Bigote's visit with Ibarvo and Flores to Mexico City. In Oconór's mind, the northern tribes would now know the route to the capital and see firsthand its defenses—an overly cautious perspective by an obsessive militarist.

Out of respect to Oconór, the viceroy asked that the matter be reconsidered based on Oconór's objections. After waiting two months for the distant Oconór to comment again, he had still not responded. Nevertheless, on

Francisco Antonio Vallejo portrait of Antonio Maria De Bucareli y Ursua, 1772. Courtesy Wikipedia Commons.

May 5, 1774, the viceregal advisers threw up their hands and decided to give Oconór the sole power to make the decision.[30] He had made his position very clear already. Fearing Oconór's reply, on May 10 Ibarvo presented an alternate request—his plan B. He asked for an exemption from the order to remain in Béxar and that he instead be allowed to return to El Lobanillo and to move temporarily to Natchitoches so he could recover his property. The viceroy saw through that scheme, immediately rejected it, and sent Ripperdá a letter making certain the governor would refuse it as well.

At this point in the process, it is unclear exactly how events proceeded. The outcome is all we have to judge what may have taken place. Whether Oconór ever received the communication asking for his final decision or not is uncertain, but he failed to act on that authority. As Ibarvo and Flores prepared to return to Béxar, Viceroy Bucareli y Ursua provided them with 202 pesos to be divided proportionally among the Adaeseños. This was in addition to the thirty-five pesos and four reales paid to Ibarvo and Flores for their expenses while in Mexico City.[31] Bucareli y Ursua sent a letter to Ripperdá instructing the governor to "assist and protect them [the Adaeseños] in everything that you feel they deserve [for the betterment] of their establishment." That letter was not delivered to Ripperdá until after Ibarvo's return to Béxar in late August of 1774.[32]

A combination of vague communications, the political cunning of Ibarvo and Ripperdá, and delays in communication with Oconór allowed the resettlement of the people of Los Adaes back into eastern Texas. Ibarvo may have simply told Ripperdá that the viceroy verbally said they could return to eastern Texas, if they would stay one hundred leagues distant from their former home in Los Adaes. Even if that was true, that was not the outcome.

When Ripperdá acknowledged receipt of the viceroy's letter on September 1, 1774, it was with a fully detailed description of how a key crossing on the Trinity River would be the new home of the Adaeseños. A decision like that was not made on the spur of the moment. Ibarvo and the Adaeseños had probably used that crossing on the Trinity River on their way to Béxar and had identified it as a desirable alternative.

Ripperdá reported to Bucareli y Ursua that the next Spanish settlement in eastern Texas would be at Paso Tomás on the Trinity River and would be named in his honor. The new home for the Adaeseños would be called Nuestra Señora del Pilár de Bucareli.

7

From Béxar to Bucareli

> [They had chosen] the place, which better than any other, enables them to engage in illicit trade and to encourage the northern Indians in stealing droves of horses.
>
> —HUGO OCONÓR[1]

The wandering Adaeseños left Béxar in the late summer of 1774, headed back to East Texas along an all-too-familiar route. Between fifty and seventy men, along with their wives and children, formed the first wave of those making the journey back along the road they had trod and suffered on not so long before, past the gravesites of those who died on their earlier trek. Some of the Adaeseños stayed behind in Béxar, unable to travel due to the lack of horses to make the trip. Others decided to remain behind and make their lives in Béxar. The Adaeseños were familiar with difficult journeys, but this time they had hopes of securing a more permanent home that was at least in the direction of their former one at Los Adaes.

Whether their relocation was taken with the full blessing of all the officials with jurisdiction over their fate seems uncertain. The viceroy and the governor required they settle at least one hundred leagues from Natchitoches, and the location they selected for the settlement on the Trinity River was only about seventy-five leagues distant from that French trading center. Nevertheless, given the dynamics and tensions of the decision to return to East Texas, this was as far east as Ripperdá and Ibarvo dared to push. The banks of the Trinity River between the Bidai and Caddo nations would be their new home. Paso Tomás, the historic confluence of roads and waters at the mouth of Bedias Creek, is where Antonio Gil Ibarvo, Gil Flores, and the Adaeseños who trusted them with their lives made their new home.[2]

On the Prairies of the Trinity

Governor Ripperdá assigned a military escort to accompany the group to the Trinity River. Lt. Simón Arocha and four of his soldiers were to provide armed protection for the caravan and serve as a set of eyes for the governor, observing the transition. To formalize and sanction the settlement, the governor appointed the group's natural leader, Antonio Gil Ibarvo, as captain and *justicia mayor* of Bucareli. Gil Flores, who had accompanied Ibarvo to Mexico City to deliver their petition, was named lieutenant, and Juan de la Mora named as *alférez*, or second lieutenant. As Blake explained,

> Gil Ibarvo found himself rather an autocratic ruler of a territory extending from [the] Colorado River on the west to [the] Red River on the east, from the Gulf of Mexico on the south to [the] Red River on the north . . . inhabited by twenty-one Indian Nations, with no soldiers or military equipment at his command, nor a single peso from the Spanish government for salary or governmental expenses.[3]

The Location

In some indigenous cultures of that period, the responsibility of searching for village sites when the tribe was ready to move went to a high-ranking member known as the *okonitsa* (one who locates). When the tribe moved, he would pay attention to all the details, including the placement and arrangement of living spaces and common structures.[4] Fertile arable lands with nearby springs, nearby hunting grounds with buffalo and deer, accessible fords, and river crossings were important. There was no *okonitsa* for the Adaeseños, but consideration was still given for the location's advantages.

The placement of the new settlement near Paso Tomás was to be on the west side of the Trinity River, the right bank nearest to Béxar. The land on both sides of the river shared similarities, but a slight advantage in elevation on the right side led to a location near but not on the river. Looking east there was almost five miles of low-lying prairie with little opportunity for a secure settlement. Despite the nature of the flood-prone plains, there was diversity in the landscape along a twenty-mile stretch above Bedias Creek and ten miles below.[5]

We can imagine the environs around Bucareli using reports from earlier Spanish expeditions, accounts contemporary to the period of resettlement, and firsthand observations from travelers and surveyors years later. The vulnerability of temporary structures, years of flooding, cultivation in prairies all along the river, and ultimately the inundation of the reservoir at Lake Livingston have reduced the likelihood of any definitive evidence of the actual location for Bucareli. The precise location remains uncertain, but research sheds light on the surroundings of the settlement.

After Bucareli was established, Spanish officials in Mexico City seemed to wonder how resettlement at that location came to be. The consensus was expressed by Commandant Gen. Teodoro de Croix some years after the beginning of the settlement. He believed that it was Ibarvo's decision. He wrote that "the new settlement of Nuestra Senora del Pilar de Bucareli [was] established, at the insistence of Don Antonio Gil Ybarbo [Ibarvo] at the site named El Paso de Tomás."[6]

Governor Domingo Cabello, the successor for Ripperdá, had the benefit of hindsight when identifying the location to others who were questioning its presence.[7] "When my predecessor Colonel Baron de Ripperdá proceeded . . . to mark-out the ground on which said Pueblo [Bucareli] was to be situated and founded, [Ripperdá] did so by declaring to his Commissioner, Don Simon de Arocha, that [the site] should be in the before-mentioned place of El Paso de Tomás, on the Trinity River." Even Cabello conceded that "even though [Bucareli] was not situated in the [most] advantageous spot in which it could have been located for its most permanent existence, [the location] was nevertheless useful and valuable by virtue of being contiguous with regions inhabited by Indians of the friendly Nations . . . also [from there, Captain Ybarbo [Ibarvo] was able to observe the conduct of their traders, which is a matter of considerable importance."[8] A letter Governor Ripperdá wrote to the viceroy explained that the location was "on this side [the Béxar side] of the Trinity River on the road that leads to the said Los Adaes and Orcoquisac."

This key crossing was not only at a point where the roads from La Bahía and Béxar merged into a single road crossing the Trinity River heading east, it was also along a road that ran north-south connecting the Caddo villages at San Pedro Creek and the mouth of the Trinity River.[9] Paso Tomás was also "three regular day's journey from the coast."[10] The distance from Paso Tomás to Orcoquisac is about 110 miles following the route Ibarvo would likely use on the high ground along the Trinity River.

A Distant Settlement

To visualize how distant Bucareli was from any other settlement, draw a line from Santa Fe, New Mexico, through San Antonio to Goliad. At the time that Bucareli was founded, there was no Spanish settlement anywhere to the north and east of that line, a vast amount of territory. The presidio at Orcoquisac

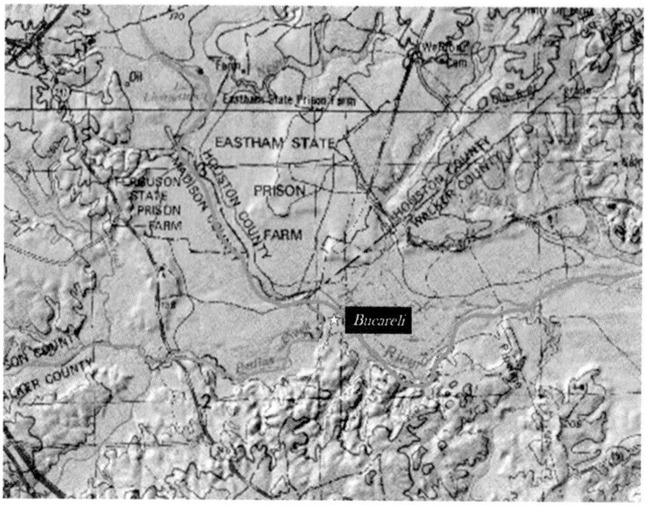

Former location of Bucareli on a modern map. Image by author.

on the southern end of the Trinity River had been closed, and the missions at Nacogdoches and Ais were shut down at the same time Los Adaes was forcibly abandoned. As the "Father President" of the missions, an elected ecclesiastical post, Pedro Ramírez de Arellano, pointed out, Bucareli was "one hundred and forty uninhabited leagues [distant from Béxar], and for the greater part surrounded with dangers."[11] Bucareli was the lone manifestation of Spanish presence in East Texas in 1774.

NEARNESS OF THE BIDAI VILLAGE

During a 1755 reconnaissance to investigate accounts of French traders along the Trinity, Spanish soldiers encountered the chief of a Bidai tribe. His villages were near the crossing of the Trinity used by the soldiers. The Spanish interpretation of the chief's name was Tomás, and the crossing there took on his name. The governor was so ingratiated to Chief Tomás that he was given a "red coat trimmed with gold braid, a red cap with tassels, shirts, powder, balls, vermilion, and other gifts."[12] His village was two leagues (five miles) south of the crossing at the mouth of Bedias Creek. The Bidai tucked their homes along a creek on the west side of the Trinity, the same side as Bucareli. Their village was described as "on the bend of the river, which opens to a wide prairie bottom to the southwest and a thick bottom of timber in the rear."[13]

The proximity of Bucareli to a Bidai village meant there were potential partners who might help the Adaeseños with defense, trade, and food during their early, difficult years of settlement. The nearness of the Bidai village and the key roads crossing nearby also called into question the settlement's allegiance to edicts prohibiting contraband. The Bidai were known to be involved in exchange with French traders, as well as with the Lipan Apache, and the placement of Bucareli nearby meant the Spanish could easily become part of that contraband trade network.

Upon their arrival at the Trinity, Ibarvo and Lieutenant Arocha were instructed to visit the friendly tribes in the area to let them know that Spanish subjects were returning to their lands with peaceful intentions. There were several tribes known to be in the region including "the Bidais, Tejas (Caddo), Quitseys (Kichai), Iscanis, Tawakonis, Xaranames (Aramanas), Taovayas, and Wichitas."[14] A Kichai rancheria was found eighteen leagues (forty-seven miles) north of Bucareli near a saline. Fifteen leagues (thirty-nine miles) to the west there was a Tonkawa village near a hill known as La Tortuga.[15] The grand plan to tour the tribal homes of their neighbors was abandoned due to "the scarcity and poor condition of the horses."[16] Both people and livestock were worn down past the point of reason. Neighborliness gave way to utter exhaustion.

THE SEMBLANCE OF A MILITIA

The designation of a group of men as a militia was in name only. There were few guns and little ammunition found among the entire group. Any concern the Indians may have had with so many Spanish subjects returning to their region would dissolve if they learned how ill-equipped the arrivals were for any armed conflict. Governor Ripperdá asked the viceroy in Mexico City for up to eighty guns with powder and shot, but those were never provided. Ripperdá was only able to supply them with one *arroba* of gunpowder, about twenty-five pounds, and two *arrobas* of balls.

Not long after their arrival at the Trinity, Ibarvo returned to Los Adaes to gather building materials and personal property, as well as arms and ammunition they had hidden at the time of their eviction. He also recovered six cracked cannons, four brass and two iron, from the poorly armed presidio. They were useless for defense but could perhaps be salvaged at some point. Bucareli later benefited from two cannons that had been at Orcoquisac before a presidio there was abandoned in 1771, and another two that were left in the possession of Taovaya Indians as far back as 1759.[17]

POLITICAL INFLUENCES

Bucareli's proximity to roads in all directions and the river was the primary advantage of its location. Most of the other advantages repeatedly named in the official correspondence among leaders were political in nature and not about the benefit to the people who would live there. The location for Bucareli was a compromise between literal orders and the extent to which they could be ignored to engage in the continuation of contraband trade across the Sabine. The location of the new settlement was claimed to be "at the insistence of Don Antonio Gil Ybarbo [Ibarvo]," but was approved by Governor Ripperdá. The governor did not want it any closer to Natchitoches, so he would not have to endure any further hostility from Hugo Oconór than he was already experiencing.[18] To Hugo Oconór the location was a blatant disregard of an order by the king.

A PLACE ON THE PRAIRIE

Bucareli's location on a large prairie, a flood plain with fertile soil, made ideal terrain for raising and keeping hundreds of horses and cattle. The later growth of rancherias would commercialize the movement of Spanish cattle into Louisiana in exchange for goods that were unavailable or too distant from the Spanish port in Vera Cruz. Even Oconór, a literalist in his interpretation of past edicts of the crown who had worked aggressively to eradicate any trade across the Sabine, recognized the reasons for the choice of the settlement. They had chosen:

> the place, which better than any other, enables them to engage in illicit trade and to encourage the northern Indians in stealing droves of horses from the Presidios of San Antonio de Bejar [Béxar], La Bahía del Espíritu Santo, and even as far as Laredo, as lately has been done . . . Hence it is concluded that the citizens established on the Trinity have better facilities than formerly [at Los Adaes] for their contraband trade.[19]

From the time that Bucareli was founded, the prairies around it became a staging area for horses, mules, and cattle that moved as contraband between Texas and Louisiana. One traveler noted:

> Arriving at the road we behold the prairies covered with cattle, mules and horses, the property of the inhabitants settled here. A few Spaniards and Americans are settled here, and it is the crossing place of all the *cavallados* [horse herds] that are driven to the United States of the north, they are frequently kept here to recruit on these prairie bottoms.[20]

OPPORTUNITIES FOR FARMING

Lt. Simón Arocha was also given an assignment to investigate the feasibility of digging ditches for irrigation to support crops for the Adaeseños. Bringing water to the crops from the Trinity River was believed to be necessary based on the experiences of farmers at Béxar. However, the banks of Trinity were too high for such methods. Irrigation was something more suited to Béxar than to the soils of East Texas.

Arocha's report to the governor when he returned to Béxar in November 1774 was not a positive one. Though the land in the river bottom was certainly fertile, the sandy soils and the elevation of the riverbanks made gravity-fed irrigation like that in Béxar impossible to duplicate. Farming was likely to take place on the east side of the Trinity, opposite the settlement, where there were some small lakes that might be used for water. The site for Bucareli was not ideal as a place for a growing settlement, and this seemed to be known and accepted by everyone involved well before it was begun.

By August 1774, the viceroy had been officially notified that the governor "had given the new pueblo the name of Nuestra Senora del Pilar de Bucareli, and that with its residents he had formed a company of fifty men for its defense, naming Don Antonio Gil y Barvo [Ibarvo] as captain and chief justice."[21]

Building Begins, August 1774

To understand the difficulty of establishing a settlement from nothing in a wilderness distant from any supplies, it is important to consider both the tasks at hand upon their arrival at the Trinity and the emotions that must have been present among the group. It is difficult for us, 250 years later, to ponder the obstacles of cross-country travel by horse or on foot, carrying everything that could be managed only to live in a place where nothing has existed before. The Adaeseños made the three-month-long trip to Béxar. They'd been met with supplies at the Brazos, and they had the expectation of the support of a populated settlement when they arrived. But there was nothing and no one waiting. They could count only on their tenacity, their will, and the kindness of their Bidai and Caddo neighbors.

One condition to which we can relate is the timing of when they undertook their relocation. August, the peak of summer in East Texas, is a brutal month. In August the heat and humidity drain the body of energy, while mosquitoes, flies, and ticks drain it of blood. The Adaeseños were indeed desperate to get away from Béxar.

The Need for Shelter

Making a home in the wilderness along a major river at a place where nothing exists is a daunting task. Wedge type tents, which had an upside-down V-shape, were in common use during this period when the American Revolution was percolating far to the east. One Adeseño was said to be living in a goatskin tent during his time in Béxar. Cowhides may have also been used to provide a more waterproof covering over an arbor of trees and limbs. It is likely that temporary shelters made from trees and grasses were their only recourse for a time.

For hundreds of years, the answer to short-term shelter in almost any frontier settlement in the Southwest came in the form of *jacales*, crude structures with a common means of construction using whatever materials are available. This type of construction was used at Los Adaes and familiar to the Adaeseños. Jacales were easily built from almost any material, they went up quickly, and with minimal maintenance could hold up long enough to be improved after a storm exposed any weak spots or leaks. The architecture of Spanish settlements, including Mission Dolores, San Saba, and many others, had long used this type of shelter. Jacales would continue to appear in Nacogdoches well into the nineteenth century.[22] A group of indigenous people were using this construction method in 1768 when a Spanish priest noted that their homes were of "good material" and "well-constructed."[23] These temporary homes could be improved upon over time with walls of mud and daub, white-washed, and made more lasting, but at their heart they were still jacales. When William Fairfax Gray visited Nacogdoches in 1835, the dwellings described earlier as "well-constructed" were just "miserable, shabby, old Mexican jacales."[24]

Pierre Marie François de Pagès—a Frenchman who visited the presidio and mission at Los Adaes in 1768, not long before the Adaeseños were forced out—found the presidio circled by "around forty miserable houses, constructed with stakes driven into the ground." When the French guest spent the night in one of the jacales, he said:

> I went to sleep in the corner of his house, which by the by, scarcely deserved that name, for the roof was only supported by a sort of piling, the greatest part of which had fallen to the ground from negligence and length of time.[25]

A jacale was a square or rectangular one-room structure with sides typically around ten to fifteen feet in length. Often, the only opening was a single door. A dirt floor, tamped down and leveled, would have been the only surface. Corner poles (*horcones*) were made of tree limbs or trunks about six inches in diameter. Three to four poles were lashed together and buried deeply. The space in the outside walls between the corners were filled with wooden poles about four inches in diameter, set a foot or so apart, upright and buried in a trench or hole. Along the Trinity, they may have found small pine trees, blackjack oaks, or even cedar limbs for this step in the construction. This use of vertical wooden supports—different from the later and more familiar cabins built with logs laid horizontally—was called the *palisado*, or palisade form of construction.

Whatever was expedient to get themselves out of the weather quickly would be a priority. A friend and colleague, Jeffrey Williams, formerly with Stephen F. Austin State University, said one thing we know for sure about the weather in East Texas in August is that it would be "bone dry until it wasn't." The mud walls and a roof made of prairie grasses or animal skins could have been blown away by the remains of a tropical storm making its way north from the coast.

Ibarvo later arranged for the construction of a guardhouse, a chapel, and even stocks should they be needed to hold a prisoner. The local sandstone, the foundation for the shoals across the Trinity, was minimally accessible, so any additional buildings were of wood with mud and grass filling the chinks, making it the only pueblo in eastern Texas with homes and buildings constructed completely of wood.[26] Within a year there were twenty wooden jacales at the site, and by the summer of 1777 there were fifty. *The Laws of the Indies*, a complex Spanish guide for laying out villages, dictated that the chapel and the guardhouse face each other on opposite sides of a plaza. If Ibarvo used that as a guide, the facing buildings would represent the options for citizens to choose either heaven or hell.[27]

After the Adaeseños arrived at the Trinity and secured some immediate shelter, Ibarvo and others returned to Los Adaes and El Lobanillo to bring back what they could salvage to use in constructing their new homes and defending themselves from any potential attack. Nails and iron from the houses and gun carriages would be prized in Bucareli.[28] Though he returned to Bucareli with three cartloads of gun carriages, iron, and nails, he also left eight carts full of iron and some cannon balls at El Lobanillo. The historian Carolos Castañeda gave Ibarvo the benefit of the doubt in saying it was for later transportation, but it is uncertain if all of it ever made it to Bucareli.[29]

Planting and Commerce

Planting corn and other crops was one of the first tasks of any new settlement, and the Adaeseños wasted no time. Their fields were on the east (left) side of the Trinity, opposite the settlement in the fertile flood plains, so crossing the river regularly would have been necessary. Flooding during their first year ruined the planting effort and left them dependent on others for their basic food needs. Their Bidai neighbors must have pitied their effort and showed the Spanish a location for planting on the right side of the river near a spring with less flooding risk.[30]

As the settlement became more stable, Ibarvo tried to secure more skilled tradesmen. When Governor Ripperdá learned of their need for wool, a weaver was sent to Bucareli within a year. The man they sent to Bucareli from Béxar was described as a "miserable mulatto negro, maker of blankets, that by his bad conduct was not producing anything useful." Ibarvo required him to teach others how to make woolen blankets to avoid dependence on his demeanor. The highly disregarded weaver found favor when he brought wool with him as well as "ewes for its continuation, and cotton seed for gathering that necessary to said making."[31] The Adaeseños at Bucareli were learning to make do with what they had. They had no other choice.

No Priest for Bucareli, February 1775

All they wanted was a priest for Bucareli.

By February 1775, the Adaeseños asked that a priest be assigned to Bucareli and for his support to be provided by the crown for ten years, the normal period for a new settlement. The two most formidable administrative hierarchies of the time, perhaps for all time—the Spanish royal government and the Catholic church—involved over a dozen people across hundreds of miles in an ongoing discussion of how to pay a holy father to save souls on the banks of the Trinity River. It took two years for their request to be heard.

Assigning a priest to Bucareli required the input and involvement of the viceroy of New Spain, the governor of the Province of Texas, the *fiscal* in Mexico City, the *commandante inspector* (Hugo Oconór, who was opposed to the whole settlement), the father president of the missions in San Antonio, the bishop of Guadalajara, the Caballero de Croix (who held two positions during the time it took), the *cabildo* of the cathedral, and the assessor general.

There was no support forthcoming. Crosses and holy water were as essential as flints and gunpowder for Spanish frontier settlements, but Bucareli received no such assistance.

A Decent Chapel, but No Priest

Undaunted by the lack of support to demonstrate their piety, the Adaeseños built a small church later described only as a decent chapel. They wanted to believe that if they built it, a priest would come. One account says that Ibarvo himself led the group in reciting the rosary at the close of each day. In February 1775 there was a brief visit by a priest from Béxar. He was given the assignment of delivering the sacred image of Our Lady of Pilár for the chapel and remaining for a few days in ministry to the people of Bucareli. When Los Adaes disbanded, the church in Béxar collected all the sacred ornaments to be stored by the governor, but the Adaeseños in Bucareli were only provided with a single object. After his work was done, the priest scurried back across the 125 leagues (almost 350 miles) that separated Bucareli from Béxar to the more comfortable confines of his mission home.

Shortly after that visit, the holy father at the mission at La Bahía offered an opinion from the religious community on the settlement at Bucareli. There was general concern among the holy that many souls would be lost at Bucareli if a priest was not assigned to watch over the people. The perception was that Bucareli attracted people with undesirable traits. From the perspective of the priests at least, people were also attracted to the distant settlement because they could carry on their lives with a certain "liberty of conscience."[32] Distant superiors believed that a dangerous and sinful life was the inevitable outcome for people disconnected from Spanish rules and Catholic influence.

Overlaid with the church's concern for their souls was the royal government's concern over the expense of a priestly appointment. The viceroy agreed that their request was "very sensible because a priest will administer to them the *Santo Sacramentos*. He may also give (such people) spiritual help, providing them the means to live in peace."[33] His polite concern was followed by an equally polite alternative that would not cost his treasury any additional funds.

With a bit of verbal sleight of hand by Hugo Oconór, Viceroy Bucareli y Ursua was led to believe that the five missions in Béxar were in close proximity to Bucareli and could cover the need for a priest. Since each of the missions had two priests already paid by the Real Hacienda, Bucareli y Ursua acted on Oconór's suggestion that one of them could also cover the settlement on the Trinity. Bucareli y Ursua authorized Governor Ripperdá to "ask the Father President of those missions, in my name, to order one of the above-mentioned priests to render his religious services."[34]

Neither the father president nor the governor wanted to give up one of their assigned priests. The head of the missions objected vehemently and explained in detail why that would not work. Out of concern for their souls, the father president suggested a secular assistant be used and supplemented by an annual visit by a priest. The arguments between the government and the church over responsibilities, costs, and resources were administratively pungent with a disregard for the real concern for the people of Bucareli.

All they wanted was a priest for Bucareli.

An Appointment, and a Bill

Despite the grim prophecy and concern from the religious brethren, it still took over a year for two missionaries to make the journey, spend a few days with the distant flock at Bucareli, and assess their need for a more permanent appointment. In January 1776, two Franciscans, Father José Francisco Mariano de la Garza and Juan García Botello, came to minister in Bucareli.[35] Both would serve the new settlement, but it was Garza who became an ongoing presence in the lives of the former Adaeseños.

The settlers' celebration over gaining a priest was quickly soured when they learned that the usual suspension of tithes for ten years had not been honored. In fact, the people of Bucareli were informed that they were two years in arrears. True to form, they complied and paid the tithe with what little funds they had, but then they quickly submitted a petition restating their many sacrifices and frequent obedience even when their interests were not served. Also true to form, it took a full year for all the levels of bureaucracy to grant their request to rescind it.

All they wanted was a priest for Bucareli.

The Church of the French Contrabandiere

The interplay between religiosity and the resourcefulness required to live on the frontier was never starker than in the contrast of having a known French smuggler pay for and construct a new chapel at Bucareli. Nicholas de La Mathe, a Natchitoches-based trading partner of Ibarvo, used the prairies around Bucareli to keep horses before moving them across the Sabine or to Béxar. It was La Mathe who paid for a new church at Bucareli and sent two carpenters to direct the construction of a chapel seventy feet long.[36] La Mathe was adept at maintaining his favor in the Spanish province by spreading good will and demonstrating his virtues to the powers that be. Appearances meant a lot. Having a church building that could be pointed to when La Mathe's motives might be questioned was a valuable diversion from his trade.

Commerce and Contraband

With Spanish supplies so distant and infrequently provided, the only practical alternative was to trade cattle and horses with the tribes or the French and accept delivery of anything needed at a lower price than by legal means. An understanding of the requisite business conditions did not take long. Commerce was as simple as the choice between an Amazon delivery to your door or traveling eight hundred miles to buy an overpriced, overtaxed commodity. Those are easy decisions, but like most of the options given to those who lived in distant East Texas, it was not that simple.

The Social Science of Contraband Trade

On January 26, 1730, a royal *cedula* (a document or pronouncement), was issued. It was firm and clear, but because it sought to control human behavior, it was destined to be challenged.

> Without exception of tolerance, proper patrolling should be given to all kinds of illicit trade . . . and to proceed against the guilty ones with the corresponding punishment ignoring their status and condition.[37]

That sounds final, but it is important to remember that economics is a social science based on human behavior, and the economics of contraband trade made sense to both buyer and seller. That simple formula would easily thwart a complex edict.

Spanish goods came to the New World by way of the port at Vera Cruz on the Mexican coast. Along the way, costs were added, and the price increased. The Spanish *alcabalas*, or excise taxes, were added at multiple points of transaction and exchange. This system was untenable when there were easier opportunities to conduct contraband trade.[38]

Goods would finally arrive in Béxar and were then somehow transported to distant settlements. That is unless there were no goods to distribute or the viceroy would not pay for them, as was the case with arms for the people of Bucareli. French merchandise coming through Louisiana cost less than the Spanish versions and was of better quality. The French would also trade guns and ammunition to the native tribes simply as a business transaction, not in some effort to arm a revolt. That resulted in situations where the only way Spanish citizens could purchase arms was from Indian tribes supplied by the French, in trade for horses stolen from the Spanish.

Among those who were happy with the Spaniards return to eastern Texas for trade were the indigenous people who lived nearby. Spanish officials noted that Ibarvo was often visited by tribal leaders eager to become favored trading partners. That posture allowed him to better understand their trading activity with the French and English. Additionally, these visits provided insight into potential threats or raids on the presidios and missions at Béxar and La Bahía, which was "a matter of considerable importance."[39] Ultimately, the cattle and horses raised on the Trinity prairies found ready markets across the Sabine, and French tobacco was a better currency than any pesos.

Official Involvement

Archaeologist and researcher Bob Skiles has studied contraband trade extensively, and contends that trade in violation of Spanish edicts may have constituted up to 75% of the total commerce during this time period; illicit trade also made up five times the revenue for church and state than permissible commerce.[40] Governor Ripperdá avoided confrontation for many years over his role in sponsoring and abetting Ibarvo and French trader Athanase de Mézières, but eventually he too was accused of contraband trade. Even if the role of the military or government officials was merely to overlook the illegal trade, at some point they would expect payment, whether in goods or money.

Priests were also not exempt from engaging in contraband trade. It was acceptable for them to provide prohibited items like tobacco to the Indians they served. What better way to develop ecumenical goodwill than to provide a chief or an official with several *varas* of fine linen or chintz? The gifts were a way to gain trust and acceptance. One would think that wearing the cloth of a Franciscan father would be a trusted passport for travel in the province. When the priest's mules were laden with goods, however, permissible trade items were often found mixed with those prohibited by the crown. The *vecinos* (villagers) most likely to be arrested for contraband were those who tried to contravene the established hierarchies and operate without the right connections. Selective arrests helped create the illusion of official compliance with the law, and they sent a message to others who may try to avoid the well-established complicity.

The Active Complaints of Hugo Oconór

No one seemed to be immune from participation in the contraband trade except Hugo Oconór, the great crusader against smuggled goods. Hugo Oconór became the *comandante inspector* of presidios in early 1773, but his experience with Texas began in 1765. Oconór removed Martos y Navarrete as governor of Los Adaes in 1767 for his role in the contraband trade with Natchitoches and spoke out negatively toward the Adaeseños new settlement at Bucareli. He was convinced that the only reason for the settlement on the Trinity was to participate in contraband trade. It seems likely that he was right, but it also demonstrated the blind spot he had regarding what it took to survive on the edge of the province with no support whatsoever from the Spanish government. Even in June 1775 after Bucareli was settled, Hugo Oconór was qualifying his letters about the settlement with language indicating he was holding out to "decide if this village has to remain or not."[41]

Oconór was opposed to the location for the settlers at Paso Tomás on the Trinity, but Governor Ripperdá was supportive. This put Viceroy Bucareli y Ursua in a position of mediating the two positions and making decisions based on their arguments. In a letter to Bucareli y Ursua on December 31, 1774, well after the establishment of Bucareli, Oconór laid out his complaints. He focused on how the location of Bucareli contributed to what Oconór believed were ongoing smuggling activities.[42]

With pressure from Oconór and others on the *Reales Juntas* (Board of Assets), Bucareli y Ursua agreed to have Ripperdá report on the situation "so that a definite resolution could be taken on this matter." The viceroy had requested a report "on the illicit trade and lack of obedience of the citizens" of Bucareli from Ripperdá months before, on July 15, 1774, but Oconór, not Ripperdá, was given the responsibility to study the circumstances and report on recommendations. In a letter to Ripperdá chastising him for his failure to report, the viceroy reminded the governor that he was required to act upon "whatever may be ordered by the mentioned *Commandante Inspector*."[43] Somehow, the full impact of that instruction was repeatedly skirted.

The Case of Marcos Vidal

Even if regular trade continued, it was important for Ibarvo to occasionally demonstrate an effort toward preventing the entry of contraband goods. In 1774, Ibarvo arrested Marcos Vidal in Bucareli for possessing a large quantity of contraband goods including clothes, playing cards, and tobacco.[44] Vidal was a citizen of Béxar and had been in the business of trade there for many years.[45] His arrest in Bucareli was a significant event not only in terms of the amount of goods, but also for the credibility of Antonio Gil Ibarvo in the eyes of the viceroy. Though the smugglers were to be punished as a legal consequence, justice for Vidal was administered differently. Following his escape from prison in Béxar, Vidal drowned while trying to cross the Nueces River. In May 1776, Governor Ripperdá arranged for an appraisal and sale of the confiscated goods. The value of the goods came to 481 pesos and included the goods listed on the following table.

PLAYING CARDS AND TOBACCO

Also on the list of Vidal's goods were two hundred packs of playing cards valued at sixty-six pesos. These items held a unique place in the contraband trade. Cards did no physical harm to Spanish citizens like trade in weapons or horses, but they were considered a financial offense against monopolies that had been in place for hundreds of years.

Confiscated goods sold at auction

Four axes	6 pesos
Six saltshakers	3 pesos and 6 reales
Six pair scissors	2 pesos
Iron pot or tin pot	4 pesos and 2 reales
Twelve table knives with deer handles	3 pesos and 6 reales
Three battered muskets	9 pesos
Ten metal door plates	40 pesos and 2 reales
Two secondhand blunderbusses	7 pesos
One arroba (25 pounds) of coffee	19 pesos
Seven mules	70 pesos

Source: "Bucarely y Ursua to Ripperdá, requesting proceedings on public auction of confiscated goods in case of Marcos Vidal," Bexar Archives, 1776-05-18, p. 7, e_bx-002505.

To exploit the popularity and widespread enjoyment of playing cards, Spain instituted a monopoly on their export in 1576—the *Estanco de Naipes* (playing card monopoly). Only a few years after that, Alonso Martinez de Orteguilla, the administrator of playing cards for New Spain, issued communications to make sure the rules applied to the colonists. In 1777 the viceroy required that all playing cards for use in Mexico had to originate in Spain.[46] By 1798 in Béxar, and likely well before, there was a position titled "Clerk of the Branch of Tobacco, Powder [gun], Playing Cards, and Sealed Paper of the Royal Treasury."[47] Sales and pricing were controlled by law, and the manufacture of playing cards was assigned by lease arrangements. As part of that cooperative arrangement, the government was to outlaw all other cards and consider them as contraband.

Vidal's tobacco was also handled separately from the other goods. There were 1,011 pounds, and 15 ounces total, of which 910 pounds was given to Father Ramírez for the missions at Béxar "since they were lacking the said commodity." The balance of 101 pounds and 15 ounces was sold at seven *reales* per pound, roughly equivalent to $125, with proceeds going to the government treasury.

ALLOCATION OF THE ASSETS

While the official treasury profited from the confiscation of Vidal's goods, participants in the confiscation did as well. The law governing such distributions had changed on December 7, 1767. Before that change, confiscated goods were split with one-third going to the judge, one-third to the informer, and one-third to the government coffers. That was abolished and changed to one-third to the judge, one-third to the informer, and one-third to the apprehender. Of Vidal's sale, 8 percent went to Antonio Gil Ibarvo as a stipend for being the *estanquero* of the *estanquillo* (keeper of the government's store), and another share went to him as judge. For each pound of tobacco, 2.25% went to the apprehenders.[48]

By August 1782 there was still no decision on what to do with the 491 pesos and four reales from the sale of Vidal's other goods. The value of two hundred packs of cards was subtracted from the total and added to the budget of the Ramo de Naipes (Branch of Playing Cards). Another share was used to pay legal expenses. The remainder was to be distributed one-third to Ibarvo, one-third to informers (including Vidal's servants), and one-third to the apprehenders who were among the militia at Bucareli. Each member of the militia received just over nineteen pesos. It was not until February 1783, however, that anyone received the allocated funds—almost ten years after the initial apprehension.

Ibarvo Makes Arrests of Lesser Smugglers

The extent to which Antonio Gil Ibarvo and other Adaeseños participated in contraband trade may never be fully known. Oconór's resistance had been circumvented at every step, but his opinions still had to be placated and demonstrations of obedience made for the crown. To maintain appearances, Ibarvo participated in arresting and judging minor smugglers caught in his jurisdiction. He did that on several occasions for cases that were relatively small but made sure his efforts were known to his superior officers. In December 1774, Ibarvo was commended by Viceroy Bucareli y Ursua for "performing his duty when he refused the admission of two bundles of tobacco." Applauding even minor enforcement, particularly in the written record, was the nature of the game.[49]

ARREST OF THE DÍAZ BROTHERS

As early as October 1774, the arrest of smugglers with little means appeared in the official correspondence. One of those cases was Lt. Simón Arocha's arrest of two brothers, Juan Antonio Díaz and José Manuel Díaz.[50] Arocha delivered them to Bucareli, where they were jailed awaiting Ibarvo's return from a visit to his Bidai neighbors. He then transported them to Béxar for trial. The story the brothers told in their hearing was a sad tale.

Juan and José left the San José mission in Béxar in early January 1774 along with a young native boy they called Juan Antonio. The father president of the Béxar area missions, Fray Pedro Ramírez, provided them with eight mules from two different missions so they could "search for a way to earn a livelihood." Surely the padre knew the way one earned a living with eight mules was to carry goods for trade. The Díaz brothers did just that, carrying three small loads of nuts, buffalo meat, and lard to Vallesillo, 225 miles south of Béxar across the Rio Grande. They sold their entire load there and then traveled another seventy-six miles south where they remained for a month.

The brothers came back to Texas with a small load of *pilonsillo* (brown sugar) and a full load of flour. After crossing the Trinity River, they encountered Tejas Indians with whom they traded the pilonsillo, two guns, one *caraza* (light body armor), some iron stirrups, two *taquimas* (perhaps boxes), and four *cavestros* (halters) in exchange for three iron pots, eight chamois, one buffalo hide, and thirty deer hides. They also were enticed to help a French trader named Gaspar who was on his way to Natchitoches with forty loads of hides. They met Gaspar at the village of the Tejas (Caddo) on Bayou Loco, not far from the Angelina River. For the next few months, they described their mistreatment by Gaspar and others. The brothers ended up on foot looking for their horses after losing mounts due to exhaustion and drowning.

The brothers became separated and ill but found each other again. The Díaz brothers were traveling with some Adaeseño families toward Béxar when they encountered Antonio Gil Ibarvo and Simon Arocha, who were traveling to their new town on the Trinity. Arocha asked to inspect their goods, and though he did not find anything on which taxes were owed he discovered they were traveling without a passport from the commandant in Natchitoches. The Díaz brothers were held and delivered to Béxar for their hearing before the governor, but they did not appear to be the type of traders about which there should be great concern.

For all their effort, the brothers made it back to Béxar with only five of the eight mules they started with, one black and one grey horse, one flintlock musket they bought from Indians, a few trunks, some chamois skins, and medicinal herbs. They never had the intent or the wherewithal to acquire goods in Natchitoches. Finding that the brothers had done nothing more than appear to be selling unauthorized goods, and "in consideration of the extreme poverty and unhappiness in which they find themselves," Governor Ripperdá freed them but only after selling all their possessions.

CONTRABAND TOBACCO FROM BUCARELI

Jacinto Mora was another example of a man engaging in a simple trade who had no larger intentions. In April 1775 he was caught with contraband tobacco from growers in Natchitoches while also accompanied by priests.[51] Mora had occasion to travel to Bucareli as an escort for one of the priests from Béxar. When Mora arrived, he found Nicholas Beausoleille (Beausoleil) there. Beausoleil owed Mora five pesos, and he repaid him with two bundles of tobacco, indirectly to again maintain appearances. Beausoleil said he would not sell the tobacco to anyone but the native tribes, maintaining a strictly legal posture. As a convenient work-around, Mora found a Bidai Indian willing to make the purchase for him.

Mora knew he was entering into an agreement to do something he should not and hid the two bundles near a chapel before coming into Béxar. Mora sold the tobacco to Marcos Hernández, who bought the contraband because he thought it was a bargain. Hernández also hoped he could trade it to visiting Lipan Apache for a mule or furs. Mora and Hernández both had their houses searched and were questioned heavily about who else might have smuggled or bought tobacco. Neither had seen anything more.

Ripperdá's intention was to deliver a harsh punishment for these men, at least in part to make a favorable impression in Mexico City. Much like the brothers Díaz, however, the social standing of Mora was particularly stark. When authorities searched his home, the only property they could find to seize was a new pair of pants made of brown wool lined with cotton.[52] The defender for Mora and Hernández pointed out to the governor that both men committed their crime out of "ignorant misery and careless blindness." He argued that their near-poverty and lack of education were what led to this transgression, and they were not in the business of smuggling contraband goods. Both were found guilty, but since Mora was unable to pay the fines, he was sentenced to fifteen days in jail.

Ripperdá then turned to Beausoleil himself. The governor had ordered that Ibarvo deliver the Frenchman to Béxar, where he was held in the guard house pending his deposition. Beausoleil explained to the governor that when Los Adaes was emptied of its citizens, he was granted a permit by the commandant of Natchitoches to trade with the Bidai Indians. He said that he traded in tobacco, blankets, shirts, strike steel, *belduques* (knives), vermilion, beads, gunpowder, bullets, rifles, and small pots. When Bucareli was founded, Beausoleil sought Ibarvo's permission to live there with his wife, claiming he did not sell tobacco or any other item to Spaniards. Contraband culture was ingrained in all commerce.

TOBACCO AT BUCARELI

Luis Cazorla, captain of the Presidio of La Bahía, was a soldier in the mold of Hugo Oconór. He was wholeheartedly invested in the letter of the law, which made the tone of his seemingly reluctant, almost apologetic, report of an incident of smuggling even more curious. Cazorla's May 1775 report to the viceroy told of an encounter civilians had while hunting buffalo up the Guadalupe River. Not far outside of San Antonio they came upon some old Frenchmen, citizens of Bucareli, carrying French tobacco.[53] Nicholas Beausoleil was one of the Frenchmen, along with Carlos Grande and Ramón Terio, and each had married Spanish women and been in trade with the tribes and others around Natchitoches.

Cazorla decided to learn more and on his return to La Bahía "made the most secret inquiries for investigating it." He discovered the purchase was just a small amount, only about four pounds, worth three and a half pesos. Cazorla assured the viceroy that he realized this was still forbidden goods, but after seeing that it was such a small amount, he produced a plan to learn more about the source rather than punish the holder of contraband.

The captain of the militia spoke harshly to the buyer about what could happen if he was violating the law. Cazorla frightened him to secure the man's help as an informant. By having the man take on an undercover mission, Cazorla learned that a substantial amount of contraband tobacco had been sold in Béxar by traders from Bucareli, where much more tobacco could be found. Cazorla's investigation continued with his interrogation of the other members of the hunting party who confirmed that the citizens of Bucareli had a substantial amount of tobacco and were trading with the French and the tribes of the north.

Cazorla, like others, believed that with Bucareli being so distant and without spiritual guidance, such vices could be expected to continue. According to Cazorla, their "deceit and liberty" were due to the lack of a priest to tend to the souls of the wayward Adaeseños and others who joined them on the Trinity. He acknowledged that trade with the Indians was important to keeping the peace through their "reciprocal barter or trade," but that over time such behavior could lead the distant Spaniards to become apostate or even worse. Cazorla even wondered if they may be inclined to join the Indians and forsake their Spanish ties.

Cazorla's report did not surprise Oconór. He knew about the contraband trade but was helpless against the silent forces that made it so common and as much a part of life as growing crops and raising a family. With Cazorla's substantiation of what was taking place in plain view, Oconór tried one more time to plead his case with the viceroy. His approach was fervent and clear—and again useless. Oconór reminded the viceroy of what Los Adaes had once been.

> [Los Adaes was] the factory of illegal abominable commerce in muskets, powder and balls provided to the Indians of the north, which they used against Spaniards, stealing their property and destroying settlements. Now the same Antonio Gil Ibarvo has been established at another distant location where he can carry on the same trade.

Oconór was unrelenting in his disgust toward Ibarvo and Bucareli. He told the viceroy he did not know which was worse for the interior provinces, the endless Indian attacks and thievery or the smuggling taking place openly between Bucareli and Louisiana.[54]

Oconór also aimed his words to the viceroy squarely toward Ripperdá when he said that despite Oconór's effort to comply with the king's orders, "others attempt, if not to prevent, to retard by their hands."[55] Oconór continued his protests with his most direct objection by saying, "The citizenship of Los Adaes is not able, in my conception, to remain in the present situation in which it is found, without causing the gravest damages." Oconór proposed the Adaeseños be evicted once again, this time from their new home at Bucareli to "free them from committing the hideous crimes that tempt them" and to "close the door to illegal commerce." Oconór's wish for this authority was not granted.

In a lengthy epistle, Ripperdá defended his decisions to the viceroy and explained that Oconór's concerns were overblown.[56] Ripperdá defended Ibarvo, claiming he was not allowing any trade in tobacco with the French in Natchitoches, nor was he providing arms to the Indians. Ripperdá credited Ibarvo with stopping contraband trade, at least enough to keep Cazorla's and Oconór's complaints at bay. As if to seal the message of goodwill, the governor's letter followed with several pages outlining the religious devotion of the citizens of Bucareli.

A Transition in Leadership

By the end of 1776, Hugo Oconór was waning both politically and physically. As a result of his poor health, he requested a less taxing post and was awarded the governorship of Yucatan. However, he lived only another two years. Though his single-minded focus on the perils of contraband trade and adherence to the king's orders were no longer centered on Texas, questions about Bucareli's role in contraband trade continued with new Spanish leadership.

In Oconór's place as *comandante general* of the *Provincias Internas* came Teodoro de Croix, titled as the Caballero de Croix. The *provincias* was a new subdivision of Texas that split off some of the responsibility of the viceroy,

Bucareli y Ursua. That arrangement occasionally left Croix and Bucareli y Ursua at odds with each other.[57] On January 1, 1777, in a shift of jurisdictional responsibilities for New Spain, Croix became responsible for Texas and Bernardo de Gálvez became the acting governor of Louisiana.

Had Hugo Oconór not been removed from his authority in Spanish East Texas, Texas history would likely have changed forever. If Oconór had his way, there would have been no Bucareli and subsequently no resettlement of Nacogdoches. Modern day Texas is fortunate that the wishes of the "Red Captain" were averted.

Ripperdá Praises Ibarvo to Croix

Governor Ripperdá wasted little time in bringing Croix up to speed and sent him detailed reports on the province. In a lengthy commentary on April 27, 1777, Ripperdá provided Croix with an overview of the settlements, including populations and current conditions.[58] When Croix assumed office in 1777, the population of Bucareli was 347 people: 125 men, including fifty-three in the militia company; eighty-nine women; sixty-four boys; sixty-four girls; two enslaved males; and three enslaved females. At that time there were over one thousand people at the presidio and villa in Béxar, and about three hundred at La Bahía.

Though Béxar and La Bahía were mentioned in passing, the letter was largely about Bucareli. It seems that Ripperdá, after the blistering parting words from Hugo Oconór, needed to defend both himself and Bucareli from further damage to their respective reputations. Ripperdá did his best to bolster an image of strategic importance for Bucareli, basing his argument on two time-tested talking points: lingering concerns about inroads of the English and French, and maintaining good will among the Indians. In addition to other tribes considered friendly to the Spanish, Ripperdá pointed out that the Bidai had their principal establishment only about two leagues from Bucareli. Even though Bucareli was "two long days" journey from the mouth of the Trinity River at Galveston Bay, its location was of "greatest importance as a means of acquiring reports of a coast as extensive as it is uninhabited."

Ripperdá also made sure that Croix heard good things about Antonio Gil Ibarvo to counter the negative reports of Oconór. Ripperdá said that Ibarvo had done well as captain and *justicia mayor*, "showing more ability than I expected, in view of his having been reared in Los Adaes." Ripperdá believed that Ibarvo's intelligence and skill with the local tribes ensured a more peaceful existence. The governor pointed out that Ibarvo had essentially been the sole financial support for the people of Bucareli by providing oxen, cattle, tools, and labor at his own expense, without saying how he gained those resources. Ripperdá also hoped to counter what Croix had likely heard about the governor himself—that he was encouraging French trade, even in Béxar. Ripperdá defended his use of French interpreters, and he complained that earlier reports of his own involvement with contraband caused him "serious calumnies" and forced him to withdraw from his open communications with Indian nations intended to foster goodwill.

With the slow pace of mail between Texas and Mexico City, Croix did not reply to Ripperdá until July 9, 1777, a delay of over two months. Croix not only encouraged patience in making changes, but also mildly criticized Ripperdá for not following his instincts in acting on relations with the friendly tribes despite Oconór's objections. Croix seemed to understand that trade relations with the Indians were the key to tranquility while living among them. Croix told Ripperdá to "proceed as one who has the facts before him," leaving Croix to "trust to your distinguished character, honor, and position."[59] Those must have been welcome words for Governor Ripperdá.

A Different View of Trade and Bucareli

Following the support from Croix, Ripperdá saw an opportunity to escape the hardline trade policies of Oconór. The governor believed the traders and their role in the borderlands should be embraced rather than interrupted by edicts and arrests. Rather than working with indigenous people as true partners, however, Spain continued a perspective that would pervade all of their interactions and relationships.

Ripperdá told Croix that one of the matters of highest importance to the Province of Texas was "obedience and subordination which should be observed by all the traders among the friendly nations."[60] The governor restated Spanish presumptions that not only did the land, which "has no limits to the north," belong to Spain, but that the tribes of the province did as well. This perspective would not serve Spain's interests in the long term, but it was so ingrained in their view of the world that it tainted those relationships for centuries. Every chief who was engaged with Spanish and French traders, even as Spain assumed control of French Louisiana, could see there was a difference in how they were treated.

Ripperdá wanted Croix to understand that embracing the facts of the contraband economy and having Spanish traders supply the Native Americans was better than refusing and then having the French or English supply them anyway. Croix came to adopt this line of reasoning and accepted Ibarvo's role in managing the settlement and the trade in distant East Texas. In so doing,

Croix tacitly acknowledged that contraband trade appeared to be a simple solution to the complexities of the borderlands.

In January 1778, Croix reappointed Ibarvo as captain of the militia for the settlement at Bucareli in recognition of "the merits he has acquired in giving a stable foundation to the new town of Nuestra Señora del Pilár de Bucareli."[61] The tides had turned in Bucareli's favor. Ibarvo's role was secured, but that change may have come too late. Antonio Gil Ibarvo was growing tired of his role and the responsibilities that came with it.

De Mézières at Bucareli

In March 1778, Athanase de Mézières received authorization to make an expedition from Béxar through the upper reaches of the Trinity, Brazos, and Red rivers on a mission for Croix, the *commandante general*. De Mézières asked to conduct a reconnaissance to the north that might improve relations with the tribes who lived there.[62] His large touring party included a lieutenant and twenty-two soldiers assigned from the presidio at Béxar, six members of the Natchitoches militia, and two of de Mézières's sons.

De Mézières's descriptions of the region are a detailed firsthand account of central and eastern Texas. Along the Colorado and Brazos rivers, he observed large numbers of birds and fish as well as an abundance of natural resources like timber and quarries of stone. He was impressed by the numbers of wild Castilian cattle that roamed the prairies and river bottoms. Large herds of mustangs never seemed to leave the banks of the rivers and streams. Between the rivers were buffalo, deer, antelope, wild boars, hares, partridges, and turkeys. The luxuriant and spacious plains and pastures were ringed by huge trees and woodlands with edibles like grapes, medlars (likely persimmons), nuts, and acorns.

Bidai and the Cruel Fever

The presence of the Bidai nearby had both positive and negative consequences for Bucareli. Though the nearness of their villages to Paso Tomás might have meant the Bidai could come to the defense of their Spanish neighbors if attacked by hostile tribes, de Mézières noted observations that were far less hopeful. He described the Bidai as a "wandering, wretched, and lazy people [who] had forgotten the occupation of hunting, on which they formerly based their livelihood." Their roaming included coming to Bucareli to beg for gifts, a behavior that only contributed to "the retrogression of the poor, sympathetic inhabitants."[63]

The Bidai population was down to around one hundred following an epidemic that cost lives at Bucareli as well. In the summer and fall of 1777 and again in the late summer of 1778, disease had an impact not only on the native populations but on the Spanish and French as well. Without an understanding of the causes for the disease, people attributed the sickness to an excessive amount of water in the floodplain, a condition that would breed mosquitoes carrying malaria.[64] Based on the symptoms they described, one of the illnesses was easily identified as smallpox. Collectively the diseases were simply known as the "cruel fever."[65]

In only about three months, Natchitoches lost fifty people out of its population of one thousand people. De Mézières reported that more than three hundred Caddo died in only a couple of months in 1778.[66] A third of the Hasinai Caddo died, including Chief Bigotes and a Nabedache chief, both of whom were important to bringing about peaceful coexistence with the Spanish.[67] A chief of the Bidai, Gorgorito, also died. El Mocho (The Maimed), the troublesome Tonkawa chief, escaped the epidemic, leading de Mézières to describe him as "the one whom it was most desired to have meet his doom."[68]

De Mézières in the Middle

It should not be surprising that the master trader, de Mézières, was supportive of Bucareli, its location, and its significance for New Spain. In a letter to Croix, de Mézières restated the case for Bucareli's continuance. It was a central location for communicating with tribes both north and south, and it was in proximity to friendly tribes who might come to their aid if needed, like the Bidai and the Nacodoche. It was beneficially equidistant from Béxar, Natchitoches, and the Indian tribes.

On September 12, 1774, almost immediately after Ibarvo and the Adaeseños arrived at Bucareli, Athanase de Mézières sent a letter to the Spanish governor of formerly French Louisiana, Luis de Unzaga y Amézaga, describing the situation as it unfolded.[69] De Mézières's letter had the air of a reconnaissance report on behalf of the governor and included the ranks of the soldiers assigned at Bucareli. The French trader's report was clearly written by someone with firsthand access to the information, and one who perhaps maintained multiple allegiances.

It is also clear from the letter that De Mézières and Ibarvo were in communication before the Adaeseños move from Béxar to the Trinity River. Where Ibarvo would end up would be of keen interest to people on the far side of the Sabine River in Natchitoches. De Mézières told the governor that "the captain

(Ibarvo) has written me, but he is not yet certain as to the place which he should select for his site." The information being reported by de Mézières came from Ibarvo himself. What reason would Ibarvo have for communicating with Athanase de Mézières if not to secure cooperative trade in the future?

The tone of de Mézières's reconnaissance report is reinforced by Unzaga's response. The governor treated de Mézières as a confidential informant and did not want that relationship to become known. In March 1775, Unzaga urged de Mézières not to communicate with Ripperdá, the governor of Texas. De Mézières was also asked to keep a close eye on the people moving toward the new settlement from Louisiana.[70]

Improvements to the Settlement

Despite the epidemic, the conditions de Mézières observed when he arrived at Bucareli in March of 1778 were much improved. In April 1776, there were only twenty houses built of timber and a few jacales for those who had not yet begun to build more lasting structures.[71] By June 1777, there were more than fifty houses of real timber, not just sticks, and a timbered palisade around the main buildings with gates they could close in the event of a threat. There was also a small cell for holding prisoners, in stocks or with four pairs of shackles if needed. Roads had been improved, and the crossing of the river made easier with a raft to use if the water was too high to cross without it. Corrals for horses and fields for planting were complete. The Adaeseños' industry and effort had begun to make their settlement along the Trinity River into a home.[72]

North from Bucareli with Ibarvo

In March 1778, de Mézières continued his expedition up through eastern Texas, traveling northward from Bucareli. He was joined by Antonio Gil Ibarvo, thirteen militiamen from the settlement, and the adventurous Father Francisco José de la Garza.[73] About forty-five miles north of Bucareli they encountered a small encampment of about twenty Kichai warriors in a "broad and fertile valley," where their corn could grow quickly and their herds of horses would be well fed. For commerce there were salines nearby to produce salt, and plenty of deer for food and hides. De Mézières said there was a road to the village with a rough track that led "over steep and rocky hills, deep glens, creeks, lakes and bogs" that gave them great difficulty in their passage. His commentary on the plant life was equally descriptive. A plant he called viper's grass was known to have curative properties as an antidote against fevers and stings.[74] He also paid homage to the sweet potato (*Convulvulus batatas*) because it "would be ingratitude to forget, they have efficiently relieved the needs of the nascent pueblo of Bucareli."

De Mézières continued westward while Ibarvo and his militia returned to Bucareli. In his letter to Croix on April 5, 1778, de Mézières heavily complimented his traveling companions from Bucareli. He appreciated the "fervent, sincere, and apostolic spirit" of Father Garza. He also made certain Croix knew that Ibarvo and the leadership of his militia "aided me so much that I acknowledge the extraordinary pleasure and benefit which I have derived from their company." He hoped that Croix would "keep them in mind, as persons capable of discharging any command they may have for its object is the service of both majesties."[75]

He was not as complimentary of the militia itself. The militiamen were sick and without proper clothing, had no weapons or supplies, and were without pack horses. The only compliment he offered for the men from Bucareli was to acknowledge their "blind obedience" to the mission on which their commander, Antonio Gil Ibarvo, had enlisted their support. Getting them back to the care of their poor families and preparing to plant corn were more important in de Mézières's mind than accompanying him on his tour of indigenous villages. Only four militiamen from Bucareli continued with de Mézières, a decision that was likely welcomed by everyone.[76] By May 2, 1778, de Mézières returned his home to Natchitoches by way of Bucareli.

Governor Ripperdá was replaced by Domingo Cabello in October 1778. Before Cabello could even assume the office, Croix sent him a clear, concise request for his input on Bucareli. It is quite interesting how a settlement where almost four hundred people had lived since 1774, four years prior to these latest discussions, was still being considered a new or temporary arrangement. In his short letter to Cabello, Croix said, "As soon as Your Lordship is instructed well about the advantages and disadvantages which are offered by the new settlement of *N[usest]ra Señora de Pilár de Bucareli* established at the persistence of Don Ant[oni]o Gil de Ibarbo at the site named *El Paso de Tomás*, [you] will inform me at the great length and clarity the concept it [the settlement] deserves."[77] It took Cabello eight months to send a reply.

The Priestly Voices

Ibarvo, Oconór, Ripperdá, and de Mézières each had their own perspective on the nature of Bucareli, its value to Spanish interests, and its role in contraband trade. They also each had interests, biases, personal histories, and obligations that may have clouded their views. Members of the priesthood were not immune from those burdens of opinion. Their schema was well known—converting the "heathen" Indians and tending their flock was how they understood their calling. As Father Zedano's arrest with contraband in 1766 indicated, the church and its representatives were not always bystanders to the movement of prohibited goods. The two priests who knew Bucareli firsthand let Spanish leaders know what they saw with their eyes and felt in their hearts.

Father Botello

Father Juan García Botello committed his life to securing souls for the kingdom of heaven, but Botello was also passionate about caring for the personal welfare of his people on earth. Father Botello had initially visited Bucareli only for a short time to deliver the church's ornaments. While Governor Cabello was learning more about Bucareli, he asked Botello for an opinion on the settlement. In Botello's letter to the incoming governor at a time of crisis in Bucareli in December 1778, the priest said he was "moved by the ruin which threatens it," and his desire to "seek the remedy of so many evils."[78]

Botello was there during the "cruel fever," the epidemic causing the deaths of significant numbers of people in 1777. In the late summer and early fall of 1777, the epidemic caused the death of seventeen persons in Bucareli, including Lt. Gil Flores. The epidemic hit Bucareli and spread to trading centers in both directions—Béxar and Natchitoches. De Mézières said the disease, "with even greater desolation entered the surrounding villages." In 1777 it looked like the scourge was over, but in 1778 sickness suddenly returned and affected Kichai, Nasoni, Tawakoni, Taovaya, and Caddo tribes.

In reporting the frightful return of the illness, de Mézières honored the misfortune of the Indian people "so adorned with such good qualities [they] should be felt as our own."[79] De Mézières's empathy was sincere. During the 1777 epidemic, de Mézières lost a son, a daughter, and his second wife all during the same week.[80]

Coming out of that epidemic, Father Botello was blunt with the governor in expressing his opinions about the future of the settlers at Bucareli. He noted that the land was fertile, but its water could not be managed by irrigation. Farming was at the mercy of the pendulum of drought and flood. Even the religious recognized that leaving Bucareli out on the fringes with no military support was not going to work, especially when the militia, as it were, did not have adequate arms or ammunition. Botello understood that any attack on the settlement could easily set the wood houses afire, and that the logs for the stockade were starting to rot at ground level.

The priest was sympathetic to the villagers and took liberties in his thoughts about where else they could live, suggesting options to Cabello. The watersheds of the Angelina and Neches rivers to the east were home to friendly tribes, and the Attoyac Bayou even farther east would be more protected from Comanche raids. The former mission sites of Nacogdoches or Ais would also offer greater security and opportunity than the current settlement on the edge of the Trinity River.

Botello spoke freely. His message to the governor was to stop pretending that having the settlement at Bucareli had any impact on preventing contraband trade. Father Botello simply wanted the governor to do something for the poor villagers of Bucareli.

Father de la Garza

The long-suffering Father de la Garza was even more direct with Cabello than Father Botello had been a month prior. His letter to the governor in January 1779 was dire and unhopeful for the people of Bucareli unless their circumstances were to change. He was deeply concerned with the "great and doleful conflict with which these my sheep in my charge are found." De la Garza's flock was "burdened with family and with miseries, overwhelmed with cares, full of necessities and fears, threats of death, and with the enemy [Comanche] at our door." The miseries of the settlers at Bucareli were many. The town's defenselessness due to its lack of arms and its distance from any military protection was never resolved and would become its undoing.[81]

Like Father Botello, Father de la Garza believed the choices regarding *Bucareli* were clear—defend it or move it east to safer territory. Both priests recognized it was essential to maintain a Spanish presence in the area where trade and Indian relations were vital. Both could see that things were only going to get worse unless something changed.

The End of Bucareli

Antonio Gil Ibarvo had been a reluctant leader ever since he became the de facto emissary representing the people of Los Adaes after their expulsion. At the time of their exit from Béxar, he had been appointed as *justicia mayor* of Bucareli. There was no payment associated with this title and no reimbursement of expenses. Tired of the constant harassment and recriminations by Hugo Oconór, Ibarvo submitted his resignation in February 1777, but Oconór had already moved on from his post and the request was simply ignored.[82] Shortly after Teodoro de Croix assumed responsibility for the province, he issued Ibarvo a commission as captain of the militia on January 12, 1778. Any thoughts of his resignation were suspended for the moment.

Ibarvo had served the dual masters of crown and contraband trade for too many years. He was tired and wanted to go home to El Lobanillo. He needed relief from the hopelessness of the Spanish goals for the borderlands and wanted to unburden himself from the obligations of the crown. In May 1778, before any official action could be taken to better care for Bucareli, the worst fears of its people began to be realized.

Fear of the Comanche

Comanche villages along the Brazos River were situated where they could easily steal horses and mules from Béxar and quickly retreat. The tribe was armed with weapons provided by French traders from Louisiana by way of the Bidai, and Governor Cabello felt powerless to resist their attacks. Comanche had stolen so many horses at Béxar he could not even give chase and retaliate.[83] Given their defenseless position on the frontier, the people of Bucareli harbored magnified fears, which were soon realized. On May 3, 1778, about thirty Comanche on horseback unexpectedly appeared on a nearby hillside.

As with many of the encounters between natives and Spanish settlers, there are different versions of this incident from both sides of the ensuing conflict. Athanase de Mézières heard about the incident from Evea, the son of the Comanche head chief. Evea told de Mézières his people had come on a friendly visit to look for the French trader, and were only resting on a hillside, having turned out their horses to graze.[84] These were seemingly not hostile actions. But when someone at Bucareli spotted the Comanche in the distance, the nature of the encounter changed completely.

The Comanche heard loud noises coming from Bucareli and saw the settlers hurriedly gather their horses inside the stockade. The tone of their fearful outcries could be heard from a distance. Evea said they became unsettled by this and departed on their own but soon found themselves being pursued by an armed group from Bucareli. Due to the settlement's lack of muskets and ammunition, leaving Bucareli with an armed party meant those who remained were left without protection other than the poorly maintained cannons at the stockade. Nevertheless, the ineffectually armed militia pursued the Comanche, killing three of them and taking some of their horses.

Upon hearing the Comanche account, Athanase de Mézières wondered why their mere presence garnered such a response. He questioned why someone in Bucareli did not pause to identify the Indians and ask, "Who were they? What were they hunting? Why [where] were they going?" Evea later told de Mézières he was "offended by the violence shown at Bucarely [Bucareli] toward the people who were going there to meet and see me [de Mézières]." De Mézières explained it to the Comanche as a mistake on the part of the Spanish, and Evea appeared to be satisfied with that answer.[85]

When Croix heard firsthand accounts of this story from Bucareli he was convinced it was an attack and not a rest stop in a nearby prairie. Mistrust of the Comanche was quickly learned on the frontier. It was not expected that a member of that tribe would approach a Spanish settlement without harmful intent. Similarly, Governor Cabello did not accept the concept of friendly Comanche. His starting position was that it was inconceivable to think that the Comanche came to Bucareli or any other Spanish settlement with good intentions. Whether the Comanches were there to kill or simply steal, he did not trust their presence based on their past actions.[86] Cabello told Croix he was convinced of the nature of the confrontation by someone whom he considered a model of religious verity—Father Fray Juan García Botello. Botello was at Bucareli when the incident with the Comanche took place and was an eyewitness to the events as they unfolded. Father Botello told the governor that by no stretch of the imagination was de Mézières's account credible. That was good enough for Cabello—he considered the event as a foiled attack on Bucareli.[87]

Only a few months later, in October 1778, the Comanche were back again, and this time their intentions were clear. They came with more than the thirty warriors who appeared in May, and their focus was on Nicholas de La Mathe's herd of horses on the prairies around Bucareli. In September 1778, Nicholas La Mathe was granted permission for the export of horses and mules to Louisiana and was waiting to herd them toward markets in the east.[88] La Mathe kept over five hundred horses on the prairie at Bucareli, and the Comanche made off with almost three hundred of them in their raid. With the help of Kichai and Caddo tribal members, the militia pursued the raiders all the way to the Brazos. After recovering their horses, they lost the stolen herd again when even more Comanche overtook them on their way back to Bucareli.

Father Garza identified with the fears presented by the situation at Bucareli and observed that "these miserable inhabitants are left in such deplorable state that they have no way to even hunt for food . . . for they cannot go out to hunt except in large numbers and well-armed, nor yet can they go out together and with their weapons, lest they should leave the settlement helpless."[89] There were only twenty-three firearms in working order for the entire settlement of over three hundred people. The cannons were nothing more than sculptures of war, representing worn out and mistaken concepts of military might and imperial dominance. Frontier rumors that Comanche would return to raze Bucareli and sell any surviving inhabitants into slavery fed into their concerns.[90] In the end, La Mathe lost horses, three Tejas warriors lost their lives, and the Adaeseños at Bucareli lost their sense of security.

No Más

Just prior to the second Comanche raid, Antonio Gil Ibarvo again tried to resign his post. His letter to Governor Ripperdá on September 22, 1778, said that he was "incapable of maintaining the position you have deemed to grant me." Ibarvo claimed his insolvency was the result of spending his personal funds to provide gifts to the friendly Indians.[91] It was the unfriendly ones who would lead to a change.

The Comanche raid and the theft of La Mathe's horses was a significant monetary loss, but the fear of further depredations shook Bucareli to its core. The people there could not bear the daily fears of their exposure to attack nor ignore the weakness of their defenses. Rumblings about leaving the settlement began shortly after the second incident with the Comanche. Father Botello heard the conversations among the people about where they could go and what they should do. Father Botello told Governor Cabello he believed that twenty-five leagues to the east would be safer: in the Neches-Angelina watershed, on the Attoyac Bayou nearer to El Lobanillo, or at the former mission site in Nacogdoches. Their lives would be more secure away from the vulnerabilities of the Trinity River. A return to Béxar was not considered. No one wanted to return to the subjugation, dismissal, and poverty of the provincial capital.

During that period of consternation, the Adaeseños at Bucareli made a brave decision. On January 1, 1779, and again on January 8, the entire village of Bucareli appeared at the dwelling of Don Antonio Gil Ibarvo, their captain and leader, asking his permission to abandon Bucareli and find a safer settlement to the east. It was on the second occasion that Father Garza wrote his own dire letter to Governor Cabello asking for either his blessing for "these miserable inhabitants" to do what they needed to do to protect themselves, or for his protection and support with military resources. The priest made sure the governor understood the desperation of the settlers. Garza told him he had seen "their miseries . . . pass before my eyes; the clamors already come to my ears; and [I am] asking of the Lord Our God incessantly for the remedy."[92] Four days later, Ibarvo wrote his own letter to Cabello informing him of the desperation of the settlers and the difficult position he was in regarding the permission they requested.[93]

The Comanche raids left them in fear. Despite the effort they had put into their current settlement, they had no other choice but to leave Bucareli.[94] Ibarvo understood their fears but lacked the authority to give them official consent. Though he was not able to offer his permission, he did give his sanction by saying if they moved farther east, closer to the protection and resources of the friendly tribes, he would explain their decision to Governor Cabello.

For the third time in only a few years, the place the Adaeseños called home was vanishing around them. Although they were forced into a decision by the raid, at least this time it was their own decision. When the village of Bucareli began its voluntary disassembly, nothing really mattered there anymore. It was significant in the colonial history of Texas that they were violating one of the core principles of the Spanish system of government by deciding where they would live without first gaining the approval of distant rulers. They did not let that stop them. The Adaeseños took matters into their own hands and decided to move to the former mission of Nacogdoches.

THE DEPARTURE

The exodus of Bucareli settlers to safer environs to the east "toward the Nation of Texas [Tejas Indians] or their borders" began on January 25, 1779.[95] In his letter to the governor reporting their departure, Ibarvo was careful to lay out the rationale. He explained that the people were unable to hunt or plant due to the lack of arms and the complete lack of support from Béxar. They moved for their own preservation. They moved to save their own lives.

Almost all the three hundred men, women, and children left Bucareli in the first group. There were not enough horses for most to ride and not enough carts on which to load belongings. Ibarvo stayed behind in Bucareli with twenty men until people could come back for belongings left behind in homes scattered along the banks of the Trinity. It would be interesting to know how the twenty-three working rifles and muskets were split between the groups. The larger group headed toward safety in Nacogdoches, and the smaller one stayed behind to protect what remained at Bucareli.

Two days later, Father Garza left Bucareli on foot with a caravan that included the sick and injured, as well at the sacred vessels and objects of the chapel. Ibarvo told the governor that he and "this poor village hopes for his [Garza's] protection." The holy father had lived through all the moments of desperation with his flock at Bucareli and was the kind of man whose faith knew no fear.

THE FIRE

The end of Bucareli would not be as simple as relocation. Official reports of a fire that followed the exit of the first group of refugees from Bucareli explained the blaze as accidental. Cabello's secondhand report of the incident to Croix wrote it off to a result caused by a chaotic and sudden withdrawal from the settlement on the Trinity. "One family [abandoned the village of Bucareli] with so much confusion that, leaving their fire-place with a fire in it, fire was communicated to the house," he explained. Then, he suggested, the flames from that wooden house jumped to another wooden house and "since the greater part of them were of timbers, they were reduced to ashes."[96] This contagion of destruction continued until half of the settlement was destroyed by fire.

There is no documentation to suggest the notion, but also nothing to dispute it, that the fire may not have been an accidental conflagration. Some of the wooden buildings would have been within the bounds of the palisade, but the walls would not have been large enough to contain half of the settlement. Given the resistance to their existence as a community, as a people, and given the indecision regarding the sanction and support they needed to exist safely on the Trinity River, it would not be unimaginable that the people of Bucareli set fire to their own homes as a way of ensuring they would not have to return. There were no casualties reported, only the complete loss of the homes caught by the fire. As the refugees looked back to the west on their first night headed toward Nacogdoches, we can imagine that they did not look upon that orange glow of their burning village on the horizon in sadness. They looked upon it as a light shining on their freedom.

THE FLOOD

The evacuation of the largest and most vulnerable part of the population before the fire was timely. Bucareli's end would not come from only one disastrous event. Two weeks later, as heavy rains fell on the night of February 14, the Trinity River left its banks with great volumes of water. The torrents flooded both sides of the river and inundated what remained of the village of Bucareli. In 1775, the group's primary plantings had been on the east side of the Trinity when they were flooded. However, the settlement itself did not flood that year, because the west side elevation was higher than the east.[97] This time everything was gone, taken away by the unstoppable flow of the mighty river. It could not be said that such a disaster was completely unexpected, as Father Juan Agustin Morfi later reported.

> The town of Nuestra Señora del Pilar de Bucareli, located on the margins of the beautiful Trinity River, must [now] be excluded from among the number of our possessions, because those residents having selected for its site a place exposed to the floods, there being within sight other admirable ones [sites].[98]

As the water left its banks it sought the lowest points, forming chest-deep pools that finally surrounded the people who remained. The overflow happened so quickly that those who had stayed behind had to float themselves out in the darkness on planks of wood from the remaining homes until they could make their way to the nearest high ground. What remained of Nicholas de La Mathe's horses were almost all drowned. Only a few horses, cattle, and domestic animals were saved.[99]

Father Garza reported that the river was two leagues wide (five miles) at Paso Tomás.[100] That measurement is roughly equivalent to the width of the second flood plain visible in current maps of the region. With the swollen and rushing Trinity River between the inundated village and their friends and family to the east, the survivors found high ground farther to the west side of the Trinity River "coming out to the highest ground for a long distance."[101] Elevations measured on the hills to the east of Bedias Creek range from 162 feet above mean sea level to just above two hundred feet. Even today, with the dam at Lake Livingston controlling the flow, current landowners report flooding can continue for up to a month, fed by flooding rains far upstream.

The indignities of the survivors did not end with their soggy escape. They were stranded on the west side of the Trinity, opposite their families in Nacogdoches and without food and supplies of any kind. Within a few days the feared Comanche reappeared, surrounding the camp where Ibarvo, members of his family, and others found themselves without defenses. What sense of mercy overtook the Indians is unclear. Perhaps they recognized Ibarvo or empathized with the group's fear and total helplessness. Whatever the reason, they left the huddled survivors alone. Instead, at sunrise on the following morning, the Comanche took all thirty-eight horses that had been spared from the flooded prairies.[102]

After the standoff, Ibarvo said the group remained on their high ground in a vulnerable position another seven or eight days before making it across the Trinity floodplain to the east side. It took another two days to get to a village of the Tejas Indians on the Angelina, with the old mission of Nacogdoches only three leagues (7.5 miles) past the village. Blake believed that the groups "traveled northeast from *Paso Tomás* along the old Bidias [Bedias] road to the Don Joaquín pass [Procella crossing] on the Angelina River, ten miles south of Nacogdoches, then turning north into the old mission."[103] The wandering Adaeseños, the unwilling Béxareños, the hopeful vecinos of Bucareli, were finally reunited at the former mission in Nacogdoches.

WITHOUT NEWS

The aftermath of the flooding at Bucareli was later observed by El Mocho, the much-despised chief with considerable survival skills, who reported what he saw to Athanase de Mézières.[104] El Mocho had been encouraged to submit himself to Ibarvo and accept the wishes of Spanish officials to make peace, settle in harmony, and cultivate crops. When he went to the Trinity River to start that conversation, he found "the settlement in silence, the houses empty, the artillery drawn to the bank of the river, and the stock scattered."

At the time of his February 11, 1779 letter to Croix, Governor Cabello had to admit that he found himself "without news of the total departure of the Captain Gil Ibarvo, nor the place fixed where he is situated."[105] Cabello lost confidence in any of the reports coming from eastern Texas and secretly hired Nicholas de La Mathe, Ibarvo's fellow trader and the benefactor who built the Bucareli chapel, to let Cabello know where Ibarvo and the citizens had gone. The people of Bucareli had vanished to Spanish officialdom.

Ibarvo had resigned his post before the second Comanche raid. In the chaos that ensued in the final months of 1778, he had no way of knowing that his request had already been denied. Antonio Gil Ibarvo was at the forefront of the future of Spanish East Texas, even more firmly and authoritatively than before.[106]

8

Color Quebrado, the Broken Color of Nacogdoches

> His [Ibarvo's] rank according to color, manner, and the opinion of the majority, he is Spanish-Indian [mestizo].
>
> —MANUEL GASPAR DE VERAZADI[1]

In a 1935 article by Karle Wilson Baker, as poetic as it is factual, she imagined that, given the thousands of years of off-and-on occupation of the hilltop between the creeks in Nacogdoches, it had never really been completely abandoned. Her thought was that the "main body of the population surged back and forth between Louisiana and Mexico in successive waves; but always somebody clung to the place, if only a dozen refugees hiding in the woods."[2]

It is not possible to know exactly what Ibarvo and the Adaeseños found when they evacuated Bucareli in favor of the "old and ruinous mission of Nuestra Señora de Guadalupe" at Nacogdoches.[3] Spanish Nacogdoches had been a fixture on the borderlands for over seventy years when Antonio Gil Ibarvo, Father de la Garza, and the scattered Adaeseños crossed Bonita Creek to the hilltop where the former mission was established by Domingo Ramón in 1716. It had been neglected for many years prior, so the conditions at the old mission were well known before the return of the Adaeseños. The ancient mounds of an earlier Caddo people were still prominent near Bayou La Nana to the east. The mission had been officially abandoned for six years—all the settlements and missions across East Texas were shut down in 1773 at the same time as Los Adaes. The mission site was familiar to many in the group since there was regular travel between Nacogdoches and Bucareli, even if only in passing through on trading expeditions to Natchitoches. Ibarvo's family maintained his ranch at El Lobanillo, and smuggling traffic continued unabated, so he had no doubt traveled there on multiple occasions.

On the way out of Los Adaes during their forced abandonment, two families, at least nine people, stayed behind in Nacogdoches and did not continue with the others to Béxar. One source reported that this was a request of the Caddo chief, Bigotes. Another report by a Spanish official suggested they may have been held hostage to try and convince the Spanish to remain in East Texas.[4] There is nothing to suggest Nacogdoches was ever completely abandoned after the mission was closed, just that it was not occupied with official consent between 1773 and 1779.

The people formerly of Los Adaes and Bucareli were in Nacogdoches hoping to remake their lives in the borderlands. They staggered in over weeks after the flooding, reuniting with their families and comforting the ill who made their way in company with the priest. Without many possessions, without stock or seeds or cultivated fields, they were vulnerable and desperate. One observer described them as being "dispersed among the heathen, carrying their meager goods and exchanging their clothing for food and hunger for nakedness."[5] So began the reoccupation of Nacogdoches; so began *las primeras familias de Nacogdoches*—the first families of Nacogdoches. Their relocation was a violation of long-held practices by the Spanish hierarchy.

Another Unapproved Location

In the five years during which Bucareli was settled, there had yet to be an official and final acceptance of its placement. At the time of the flood that led to its abandonment, there were still questions about whether it would continue with any sanction. The official uncertainty around Bucareli's legitimacy hung over it like a shadow but never seemed to interrupt the determination of its new residents. Now the Adaeseños had moved even farther from Béxar and closer to Natchitoches at a location that would inspire a new round of scrutiny.

There was little official concern for the welfare of the people who made up the settlement. The insensitivity and disdain for the people of Bucareli was revealed when one official said they were "concerned more for their own safety and convenience than for the well-being of the province."[6] Such behavior is exactly what one would expect from people in danger on the edges of the province. The authoritative and callous response implied their drive for survival was an absence of loyalty to the crown. The failure to understand that critical difference fueled the failures of the empire to control contraband trade. The authorities simply did not understand or appreciate the human factors involved with life in the borderlands.

Both Father de la Garza and Father Botello defended the newest location to Governor Cabello and pointed out the advantages to having a pueblo at the former mission site. The hilltop between two flowing creeks was well out of any floodplain and provided a consistent source of water. Fields that had been partially cleared for farming by mission Indians allowed a faster restart to cultivating crops. One of the regional features that would become significant over time was that the area was well suited for raising cattle, not just on the later, expansive rancherias, but in the woods, creek bottoms, and small prairies scattered around many springs and streams.[7]

Ibarvo added his own politically savvy commentary to promote the Adaeseños resettlement when he pointed out that the old mission chapel was already in place, allowing for the faithful to receive the sacrament without delay. Getting support from the church for their relocation was almost as important as approval by the government, and his ability to assuage those in higher authority helped ensure that message was clear.

Church Inventory Withheld

During the early months of the Adaeseños' move to Nacogdoches, Governor Ripperdá was still closing his office in Béxar on his way to his next assignment. He discovered a box that had been in his possession for six years—the remaining inventory of the chapel at the presidio of Los Adaes. He found that much of it was unserviceable. A chasuble—a sleeveless vestment of Chinese damask trimmed in gold lace—had been eaten by moths. The altar cloth and curtains suffered a similar destruction. Only the silver images and vessels were salvageable despite their damaged condition. Though the entire lot was in terrible condition, Ripperdá chose to retain the items until a final decision about the new settlement in Nacogdoches was made.[8]

Cabello Supportive

Governor Cabello, following Ripperdá in that role, tended to agree with those who supported Nacogdoches again becoming an ongoing Spanish settlement in East Texas. His March 1779 report was nine months after the request to produce it. Cabello said it was his predecessor Governor Ripperdá, not Antonio Gil Ibarvo, who insisted on the site at the Trinity despite the indications that it was unsuitable as a place for permanent residence. Cabello's conclusion gained credibility since he relied on an apparently full and frank discussion of affairs with the exiting Governor Ripperdá himself.[9] The standard list of advantages for the location of Bucareli was again itemized for Croix. The same could be true of Nacogdoches, Cabello added, saying, "The advantages which

I have explained as resulting from the settlement of Bucareli can also accrue from the place where the people of that vicinity may have become established and situated."[10] As before, Cabello pointed to a measurable weakness of the militia, both due to the distance from Béxar and the makeup of the population. A 1777 census of Bucareli counted only 125 men. Cabello recognized that was insufficient for the defense of the settlement but did not offer a solution. He only called attention to the military helplessness, something Ibarvo had been doing for years.

By mid-May 1779, Commandant General Croix had still not received Cabello's report and chastised him for that omission. Even without Cabello's input, letters to Croix from Ibarvo and the two priests who served Bucareli convinced Croix of the merits of their abandonment of the Trinity River settlement. Croix wrote that the information he gathered "prove the miserable, critical situation of its faithful, defenseless citizens, the cruelties with which the Comanches have committed hostilities, and finally that, in order not to be victims of this barbarous enemy, they rose to abandon their homes, seeking asylum among the friendly nations."[11]

While waiting for an official sanction for the resettlement of Nacogdoches, Ibarvo behaved as if gaining consent was the only possible outcome. Only two months after their escape from the flooded Trinity, Ibarvo put his son-in-law in charge of El Lobanillo, so that his attention and energy could be focused on Nacogdoches.[12] It seemed that both duty and opportunity called for it.

The Final Days of Athanase De Mézières

Croix's decision was just as Ibarvo expected—the Adaeseños could remain in Nacogdoches. He made that decision despite the impassioned letters of Athanase de Mézières strongly urging the Adaeseños return to the Trinity River. De Mézières was blunt and direct in his assessment of the abandonment of Bucareli. Considering his age and life experiences, he had little reason to withhold an opinion. As Spain's primary intermediary with the more hostile Native American nations to the north of Nacogdoches, his credibility was unquestioned but his motives were sometimes hard to discern. De Mézières's opposition to the move from Bucareli and the Trinity River to Nacogdoches could be interpreted as being based on his self-interests related to trade. Nacogdoches was clearly more practically situated to carry on contraband trade to the east, creating a potential competitor. He may have sensed there was a shift in the economic balance of cooperation and trade at play in the Texas-Louisiana borderlands that would work to his detriment.

A Frenchman as Governor of a Spanish Province?

De Mézières wrote a letter to Croix following the Frenchman's visits with Ibarvo to the villages of tribal trading partners. It represents a notable and exceptional example of De Mézières's unique perspective on the pitfalls and opportunities of Spanish rule in East Texas.[13] De Mézières ably described the boundary of the province to the north as "unknown regions," inhabited by tribes known to few other than the Tattooed Captain himself. His descriptions of the land were filled with the poetic approval of a man who had spent many days traveling its vastness and many nights under its starry expanse, leading him to say that "the serenity of the night matches that of the day." The sun was not extreme but dispensed "the soft influences which animate nature." The moisture in the dew served to "fructify the land," and somehow Texas even seemed exempt from earthquakes and epidemics in his eyes, despite his earlier personal tragedies with disease. De Mézières called attention to the natural resources, the extensive coastline, and the opportunities for trading relationships as distinct advantages to be found in Spanish Texas.

Croix's reply was laced with adjectives of praise for de Mézières's effort and exacting clarity. The commandant's admiration was not without purpose, however. As Ripperdá was preparing to leave Texas, Croix instructed de Mézières to immediately return to Béxar so he could relieve Baron de Ripperdá of the governorship of Texas. The French trader from Natchitoches was being called upon to become the interim governor of Spanish Texas.[14]

De Mézières reviewed all the opportunities for Texas as a preamble to his diatribe of disbelief that Spain was squandering it all. He chastised Croix and Spain for their failure to recognize and appropriate all the assets of provincial Texas. De Mézières explained that the local tribes Spain worked so hard to cultivate as friends and defenders were unhappy with the abandonment of Bucareli.[15]

De Mézières's admonitions came shortly after a serious fall from his horse in May or June of 1779 that caused a three-month recuperation back at his home in Natchitoches. In October 1779, de Mézières arrived in Béxar with goods from Louisiana for distribution to the Indians. Despite Ibarvo's appointment as the lone authority in charge of trade across East Texas, de Mézières reportedly bypassed the new village of Nacogdoches on his route to Béxar. The goods he delivered included hatchets, axes, knives, and hoes, as well as personal items like combs, blue cloth, shirts without ruffles, and glass beads of all colors. Unsurprisingly, the goods for trade also included eighteen bundles of tobacco.[16] Although Croix had instructed Cabello to pay de Mézières three thousand pesos on his arrival, he had not instructed Cabello on what to do with the goods, so the property was held securely while awaiting instructions.[17] Eighteen rifles, eighty-one pounds of gunpowder, and 172 pounds of rifle shot would have been among the most valued items among the trade goods held for the Indians.

This would be de Mézières's last trip through East Texas, his last chance to experience the beauty he so clearly admired. His delivery of goods ended with his death in Béxar on November 2, 1779.[18]

Consent for Nacogdoches?

Although the resettlement of Nacogdoches had not been officially approved by the government, it still gained sanction through a series of administrative actions that supported its continued existence. In October 1779, Ibarvo was appointed as captain of the militia and lieutenant governor for Nacogdoches. A salary for those positions was not approved until March the following year.[19] Ibarvo took one of his first official actions in that role when he reported on the activities of the native tribes around Nacogdoches. In May 1779, he relayed that the Tonkawa were becoming uncooperative because no Spanish traders were dedicated to their tribe. Ibarvo's recommendation to keep the peace was to establish a trading post in Nacogdoches. This would not only address the concerns of his Indian neighbors, but it would also lay the groundwork for the official, and unofficial, movement of goods through East Texas.[20] It would also likely provide cover for his unsanctioned trade across the Sabine River.

One of the final hurdles to getting Nacogdoches officially recognized was part political theater and part political survival. In this regard, it was not unlike the process surrounding the permissions the Adaeseños sought to move to Bucareli. Croix assigned a man named Pedro Galindo Navarro to provide a full and complete report on the circumstances leading up to the settlement at Bucareli and Nacogdoches. Navarro took his job seriously, reviewed all the documents and *expedientes*, and produced a thirteen-page report that was thorough, direct, and detailed.[21]

Navarro rewound the story of the Adaeseños all the way back to the September 10, 1772, edict that led to the abandonment of Los Adaes and the East Texas missions. He summarized all the prior actions and replayed the previous arguments on both sides of the issues. Navarro ultimately came to the same conclusion that others in similar appointments made—the residents should be forced to follow the regulations set out in 1772 and return to Béxar as originally ordered. He left some room for adjustment, however. If Béxar was not practical, they could go to the San Marcos River where there was much land and suitable conditions for them to settle.

After arguing for that conclusion, Navarro immediately qualified and altered it. He commented at some length about the risks of abandoning a Spanish presence among the Indians in the region. Navarro raised the concern that they could "take offence and band together to commit hostilities against the province." Navarro found an opportunity to be correct in his recommendations no matter which choice was made. To satisfy Croix's concerns, Navarro urged him to require Governor Cabello to make a personal inspection and visit the tribes himself, something he had not yet done.

Croix followed this recommendation and asked Governor Cabello to go to Nacogdoches and make the decision on its final fate. In East Texas parlance these days, one might describe the governor's response to Croix as "crawfishing"—moving backwards as fast as he could. Cabello immediately recognized the weight of the decision he was being asked to make and understood that no matter what he did someone would find fault with it.[22] Cabello first pointed out that his health prevented his effort in this regard. He had dislocated his shoulder, and he said he was suffering in pain because "the lack of any kind of assistance for its cure make[s] me unable in this wretched land to obtain any relief."

After offering the excuse, in the writing style of the times, Cabello demonstrated his servitude. He told Croix that despite his health he was willing to make a personal sacrifice in the "long and painful journey required" with no money and no assistance. In a separate reply, Cabello suggested he could instead require a "person knowledgeable in cosmography or geography [i.e., an engineer or surveyor] who could determine and choose an adequate and suitable site in which to locate and establish the aforesaid settlement."[23] He expressed his "vexation" at the thought of having to decide about the settlement on his own. Croix dismissed Cabello's idea due to the scarcity of that expertise and the distance that would be required to send that type of resource to Nacogdoches.[24] Despite Cabello's urging for technical assistance, this was not a geographical decision.

Cabello's complaints about the difficulty of the assignment were largely a smoke screen. What he really wanted to avoid was blame. Cabello was not about to wade into that trap. He knew the pitfalls all too well.

> [I know] how many intrigues occurred so as to obstruct its [Bucareli's] first establishment. Nor am I unaware of the motives voiced against its relocation. But the time will never come when my pure motives and good methods of procedure may be impugned."

Cabello tried apologizing for his limitations, making sure the commandant general knew he was just "a poor soldier [who] can do little more than substantiate events," and that he has no expert authority on whom he can rely "in the unspeakable and inexpressible wretchedness of this station [Béxar]."[25]

If anything like an official consent was granted for Nacogdoches it is not apparent from the records. With the demonstrable and practical need for what Ibarvo and Nacogdoches provided the province, the cover of an official report by Navarro, and Cabello's inaction, the resettlement of Nacogdoches continued and its pivotal role in the history of Texas fully began. As Bolton noted, "There was no one else [other than Ibarvo] who could wield such an influence among the Indians and do so much towards keeping them quiet."[26] For dozens of tribes, Antonio Gil Ibarvo was Spain in the flesh.

A People of Broken Color

The first families of Nacogdoches were the last families of Los Adaes and the refugees of Bucareli. With the move to Nacogdoches, it became their fourth home in only six years.[27] Their home in Los Adaes had been *extinguido* (extinguished); in Béxar they were not fully accepted as subjects of the crown; and their settlement at Bucareli had never quite been sanctioned before it was destroyed and abandoned. These same people found themselves living once again with an uncertain sanction in Nacogdoches. For a time, the Spanish government did not even know where the people of Bucareli had gone. History barely remembers the first citizens of the reestablished village of Nacogdoches.

Marriage Between the Castes

When Spain sought to solidify its empire in medieval Europe, its efforts to purge non-Christian Moors and Jewish people relied on a policy to preserve *limpieza de sangre*, the purity of blood. In the beginning of their moves to the Americas, there was an expectation the Spanish would somehow remain separate from the native and indigenous people.[28] Few females made the journey across the Pacific, however, and there was little prospect that Spanish desires for ethnic purity could withstand the forces of conjugal desire. The Spanish response to this cultural mixing was to classify the offspring as a defined mixture of races, creating new names for the various combinations and establishing a system of castes to install a hierarchy of acceptance and privilege around each of them.

The castes most often seen in reports from New Spain were *espanoles, mestizo*, mulatto, *coyote, lobo, indios,* and *negro. Mestizos* were the result of a union between Spanish and Indian, and mulatto the combination of Spanish and *negro* or African. *Lobo* was typically a union of a Black man and a Native American woman, while a *coyote* was a *mestizo* and Indian. The population of the resettled village also included enslaved people who had escaped from Louisiana and "useless vagabonds" with minimal skills who had worn out their welcome in Béxar. When everyday life includes people from many different nations, racial mixes, cultural backgrounds, and family affinities, it is no surprise that the makeup of Nacogdoches families mirrored that diversity. The people of Nacogdoches were a mix of races, ethnic backgrounds, and cultures formed by their lives in the borderlands, where people of all backgrounds came together in the name of trade.

The informal report by Ibarvo in 1777 stated there were about four hundred people in Bucareli, including fifteen enslaved people. He noted the ethnic classification only for the head of the household, but out of 130 households, only sixty-two were recorded as Spanish. The balance included 13 Indians, one *mestizo*, five *negros*, and forty-nine other colored groups, as defined by the census. In a later census of early Nacogdoches, one finds Spaniards married to Indians, an Apache married to a mulatto, and a Mayeye Indian married to a *loba*, along with a population of *indios*, *negros*, and mulattos.[29] Looking across additional years of marriage records for Spanish Nacogdoches, one historian found that 54 percent were across caste lines.[30]

Caste assignments were not always a fixed and inescapable assignment in New Spain. One's caste ranking could be fluid, particularly in the outer reaches of the province, allowing one to move up the hierarchy. Caste could also depend on who was doing the designation, and Antonio Gil Ibarvo is a prime example. There is general acceptance that Ibarvo's parents were from the part of Spain known as Andalucía. As a result, the 1792 Nacogdoches census noted he was *español* (Spaniard). It should be noted that was a census Ibarvo conducted himself. However, interracial marriages between Andalusians and North Africans often took place, so it left him open to later disparagement. Ibarvo was alleged to be mulatto in 1788; an official in 1791 claimed most saw him as *mestizo*; and by 1793, an officer simply left his ethnicity blank, as if it simply no longer mattered.[31]

A racial designation assigned to some during the census counts was *color quebrado*, which literally translates as broken color. It may be that was the best way to think of Nacogdoches and the borderlands settlements that grew out of the ethnic mix of people congregating on both sides of the Sabine River. Broken did not imply unfixable or unredeemable, it meant there was such a mix of ethnic blending that they lost track. It meant that the ability to document and record people's racial mix had broken, not the people themselves.

A depiction of the castes, or "Las Castas." Artist unknown. Courtesy National Museum of the Viceroyalty, Tepotzotlan, Mexico.

In the province of Texas, distance from the rigidity of Mexico City allowed priests to perform the sacrament of marriage without undue regard to the couple's backgrounds.[32] It was this mix of people and cultures, bound together by a life distant from the bureaucratic controls of Spanish rule, which became the founding families of the reestablished Nacogdoches.

By 1792 enough time had passed since the move from the Trinity River that some of the marriage records identified one of the betrothed as a "native of Bucareli." It is interesting to note that many of the matches among these people, who'd lived their entire lives in the borderlands, reflected the trading trails of the *contrabandistas*. Marriages in Nacogdoches included combinations of people of Los Adaes and Béxar, Los Adaes and Natchitoches, Los Adaes and New Orleans, Orcoquisac and Bucareli, and a Frenchman born in Paris married to a half-caste. These pairings attest to how opportunities for travel across the borderlands and the resulting contraband trade influenced the formation of families in Nacogdoches.[33]

New Homes, New Way of Life

Moving four hundred people to an abandoned mission village meant that there was again much work to do. Much of what the group acquired in Bucareli was burned or washed away by the floodwaters of the Trinity River. What they learned from building jacales and palisades at Bucareli was perhaps made easier by moving away from the prairieland into the forests of Nacogdoches. The materials for their small houses, typically only one room, were readily available. The soft rock Ibarvo used to build his stone house some years later was not initially used widely for other construction, but it was later found in the foundations for half-timbered cabins built over time.

The easiest and most productive land to farm was in the creek bottoms, but that also made it susceptible to occasional flooding that could destroy crops. Corn was the primary produce. Cattle, bear, deer, and the occasional bison provided ready sources of meat. Dove, quail, ducks, turkey, squirrels, and rabbits were more abundant. In the land around the pueblo, they could find "wild grapes, Indian peaches, blackberries, pomegranates, and melons." Nuts like walnut, hickory, pecan, and chinquapin were also seasonally available as part of the settlers' diet.[34]

Despite the minimal sanction for their presence in Nacogdoches and the desire of some to force them back to Béxar, the Adaeseños outlasted the resistance. The resettlement of Nacogdoches began a separation of sorts, an apartness that benefited Nacogdoches and vexed Spanish officials.

Ibarvo the Charitable Leader

In looking back on their first days in Nacogdoches, Father de la Garza credited Antonio Gil Ibarvo with leadership and compassion. The priest saw firsthand the good deeds of Ibarvo both in Bucareli and in Nacogdoches. The priest was effusive in reporting that "there was no other man in all these [lands with] more boldness, more honesty, move loving of the country, nor more interested in the well-being of his countrymen than Don Antonio Gil Ybarvo [Ibarvo]."[35] Ibarvo was credited with providing labor by his children and his servants to build a new chapel. He sweated with the people to clear fields and build fences. He loaned tools, seed, and oxen that had presumably been kept at El Lobanillo. Father de la Garza said Ibarvo's caring even extended to setting aside a room in his house for the sick, and occasionally for the insane, to recover from their troubles.[36]

The Adaeseños had been expelled from their homes in Los Adaes. They had resisted commands to live in Béxar and made their appeal to the highest authorities in Mexico City. At their cost and at their peril, they made a new home on the Trinity River at Bucareli. Fear of the Comanche, a fire, and a flood chased them farther from Spanish rule but nearer an enduring home with more safety and security. In Nacogdoches, perhaps the Adaeseños finally began to feel they were home again. They were closer to the ties that remained back in Natchitoches and Louisiana, and within the territory of friendly tribal trading partners. Their ability to regain control of their lives seemed more present and attainable.

The people of broken color had a new home.

9

La Mordida, Contraband and Culture in Early Nacogdoches

> You have nothing to fear, because Don Francisco Ardila
> has assured me that we would run no risk in
> transporting it [tobacco] to Nacogdoches.
>
> —LUIS GRANDE[1]

Martín de Alarcón was on a desperate assignment when he made his way from Mexico to East Texas in the summer of 1718 to resupply the new missions with food, clothing, and the necessary items for bringing religion to the indigenous people. Supplies that had been on their way to the missions earlier that year were undelivered due to flooding at the Trinity River, so soldiers hid the goods in hopes of delivering them later. Alarcón collected the hidden items and, along with goods he brought from Mexico, delivered much-needed supplies to people who had to make do without for so long.

Alarcón also had a secondary purpose for his journey. He had an obligation to reduce the flow of contraband goods into the province, a perpetual assignment for anyone accountable to the crown. Indications of how difficult that assignment would become quickly became evident. At one of the missions, Alarcón confiscated what were clearly French-made goods, including some splendid cloth, brocade trim with gold embellishments, and about two hundred pieces of fine lace. The goods were largely personal objects of borderlands finery. The unlicensed goods he impounded were like others found on lists in Spanish archives, but there was one item that triggers a series of questions history cannot fully answer.

In the name of the crown, in the wilderness of East Texas in 1718, Martín de Alarcón seized twenty-four pairs of blue stockings.

What were the stockings doing there? Who in the world would be wearing blue stockings in the summer of 1718 in Spanish East Texas? The images the confiscated stockings inspire are both curious and somewhat comical. Of all the practical items available from French traders like guns and cookware, blue stockings were on someone's wish list. In examining these kinds of questions, answers emerge from the patterns of borderlands trade. The nature of trade in prohibited items in Spanish East Texas was a very personal endeavor. Traffic in items deemed illicit by Spanish authorities were largely those either necessary for everyday living in the borderlands or finery that helped one forget that harsh reality.

The Spanish prohibition on trade across the Sabine River made no sense to people who lived in the borderlands. The suspicions, stubbornness, and petty rules of the Spanish government led to conditions that made it difficult to obtain goods people wanted to help make life more bearable.[2] In 1778, one list of confiscated goods included playing cards, sewing patterns for trousers, handkerchiefs, scissors, salt, and, oddly, ten door escutcheons, which are the decorative plates behind a doorknob.[3] Items of simple pleasure were almost always found among the wares of the *contrabandistas*. Those in charge typically presented the appearance of enforcing the Spanish restrictions, but just as often they were involved in the smuggling themselves. Trade benefitted many people and for it to be prohibited by a distant authority just meant that every now and then a competitor or someone who was not well liked might get arrested and sent to Béxar. Most of the time the goods simply flowed.

Contraband goods moving from the French to the tribal groups of the province included weapons, ammunition, and other items clearly troublesome for the Spanish. Fears and concerns over armed Native Americans turning against the Spanish were a constant reminder that Spain occupied the land of others. More often found on trade lists were goods of personal finery and private pleasures: scissors, dinnerware, bolts of cloth, tobacco, and playing cards. A recent translation of an inventory of goods held by the colonel in charge of the Presidio San Antonio de Béxar in 1760 points to the sheer volume and diversity of goods in the province, both for trade with the natives or to simply supply the troops and citizens. That list included cloth and linen of various materials and colors, red capes, fine china, silver ornamentation for clothing, tobacco, and whiskey. This single list includes 432 separate inventory items. These kinds of goods had real value in a frontier economy because they were also objects that brought comfort to a people far from any other form of civilization.[4]

Another example of the personal nature of the contraband trade involved a poorly equipped Spanish soldier. While visiting Nacogdoches, he was caught up in an investigation of the contraband goods that he and his fellow soldiers, including their captain, were taking back to Béxar. When asked what he traded for the bolt of cloth he was taking home to his sweetheart, the soldier said he traded the bridle off his horse and his breakfast biscuit. This poor soldier was willing to ride back to Béxar without food in his stomach or a bridle for his horse, and to risk arrest, simply to please his lady.[5]

Spanish dictates and edicts never seemed to consider this simple aspect of human nature. Whether for this soldier, or for the Indian chief or priest who wished to strut their fine blue stockings proudly, the real story of contraband trade is personal. Prohibited trade after Nacogdoches was resettled in 1779 certainly included arms, horses, and other items of value and purpose, but personal items of clothing and embellishment also found their way into East Texas. Even people living at the distant edge of colonial Spain wanted to look and live as well as they could. That fact of human nature is what made Nacogdoches the hub of contraband trade for the region.

On the Nature of Contraband

Obedezco, pero no cumplo. I obey, but I do not comply.

This was a commonly used expression among those who were being asked or ordered to do something with which they did not agree. Brian Stauffer, a Spanish translator for the Texas General Land Office, suggests the phrase essentially meant, "I recognize your authority over me, but I do not comply with your order because it does not make sense."[6] To fully understand this period of East Texas history, it is important to have a perspective on contraband trade that takes into account this form of noncompliance in the borderlands.

One academic definition of smuggling is "the illegal movement of goods across national boundaries to evade payment of taxes."[7] In general terms, that definition is instructive but not enlightening. Along the borderlands during this period of East Texas history, contraband trade was more about meeting the personal needs of people distant from the source of goods. The baseline of smuggling and contraband is a combination of scarcity, need, and a willingness to take a risk, but the essence of it was a very personal and transactional activity.

Spanish colonial authorities insisted on a trade policy known as mercantilism which required trade to occur only within their colonies and with strict limits and restrictions. They sought to maintain a system of passports, permits, and taxes for the benefit of the crown. One author called it "a restrictive, suicidal commercial policy" that led to a waste of the resources and abundance that was found in Texas.[8] Royal edicts could have only a limited impact on human behavior, particularly when that authority was hundreds of miles distant. The impractical expectation of Spanish authorities was that the acquisition of goods for East Texas would be focused on Mexico City and not on the simpler and more direct source only a few miles east across the Sabine River.

Goods were defined as illegal simply because the king had declared it so. Bob Skiles, the historian and former archeologist, notes there was widespread speculation about the reasons for those proclamations, both then and now. Part of the naivete of the Spanish authorities was that they somehow seemed to believe their pronouncements alone could create a change. Provincial governors on more than one occasion lamented their inability to exercise authority in the region. A governor in 1792 said that "the intervening distance between this capital [San Antonio] and Nacogdoches . . . retards the news and the receipt of requested documents." His words seem to suggest that if only his orders had reached their destination that compliance would follow. In 1779, Commandant General Croix expressed his frustration a bit more realistically in saying, "the distances [to Nacogdoches] greatly retard the usefulness of [my] determinations."[9]

It must be considered whether key officials made their decisions for a higher purpose like protecting Spain's sovereignty and right to rule, or simply for personal financial benefit. It is likely that royal underlings charged with extending Spain's contraband policies into East Texas received *la mordida*—a bite of the action.

The location of Nacogdoches and its proximity to French influences in Louisiana created an ideal environment for trade. Whether the people involved were Spanish subjects, tribal neighbors, or the many from other nations flowing in and out of the region, illicit trade was simply the commerce of the day. Nacogdoches was well beyond the reach of any effort to stem the flow of goods from French traders in Louisiana. This made the normalization of trade that the Spanish government defined as contraband much easier to carry on.

Modern Examples of Contraband

In the modern era, the word contraband conjures up images of masked raiders or vast criminal enterprises. In 2020, Texas Department of Public Safety troopers executed a traffic stop of a semi-trailer truck in South Texas. The shipping manifest said it carried used clothes, toys, and purses for delivery to Mexico. In fact, it contained 17 million cigarettes that lacked the required tax stamp. Many of the cigarettes were among brands banned even in Mexico for health reasons. When the investigation led to warehouses in Hidalgo and

McAllen, another 422 million cigarettes were seized at a value of $88 million. The operation involved parties in Mexico and Panama, and it ultimately led back to the world's largest cigarette company in China.[10]

George T. Díaz, whose research focuses on the history of smuggling across the Rio Grande, tells a story that highlights the personal nature of trade.[11] When he was growing up in South Texas, his mother pointed out empty cardboard boxes that littered the approach to the border crossing from the United States to Mexico. The box labels indicated they had contained electronics goods like stereos and radios. By removing the newly purchased items from their boxes and carrying them across the border in the open, people from Mexico could simply tell the border guards they were personal items brought with them to the United States. Otherwise, the goods would have been taxed on the Mexican side.

A boom box becoming contraband is the modern equivalent of the smuggling of cloth, dresses, and other personal embellishments that took place in Spanish East Texas. It was a simple act for one's personal benefit. Despite both acts being against the law, few considered their shopping behaviors to be criminal activity.

Actors in the Contraband Trade

The efforts to prevent banned trade focused on several distinct groups of people who might find themselves among those punished for their smuggling. The fact that smuggling was so prevalent meant that "ordinary people rarely saw smuggling as a morally repugnant or particularly severe crime." However, if smugglers on a broader scale tried to take advantage of their customers, they would find themselves as the objects of derision by the populace. The crimes of these smugglers might be overlooked for a time, but when their illegality became immoral in the eyes of the people affected, an interruption of their services could result.[12]

The second group subject to arrest were those who were poor and not well-connected, who only engaged in smuggling as a means of generating a livelihood. Provincial authorities would sometimes prosecute them simply to make an example and to show the authorities in Mexico City that an effort was being made.[13] If the *vecinos* tried to evade the system or violate the unwritten rules, they could find themselves at odds with the more powerful who had their own interests in the contraband trade. Additionally, there were the complicit Spanish officials at all levels who were engaged in the logistics of contraband either by looking the other way or being a beneficiary of the trade. As researcher Bob Skiles observed:

> The military governor in Texas was often the ringleader of the contraband trade, in the same manner as a capo of La Costa Nostra. The system was so developed at times that revenue (bribes) found its way back to the coffers of high officialdom in Mexico City, although these revenues were meticulously kept off the king's books.[14]

In 1751, Jacinto de Barrios y Jáuregui, a governor of the province in Los Adaes, supplied goods from Louisiana to four traders destined for Native American villages along the lower Trinity River, likely Bidai or Atakapan. The arms, knives, and scissors among their trade goods were exchanged for horses that were often stolen from other Spanish settlements.[15]

Another group deeply involved in the clandestine trade, and the ones getting the most attention, were non-Spanish competitors, French and English typically, who illegally crossed the border to trade with Spanish subjects and with Indian tribes of the region. These groups were alternately viewed as precursors of an invading force, unlicensed competition, or simply an undesirable class of traders.

The French had a demonstrable advantage in trade relationships. Their understanding of kinship and their personal efforts at building and maintaining relationships were an aspect of their trade behavior that the Spanish never quite seemed to figure out. One contemporaneous observer of this characteristic asked, "What room is there for doubt that the French are pleasing to the Indians?" He recognized that while others might try to base trade relationships on power or control, the "Frenchman will take off his shirt to give to them [Indians] and hold them to allegiance."[16]

Formalizing the Unmarked Boundary

Though the loss of tax revenue when goods were smuggled into the province was troubling to the crown, authorities were also concerned about intrusions by way of the ill-defined borders. When Spanish Texas and French Louisiana were separated only by an informal and unmarked boundary, Spanish fears of invasions from the east were magnified the farther one was from that space.

The residents of Los Adaes and Natchitoches had worked out a rather cozy arrangement for peaceful and gainful coexistence. The close cooperation between the people of the two villages led one writer of that period looking back over the earlier history to write, "There being no precedents, there never having been a boundary between these two provinces, [and because there was such a] small population in these adjacent places, there was never any reason for discussion about it [meaning a boundary]."[17] He and others understood there was simply no need for a boundary because it just did not matter to the people who lived there.

Back in Mexico City, different concerns lingered about the loss of Spanish territory to an invasion from the east. One would think that Louisiana's transfer to Spanish jurisdiction would have relieved those concerns. However, the aggressive and expansionist posture of English and Americans after the transfer kept boundary concerns alive. Spain believed that with Louisiana still populated largely by the French and their allies that some conflict or rebellion was inevitable despite them being newly acquired Spanish subjects. Spanish authorities widened the gulf of apartness between Texas and Louisiana when they divided their own governance at the blurred line between Natchitoches and Los Adaes. The control of Louisiana was led by officials in Cuba, while Texas remained part of the province governed by the viceroy in Mexico City. Louisiana went to leaders responsible for possessions to the east, and Texas remained in the western province.[18] That meant the two provinces were governed by two very distant leaders with little interest in each other's methods of administration or localized concerns. The Spanish territory that was Texas and Louisiana was still managed as if two separate and distinct countries.

Ibarvo in Nacogdoches

Ibarvo and the Adeseños who abandoned Bucareli in favor of Nacogdoches wasted no time in establishing a foothold and making a renewed engagement in trade across the Sabine. Their relocation had not been formally approved, but that did not deter them in communicating to Croix and Cabello that they believed their move would and should become accepted and permanent. The tacit acceptance of their presence nearer to Natchitoches was all they needed.

Within only a couple of months of their relocation, Ibarvo communicated to the governor that tribes who had been promised Spanish traders in their midst were becoming unsettled and impatient when they were not provided with their own emissaries. Ibarvo made a case for establishing a trading post in Nacogdoches to provide gifts and goods to help maintain the peace. Only a month following that request Ibarvo reported further Indian troubles and urged the formalization of a military presence there as well.[19]

As captain of the militia, Ibarvo was granted five hundred pesos a year and officially appointed as lieutenant governor of the Pueblo of Nacogdoches. In communication between themselves, Croix and Cabello understood that without Ibarvo established near the border there was no one else who could manage relationships with the natives of the region. Though Ibarvo was given a new and grander title, it was his influence with the Indians that allowed him to gain stature and exert control.[20] Authorization and funding for a paid contingent of local citizens to serve as a militia were finally granted. The militia's presence did more to calm fears than to quell disturbances. A budget for the payment of allowances to the men included twenty-two pesos per month for an officer, eighteen pesos for a sergeant, fifteen pesos each for two cavalrymen, and twelve pesos each for twenty privates. With those salaries the men had to pay for their own horses, arms, and munitions.[21] Such was life in the far reaches of the Spanish province.

In April 1780, only a year after the Adeseños returned to Nacogdoches, Governor Cabello recommended the appointment of Antonio Gil Ibarvo to "pursue contraband and illicit commerce" in the area surrounding Nacogdoches. For his effort, Ibarvo would receive one-fourth of the value of any confiscated goods sold at auction. Governor Cabello appointed Ibarvo as the singular authority over such trade in the distant province. In a lengthy letter making the appointment, Cabello referred to the king's 1776 *cedula* to:

> name men of the best qualifications to watch all shores along the coasts of their respective jurisdictions with the authority to confiscate such items as they might find, and by this means totally eliminate the age-old abuse of illicit commerce.[22]

With his edict, Cabello titled Ibarvo as the "delegate judge of confiscation and contraband in the district, territory, and jurisdiction of the Town of *Nuestra Señora del Pilár de Nacogdoches* [and the area from there down] to the northern seacoast." With that title came the authority to examine "trunks, boxes, suitcases, bags, packages, vehicles, ships, houses, and loads," as well as the authority to enter and inspect any settlements, haciendas, or camps he may encounter. Goods found without letters of permission would be confiscated. "Owners, carriers, sellers, concealers, and buyers involved in the importation of contraband tobacco . . . or other illicitly introduced goods" or without proper passports would be held and a legal disposition determined. Anyone leaving Nacogdoches with loads that could conceal contraband were to show them to Ibarvo to establish their legality and pay any taxes due. Ibarvo's power and authority over the region was codified.

To make sure Ibarvo's appointment was known to everyone, it was important to communicate it clearly. In our age of online acceptance and acknowledgment we might "click to accept" a notice from a website or a software provider. For Ibarvo's appointment in 1780 the governor's proclamation was to be published and read "to the sound of drums" in the public places of

Nacogdoches on three consecutive feast days to ensure that no one would miss the announcement. Ignorance of the decree would not be an excuse. Those moments when Cabello's letter was read to the populace are those where much could have been learned by looking toward the gathered crowd rather than at the *pregonero pùblico* (public town crier) loudly reading the pronouncement. What was their reaction, reflected in the looks on their faces? Did they naturally acknowledge the position and authority of Ibarvo to oversee trade, or were there winks of acknowledgement that contraband trade would continue and flourish?

To show his loyalty and good faith Ibarvo continued an approach that he used in the early years of the establishment of Bucareli—occasionally confiscating contraband and reporting it to the governor while allowing other efforts to continue. By March 1780 Ibarvo had already informed Cabello of his confiscation of:

> two petacas [trunks or cases] containing 29 manojos [bundles] of tobacco; an envelope of tobacco seed; a packet with five close textured Brittany cloths; four oreas [bolts] of printed calico; two iron azadones [hoes]; five axes; a small bag of wool; a shirt; a panuclo [handkerchief] with a bit of anise; and a small chest with nine pieces of Brittany cloth and three striped naguas [under-petticoats] cut out.[23]

Any impressions by modern readers of the word contraband meaning only something sinister or dangerous must be adjusted to its context within Spanish East Texas. Beyond the taxes avoided by smuggling tobacco this list has all the intrigue of a shopping trip to Walmart. The fate of the Spanish empire in the borderlands did not rise or fall on striped petticoats. It did, however, fly in the face of the Spanish desire to control all trade no matter what it might include.

INCIDENTS WITH OTHER TRADERS

Obedezco, pero no cumplo. Ibarvo was doing his part to honor his appointment. He had regularly reported the interception of contraband traders while at the same time conducting trade of his own. In the summer of 1786, Ibarvo threatened a Frenchman who had set up a trading post on the Neches River for trade with the Indians there. After Ibarvo's intervention, the Frenchman fled back to Louisiana.[24] In March 1788, Ibarvo was challenged as to why he issued passports to French traders to travel to Béxar and La Bahía with goods from Louisiana that were prohibited in the province. Ibarvo explained that the men arrived in Texas with permissions from Spanish officials in Louisiana and he saw no reason to override that authorization. Ibarvo's simple answer was,

"There never was any obstacle or order to the contrary."[25] Ibarvo saw Louisiana and Texas equally a part of Spanish territory, even when their respective leaders did not.

In late December 1789, Ibarvo found himself in the middle of one aspect of the contraband trade that was a constant throughout the region—the direct involvement of Spanish officials charged with preventing such trade. There were reports of traders from Natchitoches amid the Nadacos (Caddo) to the east of Nacogdoches. Through reports to Ibarvo from the tribal members themselves, he learned the traders were not only bringing goods that even the Indians knew were not permitted, but they were also "inciting them to various activities contrary to the good order, tranquility, and security of these subjects of the king." Typically, Ibarvo would have intervened, but he soon learned the traders were there with goods owned by Luis de Blanc, the commandant at Natchitoches.[26]

It was not de Blanc's first time to dabble in contraband trade on the west side of the Sabine to his own direct benefit. In 1783, before appointment to his official post, de Blanc had gone to the Kichai with goods. When Ibarvo's militia confronted him, de Blanc threatened to arrest them and send them all to Natchitoches for justice administered on his turf. Ibarvo knew there would be conflict if he arrested de Blanc and got into a dispute over his authority. de Blanc had issued charges in writing in the past, but the politically savvy Ibarvo hid the letters in the archives "in order to avoid greater disputes which could have affected, as can be imagined, the tranquility of both borders." The wisdom of not acting in this case demonstrated Ibarvo's practical adherence to maintaining control by not demanding mindless compliance.

BALANCING INDIAN RELATIONS

Whether to provide arms to the Indians or not was a continuous back-and-forth discussion between Spanish officials. Ripperdá and Bernardo de Gálvez had suggested that guns be provided but only those made from inferior steel. Their agenda was that the natives would then be dependent on them for parts and repairs.[27] The premise of this notion failed in the face of the way Native Americans cared for their firearms. Croix noted that the Indians were proud of their arms, took better care of them, and exhibited more skill with their weapons than Spanish troops.[28]

Indian relations were critical for the safety of both the people and the empire. A letter from Ibarvo alerted Cabello to complaints made by a particularly annoying and obnoxious Tonkawa chief named Mocho.[29] Mocho was a much-despised troublemaker who had tried to ally with Apache and Caddo to oust the Spanish from East Texas. Though Mocho told de Mézières that he had gone to Bucareli to make his peace with Ibarvo just after the abandonment of the village, Ibarvo seethed at how ungrateful and unpleasant Mocho was regarding the gifts offered him in Nacogdoches.

While Ibarvo focused on his own interactions with the indigenous people of the region, Cabello understood the bigger picture when it came to the importance of maintaining even a troublesome relationship with others like Mocho. Cabello told Croix he was unconcerned about such behavior by the chief, and that anyone confronted by Mocho personally should do their best "with a grateful reception, to again gratify him." Cabello understood that such a posture was necessary to maintain Spain's relations with the Indians, and that any "incidents of irreverence" toward Indians like Mocho would only lead to the loss of their presence in Texas. Cabello's ingratiating approach toward the unlikable Mocho was not based on kinship or commerce, but on the survival of the province.

> If the Tancague [Tonkawa] nation were to join forces with the Comanches and the two nations wanted [to attack us], in eight days no living or moving thing that was not of those tribes would remain in this place that is called a province.[30]

With gifts and trade with the region's tribes having such a critical role in maintaining a balance of power in East Texas, it was assured that trade, whether sanctioned or not, would continue largely unabated in East Texas.

VALUE OF GOODS IN 1782

As Nacogdoches took on the character of a place central to trade in the region, acts of commerce normalized and became more organized around Antonio Gil Ibarvo. To maintain consistency among the traders, it was important to establish expectations for the value of goods offered in trade. One of the primary currencies of exchange was deerskins. Most often they were processed into chamois, a very soft leather suitable for clothing and other goods. The finished product was highly prized in New Orleans trade. The skins' trade value is illustrated by their comparative value in bartering.[31] A light musket could be acquired in trade for thirty deerskins, and five musket balls with gunpowder for one skin. The cost of musket balls set a high standard for accuracy in shooting.

How items were comparatively valued offers further insight into the economy of the region. One bundle of tobacco, at eight deerskins, was valued the same as a large bell. Six small bells or six gunflints were equally valued at one deerskin. An axe or a hoe were each eight skins, and six skins secured a hatchet. One aspect of commerce and contraband that reflected how personal items were valued was the pricing for fashion. Four feet of raw cloth or a fine blanket were each available for twenty skins, and a shirt for eight. Adding a metal bracelet or some ribbon, at one skin each, would complete the wardrobe for a well-dressed East Texan.

Occasional mentions of the volume of this early trade appear in archival sources. Monthly reports of activity in Nacogdoches in 1804 and 1805 regularly mention the packhorses and mules with carts bound for Natchitoches to gather trade goods. Records from later trade ventures highlight the devasting volume of trade in hides that fed voracious appetites in New Orleans, the northeastern United States, and Europe. A US-sponsored factory, a type of trading post, at the mouth of the Sulphur River where it merged with the Red River shipped thirty thousand deerskins downriver to New Orleans in 1819 and 1820.[32] In 1828, General Manuel Mier y Terán inspected Mexican Nacogdoches and discovered that in only one year eighty thousand deerskins had been traded by the Indians, a level of killing that could not be sustained.[33]

Disorders of All Kinds

The village of Nacogdoches was the center of the universe at the eastern edge of the Spanish province. It was the lone focal point for Spanish civil life and commerce in the region. Nacogdoches was a magnet for people to live and to visit with trade in mind. With a growing number of people coming to Nacogdoches, there were inevitable issues with their behavior. Antonio Gil Ibarvo felt the need to bring some order to the chaos he saw developing and exert his authority when there was no other. When the earliest census was conducted in 1782, only three years after its resettlement, there were four hundred people in the environs around the main village. When Father Francisco Xavier Fragoso visited in 1788, he found eighty to ninety homes made of wood and between 200 and 250 Spanish and French citizens, likely an underestimate.[34] By 1790 there were 500, and in 1792 it was up to 555. By 1800, Nacogdoches was the second largest settlement in the province with 600 souls.

Intruders, Smugglers, and Other Undesirables

In 1789 a new viceroy rose to the post in Mexico City, the Conde de Revilla Gigedo. Known as a highly capable administrator, Revilla Gigedo wanted to make his mark just like every other Spanish official appointed to a new post. After only a few months of learning about the complexities of the eastern province he wanted a change that could have ended settlement in Spanish East Texas—again.

Revilla Gigedo believed Nacogdoches was an ideal location for illegal trade, and that it should be abandoned. He wanted to stop all communication and commerce between the provinces of Texas and Louisiana, despite it being ruled by Spain as well. His plan was to allow neither settlers nor vagabond opportunists to enter from the east. In the manner that Hugo Oconór had sought to thwart the trade by abandoning the region, Revilla Gigedo wanted to swing the pendulum of control by placing a stronger military presence on the border to force respect for Spanish rule and discourage an invasion, this time from the Americans and English rather than the French.

His proposal was never implemented, like similar notions before. The power of the present realities at the border was simply too strong. However, Revilla Gigedo's assessment of the character of some of the residents was apparently not far off.

Laying Down the Law

Since the pueblo was resettled in 1779, Ibarvo had sought to bring order to the distant settlement in a manner that was not quite in line with Spanish custom. He began distributing land grants of thousands of acres but did so without any official sanction and without land titles. His methods solved immediate problems but led to broad confusion over rightful ownership only a decade or so following. As the hub of commerce and citizenship in eastern Texas, to the extent that existed, Ibarvo was at the center of everything that transpired. His titles as captain of militias, lieutenant governor, judge delegate for contraband and seizures, and chief magistrate of the town and jurisdiction of Nacogdoches covered a lot of ground.

People of the borderlands were guided by the mores and customs they learned in their encounters with traders, Native Americans, vagabonds, deserters, and others who lived along the edges of governance. Ibarvo had been the sole source of influence and power for the people of a distant settlement who lived far from any external basis of law or authority for most of their lives. Given Ibarvo's influence and given that void, it seems only natural that Ibarvo would feel compelled to write a criminal code for a growing Nacogdoches. His approach would certainly get the attention of the rowdiest among them.

In the preamble of the criminal code Ibarvo compiled in 1783, he explained why the list of fifty-four separate offenses was needed. In the four years since they left Bucareli on the Trinity River, he saw "vices and crimes of every description progressing rapidly," and "disorders of all kinds spreading torrent-like amongst persons of both sexes."[35] As a practiced leader and keen observer of human nature, Ibarvo noted that when left unfettered mankind tended to "shake off the salutary yoke of the most sacred, just, and admirable laws." Ibarvo accepted that his fellow citizens were largely ignorant of criminal laws imposed by the crown, but he did not want any more excuses. There would be no pleas of ignorance when confronted with their transgressions.

Taking the time to become knowledgeable about the punishments would have been a good thing for any naive *vecino*, since about a third of the offences were punishable by death. Execution could come by various methods—by hanging, by being quartered alive and then hanged, or by being burned. One of the punishments for bestiality included death and then a burning of the offender's body along with the animal being so abused. It was not pretty. To overcome any excuse of ignorance of the law, Ibarvo determined he would have his criminal code read "in a loud, audible, and intelligible voice, for three consecutive holy days, at the door of the church." Since the non-churchgoing contingent were likely to be the most expected offenders, the laws were also read repeatedly along the road at the town plaza.

One of the non-fatal punishments was for any man who would "assent to the prostitution of his wife." If found guilty, he would "be exposed in public, being feathered, rubbed with honey, wearing a fool's cap with a string of garlic, and a pair of horns, receive 100 lashes and be sent to the galleys [jail] for 10 years." Inexplicably, Ibarvo felt compelled to consider the possibility of a second occurrence of the same offense, for which the offender would be jailed for life. Slow learners would suffer mightily. It was unclear when the offender might be allowed to de-feather.

Given the number of crimes recorded, the criminal code was either effective or not needed to begin with. A 1796 summary of criminal cases pursued by Ibarvo reportedly included only three between 1779 and 1788—a beating, a murder, and a robbery.[36] Interestingly, there was nothing in the criminal code about smuggling or contraband. Those were offenses more easily overlooked.

Ibarvo's Standoff with a Kichai Chief

There is perhaps no better example of both the simplicity of contraband commerce and the complexities of the resulting relationships than a single event in September 1783.[37] The discovery of a journal describing a confrontation between Ibarvo and a Kichai chief was one of those serendipitous findings that every historian hopes for but cannot plan. This one came by way of David La Vere, a professor of history at the University of North Carolina in Wilmington.

La Vere was looking at dozens of *legajos*, bundles of documents, at the Archivo General de Indias in Seville, Spain. Most of the documents were faded, some had holes where the ink had penetrated the paper, and the Spanish script was hard to read. The moment that La Vere found one document is memorable for him twenty-five years later.

> I turned over a page and there was this oversized report on beautiful robin's egg blue paper with the most exquisite handwriting I had seen. So large and legible. It was easy to read, and I quickly discovered this amazing journal of Grappe to the Kichais.[38]

La Vere's discovery was a detailed, firsthand account of a meeting between Ibarvo and a Kichai chief authored by a Frenchman, Francoise Grappe. In his role as an official representative of Spain, Ibarvo was to maintain good relations with the East Texas tribes so they would not ally with enemies of the crown or steal horses from the Spanish. However, Ibarvo was also a trader in his own right, with his own interests. That dual role and his official appointment allowed Ibarvo to insert himself into the trade moving through his jurisdiction. He used his granted authority to limit the unlicensed trade of others and to benefit himself personally. But this failed badly when he tried to exert that authority with a Kichai chief. Ibarvo ignored two basic tenets of commerce and human behavior—the consumer will make their choices based on what is best for them, and people do not like being pushed around.

Spain's approach to Indian relations had always been to appease the friendly tribes with gifts and goods, but only if they were peaceful, cooperative, and did not steal from the Spanish. That policy would only work if Spain could also prevent unlicensed *contrabandieros* from crossing the border from Natchitoches, along the roads that avoided Nacogdoches so they could enter the villages undetected. Ibarvo wanted to be the only source of trade for the Native Americans of eastern Texas. The Spaniards' control broke down when tribes had an alternative access to goods at a better price and without the heavy-handedness of the Spanish. Not only that, but Ibarvo was cut out of the transactions.

There was an unspoken agreement on which tribes would trade with Spain via Nacogdoches and which would trade with merchants from Natchitoches. When the Kichai, who were normally connected to traders up the Red River, moved south nearer Nacogdoches, it created a disagreement on who "owned" the trade relationship. Luis de Blanc, the grandson of St. Denis, governor, and a major trade merchant from Natchitoches, had been their trade contact when they lived on the Red River. Even though they moved to a location within a jurisdiction under Ibarvo's supervision, the tribe saw no reason to shift their trade allegiance to Ibarvo and Nacogdoches.

In a display that was an unusual show of civil and military authority, a detachment of twenty uniformed and mounted soldiers from Natchitoches, accompanied by the French journal writer, Grappe, rode toward the Kichai village.[39] As they left Natchitoches, Ibarvo was in the rear, but when they stopped at Los Adaes for the night, he was given command and the soldiers were ordered to obey his direction. Ibarvo immediately asserted his authority with the soldiers from Natchitoches, a curious and unsanctioned assumption of command.

The chief and his villagers gathered in the chief's cabin at around three o'clock in the morning and were still waiting to meet with Ibarvo at eleven-thirty. Ibarvo tried to gain an advantage by opening the discussion and showing some displeasure with the chief. Ibarvo said he had been told that the Osage, a hostile and militant tribe, had visited the Kichai along with "a number of Englishmen," both of whom were seen as a threat to Spanish authority. The chief's response was that this was a lie. Perhaps sensing that what he had hoped might gain an edge did not, Ibarvo then asked the Kichai why they traded their deerskins to Bouet Lafitte, a French merchant with operations on the east side of the Sabine. Their simple answer explained the craftiness and consumer awareness of the Indians that was often overlooked by Spain.

The chief said they traded with the French because they were given ten musket balls for each skin and the Spanish gave them only five. Viewed simply from a transactional level it is clear why the Kichai made that choice—they got a better deal. The chief told Ibarvo that "when they went to his house [Lafitte's], they ate as much as they wished, he treated them well, and that there had only been him to help when all goods were so scarce."[40]

Based on the tone of Grappe's journal at this juncture, there must have been an air of tension in the discussion that is not fully expressed in his description of the moment. The Kichai quickly tired of Ibarvo's demanding attitude. Whatever civility had been expressed in the beginning broke down when Ibarvo made threats that were completely unacceptable, eliciting a strong reaction from one of the Kichai men. Ibarvo told them he would arrest Lafitte if he came the Kichai village to ensure the tribe would trade only with Nacogdoches and only for five musket balls. He threatened to put Lafitte in shackles and jail him in Nacogdoches and would do the same with any French traders who bypassed Nacogdoches to trade directly with the Kichai without Ibarvo's consent.

In a strong reaction to the threat, one of the Kichai escalated the dialogue. He told Ibarvo that if he tried to do such a thing that the tribe would "fight until they had all been destroyed, and that when all the warriors were killed, he [Ibarvo] must also kill the women who would [also] defend the French traders."[41] This was clearly about more than the cost of a musket ball; it was family, it was personal. The Kichai had always traded with the French and said they would continue to do so. After Ibarvo tried to justify why his costs were higher and why providing them with goods came at greater cost, the Kichai could not have been more offended. They told Ibarvo that he should never come to their village again, and that they would never go to his.

At this point, Grappe's journal provided insight into one of Ibarvo's personality traits that appeared at various times during his tenure as the singular Spanish official in East Texas. In some ways, this aspect of Ibarvo's temperament was reflected in the criminal code he enacted the same year as this encounter. Grappe says that when Ibarvo was told to never visit the Kichai again that he "flew into a violent rage." Grappe's choice of words here appear to have summarized an explosive conversation in which Ibarvo's overbearing and demanding tone was utterly rejected by the Kichai.

Ibarvo responded angrily to the Kichai by telling the Indians that "all the land on this side of the Red River belonged to him." That Spanish view of the world conflicted at all levels with the perspective of the indigenous people regarding land ownership. The same warrior who said he would fight to the death "took a handful of dirt and threw it to him [Ibarvo] saying to him that since the land was his, he could take it along with him." The chief responded similarly, removing the medal the Spanish gave him from around his neck and throwing it at Ibarvo's feet. Their rejection of Ibarvo, and of Spanish trade itself, could not have been clearer. Ibarvo, ever the merchant, backpedaled and told them they could have ten musket balls in trade if they came with their goods to Nacogdoches instead of having traders come to them. They refused.

Their mistrust of Ibarvo was well-founded. One of the Kichai recounted a situation in Nacogdoches where Ibarvo had soured a trade. The story was that the Kichai and a Hainai had gone to Nacogdoches to sell skins to Joseph Marie Armand, the designated trader to the natives based in Nacogdoches. Armand wanted to pay only five musket balls, but the Indian said they were about to reach an agreement for ten. Ibarvo then came along and whispered a few words to Armand and left. Suddenly the price was back to only five. The Hainai left without making any trade at all but was so angry that he wanted to organize his tribe to attack Ibarvo and the people of Nacogdoches.

After hearing this account, the Kichai chief grew concerned that "the situation was getting a little too heated" and sent every villager away from his cabin. They dispersed, but Ibarvo must have wondered if it was only to organize an attack on him. Ibarvo quickly saddled his own horse, wrote a note commending the soldiers for them to take to their commander, and quickly left his military support behind at the village. The chief responded positively to the remaining soldiers and made sure they knew his anger was not directed at them but only at "this man who said that all the land was his." The chief welcomed the soldiers, and they stayed the night before returning to Natchitoches. Ibarvo was left to look over his shoulder and wonder if anyone was behind him on the trail aiming to do him harm.

Dispute with La Mathe

Antonio Gil Ibarvo and Nicholas La Mathe were once allies in trade. Nicholas La Mathe was a well-connected and wealthy Frenchman who lived in Natchitoches with full access to French goods by way of New Orleans. La Mathe was known to have "managed a thriving trade with the dealers for the [Indian] nations."[42] There were indications that Ibarvo and La Mathe carried on trade when Ibarvo lived at Los Adaes. After Ibarvo and the Adeseños moved to Bucareli, it was La Mathe who built the chapel. After Nacogdoches was resettled and the levels of trade increased, both the numbers of people involved and the volume of trade increased. It may have been inevitable that there would be conflict between the two men.

The troubles between them seems to have begun in 1779 over the loss of almost seven hundred horses, cattle, and mules to the Comanche raid on Bucareli and the flooding that followed. Then, around 1780, La Mathe lost direct access to the Indian trade when Ibarvo was favored by the Spanish commandant general and governor and given charge over trade in the eastern half of the province.

Croix and Cabello were working out an agreement on how to manage trade with the tribes of the north, a designation that included the Tawakoni and Tonkawa with whom the Spanish had an uneasy alliance. La Mathe proposed a system in which he would be the commissioner in charge of Indian tribute, delivering annual presents to the tribes at their villages rather than having them come to a central location.[43] Other than a process which sought to maintain peace with Spain through direct gifts, the system La Mathe proposed was clearly to his own benefit. The goods would be delivered by La Mathe and his muleteers alone, far from any watchful Spanish eyes, and they would likely include goods not sanctioned by the crown.

When it came down to a decision on that arrangement, Governor Cabello decided that having a French trader deliver goods from Louisiana to semi-hostile tribes on behalf of Spain was not the best solution. Instead, Cabello was determined to have the tribes come to Nacogdoches as the hub and central warehouse for their gifts. By doing so the trade could at least be monitored by a Spanish official in the person of Antonio Gil Ibarvo. Beyond the dismissal of La Mathe's plan, Cabello went even farther by rejecting La Mathe's list of recommended gifts for the tribal leaders as meager and deficient. The gifts Cabello added to the list demonstrated his commitment to a more generous inventory.

> Hats trimmed with imitation braid, small mirrors, awls, needles, scissors, steels, worm screws, and embroidered woolen braid with red edges. He requested ells of second-grade red cloth in addition to the usual blue Limbourg and braided as well as ordinary shirts.[44]

Cabello showed that he wanted to make sure the tribes were pleased, and not simply placated.

Father Garza's Intercession

After this rather significant shift in how trade was conducted in the region, the local priest, Father José de la Garza, observed a growing enmity between Ibarvo and La Mathe. Their disagreement was known to others and distressing to the residents who were dependent on them for trade goods. After Ibarvo's requests to resolve their differences was rebuffed by La Mathe, Father Garza went to La Mathe's home to plead for reconciliation. In the presence of the priest, the two "settled their accounts, apologized profusely to one another, and remained friends, having cleared up all misunderstandings."[45] Ibarvo had debts with La Mathe, and at their meeting Ibarvo's promises to pay were put in writing. Those promises would be the focus of a later lawsuit by La Mathe.

Garza said that a year or two after this reconciliation, another disagreement between the two traders arose about payment of commissions for gifts delivered to the Indian nations visiting Nacogdoches. For some reason, La Mathe was unable to meet his part of the agreement. When the priest again offered to mediate, La Mathe turned him down.

Nicholas de La Mathe vs. Antonio Gil Ibarvo (1782)

The brokered conciliation by way of priestly intervention was fleeting. In June of 1782, La Mathe submitted a petition to Governor Cabello stating that he had unsettled accounts with Ibarvo, and it was "imperative that I liquidate and terminate" the accounts.[46] Ibarvo owed La Mathe money for goods and had provided La Mathe promissory notes by way of "papers and obligations."

Interestingly, La Mathe's petition was delivered to the governor in person at 9:00 pm. The timing leads one to wonder what form of alcohol or stage of anger led La Mathe to the point of knocking on the governor's door after dark. To compound the problem caused by the lateness of the hour, Governor Cabello said that La Mathe appeared at a time when he "was attending to various matters which are important to the royal service." Though tempting to wonder, this historian will not speculate what matters occupied Cabello at such a late hour.

Cabello knew better than to get in the middle of a dispute between these two important traders and assigned the matter to José de la Santa, the *alcalde ordinario* of the villa of San Fernando. Cabello directed him to quickly handle the case since Ibarvo was also in Béxar at the time and needed to return to Nacogdoches as soon as possible.

When Ibarvo was served notice of the complaint, he said he would obey the governor's command to appear, but he also said La Mathe's complaints should be ignored. Ibarvo said that since La Mathe had been in Béxar, he had been "living in concubinage" and this "proves him incapable of swearing an oath which would be credible in any court." Ibarvo complained that La Mathe was a "man who is not answerable" to anyone or anything. When La Mathe was served with the notice to appear, he was informed of Ibarvo's response. La Mathe responded by changing course.

> Since the above-said captain [Ibarvo] is attempting nothing but to confound the adjudication of the demand, as one gathers from his reply which is not relevant to the matter under consideration, it is necessary that the present [La Mathe] cease and desist from his claim, only reserving his right to repeat it at a more opportune time.

La Mathe thought better of his claims and asked to withdraw his complaint, apparently not wanting to discuss his concubinage. However, the *alcalde* ignored both of the parties and demanded the two men appear and settle their dispute, likely at the urging of Cabello to be done with it. On June 28, 1780, the case proceeded. Pressed on the matter, La Mathe showed the judge the promissory notes and bonds that Ibarvo had given him, signifying his debts to the Frenchman. Some of them were signed by Ibarvo, but others were not and could only be proven by parties in Louisiana. La Mathe said those people could testify that Ibarvo agreed to pay La Mathe "in mules, mares, and deer pelts." Since it could not be settled in Béxar, La Mathe asked for a transcript of the matter so he could take it up in Louisiana where he would have a more sympathetic hearing. Little was resolved in their former relationship, however.

Governor Cabello noted in June of 1784 that La Mathe still held "implacable hatred and rancor" for Ibarvo.[47]

Faced with resistance from Governor Cabello to support his claims, La Mathe sought another audience that he hoped would receive him more positively—Commandant General Croix. Croix was so captivated with La Mathe that he allowed him to export one thousand cattle from Texas at a lowered tax rate, an example of how special favors could be dispensed by Spanish officials.[48] Croix acknowledged "the rare genius of the aforementioned La Mathe, emanating from interests in particular purposes," and called him "unbelievably efficient, industrious, and competent." The "interests in particular purposes" was no doubt La Mathe's profitable craftiness in matters of trade.

In 1784, Commandant General Croix became especially enamored with La Mathe regarding his approach to a Spanish problem along the coast. La Mathe concocted a plan to exterminate the Karankawa Indians. La Mathe's plan was to build eight canoes that would hold about twenty-five soldiers each, paddle into Karankawa territory, and ambush them in their own territory. The utter failure to build canoes that could float was only one of many indignities that led to the collapse of this effort.[49]

La Mathe's Long-Held Complaints

After the disastrous outcomes of the planned attack on the Karankawa's, La Mathe fell out of favor with Spanish officials. It seems the more he sensed he was losing his status, the more he lashed out at Ibarvo. La Mathe's determination to harm Ibarvo continued across the tenure of more new governors. With each change in governor, commandant general, or viceroy, La Mathe saw an opportunity for an uninitiated set of ears to listen to his grievances. Rafael Martinez Pacheco assumed the governorship of the province in 1787. In January 1790 La Mathe made a request of Pacheco, this one pertaining to the loss of his horses on the prairies of Bucareli eleven years earlier.[50] La Mathe was apparently not one to forgive and forget.

La Mathe was very specific in his request to Pacheco. He asked for a copy of a letter that Governor Cabello wrote regarding the "detention of my horse herd," and he wanted Ibarvo to pay the debts of his deceased brother, Juan Antonio Ibarvo, to La Mathe. La Mathe also implied that he himself had been appointed by Governor Cabello "for the purpose of seeking a better site" to settle the Adaeseños following the Bucareli disasters. La Mathe suggested that Father Garza, Ibarvo, and he were all assigned that responsibility. La Mathe also asked that eight citizens of Nacogdoches be summoned to appear in Béxar to testify in this matter at La Mathe's expense.

Ibarvo replied in full detail to La Mathe's petitions, accusations, and requests on February 19, 1790. Ibarvo said that La Mathe's request for a letter from Ripperdá to seize La Mathe's horses could not be met because there was no such letter. Ibarvo was also asked for a copy of a letter that Cabello sent him regarding the floods at Bucareli. Ibarvo again said he could not provide such a letter because it did not exist. Ibarvo said if there was a letter appointing La Mathe to help with the resettlement of Nacogdoches then La Mathe himself should have a copy.

On the request for witnesses to travel to San Antonio, Ibarvo called the named men together, reportedly in good faith with witnesses, to inform them of La Mathe's demand. Two of the men were not present—one was in Louisiana and the other was away trading with the Indians. The men responded unequivocally in a way that dismissed La Mathe's former importance. They explained, in writing, that if the request was for "some matter of royal service" they would gladly travel. However, since the "request for [their] travel emanates from a demand by a private individual solely for the purpose of his interest [and] with whom we have neither direct nor indirect business, communications, relationships, or interests of any sort" they declined. It was not a simple refusal, the men laid out ten reasons in detail as to why they would not travel to Béxar, even at La Mathe's expense.

The core reasons for their refusal centered on the time it would require to be away from their families and farms. "We have no other possible means to sustain [our families] than the productive sweat of our daily labors," they answered. In a fitting and emotional expression, surely with Ibarvo's assistance, the men summarized their feelings about La Mathe's request to travel to Béxar.

> It would be one of the greatest mistakes we ever made in the course of our lives, and would surely qualify us as insane, were we to accede to the irregular pretentions of the afore-named Don Nicolás de La Mathe

Nicholas La Mathe, former friend and trading partner, purveyor in horses and hides, and failed military schemer was rebuffed by poor farmers from Ibarvo's Nacogdoches. His influence was gone, his audiences with Spanish officials over, and his legal challenges were exhausted.

The Pendulm Swings Again

Nicholas La Mathe was not the only person wanting to make a favorable impression on newly appointed Spanish officials. From 1785 until 1789, there were five different viceroys responsible for the province prior to the Conde de Revilla Gigedo being appointed in late 1789. The rapid turnover left them little time to understand the challenges that East Texas brought to their post.

Juan de Ugalde, as commandant general, and Rafael Martinez Pacheco, as governor, were both appointed in early 1787. During his years in control of Nacogdoches, Ibarvo had endured the ire of Hugo Oconór, benefited from the good graces of Ripperdá, and gained the right to be largely left alone by Croix and Cabello. When Ugalde and Pacheco came to power in 1787, Ibarvo understood that he could seize the initiative to balance the rumors and unfavorable reports by others. Ibarvo asked for an intervention from his long-time priest, Father Joseph Francisco Mariano de la Garza.[51]

Father Garza's Letter of Recommendation

Father Garza's lengthy letter on behalf of Ibarvo in November 1787 places it at a time when newly installed officials were looking for information about the province they were assigned to govern. There are also indications in the letter that its timing was influenced by the ongoing conflicts and legal disputes between Ibarvo and Nicholas La Mathe. Garza's letter restated the history of the two men, recounting how Ibarvo had continued to try and resolve their differences. It was a preemptive effort to gain the ear of the new governor and drown out any contradictory accounts from La Mathe.

Garza knew Ibarvo as well as any of his contemporaries. They had been through many difficulties together and survived multiple challenges and hardships. From February 1775 until September 1783, Garza said, they had been together "almost continuously, except for a few days." Even in the four years since their time together in Nacogdoches ended, Garza had received favorable reports on Ibarvo through the priests assigned to the church there.

Garza's praise for Ibarvo was passionate, by his own admission, but he challenged anyone who "has been, as I, a witness to it all" to submit a rebuttal of his commendation. The priest recounted a summary of the events that led Ibarvo to his position of respect and responsibility. He offered example after example of Ibarvo's kindness, his piety, and his efforts on behalf of the citizens of the village. Garza said Ibarvo saw to it that no one missed mass, he fed and clothed the poor, insured that people worked when they had nothing, and provided for the needs of the priests and the church.

Garza's summary of Ibarvo's traits as a leader boiled down to three he admired. The first was, of course, the Christian piety he observed in Ibarvo. His examples included how Ibarvo cared for the needs of the priests and the chapel. As both an example of his stature in the community and his position,

Garza said Ibarvo "laid down his cane to take up the axe, the plow harness, and the hoe, and who, setting aside the authority of his office, donned worker's clothes to erect a house of God."[52]

The second favorable characteristic highlighted was Ibarvo's concern for the general welfare of those in his charge in Nacogdoches—the former Adeseños. Garza saw Ibarvo helping others, with tools and toil. He encouraged their industriousness, while doing what he could to prevent "gambling and idleness." Garza also pointed out a role not widely noted in the literature. He said that Ibarvo "dealt with them in such a special way that he became the judge for their trials and the arbiter of their disputes."

The third personal trait Garza admired was Ibarvo's interaction and relationships with the Indian nations of the region.[53] His trade and gifts to the tribal members were a function of his assignment, but Garza said there was much more to creating the kinship needed. At his own expense, Ibarvo not only provided gifts, but he also entertained Indians on their visits with dances and other indications of his acceptance. All these traits led Garza to state unequivocally that "among all the men whom I know in that entire province, no one could be better suited to this task than Don Antonio Gil Ybarvo."

On the same day Ibarvo delivered Garza's letter to the new governor to support his role, he submitted a second recommendation letter written in October 1786, only a few months earlier than Garza's.[54] The second letter was by Domingo Cabello, the former governor. Cabello proudly and somewhat arrogantly reminded any reader of his full title:

> Colonel in the Royal Armies, Governor and Commandant of Arms of the Province of Texas, its Missions, Conquests, and Frontiers, Captain of the Cavalry Company of the Royal Presidio of San Antonio de Béxar, and Inspector General of the Militia Corps and Presidial Troops of the said Province by Commission Conferred by the Lord Commandant General of the Interior Provinces of this Kingdom of New Spain.[55]

Cabello's focus on Ibarvo's traits was similar to Garza's but from the point of view of one in the government rather than the church. He admired the way Ibarvo "worked with such great efficiency and urgency that he has made it possible for the town [Nacogdoches] to thrive quite nicely." Cabello's attention to Ibarvo's interaction with the Indians was his ability to "make them good and devoted friends of this government."

All this effort with Governor Pacheco was short-lived. He was replaced as governor within three years. Manuel Muñoz was appointed governor of the province of Texas in April 1790 and assumed office on August 14. It took

Governor Muñoz only two days to write a letter of introduction to Antonio Gil Ibarvo. In the letter he offered good wishes and asked for "a report on the state of your town and all else that occurs to you."[56] That seemingly simple request was the beginning of the end for Ibarvo's stewardship of the pueblo of Nacogdoches and his central role in the commerce of contraband in East Texas. Indications are that Muñoz took office with the idea that a change of leadership was needed in Nacogdoches.

Signs of a Coming Change

The lack of understanding of the culture and relationships of the borderlands on the part of men appointed to govern it was mystifying and unfortunate. Their appointments were often the result of service to the crown in some distant part of the empire where the complexities of relationships, commerce, and culture were vastly different. If there was anything like a briefing or an orderly transfer of power, it seemed to be almost accidental. Each new appointee expressed shock and surprise at the extent of contraband trade allowed by his predecessor. The letter Muñoz sent to Antonio Gil Ibarvo expressed some of that, but in a more *de facto* manner. Muñoz already knew there was a problem and was restating it for Ibarvo's reading. The informant that inspired Muñoz's convictions is not known.

> I have become aware that from your province [Nacogdoches] and others, many individuals who have committed excesses there retreat to this province [Texas] under my command . . . I am also informed that many of these people have been attracted to the Indian rancherias and towns, where they live in the licentiousness that is available to them. [57]

These behaviors had been ongoing for decades before Muñoz's arrival. Nonetheless, Muñoz was determined to make his mark by eradicating such activity.

> To eliminate these evils, you must try to arrest those who might enter that town under your command without a passport, and notify me with a report of their names, country, [physical] traits, and possessions they are carrying, so that in their light [we can] determine whether they are included in the Criminal Court [of] Its Highness the Royal Audiencia, and governors and district justices of the viceroyalty of New Spain, or among those who lately have stolen some horses in these territories.[58]

Muñoz wanted to know everything, and to know it in detail. To ensure Ibarvo's reports to him were direct, clear, and accountable, Muñoz instructed Ibarvo to report "in your own hand without trusting anyone else." This instruction put the onus on Ibarvo to tell the governor everything that was going on in Nacogdoches. It could also be used to accuse him should any untruths be discovered. If Ibarvo began to feel a bit cornered, it was not without justification. What Ibarvo did not know was that the Spanish officials to whom he was making his pleas were already planning his arrest and removal from Nacogdoches.

10

The Arrest and Removal of Antonio Gil Ibarvo

My merits are so limited that I hesitated a long time between the alternative of whether I should present them at the foot of the throne or leave them submerged in the backwaters of oblivion.[1]

—ANTONIO GIL IBARVO

The village of Nuestra de Señora del Pilar de Nacogdoches was the focal point for commerce, trade, and contraband for the entire northern edge of the Spanish province. In the twelve years following the resettlement of Nacogdoches in 1779, Ibarvo and the people in his orbit knew the rules, but they also made many of their own. Though there were official edicts to follow, or ignore, their distance from Béxar and La Bahía meant the villagers were largely left to their own means for establishing the limits of commerce and culture. Though most of the official discussion around the settlements of Bucareli and Nacogdoches questioned their legitimacy, there was one Spanish official with extensive experience in New Spain who felt differently. Juan de Ugalde, who had served Spain in many roles, including as governor of Coahuila y Tejas, had his own ideas about the future of Nacogdoches. Shortly after Ugalde became commandant general of the province in 1787, he proposed three distinct actions regarding Nacogdoches.[2]

His primary recommendation involved a subject that most of his predecessors had considered but then abandoned before moving on to more pressing matters. Ugalde believed the settlement at Nacogdoches should not only be continued but ought to be increased in population. Its role regarding Spanish relations with the friendly tribes of East Texas was too important to abandon.

Secondly, Ugalde was determined that Nacogdoches should become a military settlement, with Spanish soldiers in place of a local militia. Ongoing concerns about English and American pressures from the east, as well as the enduring contraband trade, led him to finally consider that the expense of that decision might be justified. This is unsurprising for a man who had engaged in many military campaigns on behalf of the crown. To highlight his commitment to this idea, Ugalde said that any man with the necessary qualifications and commitment to be lieutenant governor of Nacogdoches should be paid 1,200 pesos a year, not the five hundred pesos per year provided to Ibarvo.

His third resolution was similarly dramatic and impactful, but on a more personal level. Ugalde wanted to remove Antonio Gil Ibarvo from his position as lieutenant governor of Nacogdoches and to cut him off from all contraband trade. Ugalde wanted to banish Ibarvo from the settlement he helped to create.

Ugalde's opinion about Ibarvo set in motion a series of events that would transform Nacogdoches from a civil settlement organized around contraband trade and led by a single person to a military outpost under closer observation and control by Spanish officials. Whether those changes had any lasting impact on the movement of contraband goods or not is doubtful, but it forever altered the nature of the community and signaled a transition that had a broader impact on the history of Texas and the United States. Ugalde's actions would forever alter the history of the Spanish occupation of eastern Texas.

The Proposal to Remove Ibarvo

When Ugalde first suggested these measures to Manuel Antonio Flórez Maldonado, the viceroy at the time, there were immediate questions and pushback. The first obstacle was that Flórez required a formal judicial inquiry into the accusations toward Ibarvo be made before acting on his removal. Flórez wisely did not wanted proper legal considerations before such a decision was made. The viceroy consulted with other leaders in Mexico City, and they agreed there was no compelling reason to impeach Ibarvo unless an inquiry suggested it was for the good of Spain. Flórez also suggested the commandant general should inform and confront Ibarvo with the charges and give him a chance to respond. Ugalde was ordered to examine witnesses "privately and secretly" should he conduct the required investigation. That approach was not what Ugalde had in mind.[3]

Flórez's second requirement was a financial one—that Ugalde specify the costs of his plan to convert Nacogdoches to a military post. Each of those requirements brought his designs on Nacogdoches to a halt while Ugalde took care of more pressing matters. In a letter on April 18, 1789, Ugalde said he would not attend to Ibarvo until "after his return from a [military] campaign" despite his opinion that "the existence of this individual [Ibarvo] is very prejudicial."[4]

Changes in Viceroy and Governor

Two major changes in the leadership of the province altered the trajectory of Ugalde's proposal. At the end of 1789, Count Revilla Gigedo replaced Flórez and became viceroy. Shortly thereafter, in early 1790, Manuel Muñoz was appointed governor of the province of Texas.[5] By the end of 1790, discussion among the changing cadre of officials who were largely new to the province was stirred again by Commandant General Ugalde, a man who seemed to harbor deep animosity toward Ibarvo.[6] At Ugalde's urging, Muñoz restarted the conversation about arresting and removing Ibarvo from Nacogdoches.

Muñoz and Ugalde believed, apparently with good reason, that the viceroy, Revilla Gigedo, would not present the same obstacles as his predecessor. Revilla Gigedo claimed Ibarvo had operated "his own clandestine trade that had made him rich." Ibarvo's wealth may have been misperceived, though in relative terms he was very well off. The viceroy claimed Ibarvo "allowed the introduction of foreign goods and the export of cattle from the province, [which was] justly prohibited in that area." Trade in cattle was permitted off and on, but their export had to include payment of the tariff set by the crown. Ibarvo was also accused of tolerating French and English traders among the Indians. This triggered the rolling concern that supplying the tribes with "gunpowder and bullets in exchange for furs, mules and horses" only continued the cycle where the tribes would steal mules and horses from the Spanish.[7]

Notwithstanding Ibarvo's many apparent merits and qualifications, he would soon learn he was an obstacle to the plans of others for the future of Nacogdoches.

A False Sense of Normalcy and a Resignation

Late 1790 and early 1791 included all the usual reports and communication between Ibarvo and his superiors. In January 1791, Ibarvo provided a census report for Nacogdoches where he identified the 524 residents within five castes: *españoles* (140), *indios* (eighty-seven), *mestizos* (seventy-five), *color quebrado* (forty-eight), and *negros esclavos*, or enslaved blacks, (sixteen).[8] In February 1790, Ibarvo asked for the church's consent to rebuild the chapel, which was "very unsightly, small, and so old that it threatens total collapse."[9] In March and for a few months following, there was discussion back and forth about concerns regarding the Apache trying to make inroads among the friendlier tribes.

Despite the continuation of seeming normalcy in his communication with Béxar and Mexico City, Ibarvo seems to have sensed a difference in the support provided by his superiors. With all the changes in government officials in charge of the province, Ibarvo must have learned that the pendulum swings in people and politics were not in his favor. Ibarvo decided it was time for him to submit his resignation—again. Where his previous resignations seemed calculated to gain some advantage or secure compensation, this one was more final. He was getting older, he was tired, and he no longer wanted to lead Nacogdoches.

Ibarvo's March 1791 resignation letter to the viceroy had little of the flowery, subservient language typical of a letter to the highest-ranking official in New Spain.[10] Ibarvo began with a resume of sorts, a history of what he had done in his life on behalf of the crown. He did not begin with his role in Los Adaes, but with his official appointment to lead Bucareli on August 7, 1774. Ibarvo listed his many accomplishments and then explained he was "tired because of his advanced age." He was over sixty years old at the time. His devotion to Spain, his relations with the Indian tribes around Nacogdoches, and particularly his founding of Nacogdoches without any expense to the government were each spelled out for the viceroy's understanding. Copies of letters of approval regarding Ibarvo's service from Croix, Cabello, and Father Garza were also sent to the governor to bolster his request.

Ibarvo's appeal seemed simple—retire at half of his present five hundred pesos per year pay and be allowed "the use of the uniform of a captain of militias." His letter for the viceroy was sent first to Governor Muñoz with a request to pass it on to Mexico City with Muñoz's blessings. In the cover letter for the governor Ibarvo explained that he had "wished to die in the royal service," but that his advanced age led him to make the request for retirement.[11] He told Muñoz that the favor of his approval "will remain engraved in me so eternally that there will be no moment in the future course of my life when I will cease to sing the gratitude of which Your Lordship will be most deserving." That form of flattery did not work with Muñoz. By the time Muñoz received the request, he was already plotting Ibarvo's removal from Nacogdoches.[12]

Muñoz's official response to Ibarvo's request, a full two months later in May, must have come as a disappointment to the ruler of Nacogdoches.[13] The governor suggested that Ibarvo "suspend the aforesaid intention for now" to achieve some unspecified aims and "perhaps to agree on a more advantageous [Indian] treaty." Munoz was still learning about the extent of contraband trade through Nacogdoches. He was also beginning to understand that Ibarvo was the only person equipped to handle the complex relationships between Spain and the numerous tribes engaged in trade through Nacogdoches.

The two-month delay in responding to Ibarvo's request did not mean that discussions of his removal were forgotten. In fact, it was quite the opposite. While Antonio Gil Ibarvo was considering a life with less responsibility, the viceroy, the governor, and both the outgoing and incoming commandant generals were communicating among themselves to coordinate a plan for his arrest.

Verazadi's Secret Report

When Manuel Gaspar de Verazadi appeared in Nacogdoches early in 1791 there was nothing particularly notable about his visit.[14] Upon his arrival he presented a permit from the governor to purchase buffalo hides and tongues. Verazadi was a European Spanish citizen of Béxar and a merchant of some success. At only twenty-five years old, his resources allowed him to sustain a mulatto maid and three servants.[15] As an active trader, particularly one close to the governor, Verazadi was someone with whom Antonio Gil Ibarvo was familiar and had communicated with regarding Apache troubles stirring in East Texas.[16] Verazadi's passport and the stated reason for his visit were part of a cover story that allowed him to spend time in the village on a secret mission. Verazadi was in Nacogdoches to investigate and report to Governor Muñoz on Antonio Gil Ibarvo's activities related to contraband trade.

As a Spaniard and a businessman, Verazadi had access to people at all levels of the village culture. As an educated man, he could also produce a written report. Frank de la Teja, a historian who has extensively researched the Spanish colonial era in Texas, notes that it was a common practice to use merchants to carry out these kinds of activities, both overtly and undercover.[17] There was a faint hint in the correspondence prior to the investigation that Verazadi might potentially be the one to replace Ibarvo in Nacogdoches should he be removed, but that never materialized.[18] Manuel Muñoz notified the viceroy of Verazadi's mission and his instructions to the covert agent to conduct himself with greatest secrecy regarding his true objective.[19] Concerns about the willingness of the people to speak freely given Ibarvo's dominance of the citizens meant that Verazadi would have to be discreet.

Instructions to Wait on Investigation

The timing of Verazadi's reconnaissance in Nacogdoches in February or March of 1791 was a bit premature based on other events. Shortly after Verazadi's trip to Nacogdoches, the viceroy instructed Governor Muñoz to wait on any further action regarding the Ibarvo investigation until the newly appointed commandant general, Ramón de Castro, could assume his post. Castro did not arrive in Saltillo until March 18, 1791.[20] Governor Muñoz communicated Castro's appointment to Ibarvo on May 14, and by June the royal cedula was posted in Nacogdoches notifying the villagers that he had been named "commandant general of the Eastern Provinces and inspector of their troops in military, political, and economic matters".[21] Communication between Muñoz and the viceroy suggests that Muñoz was not fully in agreement with the appointment of Castro. Muñoz had been chastised by the viceroy for ignoring orders to communicate the appointment, not replying to communications about Castro, and replying by improper channels.

One of Castro's first assignments was to continue the investigation into reports of unauthorized trade in Nacogdoches. Though action on anything Verazadi learned in Nacogdoches had been suspended by order of the viceroy, that did not deter Muñoz from gathering additional information.

Verazadi's Description of Nacogdoches

In June 1791, Manuel de Verazadi submitted his written report to Muñoz. Verazadi's account was descriptive not only of possible contraband trade and the suspicions surrounding Ibarvo, but also of the settlement of Nacogdoches itself. For someone from San Antonio or Mexico, East Texas was a foreign terrain. It was hilly and heavily wooded with trees forty to sixty feet tall. Anyone familiar with the layout and terrain of modern Nacogdoches would find Verazadi's descriptions recognizable.[22] The report provided a sense of how the former mission village had developed following twelve years of resettlement by the Adaeseños from Bucareli.

There is indication in Verazadi's description and in those of others that many of the primary buildings were down the hill toward Bonita Creek, northwest of the plaza within about three hundred yards. By the time of Verazadi's visit, the plaza had already been laid out and was ringed by fifteen or sixteen houses that he described as something akin to huts. The red, sandy clay that any current resident knows all too well on rainy days apparently made excellent adobe for jacales. The remainder of the fifty to sixty huts were so scattered about that they did not even form streets. By his estimation, amidst those houses and huts were about one hundred families totaling around five hundred people, a substantial population to be fed and housed.

Verazadi noted that the wooded nature of the terrain provided little immediate space for fields to plant, but that there was fertile and productive ground within three to five miles. Though the land was fertile, Verazadi said the inhabitants seemed extremely lazy and did not take advantage of the location of their village.

Contraband Trade

There was little doubt that trade across the Sabine, between Natchitoches and Nacogdoches, was ongoing and vigorous during the time of Verazadi's report. In addition to the five hundred people in and around Nacogdoches, within three hundred miles there were also dozens of tribal nations. Trade is what attracted such a diverse group of citizens, and in practical terms, contraband trade made the most sense to support themselves.

GUNPOWDER AND BULLETS

Verazadi identified the primary commerce of Nacogdoches as the bartering of powder and bullets in exchange for deerskins—precisely the type of trade that was expressly forbidden by Spanish authorities. Verazadi named the principal provider of such goods to the Native Americans to be Joseph Marie Armand (or Armant), a Frenchman from Natchitoches. Armand had been appointed an official Indian trader by the Spanish as early as 1780, and by 1790 he had been named more officially as "supplier general" to the Indian nations.

IBARVO'S STORE

Beyond controlling access to the tribes and acting as a gatekeeper for passage into and through East Texas, Ibarvo maintained a public store in the village where one could find many prohibited items including whiskey, cane rum, gunpowder, and heavily regulated items like tobacco and packs of playing cards. The royal monopoly placed on tobacco, gunpowder, and playing cards in the middle of the eighteenth century led to widespread avoidance of the tariffs on these items.[23] Verazadi noted that goods for Indian trade that were more decorative and less threatening to the crown were also available in the form of cloth with which to make breechclouts, beads, and vermilion, a deep red pigment.

Verazadi disclosed two of his confidants by reporting that Gil Morin and a man he called Little Perez told him that within the last year, Ibarvo had sent one of his road crew, Joaquín Flores, to Béxar with tobacco loaded on mules.

Francisco Ardila, a known smuggler, was also part of that caravan. Ardila's wife apparently learned that the governor had been informed of the smuggling operation and had a mail courier let Ardila know so he could avoid arrest. Ardila left the bundles of tobacco hidden near the Brazos River and returned to Nacogdoches.

The accusation of Ibarvo illegally trading in playing cards was interesting given he had issued a strict edict against gambling in his criminal code proclamation in 1783. Verazadi said Ibarvo sold the cards cheaply to promulgate their use, and then he would benefit from collecting a fine of six pesos from anyone who would violate his prohibition of gambling with the cards due to their "disgraceful excesses, in opposition with religion, good order, civilization and the welfare of the community."[24]

WHISKEY

In Verazadi's eyes, the perils of alcohol seemed to be widespread and on open display. He reported that very few villagers did not appear intoxicated in public. This was despite a proclamation posted at the guard house prohibiting trade in whiskey. Verazadi mentioned seeing the penalties for the offense posted on Good Friday, establishing his presence in Nacogdoches on April 22, 1791. Since Ibarvo was the one who sold the whiskey, he would at times remove the proclamation prohibiting its sale and offer it from his store.

"THE CAPTAIN IS NOT IGNORANT OF ANYTHING"

Verazadi upheld the image of Ibarvo as the master conductor of the contraband trade. He claimed that others told him Ibarvo knew about anything and everything that took place within the jurisdiction of Nacogdoches and East Texas. Verazadi reported that both English and Americans were allowed to come up the Trinity River to trade with the native tribes, and that French traders passing through Los Adaes and around Nacogdoches were the primary source of arms and gunpowder to the Indian nations.

Verazadi believed that garrisoning troops at the Red River and the Trinity would stop the influx of illegal goods. In doing so, he joined a long line of others who underestimated market forces and the ability of men to create clandestine routes for bypassing such attempts to stop the flow of goods. There was no stopping the commerce of the people, no stopping the economic realities of supply and demand.

Ibarvo's Imaginary Wealth

There may be a universal trait in humans to believe that those who appear well off have unlimited resources and even more wealth hidden from view. Ibarvo seemed to have access to actual money, but no one could ever determine how much, where he kept it, or the sources of it. Louis Dear, a French trader to the Indians who lived in Nacogdoches, seemed to believe that Ibarvo's invisible wealth came from his extortion of the residents or from kickbacks from the smugglers—from *la mordida*. After observing the culture of Nacogdoches and Ibarvo's place in it, Verazadi began to question that perception. The seemingly well-off Spanish trader from Béxar began to believe that Ibarvo's wealth may have been imaginary.

Verazadi reported that Ibarvo appeared to own seven hundred head of cattle, twelve herds of mares, and seven droves of mules in addition to the trading post he operated in Nacogdoches. Ibarvo most certainly had debts, the true currency of the borderlands. Verazadi also learned that Ibarvo owed more than twenty thousand pesos to his creditors, primarily to José de la Pena. One of Ibarvo's skills may have been a borderland business tactic of managing float—the ability to use debt and future promises to pay to reap present gains.

Ibarvo's Temper

One interesting aspect of Verazadi's report is of little meaning when taken only within that context. However, when considered along with other observations and accounts during Ibarvo's service, it points to one factor that may have also played into the desire for his removal—Ibarvo's temper and reported aggression toward others. Verazadi described the reluctance of others to report Ibarvo's behavior due to "the fears that they have for his cruelties." Verazadi implied that although a few reports of this may have made it to Béxar, Ibarvo was able to largely hide these incidents from discovery by the governor. Verazadi did not mention any specifics but reported he had heard accounts during his visit that suggested some citizens had endured much that went unreported.

Ibarvo's confrontation with the Kichai described in detail in a previous chapter highlights his aggressiveness and emotion when others resisted his will. That detailed, firsthand account showed how Ibarvo's attempt to impose trade requirements on a Kichai chief backfired when Ibarvo lost his cool and made demands which insulted the Kichai.[25] Even the release of his criminal code for Nacogdoches displayed a need for control by proposing harsh levels of punishment. A further matter suggestive of Ibarvo's temperament was the nature of an incident involving Gaspar Hidalgo.

Gaspar Hidalgo [Ydalgo] was an Adaeseño who was evicted along with Ibarvo and the others in 1773. He and Ibarvo would have been well known to each other. The fifty-year-old Hidalgo lived in Béxar with his wife and widowed daughter. His grandchildren, ages six and twelve, were described as Indians, and one would then assume his daughter's husband was as well.[26]

Another mention of Hidalgo listed him in 1790 among the "master masons, carpenters, blacksmiths, cart drivers, and *peones* engaged in the construction of the royal buildings of the *ayuntamiento* of this *villa* of *San Antonio de Béxar.*" His lack of skills relegated him to the list of *peones* (laborers) who earned only two pesos for eight days of work.[27]

Under circumstances that were not fully described, in 1788 Ibarvo was accused of beating Gaspar Hidalgo in a matter brought to the attention of the governor at the time, Rafael Martinez Pacheco. All that remains in the archives is a cover letter for a more complete report not yet located. Pacheco indicated it was a report on "the beating administered by the lieutenant governor of Nacogdoches, Don Antonio Gil Ybarbo [Ibarvo] to a citizen." The letter only describes that Hidalgo endured physical harm and was asking damages.[28]

Another mention in the archives on the question of Ibarvo's temperament appears in December 1789 when his public enemy, Nicholas de La Mathe, brought it to the attention of Spanish officials in Béxar. La Mathe wanted to use Hidalgo's testimony against Ibarvo in his own campaign against Ibarvo. In a letter to Governor Pacheco, La Mathe said he had information that Hidalgo had filed a petition along with testimony from witnesses. La Mathe asked the governor for a copy of that testimony. Though La Mathe swore that he did not make the request out of malice, he had been relentless in his ongoing grievances against Ibarvo.[29]

Pacheco agreed to provide the testimony and decreed that once it was located an original would be added to the official archives. Pacheco searched the archives but only found a May 26, 1788, letter initiating the complaint, which he provided to La Mathe. Pacheco explained that the additional information had been forwarded to Juan de Ugalde, but due to "natural oversight" no copy had been kept.[30] Though the incident escapes further scrutiny because of the testimony being lost, this was an event of some notoriety. The gravity of the claim, Hidalgo's pursuit of damages, and La Mathe's desire to use the testimony against Ibarvo for his own purposes all point to a charged physical confrontation that was beyond a simple dispute. If Hidalgo's claims were an indication of Ibarvo's conduct and physical confrontations, they would have matched other accounts. It would also explain why Verazadi said occurrences like these went unreported due to a fear of Ibarvo's retribution.

The Aftermath of the Secret Report

Rather than providing the evidence needed for a legal review for Ibarvo's removal, Verazadi's report offered little detail on which the viceroy could take immediate action. Ramón de Castro would later label it as incomplete. Bexar

Archives translator John Wheat returned to the original Spanish text to review the word he translated as "incomplete," calling it an interesting word choice by Castro. In Spanish it reads, "*sin perjuicio de lo que ha expuesto Verazadi en su incompleto informe.*" Wheat noted that the actual report was not unfinished but did not cover all the points needed to condemn Ibarvo.[31] Instead of descriptions of Nacogdoches's forests, farms, and houses, Spanish officials were hoping for more accusatory evidence, which the report did not sufficiently provide.

In that regard, Verazadi's report was a bit of a setback to those who thought Ibarvo should have been removed years earlier. Though the viceroy authorized Castro to suspend Ibarvo if needed, any action on the report went on hold to allow more time for the governor, the commandant general, and the viceroy to decide what to do about Antonio Gil Ibarvo and Nacogdoches.[32]

Ibarvo's Arrest

While Verazadi's secret report percolated among Spanish authorities unbeknownst to Ibarvo, his focus was on the slowness of response to his April 1791 request to retire from service. Six months after Muñoz's failure to endorse his retirement, Ibarvo made a second request. This time he did things a bit differently and more strongly.[33] Ibarvo reiterated his accomplishments for the governor but in greater detail and starting his story twenty years prior to his earlier plea. Ibarvo had served in some official capacity to the crown since 1754. Though Ibarvo did not repeat his request for half pay and a uniform, the expectation of compensation in his retirement was implicit in the letter. Ibarvo also made his plea more personal. Though he increased his use of the most flattering and effusive terms possible to the governor, it was his expression of humility that distinguished this second plea.

> My merits are so limited that I hesitated a long time between the alternative of whether I should present them at the foot of the throne or leave them submerged in the backwaters of oblivion. In this interior struggle, in which my indecisive spirit was about to proscribe them forever from my mind, my trembling quill gathered them up, inspired by the clarion call of the reputation that is made public in such sonorous voices by the magnanimity of Your Lordship's noble and merciful heart.[34]

Despite his eloquence, Ibarvo's efforts failed to have the intended effect. His retirement request and the report suggesting he be removed from office were both on hold. Only one of them would move forward. Another six months passed before any discussion about Ibarvo resumed. When Castro arrived in Béxar one of his earliest priorities was to decide Ibarvo's status as lieutenant governor of Nacogdoches. In a letter to the viceroy on the day following his arrival he said:

> I immediately asked of the Governor, Don Manuel Muñoz, for the original report of the commissioner, Don Manuel Gaspar de Verazadi, concerning the conduct of the Lieutenant Governor of Nacogdoches, Don Antonio Gil Ibarvo. And in view of it I have ordered, by common consent with the said Governor Munoz, to make Gil Ibarvo [come to Béxar]. [35]

This was an affirmation of the decision to remove Ibarvo from his post and ban him from Nacogdoches. Castro called attention not to the contraband trade but to Ibarvo's behavior and "the prejudice that the existence of the accused has in Nacogdoches, by being of evil conduct." With Ibarvo's retirement request in hand and before sending a response to Ibarvo to delay that decision, Muñoz coldly sent a letter in March to the new viceroy "proposing measures to conduct proceedings in Nacogdoches against Don Antonio Gil Ybarbo [Ibarvo]."[36] Rather than allowing Ibarvo to retire, they kept him in office so they could take an official action to remove him. That way they could keep him away from his home and family and end his tenure in Nacogdoches with disgrace.

Ibarvo to Béxar

After a review and discussion of the circumstances, Castro and Munoz decided that to arrest Ibarvo in Nacogdoches would be risky. They feared the response of residents, the local chiefs, and their traders. Instead, they came up with a scheme to trick Ibarvo into traveling to Béxar voluntarily by asking him to discuss the assignment of a permanent militia for Nacogdoches, something Ibarvo had been requesting for years. Ibarvo arrived in Béxar within a few weeks of the request. Whether in cowardice or a disregard for the magnitude of the change, Ramón de Castro, the long-awaited commandant general who ordered Ibarvo's arrest, left town before he arrived. He returned to Mexico City satisfied that the proper action was being taken.[37]

Ibarvo presented himself in Béxar on December 27, 1791, and was held in "condition of arrest" at the presidio. In a different situation when unauthorized foreigners were being detained, the viceroy directed they be held "without treating them with severity, neither placing them in shackles nor securing them in close confinement, since the measures will suffice for guarding them in a manner that they may not flee."[38] We can expect that Ibarvo's constraints may have been similarly light. Castro left Muñoz with the responsibility for determining how best to detain Ibarvo when he told him to keep Ibarvo "under the security that may appear to you, in the understanding that you will be the one who has to answer for his person."[39] The conditions of Ibarvo's detention were probably something akin to house arrest, where he was ordered to remain in Béxar but not jailed at any time.

Castro ordered Muñoz to hold Ibarvo "until the facts that have motivated his being relieved [of duty are] clarified [and] I can decide what is best."[40] Though Ibarvo's pay continued while he was held, there was still a concerted effort to make the case against Ibarvo and prevent his return to Nacogdoches in any capacity whatsoever. Recognizing the lack of authority and expertise that Ibarvo's removal would leave in the affairs of East Texas, Castro asked that Muñoz suggest the name of "a trustworthy individual who could take charge of carrying out the proceedings" against Ibarvo, and who could also potentially replace Ibarvo as lieutenant governor.[41] Both assignments would prove to be difficult to fulfill.

Cortès Appointed to Continue Investigation

The governor and the commandant general needed someone they could trust to go to Nacogdoches, gather additional information on Ibarvo, and make a recommendation on Ibarvo's status. Their standards were high. They wanted someone with "uncommon zeal, disinterestedness, impartiality, efficiency, and talent."[42] People with that reputation were not in broad availability in Spanish Texas, but there was one man whose responsibility and military service qualified him for the assignment. Castro reported to the viceroy that they would give that duty to the captain at the presidio of La Bahía, Juan Cortès. Both Muñoz and Castro believed Cortès was the only person able to perform this assignment, a reflection on his reputation and the dearth of those with trusted loyalties in the province of Texas. Castro sent Captain Cortès a copy of Verazadi's report and made clear the outcome desired.

> "The point is to prove Gil Ibarvo carried on clandestine commerce and the barter of muskets, powder and balls with the [Indian] Nations for the mules and horses which they had stolen from us. It will not be very difficult."[43]

Castro even provided Cortès with Hugo Oconór's highly negative 1776 report on Ibarvo's contraband trade written fifteen years prior. Cortès's orders were to proceed to Nacogdoches, confiscate the keys to the archive, and prepare a report detailing their contents. Castro wanted an index and an inventory of everything Ibarvo had tucked away. Ibarvo's property was to be confiscated and valued by an objective party if there was one to be found. Even more tightly focused on Ibarvo himself, Cortès was also directed to take possession of Ibarvo's personal records and papers, as well as those of any trader who may be engaged in illegal activity. While Ibarvo was being held in Béxar, his entire life in Nacogdoches was to be exposed and examined.

Concerns about Indian Relations

Spanish officials at all levels were concerned about trade with the friendly indigenous nations, as well as how to manage the more hostile tribes. Cortès was instructed to meet with the friendly tribes of the north with whom Ibarvo maintained trade relations and tell them they had to stop their trade with the Apache and make war instead. If they did not, then their annual gifts would cease. Castro feared that ending the illegal trade would also damage other legitimate trade that benefitted both the crown and the poor villagers of Nacogdoches. He cautioned Cortès to establish a trusted person to continue the preferred and legal trade, at least to the extent it could be distinguished.

Archives and Documents

Lengthy letters like the one from Castro to Cortès detailing his assignment are rich with detail and instruct historians about aspects of these pivotal moments that would otherwise be lost.[44] In this case, however, the letter is also a cruel tease regarding what is lost or not yet found in some distant archive. Ibarvo's records and files, *cedulas*, correspondence, and other official papers in Nacogdoches were kept under lock and key. Cortès was to take over the keys and send Castro a certified copy of an index listing what he found. We must assume that Cortès fulfilled that order, and a copy of that index was sent. We can also hope that it may someday still be found.

Cortès was to also take possession of Ibarvo's private papers. There may have been a listing of the seizures of contraband made by Ibarvo, an inventory of his stores, and journals showing the items acquired, sales, and payments. The prospect of finding those in a dusty archive is dim, but it would be a moment of revelation for the history of Spanish East Texas.

Castro also sent Cortès information with which to conduct his follow-up investigation. He told Cortès, "In a separate official communication of this date I enclose to you the complaints which various citizens and inhabitants of Nacogdoches have presented to me in *San Antonio de Béxar* against the same Lieutenant Governor."[45] Cortès himself was to gather similar complaints when he traveled to Nacogdoches, but there is no extant documentation of that effort. Were any of these written communications found they would greatly inform our understanding of the interplay between Spanish officials and the means of determining the fate of Antonio Gil Ibarvo. To date all these records have evaded discovery.

Delays in Beginning the Investigation

Despite the urgency expressed by the commandant general and the governor and the communication to the viceroy of the measures to be taken, nothing happened for the first three months of 1792. Cortès was assigned his duties on January 10, and by February 7, he had not even been able to leave La Bahía due to daily rains and flooding. In a report to the viceroy on March 20, Castro had to admit that he still did not have any news from Cortès.

During that delay, Ibarvo was still being detained in Béxar. It would be hard to believe that he was not finding a way to communicate his dilemma and his wishes back to his allies in Nacogdoches. After being appointed as the person responsible for gathering evidence, Cortès said he would keep his effort confidential, but there is little expectation of that given the circumstances. Ibarvo was being detained in Béxar, and people back in Nacogdoches would eventually ask questions. It is unclear what the population of his village knew or did not know about what was happening to Ibarvo at the time. It is unknown who may have filled the leadership void as Ibarvo's proxy in the contraband capital of Texas.

Although Ibarvo was removed from Nacogdoches, both he and the Spanish officials in Béxar who removed him often behaved as if it was a temporary circumstance and he still held his office. In April 1792, the viceroy asked Muñoz for a report on the foreigners living in Nacogdoches. He wanted to know who they were, where they came from, their livelihood, and even their marital status. Muñoz knew he could not answer without help, so on May 12 he asked Ibarvo for the information. Ibarvo provided a detailed answer on the same day as the request.[46] Ibarvo named forty people, predominantly French and some with families, who had either come for trade or moved into his jurisdiction following the eviction at Los Adaes. He told Muñoz that for the most part they had come and "formed cattle ranches, cultivated the lands and cornfields [and] homes, establishments with their families and enslaved people [those who had them], and otherwise [for] the trade with the Indians." Among those named were Joseph Marie Armand, Louis Armand, Stephen Goguet, and Nicholas de La Mathe. All were significant players in the commerce of the day.

Some insight into Ibarvo's personality can be found in what he told the governor about his adversary, Nicholas de La Mathe. Ibarvo had an opportunity to sully La Mathe's reputation with the governor, but he provided him only the facts. He told the governor that La Mathe came with passport to Bucareli "for the purpose of complying with a promise that he made to Our Lady of the Post (Nuestra Señora del Pilár) for building a wooden church" but remained in Bucareli even after not having completed that structure.[47] Either Ibarvo's honesty shone through, or he realized that if he explained La Mathe was keeping hundreds of horses with suspicious origins on the prairies at Bucareli it would further stain his own reputation.

Captains of Contraband

In appointing Juan Cortès, the captain of the presidio at La Bahía, to conduct the investigation into Ibarvo, the viceroy and the commandant general wanted to believe their high expectations were met. They wanted someone to follow up the investigation into Ibarvo's behavior who would act with high ethical standards. They got was the closest person they could find.

Cortès and several soldiers set out for Nacogdoches from La Bahía on February 9, 1792. They arrived on March 6 and remained in Nacogdoches for over three months. During that time Cortès acted as the interim lieutenant governor of Nacogdoches. Though the governor wanted someone beyond reproach, what they got instead was a man who immediately engaged in the same type of smuggling he was supposed to be investigating.[48]

The Investigator Becomes the Investigated

On June 17, 1792, the very day that Cortès and his soldiers arrived back in Béxar from their months in Nacogdoches, Antonio Gil Ibarvo reported to the governor that Cortès himself was engaged in smuggling contraband goods.[49] Ibarvo wasted no time in reporting this behavior to the interim governor, the Conde de Sierra Gorda. Sierra Gorda was briefly sent to the province in 1792 to examine the administration of Manuel Muñoz and during that time served as an acting governor. Although Ibarvo had been removed from Nacogdoches, he had not yet been removed from service. Ibarvo signed the letter of accusation as the "captain of militia and lieutenant governor" of Nacogdoches.

Ibarvo reported that within only three days after arriving in Nacogdoches to begin his investigation, Cortès teamed up with Ibarvo's enemy, Nicholas de La Mathe. Cortès sent one of his sergeants and a private to Natchitoches where they met up with La Mathe and then came back with "many loads of goods" that included tobacco and playing cards, along with other regulated commerce.

They also collected some of Ibarvo's mules, which were seized while he was held in Béxar. In May 1792 Captain Cortès went to the home of Joaquín de Cordova in Nacogdoches and asked if he had mules belonging to Ibarvo, which de Cordova did. Cortès told him that the mules were being seized and ordered de Cordova to hold them until Cortès needed them. In a letter to Ibarvo, de Cordova described how after leaving Cortès's house in Nacogdoches, he encountered Nicholas de La Mathe, who told de Cordova to give him one of the mules. When de Cordova complained about doing that and explained the order from Cortès regarding the mules, La Mathe went to Cortès, who then ordered de Cordova to give La Mathe one of Ibarvo's mules. La Mathe may have justified taking Ibarvo's property because of Ibarvo's debt, but Ibarvo implicated Cortès himself for the unlawful transfer.

There are two interesting aspects of this complicated matter. The first is the chain of debts and payments that became triggered by the exchange of the mules. The details of how one person owed another and how notes were held as debt, how long the notes were held, and how they were paid by pesos or property attests to a frontier commerce based on the exchange of goods for future promises.

The second item of note is a comment made by de Cordova. When explaining to Ibarvo about what had happened with his mules, de Cordova said, "I found myself being compelled to provide them, and since they put so much fear into us here, I said I would provide them."[50] Intimidation and threats as a means of control were instruments of authority in the borderlands. Ibarvo himself displayed some of that in his dispute with the Kichai chief who tossed a handful of dirt toward him. Here it is seen expressed during the void in leadership following Ibarvo's removal—a time when Cortès, La Mathe, and others were jockeying for more influence and control.

Ibarvo suggested that Sierra Gorda act quickly so Cortès would not have time to conceal the goods he had taken. Not only did Ibarvo report the smuggling, but he also suggested who Sierra Gorda should depose when he investigated. Though Ibarvo was prevented from leaving Béxar, he was clearly not barred from having contact with others. Someone loyal to him, someone on whom he counted as an informant and contact, must have told him about the behavior of Cortès and La Mathe while in Nacogdoches. Ibarvo said "they acted in a prejudicial manner with such outrages, vested interests, and lack of Christianity, ignoring [his] lawful rights."[51] Reporting them for smuggling was a fitting form of retribution for Ibarvo and an opportunity to polish his image with the officials who had him removed.

Given that Cortès was in Nacogdoches to investigate the contraband trade of Ibarvo, Cortès's actions and illegal acts were an affront to the royal decrees to control trade in certain goods and property. The governor agreed with Ibarvo's assessment of the troubling situation with Cortès. Within three days of Ibarvo's report, Sierra Gorda himself was taking depositions.

Depositions Begin

Based on Ibarvo's report, Sierra Gorda immediately ordered that the goods in question be found and seized from Cortès and any of the men who accompanied him. He also discreetly sent Lt. Bernardo Fernandes and ten soldiers to La Bahía. Some of the men Ibarvo named were in Béxar, so the investigation began quickly on June 20, 1792. Sierra Gorda's questions focused on the goods brought to Nacogdoches by Frenchmen from Natchitoches, on whose authority they were transported, the means used to purchase them, and where the items went. He took initial depositions from the following men:

- Sergeant Antonio Trevino (43 years old, married)
- Corporal José Ylario Maldonado (46 years old, married)
- Private Antonio Gomez (28 years old, married)
- Private José de Trexo (21 years old, single)
- Private José Antonio del Rio (42 years old, married)

Each of them, based on their assignments during the time the goods were brought to Nacogdoches, had a different perspective on the matter under question.

In general, the story they told was that within three days of their arrival in Nacogdoches, Captain Cortès ordered some of his men to travel to Natchitoches with a few Frenchmen to purchase goods. The testimony of the soldiers, particularly that of Sergeant Trevino, reported a large amount of tobacco, two kegs of *aguardiente*, two kegs of gunpowder, many bullets, and a cask full of large knives. Food items included two casks of lard, salt, corn, sugar, and one sack of beans. There was also uncut fabric and vermilion for making clothing and beads for adding decoration. Trevino reported seeing seventeen mule loads arriving from Natchitoches in three separate travel parties. One of the soldiers noted that the Frenchmen who went to Natchitoches also carried a load of buffalo tongues for trade.

Part of what angered Ibarvo was the apparent fact that the purchase of these items was paid for with two hundred deerskins that were among his confiscated property. His property was to be held while his case was pending. Sergeant Trevino confirmed that the skins were Ibarvo's.

Each of the soldiers deposed in the matter reported that though some of the goods went to the home of Louis Armand, the French trader to the native tribes, the bulk of the goods went to La Mathe's house. From the testimony, however, not all the goods stayed with La Mathe. As much as half of the seventeen loads of goods were given to Capt. Juan Cortès. Perhaps to ensure his soldiers remained silent, Cortès, Armand, and La Mathe shared with them rather liberally and encouraged them to conduct their own trade with the Indians. One soldier said that Armand supplied him and others with quantities of tobacco and "other assistance for his sustenance" by order of Captain Cortès.

In some cases, the soldiers were given deerskins, the de facto currency of trade in East Texas, which they then exchanged for other items. Sergeant Trevino said that La Mathe had given him skins and that some of the other soldiers traded for skins in the Indian villages in exchange for tobacco and knives given them by La Mathe with Cortès's approval and consent. During the months they were in Nacogdoches, a single soldier said he received about four *manojos* of tobacco (about twenty pounds). Another soldier estimated that they had each been given about one pound of tobacco every two weeks. Some of the tobacco was for personal use, but the soldiers were given enough extra tobacco that it could be used to trade for deerskins. Private Trexo said he acquired a valued deerskin by trading what he could muster—he swapped the bridle off his horse and a biscuit he saved from breakfast. This is perhaps the truest expression of the power of forces driving contraband trade, and the basis for the title of this work.

Harsh Judgment for Sierra Gorda

Ramón de Castro, the commandant general, did not learn about Sierra Gorda's investigation of Captain Cortès until July 14. Castro received an initial set of documents from Sierra Gorda including a long list of goods confiscated from each of the members of the troop. The baggage of Captain Cortès alone contained yards of blue, yellow, and red cloth; cloth for jackets and skirts; playing cards; axes; buttons; coffee; and eighty pounds of French tobacco. On that list were items that were clearly prohibited, including playing cards, tobacco, and uncut cloth.

A glaring omission from the documents was the testimony of Capt. Juan Cortès. Sierra Gorda had interviewed only the few members of the group who were already in Béxar. Sierra Gorda had not questioned or deposed Cortès himself after the initial testimony by the sergeant and privates who accompanied him to Nacogdoches. Nor had he questioned Cortès's brother-in-law, José de Jesus Alderete, who was also involved.

Sierra Gorda may have thought he was finished with the matter, but Ramón de Castro was just getting started. Castro's response to Sierra Gorda was forceful and direct. Castro said that simply based on the initial report, Sierra Gorda had enough information to immediately arrest Cortès for smuggling, but he failed to act. Castro scolded Sierra Gorda by saying that he was "obliged to act with utmost purity [but] since you have not done so, I see no reason for you not to be judged harshly."[52] With strong words of rebuke, Castro instructed Sierra Gorda to carry on toward a verdict that could then be passed on to the viceroy for approval. He was to also keep the confiscated goods safely isolated and wait for a decision regarding their disposition. As further evidence of Castro's lack of trust in Sierra Gorda, he remarked that someone else may have to be sent to Nacogdoches to confirm what Sierra Gorda was reporting and to clean up the mess.[53]

Capt. Juan Cortès Delays his Deposition

Sierra Gorda sought to correct his initial oversight by bringing Cortès and the soldiers back to Béxar from La Bahía. He sent Cortès a letter in August 1792 ordering them to come to the capital. Antonio Trevino, promoted from sergeant to lieutenant since the confiscation, obeyed the interim governor's order and was immediately en route with the summoned soldiers, lacking only a couple who were legitimately unavailable.

However, Capt. Juan Cortès did not immediately comply with the order. His letter of August 19, 1792, said he had a ruptured swelling, possibly a tumor or cyst of some kind, in his left arm that rendered him unable to ride a horse. Cortès effectively called in sick for his legal proceedings, an unusual response to a superior officer. Given that his condition still required treatment six months later, it seems a legitimate complaint while still a surprising rejection of Sierra Gorda's interim authority.[54] Cortès was also prepared with a second excuse that was not quite as reasonable. He said he had some paperwork to do with a pressing deadline. The *havilitado*—the regiment officer in charge of payroll and other administrative duties—was leaving his post, and Cortès had to do an audit of his work so that the incoming officer would have a starting point. Rather than the usual flowery closing and typical wishes that "God grant your Lordship many years," Cortès simply said he hoped Sierra Gorda "will please pardon my unavoidable absence."

It was not until September 10, 1792, three months after Ibarvo's report of wrongdoing, that Capt. Juan Cortès made it to Béxar and was finally compelled to respond to the charges. As one might imagine, given the time elapsed since the deposition of his soldiers and Cortès's role in the incident, his testimony provided both additional details and a bit of an alternate reality in opposition to the statements of his soldiers. Cortès's story differed from the very outset of the questioning.

When Cortès was asked why his soldiers went to Natchitoches, he placed the responsibility on Sergeant Trevino rather than himself. Cortès said that Trevino asked permission to go to Natchitoches to collect a debt. Cortès said he told the officer it was up to him if he wanted to go, which is not a response one would expect from a commanding officer. While that may have initially been true, Trevino also traveled to Natchitoches—contraband central—a second time with Nicholas de La Mathe. That the captain would allow his sergeant to leave their assignment in Nacogdoches seems an aberration in his military duties. La Mathe, with Trevino, left Nacogdoches on May 21, but returned on May 25 after finding the Sabine River too flooded to cross.

When asked about the loads brought into Nacogdoches by the three Frenchman, Trevino said there may have been two or three loads brought in, but he knew about only one. Cortès said the load that went to La Mathe's house contained tobacco, scarlet and blue cloth, vermilion, glass beads, knives, mirrors, gunpowder, and bullets. Cortès also added that La Mathe used the goods as "gifts to the [Indian] Nations that came to visit him at the town of Nacogdoches." Was La Mathe working to replace Ibarvo on his own, or was he simply gaining favor with the Indians to carry out his usual trade?

Cortès's admission that he did not recall or notice how many loads of goods La Mathe brought from Natchitoches suggests that Cortès, who'd been sent to investigate contraband, was either looking the other way or was involved himself. In his deposition he sought to evade a direct question about the goods.

> Asked if he knows of the repeated superior orders that have been issued to this province prohibiting trade of all kinds with the French, and that there can be introduced into this province only the fabrics and goods brought in through the port of Beracruz [Veracruz] and others authorized by Our Lord, the King, he said: That he is not aware that there exists in the archives at [La] Bahía del Espíritu Santo orders that address this particular, and if there are, he is unaware of how he might have disobeyed them.[55]

Even Cortès's sergeant had admitted knowing that playing cards, tobacco, and uncut cloth was contraband. That Cortès seemed to plead ignorance was surprising. His answer to the most telling question posted to him by Sierra Gorda seems either disingenuous or simply another example of the Spanish custom of *obedezco, pero no cumplo.* I obey but I do not comply.

Questions about the tobacco, the cloth, the buttons, and other items found in Cortès's possession were explained away. Cortès also tried to absolve himself of any blame by stating that he purchased none of those items in Natchitoches, but rather in Nacogdoches. He argued that he was not guilty of contraband trade—even though he traded for items he knew were disallowed—because he was not the one who brought the goods into Nacogdoches.

Ratification of Testimony before Muñoz

By September 1792, an impatient Manuel Muñoz was back in the governorship. Sierra Gorda had either finished his temporary assignment in Texas or had been pushed aside from the investigation because of his failure to act. Muñoz now wanted to question Cortès and the other witnesses himself, so he called each of them back to review their testimony firsthand. Muñoz began his questioning on September 25, 1792, and was much more pointed in his questioning than Sierra Gorda, learning additional details about the goods that had not been exposed.

Lt. Antonio Trevino had nothing to add or delete from his earlier testimony, which had been detailed and forthcoming. Cpl. José Ylario Maldonado, after affirming his previous testimony, added details under the hard questioning by Muñoz. Maldonado admitted he had received as much as twenty pounds of tobacco from Louis Armand, the French trader, during their three-month stay in Nacogdoches. He also acknowledged using a common method to avoid the ban on possessing uncut cloth by having clothing made. Having a tailor was like have someone who could launder stolen money. Maldonado also recounted several examples where Captain Cortès provided him with known contraband goods or permitted trade that they both knew was prohibited.

The deposition of Pvt. Joaquín Galan revealed he was quite actively engaged in trade. He did not travel to Natchitoches but benefitted from the trade of others, and his earlier testimony differed from his updated admissions. Galan admitted he had misled Sierra Gorda about how he turned cut cloth that was illegal into completed petticoats, skirts, and other finished clothing that was legal. His goods included chamois and a buffalo skin he had purchased in trade for an old waistcoat and a *zarape*, and other items he had won in a card came called *malilla*. Captain Cortès had also given Galan a horse to trade, and Galan somehow acquired two other horses on his own.

Galan also shed some light on Cortès's attempt to hide the contraband and avoid detection on their way back to La Bahía. Muñoz asked Galan if it was Cortès's intent to bring the goods he carried from Nacogdoches to Béxar for inspection, or if he planned to secret them off to La Bahía. At a critical intersection in the road from Nacogdoches, Cortès had Sergeant Trevino take the road to La Bahía with the loads of goods, while Cortès and a few soldiers continued to Béxar. Their separation would likely have come just across the Trinity River on the west side of Paso Tomás near the former site of Bucareli, abandoned thirteen years before.

Another soldier, Pvt. Antonio del Rio, knew the tobacco and playing cards he acquired were contraband, but he said he thought purchasing the other goods in Spanish Nacogdoches made them legal. He disregarded that they were illegal goods or delivered by illegal French traders. According to the private's uninformed experience, the source of the goods did not matter once they were sold to someone like him in Nacogdoches. The more the private answered Muñoz's questions, the more he painted himself into a corner with his answers. Castro became incensed when del Rio claimed not to know the origins of the tobacco he purchased in Nacogdoches. Muñoz's report said that the privates answer caused "the present governor some difficulty."

Munoz increased the intensity of his questioning, asking del Rio where he was born, when he left Los Adaes, and how long he had been in the military. Del Rio answered each question. In reply, Muñoz wondered aloud how he could not know the tobacco was French given del Rio's history in Los Adaes, Natchitoches, and the presidios of Orcoquisac and La Bahía. From the tone of the report, Muñoz's questioning was no doubt withering for the forty-two-year-old private. Muñoz even asked del Rio at the end of his deposition if he had been coached on any of his answers. Muñoz did not trust the private's replies, which sounded too similar to those offered by Cortès.

Several soldiers who had not been part of the initial round of depositions were summoned to testify before Muñoz on September 28, 1792. Pvt. Salvado Sierra's lengthy testimony added details to what Muñoz had already gleaned from others. Sierra was the first one to name others who were on the assignment in Nacogdoches. He also admitted he began the trip by planning to trade as soon as he arrived, bringing four pairs of women's shoes with him to Nacogdoches. Sierra also had yet another variation on how he determined something might be contraband. He claimed it was his understanding that an item was not contraband if it was used rather than new.

Whether Muñoz had decided Cortès would have little more to say, or doubted he would tell the truth, he had few questions for the captain of La Bahía. Cortès affirmed his testimony, adding only a few other items he had in his load, but he dismissed further details by saying, "If there is anything else, it would be of such little consequence that he cannot recall it." Cortès was dismissive.

A Decision and an Auction of Goods

Although Munoz was cleaning up the investigation done by Sierra Gorda and gathering his own testimony, the information that had already reached Viceroy Revilla Gigedo was more than enough for him to issue orders on how to proceed with the case. Based on the results of Sierra Gorda's initial depositions, which the viceroy received on July 2, the viceroy issued orders to Governor Munoz on how to proceed in a September 1792 letter.[56]

The seized tobacco was to be sold in the *estanco*, the government's store. The viceroy also decided that all the skins, other than those in the possession of Cortès and his brother-in-law, José de Jesús Alderete, should be returned to those from whom the goods were confiscated. However, Cortès and Alderete were to be further punished by the loss of goods, because "they are the culprits in this contraband." Finally, the viceroy ordered that all the textiles, gunpowder, playing cards, and other contraband goods be sold at auction for the benefit of the royal treasury. Public announcements of the auction by Governor Muñoz went out, and the goods were put on display.[57]

The auction on November 17 produced a little over 958 pesos in revenue for the crown. The eighty pounds of French tobacco sold in the store produced 135 pesos, but it was the uncut fabric that brought the most revenue at about 286 pesos. Cut cloth, finished skirts, and trinkets such as buttons, ribbons, and belts brought 373 pesos. A nice kerchief and an axe both sold for four pesos each, while skirts and blankets were each about six pesos. For two pesos, one could have purchased a buffalo hide or an iron pot. Anyone in the market for a moth-eaten deerskin could have had one for only two reales, one-fourth of a peso.

For Captain Cortès, Lieutenant Trevino, and the other soldiers, there were no other legal repercussions beyond the loss of their goods. They all remained in their posts, chastised but not punished. Cortès continued to report on encounters with Apache and investigations of the coastline in search of any invading French force. For all its bluster and prohibitions, the Spanish laws on contraband were not necessarily meant to eliminate such trade but to control it in a way that created revenue for the provincial government in New Spain. The usual deterrents to contraband trade were hardly a slap on the wrist.

A Replacment for Ibarvo

Focus on the smuggling and contraband trade of the formerly trusted Capt. Juan Cortès may have taken the spotlight from Antonio Gil Ibarvo and his reported transgressions for a time. In late 1792, After Juan Cortès's failures in

Nacogdoches, the sixty-two-year-old Cristóbal de Cordova was appointed as the new commander and justice of Nacogdoches.[58]

Even though Ibarvo had been replaced in Nacogdoches, he performed acts as if he were still installed. In October 1792, Ibarvo was in the home of Governor Muñoz along with Bernardo Fernández, newly appointed as second in command to Cordova at Nacogdoches, and Xavier Menchaca, the second lieutenant of the Presidio of San Antonio de Béxar. Ibarvo continued to try and curry favor with the governor by reporting others engaged in contraband trade. In December 1792, Ibarvo told Muñoz a few citizens of Nacogdoches were suspected of having loads that included some "illegally imported goods."[59] Ibarvo also said there was a priest traveling with them, and that he too had contraband among his other items carried "without regard for the various royal orders published in that town [Nacogdoches] against such an abuse." Likely using Austin's "old road" and the other former Bidai trails that helped avoid detection, they intended to branch off toward La Bahía, Ibarvo said. Once there, the smugglers would hide their goods in the mission or in the home of one of the Indians.

Given his position and allegiance to the crown, Muñoz felt compelled to investigate. Oddly, he again assigned the responsibility to Capt. Juan Cortès, even though La Bahía was implicated by the complicity suggested in Ibarvo's report.[60] The small trunks carried by Father Francisco Gamarra and the others from Nacogdoches were delivered to Cortès in December 1792. The group had *guías* (licenses) for certain goods issued by Cristóbal de Cordova, the new commander in Nacogdoches.

Cortès assumed this would be a simple matter and delegated the inspection to Lt. Manuel de Espadas. Espadas's assignment was to see if there were any other items not listed in their permits. Cortès's letter to Espadas hinted at some disdain for the governor's order. Cortès told Espadas that his action was to "give satisfaction to the Señor governor of the province."[61] The follow-up to Ibarvo's report was taking on the air of soldiers simply going through the motions.

Is It Contraband or Is It Not?

Espadas wasted no time conducting his inspection of the loads, which had been locked in the guardhouse at La Bahía. Espadas did not find anything in the trunks other than what was listed on the *guías*. The loads were found to have been legally transported, and Cortès ordered the goods returned to the owners the same day.[62] It was surprising that Cordova gave permission for the transport of uncut fabric and cloth found in the baggage, items that had been considered as contraband in earlier matters.

Cortès forwarded the *guías*, his orders, and Espada's report to Governor Muñoz in mid-January 1793. Although his letter was brief, Cortès did not hesitate to pass up the opportunity to take a verbal swipe at Antonio Gil Ibarvo. He told Muñoz, "The accusation that you received in writing did not accomplish the purpose sought by the accuser [Ibarvo], because [the results] were quite contrary to what he was thinking."[63]

Muñoz had a different perspective, however, and he challenged Cortès's view.[64] In the letter Muñoz told Cortès that his decision was "thought to be rash." Muñoz believed the skirt cuttings should have been confiscated and held until the viceroy could make a declaration. What Muñoz preferred Cortès do was to inspect the loads himself, register what they contained, and then hold the goods under guard until Muñoz made a ruling on their disposition. Cortès may never have seen the letter from Muñoz. A note in the margin indicating it was "not sent" may have meant that Cortès avoided the governor's chastisement, or Muñoz simply believed it just was not worth sending.

As the testimony of the soldiers in the Cortès matter illustrated, the understanding of what goods were prohibited and what was acceptable was a fluid definition largely based on one's personal experiences. The question of what was and wasn't contraband lingered much longer than one might expect among men in key positions in the province.

Where one would not expect a lack of clarity about what was considered contraband was with a commandant general, a Spanish governor, and the captain of a presidio—Pedro de Nava, Manuel Muñoz, and Juan Cortès. For a couple of years, Pedro de Nava and Ramón de Castro had jointly governed a large jurisdiction called the Eastern Provinces. When the Provincias Internas were separated into smaller jurisdictions, it was de Nava who served as commandant general. In October 1793, de Nava felt the need to again redefine what commerce was acceptable. He had probably already learned about Cortès's role in a few controversial acts. De Nava reiterated that the presidio at La Bahía was not allowed to accept <u>any</u> items from Nacogdoches, and Muñoz passed on that edict to Juan Cortès at the presidio. After Cortès briefly agreed he would not allow any goods from Nacogdoches to come to the presidio at La Bahía, he asked a question that showed his own uncertainty about what was and what was not acceptable when it came to trade. Cortès's question to Governor Muñoz reflected his ambiguity and frustration.

> You will please to tell me whether one who brings in a guía from the justice [commander] there [Nacogdoches] should be treated in a similar fashion with a confiscation, because I know full well that with [a guía] some

> [contraband goods] have been introduced into that capital [Béxar] and were not seized. Thus, in order that I make no mistake in its observance, I will merit your telling me what is best.[65]

Cortès statement is a striking example of the persistent duplicity in the enforcement of edicts against the import of contraband goods in the province of Texas. Selective enforcement, geographic inaccessibility, indefensible laws, and international commerce would never stop what was essentially, in any other setting, the routine activity of everyday life. Cortès succinctly defined the issues of the day.

Muñoz challenged Cortès to provide examples supporting his allegation and state who had allowed that to happen. When Cortès did not do so, Muñoz refused to let an empty accusation go unchallenged. He instead reminded Cortès that he still expected to hear about examples of impermissible contraband goods being brought to Béxar. Cortès again did not provide specific examples, but instead he taunted Muñoz by telling him he would answer Cortès's question "at the appropriate time," without stating when that might be. He also implied that when, or if, he did so it might scandalize the governor himself. Cortès closed his end of the conversation with a comment that was remarkably bold and direct when spoken to a superior official.

> Since [you] have not earned your living with anything other than the king's salary, as have I, and not with contraband, it is necessary to clarify what is still [shrouded] in malicious reports, which will be clarified someday.[66]

The implications of Cortès's statement remain a mystery, known only to him. Whether the reports he thought would be clarified were the accusations against him by Ibarvo, or the general nature of inconsistent efforts toward contraband trade is not known.

What seems to be clear is that Cortès's commitment to serve the crown and to report to a succession of rotating superior officers was nearing an end. The underlying message of Cortès's letter implied that he had had enough. He would continue to serve the crown in his post because, as he said, he had never earned a living otherwise.

11

"It Is Just That He Suffer," the Case Against Ibarvo

I humbly beseech you, to issue a new, prudent, and cautious order that suffices to overcome the odious delay that I am experiencing in my affairs on the part of this señor governor.[1]

—ANTONIO GIL IBARVO

While verbal sparring and investigations into smuggling by presidio captains and Spanish priests drew away attention, the case against Antonio Gil Ibarvo languished. His removal from Nacogdoches was the primary goal, so there was little pressure to resolve the matter other than what Ibarvo applied himself. Though he was ostensibly held in Béxar awaiting charges, his full pay continued even if his earlier life did not. While Ibarvo was held in Béxar, two of his sons died within a three-day period in December 1792. One died from natural causes and the other from "blows that a drunken mulatto gave to him."[2] History can easily forget that famous figures of the past were also fathers, husbands, and friends.

The fact of Ibarvo's removal from his post was certain. Governor Muñoz communicated with Pedro de Nava in July 1793 about the need to find a replacement for Cristóbal de Cordova, the old soldier who had been put in place in Nacogdoches a year prior. Ever hopeful he would find the right person, Muñoz still sought:

> an official who is capable, disinterested, and free of the passions which may show a bad example to its citizens and Indians who may repair to it, and not having a subaltern of these qualifications in this province, nor of the ideas that are adaptable for the Indian trade, nor to acquire from them the news that we are able to crave.[3]

In September 1793, Muñoz repeated his plea to de Nava for help in finding a replacement after the commandant general ordered Muñoz to do so. Muñoz again said he knew of no one in the province of Texas or in any of the military officers within Coahuila. He also pointed out that whoever was appointed would not succeed without the support of additional troops in place in Nacogdoches to cut off all the contraband routes toward the villages nearby. Those routes were where illicit trade was most prominent and were former Bidai trails and trade routes.

Muñoz also pointed out to de Nava, not very subtly, that Ibarvo himself had repeatedly pointed out the need for additional troops to Ramón de Castro. In fact, the ruse used to lure Ibarvo to Béxar had been based on just that—his continuing request for troops.[4] By informing de Nava of the need for a person with specific traits, Muñoz had to wonder why the opening existed at all. The qualifications listed sounded exactly like the man he had removed. Muñoz admitted there was no one like Ibarvo in the entire province; there was no one who could do what Antonio Gil Ibarvo could do.

It is only a hint, but perhaps there is one aspect of those qualifications that had caused Ibarvo to lose favor, both with his superiors and even with the people of Nacogdoches. Muñoz said he needed someone who is "free of the passions which may show a bad example to its citizens and Indians who may repair to it."[5] Similarly, de Nava urged they do not install anyone who may "vex the citizens."[6] There was also a suggestion that the tribes would not mind much if Ibarvo was removed. Ibarvo's alleged beating of one or more citizens of Nacogdoches pointed toward the notion that he, like many in positions of power over others, had worn out his welcome. Despite his other favorable qualifications, there would be no going back.

One thing was certain—Cristóbal de Cordova was not the man for the job. Cortès's leaving him as the interim lieutenant governor in Nacogdoches was a stopgap measure. Muñoz told de Nava that Cordova was not equipped for the role due to "his kind nature, as well as the smallness of his abilities."[7] It would take another year and a half to find—or convince—someone to take his place as the de facto leader of the Spanish pueblo at the center of contraband trade. Despite his shortcomings, Cordova remained in the post until January 1795, a service of over three years in Nacogdoches.

Cordova's replacement would be Lt. Bernardo Fernández, who had been engaged in the investigations and was second in command for a time. In de Nava's letter regarding the appointment, he instructed Cordova to turn over the jurisdiction and archives to Lieutenant Fernández along with the "instruments of war."[8] Fernández began his trip to Nacogdoches from Béxar in early

January 1795 with additional troops and gifts for the Indians, and by February 21 Fernández was in command.[9] One must wonder if he knew what he was in for.

Three Books

Early in their tenure, each new commandant general or viceroy for the Province of Texas seemed convinced that with a few pronouncements and edicts they could tidy up whatever mess they inherited. In his letter to Governor Muñoz in late November 1793, Pedro de Nava seemed confident he could quickly finish up the Ibarvo matter. It had been two full years since Ibarvo was removed from the center of contraband culture in Nacogdoches. De Nava gathered all the charges and testimony together in three books and sent them to Governor Muñoz for his consideration. He was certain it was all Muñoz needed to "proceed as soon as possible to its execution and compliance with the writs that it advises for its final determination."[10] The final determination was a decision about Ibarvo's status.

That optimism by the commandant general for a swift resolution was unfounded. Almost a year later, Ibarvo sent the first of a series of complaints to de Nava about Governor Muñoz's slowness in bringing his case to a conclusion. Ibarvo added that Muñoz had made insulting remarks about toward Ibarvo. In a testament to that slowness, Ibarvo's letter sent to de Nava in August 1794 was not forwarded to Muñoz until late October, and Muñoz did not reply to de Nava until early 1795.[11] Muñoz's reply to de Nava spelled out the reasons—the excuses—for not coming to a final determination.

De Nava's impassioned convictions appear to have had little impact on Muñoz's delays. Ibarvo again wrote de Nava in January 1795, and de Nava wrote Muñoz a second time reminding him of the order issued in the previous October.[12] De Nava wanted it finished, and Ibarvo wanted it finished. Muñoz seemed to simply want to move on to other matters.

Muñoz's Excuses

Muñoz wrote a lengthy letter in response to de Nava's continued orders to conclude Ibarvo's case. It was made lengthy by the extent to which Muñoz went to deflect blame away from himself, and in some cases, place the blame on Ibarvo.[13] It was Muñoz's efforts to blame Ibarvo for the slowness that exposed not only that Muñoz's delays were likely intentional, but they also showed again his disdain for the former lieutenant governor. Muñoz said that although Ibarvo grumbled about the harm done to him by the delay, Ibarvo complained "without thinking that his excesses were the cause of the charges being made against him." Muñoz thought it was only fair that Ibarvo suffer.

> The harms that Gil Ybarbo [Ibarvo] is protesting result to him, and as the cause of them by his disorders [his behavior], it is quite just that he suffer them, until he offers other evidence in support than the ones that run in the proceedings.

Muñoz also noted that when word began to circulate that Ibarvo could possibly return to Nacogdoches, some of the citizens who had submitted written testimony unfavorable to Ibarvo wanted to retract their depositions out of fear of retribution.

Ibarvo had complained Muñoz was doing him harm by propagating a statement made in the Verazadi report that Ibarvo was not really a Spaniard, but a mulatto, a mix of Spanish and African descent. Muñoz told de Nava that it was apparent based on Ibarvo's skin color and was easy to prove. Muñoz also said that the documents Ibarvo submitted to disprove the allegations of his race were suspect testimony issued only to try and "obscure his genealogy."[14]

De Nava was having nothing of Muñoz's complaints and excuses. He called Muñoz's delay "contrary to justice," and noted that it was not right for "this individual to experience such a long imprisonment when it is not known if his offenses, when judged, will merit such punishment." Muñoz went to some pains to clarify that Ibarvo's "imprisonment" was more akin to a house arrest, with limits on his comings and goings.

> The latter has not been under rigorous arrest, as he claims, nor has he suffered any other than the freedom to go from house to house in this villa, according to his pleasure and will. And he has been improperly receiving his salary up to today's date, even though he is suspended from his office, which [salary] he has been enjoying because no action has been taken, nor was this point addressed by the most excellent senor viceroy of Mexico, or the former commandant general of the Eastern [Interior] Provinces, Ramón de Castro, for which reason the governor [Muñoz] thought it best not to deal with this matter.[15]

Muñoz also contended that the document with which Ramón de Castro placed Cortès in charge of the investigation and laid out his assignment should be confidential and withheld from Ibarvo. He made the same argument for confidentiality for the Verazadi report. De Nava found that unacceptable, saying, "No one suffering imprisonment should be deprived of the recourses necessary to their legal defense."[16] The evidence must be shared with the accused.

The Case Finally Progresses

Once Muñoz committed to completion rather than complaint, matters seemed to progress more quickly. After Muñoz finally presented his evidence to the government attorney, the counsel asked the testimony of witnesses who were interviewed three years earlier by Juan Cortès be ratified to ensure they were not coached or coerced. Muñoz sought to excuse three years of delay by saying that if he now imposed on these witnesses to be interviewed, he would somehow deprive "those unfortunate ones" from doing the planting they needed to survive.[17] That complaint was ignored.

By mid-May 1795, Muñoz arranged for the witnesses available in Béxar and Nacogdoches to come forward to ratify their earlier testimony or modify it from what they said before. There were seven witnesses in Béxar, and another group in Nacogdoches. After hearing their testimony, Muñoz said the witnesses examined in Béxar corroborated their earlier testimony and did nothing to acquit Ibarvo.[18] Lieutenant Bernardo Fernández was to conduct the interviews of those in Nacogdoches. Muñoz sent Fernández copies of the earlier proceedings by June 5 so he could compare new statements with what had been earlier stated. De Nava continued to issue orders to resolve the matter to Muñoz since nothing had been decided by mid-July.[19]

Charges Delivered

October 1, 1795. That was the date Antonio Gil Ibarvo finally received the compilation of charges against him. It was two months shy of four full years that he had lived in limbo in Béxar, an unwelcomed guest and a commander without a jurisdiction to command. What had been three books of documents regarding Ibarvo's behavior in the past became four. Ibarvo's request for those volumes had been approved by de Nava, and they were finally delivered. Apparently, they still did not yet contain all the testimonial details. There were older complaints alluded to in the third book but not provided, including remarks attributed to Hugo Oconór, Juan de Ugalde, and the Verazadi report itself. Ibarvo requested those documents so he could prepare a defense. Despite all the activity, the case was still not yet resolved. De Nava gave up on issuing orders that would simply be ignored and resorted to pleading with Muñoz to resolve the case.[20]

> You well know how important it is to conclude Gil's case. This individual is suffering punishment from which he should be freed if he does not deserve it or increased if he so deserves; the budget bears a salary that is not due; and justice continues to be illusory at any rate as long as the

> proceedings have no resolution. Therefore, I charge you most especially to seek to finalize the aforesaid case without further delay than that already experienced.[21]

Either de Nava's plea had the intended effect or Muñoz was tired of addressing it. Progress on completing the case against Antonio Gil Ibarvo finally picked up pace.

Administratively Concluded

The deaths of two of Ibarvo's sons while he was banished to Béxar were not the only family tragedies. His wife, María Padilla, died in Nacogdoches on January 21, 1794.[22] She had requested her belongings be kept by her grandson, Gregorio Mora, until Ibarvo could arrange for their disposition. Ibarvo asked that his daughter, María Antonia, deliver to him some of the items he had given his wife. The conditions of Ibarvo's arrest apparently did not prevent him from making new relationships or social contacts. Two years after his wife's death, Ibarvo remarried in early 1796. Since he was still considered under house arrest, Ibarvo sought permission from Pedro de Nava to marry María Guadalupe de Herrera in Béxar.[23]

An Ending Without a Conclusion

It was early in 1796 before the troubles of Antonio Gil Ibarvo began to work their way toward a legal conclusion. The delays in his case were not always caused by others. After finally coming to the point of appointing a judge to administer justice in his case, Ibarvo rejected the first appointment, which forced the selection of a second person to hear the case. The governor appointed forty-two-year-old Juan Martín de Amondaraín, a merchant of Béxar. Though not an attorney, his stature led Muñoz to call him "the only one who could carry out the duties of this position."[24] Amondaraín had his own complicated legal difficulties a few years prior. A complex case over his appointment as guardian of the children and manager of the assets of Fernando de Veramendi led to his "unauthorized absence" from the jurisdiction. He had also served briefly as lieutenant governor under Martinez Pacheco.

With four books of letters, documents, and depositions in hand, the proceedings crawled toward a final decision. In the letter from Governor Muñoz to Pedro de Nava on March 14, 1796, the governor explained that Amondaraín had come to an opinion on the matter and transmitted the files to de Nava for a final decision. De Nava acknowledged receipt on April 4 and passed them on to the legal authority there in Chihuahua.[25] Another six months passed before de Nava brought the case to a conclusion.

> In view of the case brought against Don Antonio Gil Ybarbo [Ibarvo], former lieutenant governor of the town of Nacogdoches . . . regarding malfeasance in his office and his having concealed the introduction of contraband goods, although such excesses have not been fully substantiated, I have resolved by a decree of this date—in accord with an opinion of the senor military asesor [assessor] of this commandancy general—to consider it administratively concluded in the state in which it exists, but without him being able to continue in that post. This determination you will make known to the interested party, setting him free immediately and ordering that he be returned all the property that might have been confiscated so that he might settle wherever it suits him.[26]

It took a full month for news of de Nava's September decision to reach Ibarvo. On October 21, 1796, Ibarvo learned that his case was over. After five years, Ibarvo was found neither guilty nor innocent, he was not convicted or cleared. His case was simply "administratively concluded."[27] De Nava admitted in his letter that although Ibarvo was investigated for malfeasance in office and for introducing contraband goods to the province, that his "excesses have not been fully substantiated." The commandant general instructed Muñoz to immediately release Ibarvo from any custody or limitation of movement and to return all his property that had been confiscated five years earlier. De Nava also made clear that Ibarvo could not continue in his official post but could live anywhere he chose. In a separate letter on the same date, de Nava instructed Muñoz to immediately stop Ibarvo's pay.[28] Freedom had its costs.

One can only imagine the scene when Ibarvo and Muñoz signed the document ending Ibarvo's long suspension and removal from East Texas. Their relationship had been tenuous throughout the ordeal, and it was Muñoz's foot-dragging that delayed a final decision. The witnesses to the signing, José Gervacio de Silva and Gabriel Gutièrrez, appeared frequently for signing official documents. José Gervacio de Silva was the first *alférez* (a rank of second lieutenant) of the presidial company of San Antonio de Béxar, and Gabriel Gutièrrez oversaw the *abilittación* (the office of paymaster) for the presidio.

Did Ibarvo feel relief? Was he surprised about losing his pay and title? Was there a sense of satisfaction with what was essentially an acquittal, or did his anger and temperamental nature appear once again? Our only guides to his thoughts are the actions he took that remain recorded in the archives. From those we see that Ibarvo wasted no time in working to regain his property.

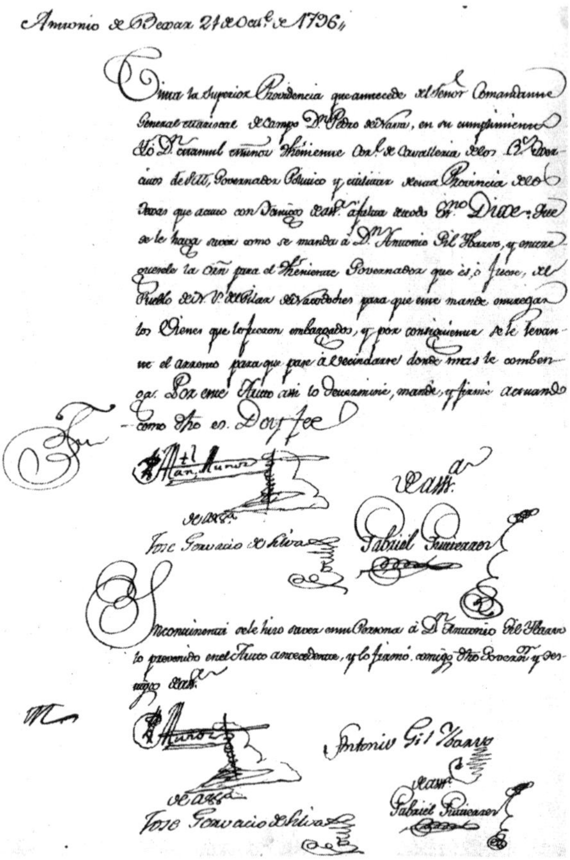

Document and signatures indicating the end of the case against Ibarvo. Courtesy Bexar Archives, e_bx_011624_0003, The Dolph Briscoe Center for American History, The University of Texas at Austin.

Reclaiming his Property and Assets

After all the secret investigations, confidential documents, depositions, petitions, and delays, Ibarvo was free of the burden of further legal action. There were still many consequences from his years removed from his post and stresses within his family from which he had to recover. Primary among those was recouping what was left of his property and assets. During his banishment from the region, three families of enslaved people helped maintain Ibarvo's Rancho Attoyaque between 1792 and 1799.[29] Most of his confiscated assets had been held in Nacogdoches and La Bahía, and each required that he interact with people who had treated him badly.

MORE CHANGES IN NACOGDOCHES

On the same day Muñoz informed Ibarvo of the dismissal of his case, the governor sent a detailed letter to Bernardo Fernández in Nacogdoches. Muñoz let Fernández know about the decision and began the process to relieve Fernández of duty. Bernardo Fernández surrendered his role as interim lieutenant governor in Nacogdoches to an ambitious young cadet, José María Guadiana. Guadiana had asked the commandant general for a promotion only a few months prior.[30]

Guadiana was already serving in Nacogdoches, and in fact, Muñoz said that it was Guadiana who had "contributed to the greater part in the best duties of his predecessor," Bernardo Fernández. In praising Guadiana, Muñoz also provided a very negative performance review of Fernández and the officer corps saying that Fernández, "like the rest of the officers that the companies of this Province have, are not truly competent to be able to direct, by themselves alone, such commissions."[31]

For his transition out of office, Fernández made a record of the contents of the archives, including the hundreds of letters he had sent and received during his tenure from January 1795 until October 1796. He also turned over fetters, shackles, and handcuffs, along with four bronze and iron cannon, and two prisoners.[32] Fernández turned over command in Nacogdoches to Guadiana on October 16, 1796, and was on his way to Béxar by October 24. Things were changing in Nacogdoches in more ways than one.

PROPERTY SCATTERED ABOUT

Within a month of assuming command, Guadiana affirmed the order to allow Ibarvo or his agent to receive the confiscated property "under the requisite formalities."[33] The status of Ibarvo's confiscated property in La Bahía was no less complicated. It also involved interaction with the man who had been assigned to investigate Ibarvo and wound up accused himself of contraband trade—Capt. Juan Cortes. On November 15, 1796, Ibarvo petitioned Governor Muñoz to assist with the return of his property.

Muñoz's letter to Cortès was very direct. Cortès was to "arrange that the goods and valuables stated in his [Ibarvo's] petition be returned to him in their entirety, with complete satisfaction of the other charges that he mentions . . . so that he may freely settle where it shall suit him."[34] Cortès's response to the governor reflected emotions of resentment and impatience with Ibarvo and his claims. His letter was essentially a rebuttal to Ibarvo's petition. Cortès called attention to the low value of the mules and their "useless gear," and how many had been lost due to "stampedes, death, or being lost for reasons that I do not know."[35] Cortès explained in detail how the two cows Ibarvo named were only one cow and a bull, and there was no ram, only a ewe. Cortès had the bull and cow butchered to feed the people who went without pay to Ibarvo's Rancho de Attoyaque to brand the cattle and horses. Cortès even argued that a bottle cabinet Ibarvo said was valued at twelve pesos was only worth ten. Five years after the confiscation, this was the best Cortès could do. The tone and tenor of the communications was an indication that these lingering disagreements would not diminish.[36]

Ibarvo Can Live Anywhere . . . Except Nacogdoches

With Ibarvo's release there were rumblings about the possibility of his return to Nacogdoches and the concerns over him trying to reestablish his role and authority there. In the orders for the closure of Ibarvo's case, de Nava had initially said that Ibarvo "will be able to become a citizen where it may suit him, without prejudice to the peace and tranquility of that neighborhood." De Nava would soon change his mind.

Governor Muñoz expressed his concerns to de Nava saying, "It appears to me his [Ibarvo's] assistance [in Nacogdoches] will not be advantageous to anyone, since the nearness of his relatives and partisans, who have managed, with great diligence, to cause affection in these last times, with the purpose of re-establishing himself in the command."[37] Based on Muñoz's report, in November 1796 de Nava reversed his earlier ruling. Like Muñoz, he worried that Ibarvo's presence in Nacogdoches would cause "movements contrary to the union and good harmony of its inhabitants."[38] De Nava decided that Ibarvo may not return to live in Nacogdoches, and that Muñoz should direct someone to gather his property there on Ibarvo's behalf.

Ibarvo continued to live in Béxar during 1796 and 1797. A snapshot of his circumstances is found in the census reports for those years. The years of detention in Béxar had left Ibarvo with sufficient means of support to maintain nine people in his home. In 1796 the census recorded the sixty-three-year-old Ibarvo living with his thirty-year-old wife, a young orphan from Nacogdoches, a Spanish serving man, and five enslaved people. By the end of 1797, his household had grown to eighteen.[39] There is no indication how Ibarvo increased his household in one year or what activities or labor engaged everyone daily.

A UNIFORM BUT NO PAY

De Nava went to great lengths to show concern about Ibarvo's circumstances. He allowed Ibarvo's pay to continue while the investigation was underway, he pressured Muñoz to conclude the case, and he ordered Ibarvo's property be returned to him. De Nava also ordered Muñoz to prevent Ibarvo's return to Nacogdoches, but that it be done "without embarrassing him."

Perhaps in deference to his service, de Nava also instructed that Ibarvo be able to continue wearing his uniform and retain the benefits of his title as captain of the militia. In addition, he was to retain his *fuero* (privileges) as a military officer. *Fueros* were organized in a way that created layers of citizenry who were held to different standards and allowed certain privileges. Those privileges may have included exemption from certain taxes and levies, charges for quarters, and some relief from responsibilities of citizenry.[40] What that meant for Ibarvo is not known. Wearing his captain's uniform would certainly make sure he stood out among the others.

IBARVO COMPLAINS OF MISTREATMENT

Ibarvo endured his paid suspension of almost five years with a fair amount of patience, but his petitions and complaints increased when his pay stopped. By July 1797, ten months had passed since de Nava ordered Ibarvo's assets returned, but there was still little progress. Ibarvo wrote a letter of complaint to de Nava, bypassing Governor Muñoz, in which he asked for help in a way that fully displayed Ibarvo's skills at diplomacy. Every sentence was filled with deferential language meant to gain the favor of the commandant general. Ibarvo noted de Nava's superior and commendable kindness, his proven mercy, and his issuance of prudent and cautious orders. Ibarvo apologized for intruding upon de Nava's bigger concerns but proceeded to ask for his help to address his complaints. The first of his complaints was regarding Manuel Muñoz, the governor who had plagued him during the entire ordeal.

> I humbly beseech you, to issue a new, prudent, and cautious order that suffices to overcome the odious delay that I am experiencing in my affairs on the part of this señor governor, who does not cease to do public outrage to my person and honor, nor does he cease to send his orders to his lieutenant at that post [Nacogdoches], all of them aimed at my total perdition.[41]

Ibarvo's temperament began to show in his communications, but his lack of transparency did as well. The man who managed to own several enslaved people in a household of eighteen looked for Nava's pity, saying these circumstances may find him "forced to beg and live on alms."

Ibarvo also used his letter to complain about an effort by some of his grandchildren while he was held in Béxar to prevent him from inheriting property owned and maintained by his first wife. This dispute over his wife's assets arises often in the Béxar Archives but is only mentioned here to illustrate that Ibarvo's troubles originated from many sources. Ibarvo believed his grandchildren were pursuing a misguided and unjustified legal effort because of their embrace "of the counsel of my adversaries, who aspire to nothing other than my total ruin." Another influence on his grandchildren could have been that Ibarvo's second wife was only in her thirties—closer in age to his grandchildren than to her husband—perhaps stirring their resentment.

Ibarvo's letter struck a chord with Pedro de Nava, an Ibarvo sympathizer who had shown respect for Ibarvo's service and insisted on fairness in his case. In de Nava's letter to Muñoz the following month, the commandant chastised his governor for Ibarvo's continued difficulties. One can see not only some irritation with Muñoz but sense de Nava's frustration with the whole matter in general. De Nava begins his brief letter by telling Muñoz that he does not want to hear from Ibarvo again on this matter.[42] Muñoz was tersely ordered to be done.

The commandant general accepted Ibarvo's complaints without question, and it is likely he had his own experiences with Muñoz that convinced him of their truth. De Nava pointedly noted that "in light of the repeated orders that I have issued on their [Ibarvo's] behalf, I cannot help but believe that there is a failure there [in Nacogdoches] to observe them." De Nava's position was that Ibarvo was being denied "the fairness and pity which he deserves because of his age, for his current state [of health], and for how much he has suffered in the prolonging of his case."

Muñoz had no other choice but to respond in affirmation to his superior commander, but how he did that reflected his own disgust. After the usual florid expressions of submission that began official communications, Muñoz coyly told de Nava that Ibarvo "will find no impediment whatsoever of my part."[43]

Obedezco, pero no cumplo. I obey but I do not comply. The Spanish custom was strong.

PERMISSION TO GO TO NACOGDOCHES

For months prior to Muñoz's decision to allow Ibarvo to recover his property in Nacogdoches, the lieutenant there, José María Guadiana, had complained to the governor about the "restless activities" caused in Nacogdoches by Ibarvo's relatives. Letters from Muñoz to de Nava in November 1798 and again in January 1799 lamented the continued troubles being caused by the Ibarvo clan in East Texas.

Ibarvo finally availed himself of the services of an agent to collect his property in Nacogdoches but with little success. After Ibarvo's agent, Juan Ignacio Guerrero, was met with obstacles and faced his own personal problems, Ibarvo wrote Governor Muñoz to complain in August of 1798. Ibarvo said his assets, particularly his cattle and horses, were "very much dispersed around the countryside," as much as twenty to thirty leagues (seventy-five miles) distant from Nacogdoches. Ibarvo asked permission to go to his former home to collect the property himself because it was "the only material comfort I have to maintain my large family."[44]

Muñoz knew he could not make that decision on his own and forwarded Ibarvo's petition to de Nava in mid-September of 1798, almost two years after the order that Ibarvo's property be returned.[45] By mid-April 1799, Muñoz finally granted permission for Ibarvo to return to Nacogdoches and did so despite his concerns that Ibarvo's presence there would incite old fears and unrest. Muñoz said he had let Ibarvo know "how important it is [for him] to desist from the disturbing principles he has followed up to now."[46] Ibarvo was no saint, and his anger with his lack of control over the situation would have been palpable.

The Punctual Performance of His Duties

The communication among Pedro de Nava, Manuel Muñoz, and Antonio Gil Ibarvo revealed the tension that existed among the three men. In early 1798, Ibarvo asked the governor's permission to travel to Saltillo on personal business, a request which Muñoz denied. Though Ibarvo was ultimately prevented from returning to Nacogdoches, de Nava's orders specified that he not be restricted in his travels anywhere else within New Spain. Nevertheless, Muñoz denied his request. When Ibarvo complained to de Nava about Muñoz's refusal to approve a passport for his travel, the commandant general bluntly restated his position to Muñoz saying, "that for no reason are you to prevent him from leaving that province."[47]

Muñoz's rebuke from his commandant general regarding the troublesome Ibarvo came at a time when Muñoz was in decline, enduring several years of ill health. When de Nava had asked Muñoz to show pity for Ibarvo due to his age, his health, and his suffering, those conditions applied to Muñoz as well. Muñoz apologized for inaction on a particular matter by blaming "the dreadful constitution in which my illness has left me."[48] His accelerating inability to perform his duties coincided with the conclusion of Ibarvo's legal status.

Even without de Nava's challenges and doubts, Muñoz realized he could not continue in his post. De Nava first learned that Muñoz's health was in decline two years prior. By November 1796, shortly after the decision on Ibarvo's status, de Nava noticed a lack of correspondence from the governor and was left to wonder if he was able to manage his role. In a letter questioning Muñoz about his condition, de Nava asked whether his health "impedes the punctual performance of [his] duties." He asked Munoz if he should appoint someone "with the proper energy" to replace him until he could recover.[49] A series of planned replacements for Muñoz failed to materialize and led to the need for him to remain in office much longer than planned.

Muñoz's health continued to worsen. He petitioned de Nava for permission to retire, and by August 1798 the viceroy approved it. When Muñoz received the approval for his retirement, he had been "bedridden for some time as a result of [his] infirmities and age and prevented from carrying out [his] duties."[50] Muñoz would be allowed to retire with a rank of colonel, one-third of his four thousand-peso annual salary, and with the matching *fuero* (privileges) for his position.[51] When Muñoz became bedridden, Juan Bautista Elguézabal worked with Muñoz as his assistant while they waited for a royal appointment of his replacement.

The Candor of a Dying Man

This discussion of the end of Muñoz's career is intended to preface what this researcher believes is the most telling and informative communication in this entire Ibarvo saga about the relationships within the culture of contraband in Spanish East Texas. In May of 1798, Manuel Muñoz replied to de Nava's reproach of his decision to prevent Ibarvo from going to Saltillo.[52] Muñoz's letter is amazingly personal and free from formality. His words to de Nava came at a time when he knew his "advanced age and serious afflictions have given my constitution nothing to hope for, much less to wish to alter that conduct." It feels like the voice of a man who has done all he can and is tired not only of Ibarvo's many complaints, but also of the aggravations brought by his role as governor.

The letter feels as if the aged and ailing Muñoz, bedridden at the time, spoke the words personally. It can be read as if it were literature, the sad soliloquy of a character in a Shakespearean tragedy. The long-time translator of the Béxar Archives, John Wheat, has accomplished not only the difficult task of translation from the Spanish, but crafted a magnificent interpretation that captures the richness and emotion of this moment in history. To fairly represent the significance and emotion of Muñoz's communication, much of it will be quoted verbatim from Wheat's translation.

Subordination and Blind Obedience

Muñoz opens his lengthy correspondence by reviewing his own performance and explaining his lifelong approach in his service to the crown.

> An inseparable circumstance to the exactness with which I have sought to carry out the matters of the king's service that have been entrusted to me, has always been the greatest subordination and blind obedience to carrying out the orders of my superiors, and never have I looked upon them without the respect that is justly due them.

Muñoz described his lengthy service to the crown as one who sees the end of their career, or perhaps their life, approaching. He was uncomfortably uncertain about the leadership in the province who might follow him and hoped that "command be assumed by an individual capable of properly achieving the important objects that are peculiar to it." His experience was that the pool of candidates would have difficulty "carrying out certain matters where their intelligence comes into play." Muñoz bluntly stated that he thought their "lack of prudent zeal might be one of the essential causes that have contributed to the decadence that [we] have experienced."

Muñoz worked to preface the rest of his letter by establishing that de Nava should not question the integrity with which he acted or the deference to authority required of his post. That is not to say Muñoz did not have challenges in maintaining that posture, particularly in the conflict with Ibarvo. Muñoz also explained how difficult that was to do when edicts came from superiors who were ill-equipped to deliver them. Muñoz said he obeyed such orders "even though (as often occurs) they were born of the erroneous notions in which they are placed by the distorted reports of those who have served and continue to serve poorly under the cloak of flattery and superficial merits."

Without stating directly that he considered de Nava to be one of those who were influenced by "flattery and superficial merits," that method is precisely what Ibarvo used in his letters of complaint. Ibarvo had mastered a combination of a subservient deferential style with a demanding presence, a style he frequently used when bypassing Muñoz to complain directly to the commandant general.

Complaints About Ibarvo

After establishing his motives and his loyalty, Muñoz recapped his experience with Ibarvo from the perspective of a governor trying to follow orders and represent Spain well in carrying them out. Muñoz bemoaned the leeway given Ibarvo during his confinement and after his release.

> This government has been greatly inconvenienced by the effects of his [Ibarvo's] troublesome conduct, whether by the clever scheming that he foments among these citizens, or as well with his repeated denunciations made against me for the poor attention that he criticizes in my decisions and actions.

Unlike Muñoz's earlier generalized comment about obeying orders from those who are ill-informed, Muñoz this time blames de Nava directly for some of Ibarvo's contentious conduct. Muñoz believed that Ibarvo was "emboldened by the excessive clemency with which Your Lordship has distinguished him."

> This does not surprise me, because being accustomed to run down the honor of other commanders of higher rank and distinguished merit than my own, he [Ibarvo] has reaped more satisfaction than his excesses called for.

A Shadow of the Truth

Muñoz believed that Ibarvo's misrepresentations and maneuvering could have been easily understood if only de Nava had paid attention to the reports of "impartial individuals who have observed in practice the same bad qualities about which I must justly complain." Muñoz himself seemed to want to take responsibility for ensuring a full consideration of all the facts of what happened, but the reality of his health stood in the way.

> This I will do [prepare the facts] at the proper time and in detail, when allowed not only by the afflictions that beset me but also by the duties that I have at present, preferential, no doubt, to the odious response called for by such unfounded petitions that, based on false principles, are solely aimed at surprising that superior office with the claim of supposed damages, which are given credence by the lack of preparedness and poor knowledge of the one in charge.

These were critical words to a superior officer by a man who knew he was dying and who became bolder the more he continued.

Muñoz's disgust with Ibarvo's accusations and lies, particularly those made toward him, began to boil over. The emotion Muñoz showed in his letter is truly remarkable, especially considering the purpose of his letter was to simply answer de Nava's question about why he prevented Ibarvo from going to Saltillo. Before taking care of that single task, Muñoz unloaded years of resentment and bitterness. Not only did he want to answer de Nava's question, he also wanted to confront de Nava about Ibarvo's abuses and de Nava's failure to look at the situation with a broader understanding of the truth. As Munoz felt the end of his life approaching, he wanted to defend his honor.

> The truly limited insinuations that I have made previously [against Ibarvo] are insufficient, and rather, the matter calls for extended discussion, being of no less importance to the honor of my office and the honorability of my person. I am provided sufficient material by the excessive indulgence with which (so as not to be consumed by passion) I have tolerated his [Ibarvo's] outbursts during the time that he has resided at this capital, [and] no less by the dishonesty that he manifested before I took command of the province. No lesser a reason is provided by the continual statements of the [current] lieutenant governor of Nacogdoches, complaining of the bad conduct of [Ibarvo's] relatives, who, at his instigation, disturb the peace and good harmony of that post.

Concerns About Ibarvo's Return

Muñoz was continually concerned about Ibarvo returning to prominence in Nacogdoches, whether officially sanctioned or not, during the many years following Ibarvo's removal from office. Muñoz received a steady stream of reports, particularly from Lieutenant Guadiana, with suspicions that Ibarvo's relatives were trying to clear a path for some type of triumphant reentry and were stirring up the tribes to make demands for Ibarvo to be their intermediary for trade and relations with the Spanish. Muñoz asserted that the Ibarvo clan was "accustomed to the tolerance and abandonment with which they used to live," and because of that, "all subjection necessarily must be repugnant to them."

> [Ibarvo's relatives were] sowing among the tribes of Friendly Indians ideas contrary their tranquility, although [his kin] are working together to achieve his personal ends and his restoration to his former position. I had these incidences well in mind when I told Your Lordship that they would result if ever he were permitted to establish himself in that jurisdiction.

Muñoz heard Guadiana's calls to alarm. Muñoz did not always pass on the information he received from Nacogdoches to de Nava, knowing that it would often be dismissed. Muñoz felt enough was enough, however, and now he was ready to feed De Nava every detail.

> In order to provide the remedy called for repeatedly by the aforesaid lieutenant governor [Ibarvo], I have told him [Guadiana] to gather in full detail the corresponding information and to forward them without delay to me in order that I might do so to Your Lordship, which I will do, enclosing to you the [reports] that I deem sufficient, so that [you] might please to make the just decision that you think best, and so that you might be aware at the same time of the fairness of my actions with regard to the affairs of this individual, to whom, far from regarding him with the passion that he argues in his petitions, I have treated with more favor than I should have.

Muñoz kept his promise to inform de Nava of the details of Ibarvo's disruptions more fully in communications in November of 1798 and again in January 1799.[53] One of Muñoz's letters concerned a series of incendiary *décimas* that Muñoz attributed to Ibarvo's kin. *Décimas* were a form of Spanish poetry with five verses set to music and filled with humorous and biting denigrations of others, particularly those in positions of authority. Muñoz wondered what motivation Ibarvo had "in satirizing indiscriminately the activities even of persons he has no reason to offend."[54]

Finally . . . About Saltillo

After Muñoz had gotten things off his chest, he finally got around to a brief, half-hearted explanation of why he prevented Ibarvo's travel to Saltillo. Muñoz's justification for that decision was simply that the transfer of Ibarvo's property back to him was still in limbo. There was conflict in coming to an agreement on what that property included between Ibarvo's agent and the trustee in charge of it. Additionally, the legal challenges by some of his children and grandchildren to Ibarvo's right to possessions of his first wife complicated matters considerably. Other than that, the only reason Muñoz gave for his refusal of Ibarvo's travel was that the former lieutenant governor "did not explain the purpose for which it was aimed or the time he must spend on it." Munoz left unstated what was perhaps the real reason he refused permission—because he could.

Muñoz's Curtain Call

At the time Muñoz penned his very personal and emotional response to his commandant general, his wife had died a few years before, his health was failing, and he had little to lose. He knew he had crossed that invisible boundary between himself and a superior. His accusatory tone was unapologetic yet respectful. Still, he sought to gain acknowledgement from de Nava about the motives that guided the ailing governor's career in service to the crown.

> I beseech Your Lordship to please to pardon me if, my discussion having strayed from the principal object to which your order is aimed, I might have gone to excess and incurred some defect of too much candor. I have always dealt in that way with the commanders who have governed me, without detriment to the respect that I have devoted to them in excess, and in the same fashion, I will manage to disencumber myself of the offense made to my honor by despicable individuals and provide, in the performance of my duty, the good offices demanded by justice, and to promote, insofar as I am able, the happiness of these provinces, the ultimate service with which I can repay the satisfactions that the King's mercy has dispensed to me.

Muñoz had accomplished his purpose in his response to de Nava. He sought to clean up his reputation, make clear the difficulties caused by Ibarvo and his family, and answer de Nava's question. Muñoz would never make it to his retirement; he died in San Antonio on July 27, 1799.

Another "Retirement"

During the period of Muñoz's inability to fully perform his duties, another key player in the Ibarvo saga ended his military service. In June 1798, Pedro de Nava approved the retirement of Juan Cortès who'd been the presidial captain at La Bahía since 1791, but his departure from service to Spain was not altogether smooth.[55]

In February 1797, questions about how Cortès and Juan Timoteo Barrera managed the tobacco stores of La Bahía led the auditor to question Cortès's veracity. Cortès's answers to the auditor's questions were suspect, and the auditor found "little cause to consider his excuses to be true."[56] There were also issues with how Lt. Manuel de Espadas managed the finances of the presidio while he was *avilitado* (paymaster). An investigation led Pedro de Nava to state that the evidence submitted by Cortès "does not dispel the notion that he [Cortès] handled this matter with little activity," and that Cortès sought to conceal the evidence and interfere with the investigation.[57]

By March 1797, Cortès was removed from command at La Bahía. De Nava called on Juan Bautista Elguézabal to fill in temporarily and try to clean up the mess caused by Espadas and Cortès. Cortès was transferred to the presidio at Béxar under the direct command of Governor Manuel Muñoz. Espadas remained in La Bahía to help with the investigation and was then transferred to Béxar under conditions of arrest. For his part, Cortès was found culpable in the financial misdeeds. Two-thirds of his salary of one thousand pesos per year was withheld until he repaid the 3,356 pesos lost in the mismanagement at La Bahía.

Even before Elguézabal concluded his investigation, de Nava believed there was a "well-founded suspicion that he [Cortès] has behaved carelessly in the command, government, and training of his troops, in the fulfillment of his respective duties, and in that of the orders that have been sent to him." De Nava's loss of confidence in this matter was final. De Nava's approach to Cortès's shortcomings were also much different than that of Sierra Gorda in 1792 when Cortès smuggled contraband goods from Nacogdoches. For smuggling skins, tobacco, playing cards, and fine cloth, Cortès lost the goods; for mismanaging his direct reports and mismanaging thousands of pesos in presidial funds, he was pushed aside and ordered to repay the losses.

In April 1797, de Nava transferred Bernardo Fernández to La Bahía in preparation for Elguézabal to complete his investigation. The commandant general wanted Elguézabal to advise Fernández about what he was walking into, telling him fully about La Bahía's "poor state of instruction, discipline, and subordination."[58] By the time Fernández arrived at La Bahía on May 27, 1797, Captain Cortès had already left for Béxar the previous week. Before he left the presidio he had served since 1791, Cortès turned over the archives and weaponry and reviewed the fifty-three men that remained. Cortès and his wife, María Catalina de Urrutia, had no place to live in Béxar, so de Nava gave his approval to stay at the Mission San Juan.[59] Within a month, Elguézabal decided to proceed with the formal seizure of all the assets of Cortès and his wife, and that the remaining amount of his ungarnished salary would be received while he was effectively under house arrest in Béxar.[60]

On June 14, 1798, José Miguel del Moral, the replacement commander for La Bahía, officially removed Juan Cortès from active duty.[61] Interestingly, Cortès wished to retire to Nacogdoches, the center of contraband trade in the province of Texas.[62] De Nava did not think that was a good idea and promptly responded to the request in July 1798.

> But deeming it inopportune to allow him to settle there, because as a result of the time that Cortés was on assignment in that place, when he returned to the aforesaid presidio of La Bahía, several effects that he brought were confiscated from him.[63]

De Nava smoothed over the concerns about Cortès's earlier involvement in contraband trade by also pointing out that Nacogdoches was "usually commanded by a junior officer and at times by a sergeant," and therefore Cortès's presence there would be beneath his rank.[64] A tactful refusal for a man whose career may not have deserved such deference.

End of an Era in Spanish Texas

By the end of the eighteenth century, there was a sea change in Spanish Texas and its leadership. The authorities had removed Antonio Gil Ibarvo from East Texas, limiting his influence, removing him as a focal point for East Texas commerce and trade, and scattering his assets. Manuel Muñoz, the governor who pursued his removal, was dead, and for years before his passing his own role had been reduced to that of a bedridden man only able to dictate his thoughts to an assistant. Juan Cortès, the captain at La Bahía who investigated Ibarvo in Nacogdoches, became implicated in smuggling goods while there and later for mismanaging the presidio of La Bahía. He too was dead, leaving his widow to settle some of his debts.

Though the documentation that remains in archival sources tends to focus on these men in positions of command or wealth, we must be constantly reminded that the growing numbers of farmers, laborers, soldiers, traders, and others who made up these distant settlements had stories of their own. Poverty was rampant. Indolence and laziness were commonly reported, but those reports came from the perspective of military leaders or priests, who generally had an easier life on the frontier. There were times when food was scarce. Almost everyone participated in some way in the chain of contraband trade, but very few benefitted from it financially.

Spanish soldiers were no better off. They had to provide their own arms, horses, and clothing. At times their commanders treated them like servants, assigning them tasks solely for the private benefit of their captains and lieutenants. In one case, soldiers in Nacogdoches who complained about a lack of horses were found to have sold them before claiming the animals were drowned in a river crossing or stolen by Indians.[65] The lack of paper was a constant complaint. In La Bahía an auditor learned that paper from the account books had been used to make wadding for soldiers' ammunition.[66]

A new century for New Spain would begin with many changes and dangers. Conflict from within Mexico itself would surpass any fears of French or American incursions. Tensions in the borderland regions of East Texas would boil to overflowing in the coming years. One thing was a constant, however—commerce would continue, and the malleable *contrabandistas* would quickly adapt and evolve.

The culture of contraband trade in Nacogdoches would hardly miss a beat.

12

When Nations Intervene

Up until today there has not occurred at this post,
its jurisdiction, or over in Natchitoches anything
worthy of communicating to your Lordship.
—JOSÉ MARÍA GUADIANA[1]

In December 1796 when Lt. José María Guadiana submitted his report to the governor on conditions in Nacogdoches, his summation belied the complex realities of the borderlands. He had spent time in Nacogdoches prior to his official appointment, replacing Bernardo Fernández in the succession of lesser officers assigned to the post after Ibarvo's removal. Guadiana's "I got this" response was bred by his enthusiasm for the role and his underestimation of what was required of him. His untested leadership may have overtaken his ability to perceive the difficulties of what he faced. One hopes that Guadiana enjoyed his momentary lull in the action, because he and others who followed him would have seen nothing like what was to come in Spanish East Texas.

The focus of this work has been the unique period of Texas history that includes the closing of the mission and presidio at Los Adaes in 1773 and the expulsion of Antonio Gil Ibarvo. With the United States' increasing pressure on Spanish sovereignty from the east in the early nineteenth century, this period of history is a distinct slice of time where multinational, multicultural, cross-border commerce was based on a rather simple societal norm—goods considered as contraband were absolutely necessary for living in the borderlands and all across the province of Texas.

During Ibarvo's time in East Texas, he was the dominant force overseeing the movement of goods and managing trade relationships with the local tribes. Having him in that role meant the region was able to largely maintain a cooperative and workable economy in a diverse community of borderland settlers. To call the region a diverse community is perhaps a bit too overladen with current perceptions and language. Nacogdoches was an extraordinary assemblage of people from many countries, many races, and many backgrounds gathered along an ill-defined border. German, French, English, Spanish, African, Irish, and Native American people mixed, mingled, traded, intermarried, and engaged in whatever labors they could to scrape out an existence. Governed by a culture that classified people by race and caste, the odd mixture of human relationships challenged colonial classification to the extent that a particular name had to be applied to those whose racial mix did not fit categorization—*color quebrado*, or broken color.

With Ibarvo permanently removed from East Texas, Spain relinquished the experience of a man who was born of the borderlands. He knew inherently how things worked. Spanish leaders from Mexico City, Saltillo, or Béxar who took orders from a distant royalty would never quite understand why they could not govern East Texas in the same way they did other parts of the empire. Ibarvo's approach to maintaining peace would never fit their perspectives of New Spain.

If it had been solely up to Spanish authority, there would have never been a resettlement of Nacogdoches. Ibarvo and the evicted Adeseños had made an impermanent life along the Trinity River. When they were forced to leave after a series of difficult events, they did not ask permission to go to the former mission of Nacogdoches, they simply went. Nacogdoches was a consequence of a people whose entire lives had been distant from the seat of power. Whatever authority they needed, Ibarvo provided. Somehow, for almost twenty years, all the factors involved fit together to support a faraway settlement where commercial and cultural relationships supported an untidy and sometimes unlawful style of living. Spain may have tried to rule East Texas, but in the borderlands, commerce was king.

Closing the Door

Antonio Gil Ibarvo did not invent contraband trade, but that trade certainly created him. Contraband was a way of life. Spanish law made the importation of everyday items from across the Sabine an illegal act. Fears that Ibarvo would somehow reconstitute his earlier hold on power and regain control of contraband trade in the region never came to fruition. Contraband trade continued, and in many ways became more institutionalized under the series of military leaders assigned to the post after his removal. Whether Antonio Gil Ibarvo was in Nacogdoches or not mattered little to the increase or reduction in contraband trade. When it came to contraband, all that changed after Ibarvo's removal was who was involved, who benefitted, and who got caught.

In his multivolume history of Spanish influence in Texas, historian Carlos Castañeda titled a section of the work to explain this transition beyond the Ibarvo era in a fitting way—"Difficulties in Closing the Door." Every freshly appointed and ambitious commandant general, governor, lieutenant governor, or presidio captain continued to issue edicts prohibiting the exchange of goods across the Sabine to Louisiana. Castañeda noted that although leaders in both Natchitoches and Béxar in 1793 knew that traders "entered clandestinely, killed wild cattle, stole horses, traded with the Indians, and committed numerous outrages" they also knew they were helpless in enforcing any restrictions on trade.[2] Clandestine trade went merrily on, no doubt connived by some of the local authorities and greatly enjoyed by many of the settlers.

Official Doubts About Guadiana

Ibarvo's initial replacement, Cristóbal de Cordova, was an old soldier and a stopgap placeholder in Nacogdoches. Cordova's replacement, Bernardo Fernández, was younger but still a lesser choice. He was criticized by Muñoz as being incapable of handling the responsibilities of the post. José María Guadiana showed some initial promise in following Fernández. He was an ambitious cadet who had communicated his request for consideration of a promotion directly to the commandant general. As with others in new assignments, Guadiana was confident he could undo any damages caused by the incompetence or ineptitude of his predecessor and somehow avoid the traps and pitfalls that led to their reassignment. Instead, he succumbed to the same influences as others and became involved in the trade he was sent to prevent.

Suspicions

As Guadiana grew into the office he held, he began to learn the dynamics and relationships of frontier commerce. By March 1798, two years after his arrival, suspicions of Guadiana's complicity in allowing foreign traders to enter the province in violation of Spanish law made their way to de Nava and Muñoz.

Both those suspicions and their own observations led Governor Muñoz to caution Guadiana to improve.

> With the increase these days in news regarding the suspicious nature of the introduction of foreigners into that province, I am instructing you to see to the strict fulfillment of the orders that are sent to you about this important matter, and that whenever someone arrives at that town or its environs, you question him as to the origin and purposes of his travel and arrest him whenever he fails to present a passport. And if he does present one, you will have him withdraw without allowing him to deal or communicate with the citizens and report everything to me for my resolution.[3]

The citizens of Nacogdoches noticed that Guadiana was no different in how he administered trade. Like others, he used his position to benefit from the illegal trafficking of goods from Natchitoches.

Testimonials

Reports about Guadiana surfaced with rumors of his selective enforcement of laws regarding entry into the province and trade within the region. As an indication of the lack of respect others had for Guadiana, he was the subject of those provocative songs known as *decimas*. Embarrassing rhymes sung about men in prominence signaled a groundswell of rebuke for those in authority. Guadiana took advantage of his standing as a military officer in a manner that was an overreaction to the gravity of the issue. He conducted a wide-ranging investigation into the "incendiary verses" aimed at himself and at the Italian merchant Vicente Micheli. Guadiana hoped he could recoup some of his standing with his superior officer by gathering testimonials to his character to send to the governor.

> I am sending to Your Lordship six testimonials issued in my favor up to now by the citizens of this post [who are] named in them, among whom are several elderly and upstanding [citizens]. Some others have promised to give me the same through the persons who voluntarily assumed responsibility for seeking them.[4]

Guadiana also named Gregorio Mesa, José Flores, Ramón Córdova, Gregorio Soto, and Mariano Mora as a group that initially said they would support him but backed out when it was time to fulfill their promises. In addition to those, Guadiana knew that Ibarvo's agent Francisco Guerrero and others who were associates of Ibarvo "will not give me [a testimonial] for no other reason than their miserable passions." Undoubtedly there was an equal number of residents who had nothing to say or would not have provided a positive review.

One of Eighteen

Nacogdoches was too much for Guadiana. He already knew he was on the way out in Nacogdoches, so the testimonials were meant to aid him in his next assignment, not to retain his current one. De Nava and Muñoz each had their favorites for his replacement. Muñoz supported Lt. Sebastián Rodríguez and de Nava was in favor of José Miquel del Moral.

As might be expected, de Nava made the decision to install Moral and suggested Muñoz could decide on the next one, a nod toward the fact that each knew it would not be long before he had that opportunity. De Nava was not simply being fair to the governor; the two had already decided there would be continuous turnover in posts like Nacogdoches and La Bahía because of their role in monitoring the movement of goods between Louisiana and Texas. The two leaders decided that any future commanders would not hold the office more than four to six months. The rationale being that they could then "avoid their acquiring any prejudicial connections."[5]

Their history with Ibarvo in Nacogdoches and Cortès at La Bahía demonstrated the challenges of filling those posts. What they gave up was having a leader in place who, like Ibarvo, could build the relationships among traders, native tribes, and foreigners to make the contraband commerce of East Texas work. What they got instead was the barely detectable influence of eighteen different military commanders in Nacogdoches between 1791 and 1812.[6]

The Jurisdiction of Nacogdoches

Since it's resettlement by way of Bucareli, Nacogdoches had been led by an autocrat and patriarch capable of being a go-between for the relationships that kept the tenuous peace. Since Ibarvo's removal, the Spanish model for Nacogdoches was that it needed to be a military post led by an inexperienced junior officer capable of scouting any intrusions on Spanish territory and turning them away. Lest one begin to believe the concerns about Nacogdoches regarding contraband and the entry of foreigners were solely due to Ibarvo's leadership in Nacogdoches, one must recall the nature of the uncertain boundary and the vast jurisdiction of Nacogdoches. A simple question by the priest assigned to the church in Nacogdoches exposed the lack of definition about when the boundary was crossed.

An Unburdening of Conscience

Father Bernardino Vallejo, the parish priest for Nacogdoches, asked for help with some painful observations.[7] Father Bernardino noticed that those who lived to the east of the Sabine River would not participate in their "annual obligations of Confession and Communion." The largely French and English occupants, some of whom were not even Catholic, told the priest they were not part of the jurisdiction of Nacogdoches but were instead within that of Natchitoches and Louisiana. Lent was approaching, and the resident father did not want these neighbors to the east to miss their annual opportunity for the "unburdening of their consciences."[8]

The priest's letter to the commander at Nacogdoches was not intended for commiseration but for clarity. Father Bernardino wrote Guadiana to ask that he clarify whether those cabins to the east of the Sabine were in the province of Texas or not. Bernardino was no novice to the borderlands, so he probably understood that his question involved broader and more complicated issues. Nevertheless, he straightforwardly submitted his question to Guadiana. The priest wanted to know if those across the Sabine River were part of his flock or not.

> It is highly important that you clarify the point as soon as possible, bringing to the light the corresponding instruments [i.e., documents] that will show us the limits or borders of this jurisdiction with that of Natchitoches.[9]

Guadiana's reply to the priest a week later showed both the ambitiousness and naivete of the young cadet. He diligently replied to Father Bernardino with a report he had prepared by interviewing the oldest residents of Nacogdoches who were part of the original group of Adeseños evicted from their homes. Guadiana relied on their "accurate knowledge of the frontier of this province with that of Luiciana [Louisiana]." In addition to his immediate reply, Guadiana sent the request, his reply, and his report to the governor, repeating the request for any documentation.[10] Given that Manuel Muñoz was the governor of the province and the fact that Spanish Louisiana was still treated as if governed by a foreign power, Muñoz' reply a month later was somewhat surprising in its brevity.

> I have now searched the archives of this government for the documents that should bear on the matter, without my efforts producing any results.[11]

Muñoz's answer was that he had no idea where the border might be.

Not Everyone Wanted a Border

The good father's seemingly simple question exposed the true nature of the borderlands around Nacogdoches and the intractability of the problem of goods and people moving back and forth across the Sabine River. For the people who lived in the Natchitoches-Nacogdoches-La Bahía trade corridor or benefitted from its fluidity of commerce, the notion of a defined border with limited access was not a desirable state.

Since the earliest days of Spanish occupation at Los Adaes, trade was what mattered most. In his outstanding history, *Los Adaes, The First Capital of Spanish Texas*, historian Francis X. Galan called the borderlands a "smuggler's paradise." He noted, "The remoteness of *Los Adaes* from legal ports of entry in New Spain made the region a smuggler's paradise where governors monopolized commerce and Spanish officials could not entirely stop the burgeoning contraband trade as they sought to determine the border between Texas and Louisiana."[12] Although Los Adaes had been put in place as a military post to impede the flow of goods, it was often those charged with that responsibility who engaged in the trafficking they were supposed to stop.

The People, 1793

The population of Nacogdoches continued to grow at the end of the eighteenth century and into the nineteenth. Census reports submitted by Ibarvo between 1783 and 1792 showed an increase in population from 349 to 555. At any given time, there were fifty to seventy-five foreigners among the tallies. A census at the end of 1793 by the newly installed Cristóbal de Cordova showed a population increase from 487 in 1792 to 536 in 1793. The report went beyond simple numbers and provided more detailed information about the inhabitants of the town. In an acknowledgment of their positions of importance, the census begins with the sixty-six-year-old Cordova, two unnamed clergy, and María Padilla, the first wife of Antonio Gil Ibarvo.

One aspect of the history of Nacogdoches that is often forgotten is that most of the residents were from Los Adaes, including Cristóbal de Cordova, the lieutenant first assigned to Nacogdoches after Ibarvo's removal. The roots of Nacogdoches were firmly planted in the culture of the borderlands. The mix of others attracted to the town included French, Irish, English, and Native Americans. *Mestizos* were married to *coyotes*, and mulattos were joined with Apache. Many women were identified as widows, and others simply noted that their husband had been gone for years. Most of the residents were classified as farmers, but there were also cowherders, muleteers, blacksmiths, hunters, shoemakers, shepherds, laborers, and servants. There were also those listed as traders, mostly Frenchmen with connections to Natchitoches.

The histories from which we learn about people and events are commonly a history of the adults. It is the census reports that allow us to learn about the children who lived in these frontier spaces. Life goes on no matter where it exists, and in the Nacogdoches census of 1804, there were newborns reported in the census. Seven girls and two boys under six months of age were among those listed. Ponciano Ybarbo, a seventeen-year-old boy, was married to a twelve-year-old girl, María Padilla.

The numbers of older residents may surprise those who think that life expectancy was universally bleak during that period. Many of the residents were in their sixties. Dimas Maya was the oldest resident. The eighty-five-year-old native of Monterrey was listed as a farmer married to his sixty-seven-year-old wife, María Rafaela Sanchez.

The Town, 1804

José Joaquín Ugarte came to Nacogdoches in 1803 as the military commander of the Nacogdoches District. His "Statistical Report on the District of Nacogdoches belonging to and situated East of the Province of Texas" provides a snapshot of the conditions in the settlement.[13] Ugarte counted 791 people in the population covering over eighteen thousand square leagues (about eighty million acres). The only members of the military assigned to prevent smuggling from Louisiana were the thirty soldiers stationed in Nacogdoches. They were intended to cover land all the way to the coast and the mouth of the Sabine River. Ugarte's estimate did not include what he called the northern section, which was "unknown and unpopulated," at least by the Spanish. He said there were no public roads in the district, "only two trails leaving here, one to *Béxar*, and the other to *La Bahía*."

As for commercial promise, there was little which could be considered profitable. Salt had been harvested from saline soils for centuries, and iron-based rocks were known to exist but were not being worked. There was no lead, copper, or gold, but the Spanish were never quite able to give up on discovering silver, which Ugarte reported was "supposed to exist." Goods from Spanish territories, Asia, or China were not making their way to Nacogdoches. The staples of coffee, sugar, and flour were the primary articles of trade. Skins were still the most reliable and available currency, other than the two thousand pesos a year that paid all the troops.

At the time of his report, Ugarte had only been in his position for eleven months. His visibility into smuggling in 1804, which slowed down following the United States' acquisition of Louisiana in the Louisiana Purchase in 1803, only mentioned the less dangerous or more taxable goods. He said that "as far as I could ascertain during a residence of 11 months, muslin, cotton, velvet, prints, silk and cotton hosiery, cotton and linen goods, shawls, saddles, and bridles" were the primary items still entering from Louisiana. This volume of traffic may explain why sixty Nacogdoches residents were identified as mule, horse, and cart drivers. The trade traffic was brisk.

Foreigners in Nacogdoches

The number of people in Nacogdoches in 1796 who were French, either from France or by way of Canada, was very small—only ten.[14] The two carpenters, shoemaker, and tanner among them would be welcomed by any settlement outpost. Two of the laborers had been in the region for twenty-eight and thirteen years, respectively. The two merchants named had only come to Nacogdoches after Ibarvo's removal and were likely traders filling the void.

A census of foreigners living in Nacogdoches in 1805, however, demonstrated how much had changed since Ibarvo's removal, and how much the entry of foreigners increased after that transition. Among the forty-eight new foreign residents, there were citizens of France, Louisiana, the United States, Ireland, England, Canada, Italy, and Germany. Of those, France, Louisiana, and the United States were the origins of thirty-nine of the forty-eight people named. Only six of those named were present in Nacogdoches during Ibarvo's tenure prior to 1792, and each of them had French roots. Following Ibarvo's removal, the pace of foreign migration to Nacogdoches increased with thirty-three new additions between 1792 and 1798. That pace came to an abrupt stop in 1799, and there were only nine new additions between 1799 and 1803.

Spanish concerns about foreign traders were not unfounded. Though most of them were in Texas as merchants of commerce rather than as the frontline of some planned invasion as Spain feared, their disruptions of relations with the tribal nations were reason enough to apply restrictions. When the Indians showed favor to foreigners over the Spanish, the governor and commandant general imagined all sorts of reasons for that undesirable behavior. One such thought was that perhaps the tribes recognized the military weakness of Spain and were preparing a major attack. Fears like that led to a general ease in the treatment of some tribes. One governor strongly disapproved of any action against the Native Americans that involved arms or force, saying instead his lieutenant should use their potential loss of annual presents as leverage. Foreign traders were often treated less strictly than the edicts required because officials worried they might be angered enough to incite their tribal trading partners.

Contraband trade was a no-win situation for Spain. As occupiers of indigenous territory, the Spanish had to balance cooperation and authority. The willingness and cunning of inbound traders, the availability of clandestine trails to move goods, and a ready market for skins and furs composed a commercial combination that could not be deterred.[15]

Despite seeming acceptance of the presence of foreigners in the province, Spanish authorities' position toward them continued to seesaw. One year there was an edict to evict or deny entry; another year, and for certain individuals, there was a tenuous acceptance. Historian Mattie Austin Hatcher noted that the Spanish never fully lost their distrust of immigrants from other countries. She went as far as to suggest that perhaps the officials, mostly local, who held open the door of access to Texas for foreigners may have triggered the beginning of the end for Spanish Texas.[16]

There were several notable foreign traders who had an outsized impact on the region. Extensive work is available on their histories and influence, and they are mentioned here as a reminder of their role in the commerce of the day.

Philip Nolan, Mustanger

Over time, cases where traders had an ulterior motive for entering Spanish territory increased and served as excuses for a more aggressive Spanish response. The case of Philip Nolan was a prime example. Born in Ireland, Nolan became a protégé of US Gen. James Wilkinson while living in Kentucky. After first coming to Texas in 1791 with a trading wanderlust, Nolan lived with indigenous people for a couple of years. Nolan wrote to General Wilkinson, saying that he was somewhat enamored of that life, but could not "altogether Indianfy (sic) my heart."[17]

Nolan also lived for a time in Nacogdoches. Though he may have begun his excursions in Texas for the lifestyle it offered, he quickly learned he could engage in trade in horses in large numbers. Texas mustangs multiplied rapidly along the fertile prairies south of the Red River. Zebulon Pike in 1806 noted that "the wild horses are in such numbers as to afford supplies for all the savages who border on the province, [as well as] the Spaniards, and the vast droves for other provinces of the United States."[18] Thousands of horses were there for the taking, even while still considered property of the king. A passport from the governor of Louisiana allowed Nolan back into Texas to capture mustangs for the military.

Nolan returned to Louisiana with 250 Texas mustangs in 1794 and over 1,200 in 1799. When Nolan made his last trip into Texas in 1800, he learned that the Spanish were suspicious of his motives and planned to arrest him. Commandant Gen. Pedro de Nava wrote the new governor, Elguézabal, in August saying that Nolan was not what he appeared to be.

> Having received reliable reports that Don Felipe Nolan is an Anglo American and a man whose conduct raises serious suspicions that when he entered that province, he did so with intentions very different from the ostensible ones shown on the passports and the personal matters that he said had brought him there [to Texas].[19]

Nolan and his party of over thirty well-armed men bypassed Nacogdoches to the north bound for the prairies south of the Red River where thousands of mustangs roamed freely. Spanish concerns worsened, and the military mission for Nolan moved from capture to elimination. They believed that "grave consequences" would result if he was not stopped. In a skirmish documented by Peter Ellis Bean, a member of Nolan's party, and Spanish commander Miguel Francisco Músquiz, Nolan and most of his group were killed in late March 1801. Nolan was stopped, but there would be little pause in the progress of others in the Spanish province of Texas.

The House of Barr and Davenport

While Nolan was beginning his effort to capture horses, another Irishman, William Barr, was starting his chapter in East Texas history as a purveyor of stock for export along a more legally acceptable path. Barr had come to Nacogdoches in 1793, after Ibarvo's expulsion, and became a designated agent for trading with the local tribes. In 1798 he registered his official cattle brand for Barr and Company, and by 1799 Pedro de Nava permitted him to export mules from Texas to Louisiana.[20]

In 1800, Barr became associated with a man who also came by way of Louisiana, an American named Samuel Davenport. When Barr and Davenport joined forces in sanctioned trade, they formed a formidable commercial force in early Nacogdoches. During the period of 1798 until the filibustering expeditions in Texas in 1812, Barr and Davenport were the primary agents of trade in Spanish Texas.[21]

Barr and Davenport served several major purposes for the Spanish government. Spain believed that the presence of Indian trade partners—nurtured by their association with Barr and Davenport—along the uncertain boundary between Louisiana and the United States would provide a buffer and a deterrent to immigration by unwanted Americans and their interests in expanding their empire. Barr and Davenport, because of the many benefits they accrued being monopolistic purveyors of Spanish trade, were able to be liberal in their gift-giving. Their gifts to the tribes included "muskets, gunpowder, knives, scissors, axes, hoes, combs, glass beads, war paint, mirrors, wire, copper and iron pots, ribbons, coats, bells, needles, belt buckles, ramrods, hats, and various kinds of cotton goods, tobacco, and occasionally rum.[22]

The horses and cattle they received from the Indians in trade were legally exported to Louisiana. In one trip, horses sold in Louisiana and west Florida netted $3,944 (2,720 pesos), generally about ten pesos per head.[23] In addition to the Indian trade, Barr and Davenport supplied Spanish military endeavors and soldiers posted in all the Spanish settlements and presidios. Flour, beef, salt, soap, candles, and even chili were part of the supply chain. Barr and Davenport operated for some time out of Ibarvo's Old Stone House constructed on the *plaza principal* in Nacogdoches. The establishment of a large trading enterprise by Barr and Davenport represented a transition away from the more simplistic and less ambitious control of trade as practiced by Ibarvo, La Mathe, and others.

Vicente Micheli, "The Merchant of Venice"

Another contemporary of Barr and Davenport was the Vicente Micheli, an Italian. Micheli had come to Nacogdoches around 1793, also after Ibarvo was removed. By 1797, Spain awarded Micheli a land grant of five and a half leagues, or twenty-four thousand acres. Micheli was also the object of several *decimas*, which one official called "scandalous couplets, insulting, and directed towards altering the public tranquility."[24]

For a time, Micheli worked for Barr and Davenport as one of their affiliated traders. Land grants that Micheli sought put in him proximity to the Bidai, both along the Trinity and Bedias Creek, as well as on the Neches River adjacent to Bidai villages to the south of Nacogdoches. Over time Micheli became a wealthy man in his own right. He was the only bidder when Ibarvo's enslaved people and livestock were sold at auction to pay off debt. The total sale was for 3,624 pesos, leaving only three pesos that Ibarvo had to pay to complete the repayment of a debt.[25] In 1798, Micheli provided 310 pesos to Lieutenant Guadiana in Nacogdoches to pay the troops when a shortfall in funds needed to be covered.[26] By 1801, however, Micheli was in dire straits financially.

> Don Vicente Micheli, a citizen of San Ant[oni]o de Béxar and resident in this villa, with the deepest respect makes known to Your Lordship that due to the unavoidable misfortunes that he has suffered in his business, finds himself reduced to the unfortunate necessity of ceasing his business activities at a time that, by an agreement made with his creditors, he is needing to repay them, during a term that he has stipulated, the considerable sum of more than ten thousand pesos that he owes them, and that perhaps he will be unable to pay them without sacrificing the last remnants of his industry and labor.[27]

This opening to Micheli's letter to de Pedro de Nava was followed by a request to bring a cotton gin to Béxar with five years exclusivity for its use in exchange for financial support from the government and the government's promise to promote the growth of cotton. Political favors and financial preferences are not new.

Shortly after Ibarvo's removal, the nature of commerce in Nacogdoches changed in dramatic ways, and not to the benefit of Spanish interests in the long term. These three traders—an Italian, an Irishman, and an American—gained favored status as sanctioned traders of goods and livestock between Indian nations, Spanish Texas, and Louisiana. They each made their motives clear—they were in Texas for the money.

The World Changes Around Them

Though the focus of this work has been on East Texas and the influence of early Spanish leadership on the formation of Nacogdoches's commerce of contraband, one must still acknowledge that many outside factors were at work beyond the control of Spain. Though somewhat immune locally to the machinations of nations in Europe, Spanish leadership in Mexico City could not ignore changes in the alignment of nations around New Spain.

While Ibarvo and the Adeseños were establishing themselves in jacales and huts along the Trinity River in 1776, colonists in New England declared their independence from the king of England. In 1779, while Nacogdoches was being resettled at a run-down former mission, Spain declared war against England. When tensions between the United States and France grew in 1799, there were Spanish concerns that their own close relations with France could lead to US aggression toward Spain in Texas. Spanish officials suggested the installation of a post to the east of Nacogdoches to maintain a watch of activity in that direction, an instruction that was not followed.[28] No attack was forthcoming, but the vigilance in Nacogdoches continued nonetheless. In 1800, the captain in Nacogdoches informed the governor that fortifications included a reconstructed stockade and that poorly maintained artillery had been repaired and mounted for use.[29] Spain liked to think they were prepared for what may come their way from the east.

Louisiana Purchase, 1803

The killing of the mustanger Philip Nolan in 1801 was one of the earliest signals that United States interests in expansion to the west would not stop with their current land holdings. In the language of cable television, what came next was the biggest "property flip" in US history. In 1762, Spain acquired the all-important Mississippi River valley and the vital port of New Orleans from France. Despite Spanish "ownership" of the territory, New Orleans was still indisputably French and was never quite comfortable being part of Spanish colonial rule. French traders from Spanish Louisiana were at the heart of contraband trade into Spanish Texas. A secret agreement between Spain and Napoleon Bonaparte, the ruler of France who had only recently come to power, retroceded almost nine hundred thousand square miles of land in the heart of the continent. The retrocession was accomplished on October 15, 1802. Word of the transfer came to the surface through a proclamation issued by the Spanish governor of Louisiana, Manuel de Salcedo, in May 1803.[30]

This action greatly troubled US President Thomas Jefferson, who feared that French control of New Orleans and the mouth of the Mississippi River would practically eliminate any access to the bounties of trade offered by the Mississippi River valley and transportation down its waters. By October 1803, Napoleon traded whatever visions he had of a French presence in North America to the United States for $15 million. Of course, all that territory was not truly French—it was long occupied by numerous indigenous peoples. Ownership of land that was home, farm, and cemetery to the native inhabitants was something all three European countries were skilled at ignoring. However, even Jefferson appeared to acknowledge the claims of the native people.

> The territory acquired, as it includes all the waters of the Missouri and Mississippi, has more than doubled the area of the United States. I presume the island of N. Orleans and the settled country on the opposite bank, will be annexed to the Mississippi territory. The rest will probably be locked up from American settlement, and under the self-government of the native occupants.[31]

After the ratification of the purchase, mapmaker Juan Pedro Walker so hated the Americans that he abandoned his beloved Spanish/French Louisiana for Spanish Texas.

> America has acquired from France all of Louisiana, and if they arrive to take possession clear to the boundaries that divide this province from that [Spanish Texas], God help us! This is the most ambitious, restless, lawless, conniving, changeable and turbulent of all the Governments in the Universe. I am so disgusted with hearing them that I can hardly wait to leave them behind me.[32]

The border between Louisiana and Spanish Texas was verbally pushed and shoved back and forth in diplomatic communications and challenges. At various times in the negotiation the United States wanted the boundary to be much farther south at the Rio Grande, the Guadalupe, or the Colorado rivers. The US finally came to contend that the Sabine River should be the boundary.

Spain made a case for the boundary being farther to the east along the Arroyo Hondo, almost to the extinguished former capital at Los Adaes. The continuing disagreement over the location of the boundary led to a break in diplomatic communications and the perceived threat of a conflict with the US at the edge of the province. It also led to another Spanish settlement built from nothing on the edge of the Trinity River.

Trinidad de Salcedo, 1805

The US acquisition of Louisiana in 1803 set urgent Spanish responses in motion, at least to the extent that the empire could muster them.[33] As tensions grew, Nemesio Salcedo, the commandant general of the Internal Provinces, knew he had to take defensive action. Following numerous proposals for settlements along the coast and allowing the entry of non-Catholic foreigners to increase colonization, a formal proclamation was issued for the development of a new settlement on the Trinity River near the El Camino Real crossing toward Béxar and to La Bahía, miles north of the former location of Bucareli at Paso Tomás. It would be named Santísima Trinidad de Salcedo, honoring the commandant general.

WHY ON THE TRINITY?

One may wonder why the Spanish would build another settlement on the Trinity when Nacogdoches was already established and populated with around seven hundred people at the time. Governor Elguazabal himself admitted that "the government ignored their existence until the year 1795" when Ibarvo was excluded from reentry.[34] After a visit to Nacogdoches in the summer of 1805, Antoni Cordero y Bustamante could plainly see that the Province of Texas was defenseless. A small advance post on the Arroyo Hondo was there for observation, but the soldiers would have to retreat to Nacogdoches should any threat approach. Nacogdoches was built for trade, not for defense. Any invading force would overtake Nacogdoches with little effort or armament. If Nacogdoches fell to the Americans, there was only the road to Béxar ahead of them. Spain's need for a defensive position led to an 1805 decision to build both a military and a civil settlement on the Trinity River upstream from Paso Tomás and the former site of Bucareli.

In mid-December 1805, Salcedo approved the plans for a settlement at the Trinity River. However, the actual threat of attack from the United States was likely not as strong a possibility as the Spanish feared. In a speech to Congress in December 1805, President Thomas Jefferson said a war with Spain was not necessary.[35] Jefferson did not seem inclined toward anything like an invasion but did understand that a show of force might encourage Spain's agreement with their diplomatic demands regarding the boundary.

POPULATING TRINIDAD

The civil settlement authorized was farther downstream from the presidio and was not located on the road between Nacogdoches and Béxar. Cordero knew that protecting the territory between the Trinity and the Arroyo Hondo would take more than a military presence. To ensure more permanence, Spain needed a settlement. Having civilians nearby to support the military presence provided craftsmen, stock-raising, and food cultivation, freeing up the soldiers for their military roles. The next question to be solved was who those civilians would be and where they would come from.

By December 1805, 120 soldiers from San Antonio arrived at the Trinity and set about building a chapel and barracks at a site on the east side of the river where nothing had existed before. Fueled by concerns about an invasion from the US, the military contingent quickly grew to almost four hundred men. When the perceived threat began to lessen, the number of soldiers went down to around one hundred. Hundreds of acres were also identified and set aside for civilian use, including one large tract for private property and another for shared pasturage, water, and timber.[36]

Ideas about how to bring people to the new settlement largely looked to attract Spanish subjects from other provinces beyond Texas or even from Spain. People who wanted to live in such conditions were hard to find, and it was difficult to convince people to leave homes in Béxar or other established settlements regardless of any troubles they may have been experiencing. By January 1806, only five families from Béxar responded to the invitation to settle, but twenty people from Louisiana were among the first to arrive.[37]

As tensions rose with the United States over the boundary, the soldiers went through the motions of being prepared for their duties and the possibility that they may be called to defend Spanish Texas. They would indeed be called to arms but not for another five years. Another kind of conflict was coming.

Neutral Ground Agreement, November 1806

The western fringes of the United States were like the leading edge of a lava flow, surging slowly but nonetheless certain to overwhelm anything in its path. The people might outrun it, but the land would never be the same. In 1801 there were only about two hundred Spanish troops in Texas presidios, but by

1806, the number had reached 1,368; they were brought to the province to "protect what was now New Spain's border with the land-hungry United States."[38]

US Gen. James Wilkinson described the disputed territory between the Spanish province of Texas and the land acquired by the United States in the Louisiana Purchase as "inhospitable wilds." A dividing line was not agreed upon, yet each nation wanted to assert what little sanction, authority, and military strength they could scrape together to settle that question to their favor.

The eastern perimeter of Spanish Texas was not the only place where tensions were putting the Spanish on edge. Early in 1805, President Jefferson appointed Thomas Freeman and Peter Custis, a surveyor and a naturalist, to explore the Red River north from Natchitoches. It took until May 2, 1806, for them to begin their expedition up the river. Impeded by the Great Raft, a huge log jam, they pushed upstream through amazingly difficult conditions. When word of this American intrusion reached Spanish officials, the captain at Nacogdoches, Francisco Viana, was sent north to intercept the group and turn them back. He did that on July 28, 1806, at a point on the Red River now known as Spanish Bluff.[39]

"They Would Absolutely Starve"

The ability of Spain to mount a military response to such threats was an open question. The commander in Natchitoches in 1804 saw that "the inhabitants between here and there [San Antonio] do not raise Sufficient Provisions to carry them through half the year. If it were not for the Supplies they get from this District [Natchitoches] they would absolutely starve."[40]

The Spanish understood these weaknesses all too well. Manuel de Salcedo issued an edict in 1805 ordering the cessation of all trade toward Louisiana. His proclamation of the death penalty for anyone selling horses and mules to Americans got the attention of traders in Nacogdoches. Despite the threatened punishment, his orders were resisted by the people of East Texas, and their dependence on supplies by way of Natchitoches continued. By November 1805, Cordero explained to Salcedo that he could not get enough provisions from San Antonio to supply the seven hundred or more residents of Nacogdoches and asked to be able to continue trade in Natchitoches. This created an interesting dynamic. Although there was no present military conflict, provisions were being purchased in the territory where armed conflict was expected to begin. Supplies to feed Cordero's troops in Nacogdoches were coming from his potential enemy.[41]

A FINAL STANDOFF

Building tensions at the border with what became United States territory continued through 1806 with feints and bluffs between the two sides like two boxers who do not want to deliver a punch. In January 1806, the US commander at Natchitoches, Moses Porter, wanted his counterpart in Nacogdoches, Sebastian Rodriguez, to commit to no aggression on the east side of the Sabine. Rodriguez tacitly agreed but explained his orders were to prevent contraband trade and the removal of horses from the province, and to accomplish that he must patrol the area of the Arroyo Hondo, a small stream near the old location of Los Adaes.

Sixty United States soldiers removed a Spanish patrol from Los Adaes in February 1806. Governor Claiborne of Louisiana fanned the flames by spreading false rumors about the presence and number of Spanish troops and their impending invasion. Governor Salcedo even reached out to Claiborne himself, assuring him that Spain would not be the aggressor and asserting that his assumptions about Spanish intentions were not valid. He told Claiborne that the Americans had no "cause for unsheathing the sword."[42]

A THIRD NATION

It was not just these two nations that were on edge—the third largest nation of the region, the Caddo, were also concerned about the outcome. Chief Dehahuit had been in communication with Governor Claiborne of Louisiana and reasserted Caddo neutrality. Like the Kichai chief who rejected Ibarvo's claim to land occupied by the Indians as "his land," Dehahuit tried to explain a concept to the governor that neither Spain nor France understood fully—those new nations were in the land of the Caddo. "My words," Dehahuit explained, "resemble the words my forefathers have told me they used to receive from the French in ancient times. If your nation has purchased what the French formerly possessed, you have purchased the country that we occupy, and we regard you in the same light as we did them."[43]

SAFE SPACE FOR BANDITTI

In October 1806, Gen. James Wilkinson, discovered later to be both a US commander and a spy for Spain, arrived in Natchitoches to take command. Shortly after his arrival, Wilkinson told the Spanish he was advancing to the Sabine River but then did not do so until later in the month. Porter for the US and Herrera for Spain had already worked out an arrangement that placed Spanish troops on the west side of the Sabine and the US on the east side of the Arroyo Hondo. Wilkinson finally acceded to that agreement and formalized a proposal on October 29, 1806, to Governor Antonio Cordero by way of Simón de Herrera, the Spanish commander.

In his proposal, Wilkinson explained how soldiers like himself must follow orders, however Wilkinson the diplomat made a proposal. He was not authorized to make a treaty but suggested there are times like this one where battlefield decisions must be made without waiting for higher authorities to make them at their distant posts. Wilkinson told Cordero he was therefore "willing to risqué the approbations of my Government to perpetuate the tranquility of the inhospitable wilds."[44] Herrera's reply on November 4 affirmed Wilkinson's wisdom, and their actions created the infamous "Neutral Ground" between Spanish Texas and American Louisiana. The agreement kept the peace between their nations but created a disquieting strip of land 30 to 40 miles across where only the ungoverned would roam.

Over time, contrabandistas, deserters, and enslaved runaways flocked to the zone where no soldiers were allowed. Spanish officials were determined to clear the neutral zone of anyone classed as undesirable, but there were just too many miles, too many river bottoms, and too many woods to make a difference. Spanish soldiers burned any homes they found, but people persisted in living along both sides of the Sabine. Those hiding out there knew that setting foot inside the neutral zone gave them some advantages.

Trafficked goods still flowed between Nacogdoches and Natchitoches. As a result, caravans were constantly being robbed and people killed for their goods. Commerce and contraband took an uglier turn and continued to worsen, and by 1812 had grown intolerable.

> The commission of robberies on the Territory West of the Arroyo Hondo, and East of the Sabine River, and as your memorialists believe within the limits of your Excellency's Government, has become so frequent, that it is no longer safe to travel on the highways & roads through which the commerce of this Parish with the adjoining Mexican [Spanish] provinces have hitherto been carried on . . . on the second of January last a Company of Spaniards, whilst travelling on the highway leading from the Sabine to Bayou Pierre, were attacked by a party of Said Banditti about thirty in number, with their faces blacked, and otherwise disfigured, who fired upon them, killed one man, wounded several, one it is supposed mortally so, and robbed them of all their horses, mules, baggage and about six thousand dollars in specie.[45]

The paternalistic controls and the culture of contraband trade practiced by Antonio Gil Ibarvo would seem distantly quaint to anyone forced to fear for their lives and livelihood just to cross the well-traveled roads toward Natchitoches.

The borderlands had become a smuggler's back alley in a no-man's-land at the edge of two nations.

Conditions in Nacogdoches, 1805–1810

Direct conflict with the United States may have subsided after the acceptance of the Neutral Ground Agreement but that solution to the problem created another one. Thousands of ungoverned acres—where lawlessness had become codified and where civil and military authority had no place—was an attraction to an undesirable class of people. Concerns about the inhabitants of the neutral zone grew; fears about foreigners in Spanish territory remained. In 1810, Spanish leaders looking for ideas and information asked for updates on conditions in Nacogdoches.

MONTHLY REPORTS INDICATE DIFFICULTIES, 1804

Regular monthly reports from José Joaquín Ugarte detailed the concern over conditions along the borderlands following Ibarvo's removal. The state of military diligence and readiness was regularly reviewed and reported to the governor. In the report for January 1805 detailing activities for the month prior, Ugarte reported there were fifty-one soldiers on assignment in Nacogdoches. The companies of Béxar, La Bahía, and San Carlos de Parras surrendered troops in equal proportions to the post. Ten of the soldiers were assigned to "reconnoitering the roads which lead to Louisiana" through a dangerous no-man's-land. Another four soldiers were assigned to the roads toward Béxar and La Bahía. Interestingly, eighteen of the men were listed "with no assignment" that month.[46]

The daily diary was a detailed listing of what was, or was not, happening in the entire Nacogdoches district. On the third of December in 1804, Señors Rocha, Estrada, Renglan, and Ernandes "left to capture *mesteñas* from the herds, and to hunt beaver and deer on the banks of the Brazos River." On the fifth, Juan Fonten and Luis Sarnac left for Natchitoches with carts to bring back flour. Only four days later, Manuel Flores and another man went to Natchitoches with "seven mules and horses for freighting flour."

Nacogdoches continued as a busy hub for local tribes looking for trade goods or gifts. On December 4, a Nadaco chief came with "twelve braves and eight squaws" and were given "the most essential supplies or their maintenance." On the eighth, eleven Ais came and "asked that they be given food." Eighteen Bidai people came to the post on December 24, also in search of gifts and sustenance.

The military patrols of both the main roads and the contraband routes occasionally turned up unauthorized goods and livestock. On December 15, two soldiers returned to Nacogdoches with "six horses and three mares they found hidden in a motte (a mound) where, signs indicated, someone was taking care of them there." On the last day of the year in 1804, and sprinkled throughout the diary accounts for the month, Ugarte reported with some relief that "the day was spent without unusual incident." If only he knew then what changes were to come for East Texas.

PRIESTLY OBSERVATIONS

Father Mariano Sosa had only recently been assigned to the chapel at Nacogdoches in May of 1810. Though his brief experience in Nacogdoches could have offered him a ready excuse to avoid reporting any observations worthy of consideration by the governor, Sosa instead penned a lengthy letter with his opinions about the moral state of the most distant settlement in Spanish Texas. His first impressions were more than sufficient for him to make early judgments about his flock.

In his view, Nacogdoches was a "village without order, without morality, and without Christianity in general" on the border of a region that was "strewn with various pernicious libertines." Lacking proper education in the law or in basic morality, the residents simply did what those who came before them had done, putting them in a state of the "crassest ignorance [whereby] they are persuaded that they know everything." Sosa had no shortage of opinions; his missive went on for pages after that attention-getting opening.[47] Father Sosa acknowledged the actual conditions that led to much suffering by the population. He noted the primary occupations of farming and cattle raising, making sure to include contraband trade on that list of occupations. He suggested that were it not for their laziness and dishonesty, they may have been able to be better purveyors of their goods and services.

Sosa found the military as much to blame as the citizens. He found them to be petty thieves, suggesting that improving their pay would be a solution. Soldiers not only had to buy their own supplies, but they could also only make legal purchases from the military commissary. Soldiers were at the mercy of their commanders, and that authority was often abused. During Governor Ripperdá's tenure, Sosa said, the governor forced his soldiers to purchase "useless" items like mirrors, pins, and door locks directly from him at two times the usual cost.[48]

Sosa believed it would help both the soldiers and citizens if they could use some form of specie to buy from local merchants. Sosa's recommendations reflected a keen understanding of the pressures of supply and demand, but a naivete about how things worked in the borderlands. Sosa expressed concern for the "patronesses" the soldiers used for services and favors, and for the wives of men who left for days or weeks in hunting or trading expeditions who were left only with their bodies to make a living.

With all his observations of the ills of Nacogdoches expressed, Sosa boiled down his suggestions for improvement to three primary focal points: "a public school for Christian education; another mode for maintaining the troops; and another means in order that this village may have an outlet for its produce."[49] Though a man of the church, Sosa's recommendations were focused on an improved civil society. Had he removed the garments of the priesthood, Sosa might have made a fine leader for the struggling frontier settlement.

A MILITARY VIEW

Like Father Sosa, Lt. José María Guadiana sensed the gravity of the governor's request and responded with a lengthy, detailed description of the conditions in Nacogdoches. However, the styles used by each of the respondents could not have been more different. While Father Sosa's letter was filled with descriptions that began with the trained emotional observations of a loyal servant of the church, Guadiana took a "just the facts" approach focusing in large part on the land, rivers, and roads. While Sosa was not shy in offering his opinions about what needed to change, Guadiana simply reported the circumstances and did not make a single recommendation for change, perhaps for fear of being wrong.[50]

Like Sosa, Guadiana noted that there was much more agricultural opportunity left untouched due to the residents' lack of industriousness. Corn and beans were common, wheat was less so. He believed that cotton, tobacco, flax, hemp, and grapes could be grown more commercially even though the terrain meant that none of the rivers were suited for irrigation.

When Guadiana's report came to his account of the people of Nacogdoches, one can begin to sense his frustrations with both the people and the conditions under which they must survive. In his view, the people of Nacogdoches had little to offer.

> These citizens absolutely lack all commerce, active as well as passive. They do not trade with anybody, nor does anybody trade with them . . . Because what are they able to bring to this that they have account?

Guadiana listed out all the possibilities and also the obstacles that prevented the populace from finding opportunities for improvement. No matter where Guadiana looked for commercial options, there were limitations. Furs, grains, and pelts had costs that were barriers to their participation. If they did manage to grow enough food to sell any excess, it was more often thrown away "through not knowing what to do with it." To acquire basic goods from

Natchitoches, they were forced to travel through the neutral zone "at a cost of losing themselves if they are surprised by any party."

Guadiana's Nacogdoches was trapped in a set of circumstances made worse by the limitations on trade across the Sabine. Where Ibarvo's Nacogdoches had once found a balance among the Spanish, French, and Native American interests for a somewhat cozier arrangement in trade, Guadiana's Nacogdoches was having its life drained by the disparities between nations.

CONTINUED USE OF THE OLD ROADS

If there was commerce, there would be roads to move and transport it. The "public" roads—those like El Camino de los Tejas and the contraband trails that were lesser used—each served their own purposes. In early 1802, Lieutenant Guadiana had updated the governor to let him know that "frequent clandestine extractions of horses are made along the road that runs from La Bahía to Luisiana," one of the three Bidai trails covered in an earlier chapter. Guadiana tried to reassure the governor that he was doing the best he could to patrol "those [roads] that, from those two communities, flow into this post and ranchos and its jurisdiction.[51]

The problems with alternate routes continued in 1809. Guadiana noted that John McFarland, a known troublemaker, was believed to be using what was called "the Lower Road" and that he "had crossed the Sabine River, and there is no doubt that it is with the intention of going to Louisiana."[52] In 1810, from the presidio at Trinidad de Salcedo, Lt. José Antonio Cuellar, along with a sergeant, a corporal, and nine soldiers, headed south "for the purposes of patrolling the roads, paths, and sideroads by which contraband of goods or herds of horses may be able to be carried toward foreign dominions."[53] They passed Bedias Creek along the way and crossed the "road of the Cosshattas (Coushatta)" at a hard crossing on the river they called the "place of the *calichitos*," likely a caliche-like mixture of light rock, sand, and clay with just enough of limestone to make it appear hard like cement.

Feeble attempts to seal off similar crossings were short-lived. In one attempt to stop up a crossing at the "second falls" of the Trinity River, soldiers piled timber in the cuts in the crossing's riverbank to the water level. If the next rush of water down the river did not remove the debris, then another crossing would be found.[54]

All Things Must Change

In 1779, shortly after his arrival to resettle Nacogdoches, Ibarvo made a declaration that he was taking ownership of land along the road from Nacogdoches toward El Lobanillo. Ibarvo immediately assigned the land to his son-in-law Juan Ignacio Guerrero and his daughter María Antonia. This site, La Lunaca—most often seen translated as The Cresent or The Half Moon—was about ten leagues from Nacogdoches, so the cattle there were closer to Natchitoches and did not have to pass through Nacogdoches. As a result of changes to the course of the Attoyac Bayou, a place called "the island" was created—a low valley between high hills on the east and on the west. At one time the river forked and ran on both sides of the ranch, with the main flow to the west. When the main flow moved to the east side it created a crescent-shaped piece of land almost a mile across in some parts.

Pedro de Nava allowed Ibarvo to move there in late 1809 or early 1810, shortly before his death. His poor health was likely the reason that de Nava relented. Whether Ibarvo passed through the village of Nacogdoches as described by Sosa and Guadiana or quietly used one the roads around is not known. His passage through the region he helped define came before the turmoil and disassembly of all that had been gained.

The Demise of the Bidai

Some historical accounts describe the state of the Bidai at the beginning of the nineteenth century as depleted and desperate, "living a wandering life and obtaining food where they could."[55] In 1804, the Bidai under Chief Prieto (Dark Skin) were living along the Trinity in an area later inhabited by the Coushatta, one of the Louisiana tribes that migrated into Texas and would quickly fill the role of trading middlemen formerly held by the Bidai.

Following Prieto's death in 1808, the Spanish captain of the fort of Atascosito near present-day Liberty appointed Nicopí as the medal chief of the Bidai.[56] Despite the official designation, the Bidai began to lose their identities and assimilate into other tribes. The Bidai merged with the Coushatta and other Atakapan tribes from Bedias Creek southward along the Trinity.[57] Colonists among the early members of Austin's colony in 1821 described them as a "beggarly tribe." By 1834, there were almost nine thousand Anglos in East Texas, overwhelming the numbers of indigenous people native to that ground.[58]

Revolution in Mexico, 1810

Perceptions of the region by Nacogdoches residents were quite different than those of distant authorities. Local knowledge was fueled by a daily exposure to present reality. Distant Spanish leaders feared all foreigners and saw them as forerunners to a future threat of invasion. In fact, during the years between 1803 and 1810, after an initial inflow, settlers were abandoning East Texas and going to Natchitoches or New Orleans in numbers that became a concern. Worried that the eastern half of Texas would be emptied of its residents, Governor Salcedo issued a proclamation on July 29, 1810, offering what amounted to a pardon for anyone accused of contraband trade.[59]

Rumblings of revolution in Mexico against royalist Spain was the reason for the exodus of residents. The Mexican struggle for independence from Spanish rule began in 1810 with a revolt led by a Spanish priest. It did not officially end until 1821 when Mexico was granted independence.[60] In early 1811, Capt. Juan Bautista de las Casas, a militia leader in San Antonio, arrested Governor Manuel Salcedo and sent eighty soldiers to Nacogdoches to install a revolutionary government. That action led to more arrests and the confiscation of property in Nacogdoches. After backlash led to the arrest of Casas, extreme measures were taken to let the insurgents know that their actions would not go unpunished.

> As a reminder of punishment adjudged to insurrectionists, Antonio Cordero shipped Las Casas' head in a box to Béxar, where soldiers displayed the gruesome object on a pole in the military plaza.[61]

The instability of the government in Mexico City and the continuing pressures of revolutionary ideas and actions had Spain focusing inward, distracted from problems at the Texas-Louisiana border.

Gutièrrez-Magee Filibuster, August 1812

The word "filibuster" in today's lexicon evokes images of a stalemate in the US Senate. In less divisive times, the filibuster required a verbal takeover of the floor, with the senator speaking as long as physically possible to stall legislation. During the late eighteenth and early nineteenth century, the word had an entirely different meaning. Ed Bradley, in his outstanding work *We Never Retreat—Filibustering Expeditions into Spanish Texas, 1812–1822*, reported on the application of the word to 1812 Nacogdoches.

> Persons who, lacking either the explicit or implicit consent of their own governments, planned, abetted, or participated in private military invasions or intended invasions of foreign nations or dependencies with which their own countries were at peace.[62]

Nacogdoches was a weak and failing settlement in 1812. The soldiers lacked horses, shoes, flour, and funds. The troops included men who were untrustworthy, disabled, or were undesirable elements. The couriers responsible for mail service were often on foot, forced to abandon lame or ill horses, and faced the constant threat of hostile attacks. It was widely known that Nacogdoches was indefensible, and the military resistance that might forestall any invaders from the United States was untested and uncertain.[63]

The pace of revolutionary resistance to Spanish rule within Texas continued to arouse the populace. When a rebel entourage led by José Bernardo Gutièrrez de Lara crossed the Sabine River on a smuggling road into the Neutral Ground in September 1811, it began a series of events that led to the depopulation of Nacogdoches. The unfounded hope of US-sanctioned military support for the takeover remained in the background.

In Louisiana, Nashville, and Washington, DC, Gutièrrez sought money, guns, and backing for an invasion of Spanish Texas to dislodge the royalists and form an independent republic. In Louisiana, Gutièrrez brought other prominent men and borderland civilians into his cause. One of those was Augustus William Magee, a graduate of West Point and a US Army officer. He resigned from the army to lead a force of 150 men into Nacogdoches in August 1812 beneath a flag of solid green. When those retreating to Nacogdoches in advance of the armed contingent told the citizens there about the approaching conflict, the Spanish commander ordered a retreat to Béxar. All but about ten to twenty of his soldiers deserted during the retreat. Magee and his contingent took Nacogdoches without firing a shot.[64]

The presidio and villa of Trinidad de Salcedo on the Trinity River fared no better. Despite the addition of Spanish troops from Orcoquisac and the restoration of defensive fortifications, there was no resistance at Trinidad either. In the face of Magee's force, thirty-seven of the soldiers surrendered while the remainder abandoned the post. Civilians of the villa were already inclined to support the revolution and they joined with Magee, along with some of the Spanish soldiers.

Pichardo's map of 1811 used simple, compelling words to assign the location of the former home of the wandering Adeseños—*Bucareli extinguido*—the extinguished site of Bucareli.[65] The same words could be used to describe the fate of Trinidad de Salcedo. There are numerous historical accounts that detail the successes and failures of the Gutièrrez-Magee expedition and its brief establishment of a republic in Spanish Texas. The insurgent's attempts at filibuster ended with their slaughter at the Battle of Medina in 1813. The royalist forces did not end their violence against any remaining revolutionary notions there, however. Under orders from Juan Arredondo, soldiers marched toward East Texas intent on executing anyone who might still hold thoughts of separating Texas from Spanish rule.

As Spanish troops approached the Trinity River from the west, opposite Trinidad de Salcedo, they were restrained by a natural event often memorialized in early Spanish diaries—the Trinity River was flooded, swollen, and impassable. Stopped by the grand river for several days, the sympathizers that the soldiers were ordered to execute looked back at them from across the Trinity. There was plenty of time for the citizens and soldiers there to escape to the east toward the United States.

The fate of the Spanish settlements on the Trinity River, Bucareli and Trinidad, were determined by similar events. The flooding that inundated Bucareli spared Trinidad from Elizondo's immediate entry by being built on higher ground. Trinidad did not escape the elements; its barracks and jail had been earlier destroyed, likely by the remains of a Gulf of Mexico hurricane.[66] An attack on Bucareli by the Comanche was mirrored in Trinidad by an attack by Spanish royalist forces. Fire was also part of its demise. After finally being able to cross the river, Spanish forces set fire to both the villa and the presidio, burning them to the ground. Only forty years after the burning of Trinidad de Salcedo, a visitor found the site "covered with wildflowers and grapevines."[67]

Nacogdoches was emptied by the time Spanish forces arrived. Those remaining had escaped to Natchitoches or within the neutral zone. It would be years before many would return to the hills between Bayou La Nana and Bonita Creek.

Conclusion

Following the attempts of American filibusters to take over Spanish Texas, the nature of East Texas changed in dramatic ways. Although Spain continued to shore up its defensive posture and attempted to boost its projection of strength, those perceptions were illusory and temporary. Like the false front of a movie set, things might look substantial and real at face value, but when you peer around the corner the entire thing is propped up with boards and nails that look too weak to support the structure.

Over time, Nacogdoches and East Texas became the entry point for those with bigger goals than trading horses and skins. Dissatisfaction with whomever was in charge at the time turned into rebellions, opportunities to settle and colonize turned to greed, and desires to control commerce were routinely acted upon. Beneath it all was the land. People who had not lived on the land for centuries, as people indigenous to East Texas had done, decided they were the owners. Instead of land jointly claimed by tribal groups as a shared resource, boundaries and ultimately fences were devised. The land was claimed by Spain, claimed by Mexico, and claimed by the Republic of Texas. It was occupied by the force of arms and shaped by Anglo plows and axes.

The new occupants changed the names of rivers, streams, and sacred places to Spanish and then English versions that were dissimilar and odd-sounding to those who first walked them. When Spanish descendants from the Mora family joined the army in World War I, the military even anglicized his name to Moore.[68] Over time, even the more seemingly permanent places were altered. The Mountain Cemetery near Chireno, where names like Cordova and Y'barbo are found, has had its boundaries altered. A road near the cemetery was once known as "the smuggler's road." Gerald Mora said that before the county straightened Texas State Highway 21, the old route of El Camino Real, "it was so crooked that you might see your own shoulder coming from behind."[69]

Borders, Not Boundaries

If a boundary is thought of as a line separating two countries, then a border is a perpendicular line that connects the two sides. Though borders have been defined and altered over the years, they have rarely stood as obstacles to travel and trade. Their porous nature exists because of the necessity of trade, the endurance of commerce, and the ingenuity of those who wish to cross.

To illustrate that difference, three Native American artists constructed a two-mile-long artwork that crossed the US-Mexico border. In 2015 they installed twenty-eight helium-filled balls tethered to the ground along an imaginary line extending one mile on either side of the border. The bright yellow spheres each had a design they called the "open eye," harkening to a symbol that has existed in indigenous cultures for thousands of years. They described the work as "a metaphorical suture stitching together cultures that have inhabited these lands long before borders were drawn." This artistic work sought to illustrate how boundaries are simply imagined lines and that the people on either side are inextricably joined.[70]

An author used a similar method to recast our thinking about boundaries. In his 2008 book about the borderland history of the United States and Mexico, Samuel Truett expands on the concept of "fugitive landscapes," which was coined by Cornell University's Raymond Craib. Fugitive landscapes are those along the borders of nations that defy efforts to be tamed or controlled. Truett makes the case that the nature of borderlands history contradicts the nation-centered histories with which we are most familiar. He argues that borderlands both divide and connect the people, places, and commerce within them. Boundaries can be defined, changed, refined, or abandoned, but the social networks continue unchanged no matter how the boundary is defined. Truett says, "Border people cannot forget nations, but nation-bound histories often forget border people."[71]

An Image from the 2017 documentary *Through the Repellent Fence*, about an art project calling attention to how cross-border cultures inhabited lands long before borders were drawn. Image courtesy of Cristóbal Martínez and Kade L. Twist through their art collective, Postcommodity.

In June 1811, Spanish authorities conducted an extensive investigation to determine the source of ongoing plots to overtake Nacogdoches from across the Sabine River. They took the depositions of several men who lived in the Neutral Ground regarding what they had observed. José Miguel Crow, an outspoken ferry operator on the Spanish side of the Sabine River, was in a position where he could see the comings and goings across the boundary. When asked of what nation he was a subject, he said that since he had lived in the Neutral Ground for almost ten years, he was not able to answer that question—he no longer knew the answer to the question.

When rumblings of revolutionary intruders picked up pace, Crow was arrested and interrogated after a group of armed men with bad intentions crossed the Sabine. He had seen that there were men who were thinking of "raising a revolution and gaining this place, for afterwards insinuating themselves in the kingdom." Crow implied that this was being done with the involvement of a priest he called the "Fat Father," a Father Huerta in Nacogdoches, and the former commandant of Nacogdoches, José María Guadiana.

Crow pled ignorance of all but the general perception that something was afoot. Though he professed unfamiliarity with any revolutionary plans, Crow was sure about one thing. His interpretation of what he saw happening was a perfect summation of the nature of contraband in the East Texas borderlands.[72] Crow told his Spanish inquisitor:

"This revolution was for commercial purposes."

APPENDIX A

Castes

These are the most common caste assignments seen in the Nacogdoches census reports. These are in descending order of status assigned to each group.

CASTE	DEFINITION	CHILD OF	
		MALE	FEMALE
Spanish (espanoles or peninsulares)	Spaniards who claimed to have pure Spanish blood	Spanish	Spanish
Indian (indios)	Indigenous	Indigenous	Indigenous
Mestizo	Of Spanish and native ancestry	Spanish	Indigenous
Mulatto (color quebrado)	Broken color; could be multiple mix of populations	Spanish	African
Africans (negro)	Black Africans; if enslaved, the name given might be negros esclavos	African	African

Caste usage often varied by location. In Los Adaes, other castes were also mentioned.

They were also of a diverse background and castes with 44 *espanoles*, 31 *mulattoes*, 21 *coyotes*, 17 *mestizos*, two *castizos*, one *lobo*, one free *negro*, and one *Indio* represented in the population.

Sources

Avery, George. "Archival Investigations of the People of Los Adaes," *Southern Studies* 7, no. 1 (1996): 65-88.

McReynolds, James M. "Family Life in a Borderland Community: Nacogdoches, Texas, 1779-1861." PhD dissertation, Texas Tech University, 1978.

Townes, J. Edward. "Invisible Lines: The Life and Death of a Borderland." PhD dissertation, Texas Christian University, 2008.

APPENDIX B

Measures of Distance, Land, and Volume in Spanish Colonial Texas

Land Measurements

The Spanish *vara* was the common measure of distance during the colonial period and after Mexican independence. The equivalent measure is 33.3 inches. Measurement conversion tools are available.

A league of land (or *sitio*) is 4,338 acres, and a labor is 177 acres. A league is also a measure for travel distances.

TRAVEL DISTANCES

When measuring distances traveled, the Spanish league is used. The equivalence is 2.6 miles.

VOLUME

Arroba could be used to measure either weight or volume. One arroba in weight is 25.36 pounds; in volume, it is 4.26 gallons.

Sources

Chardon, Roland. "The Elusive Spanish League: A Problem of Measurement in Sixteenth-Century New Spain," *Hispanic American Historical Review* 60, no. 2 (January 1980): pp. 294-302, https://doi.org/10.1215/00182168-60.2.294.

"Convert Vara [Texas] to Foot [Survey]," ConvertUnits.com. Accessed July 13, 2022, https://www.convertunits.com/from/vara+%5bTexas%5d/to/foot+%5bsurvey%5d.

"Quick Conversion Tables for Basic Colonia Measures," Faculty homepage: Dr. John E. Worth (website). University of Western Florida. Accessed July 13, 2022, https://pages.uwf.edu/jworth/jw_spanfla_measures_conversions.html#Spanish_Varas.

APPENDIX C

Distances Between Locations

These distances are generally expressed from west to east.

FROM	TO	SOURCE	LEAGUES	MILES (× 2.6)	HIGHWAY MILES
Bucareli	San Antonio	Morfi, vol. 1, 1777	125	325	226
Los Adaes	El Lobanillo	Blake, vol. 34	18	47	47
Los Adaes	La Bahìa	Breve Compendia Blake, vol. 34 34	200	520	371
Los Adaes	La Bahìa	West, 1907	240	624	371
Los Adaes	Mexico City	West, 1907	600	1,560	1,227
Los Adaes	Mexico City	Blake, vol. 34	600	1,560	1,227
Los Adaes	Mission Dolores	West, 1907	20	52	64
Los Adaes	Mission Dolores	Blake, vol. 34	20	52	64
Los Adaes	Nacogdoches	West, 1907	47	122	98
Los Adaes	Nacogdoches	Blake, vol. 34	47	122	98
Los Adaes	Natchitoches	Blake, vol. 34	7	18	19
Los Adaes	Orcoquisac	West, 1907	150	390	177
Los Adaes	San Antonio	Blake, vol. 34	240	624	409
Mission Dolores	Bucareli	Blake, vol. 44, p. 212	39	101	129
Nacogdoches	Orcoquisac	West, 1907	126	328	117
Nacogdoches	San Antonio	Blake, supplement 3	160	416	292

(*continued*)

FROM	TO	SOURCE	LEAGUES	MILES (× 2.6)	HIGHWAY MILES
Natchitoches	Los Adaes	West, 1907	7	18	15
San Antonio	La Bahìa	West, 1907	40	104	93
San Antonio	La Bahìa	Morfi, vol. 1, 1777	32	83	93
San Antonio	Mexico City	1907, West	370	962	869

Sources

Blake, Robert Bruce. "Robert Bruce Blake Research Collection, Supplements." FamilySearch. Salt Lake City, UT: The Church of Jesus Christ of Latter-Day Saints, 2009. https://www.familysearch.org/search/catalog/1622067.

Morfi, Juan Agustín. *Provincias Internas: Antología, ed. Guadalupe Curiel.* Mexico City: Universidad Nacional Autonoma de Mexico, 2003.

West, Elizabeth Howard, and Marques de Altamira. "Bonilla's Brief Compendium of the History of Texas, 1772 (An Annotated Translation)." *The Quarterly of the Texas State Historical Association* 8, no. 1 (July 1904): 3–78. https://doi.org/http://www.jstor.org/stable/30242842.

APPENDIX D

Spanish Leadership in the Province of Texas

The following table is an effort to chronicle the many changes in Spanish leadership at all levels of government in the late 1700s and early 1800s. When a calendar year saw more than one appointee in a given post, there is an "a," "b," or "c" after the year. Credit to Donald Chipman for his lists of viceroys, commandants general, and governors.

YEARS	VICEROY	COMMANDANT GENERAL	GOVERNOR	COMMANDANT NACOGDOCHES
1770 a	Carlos Francisco de Croix	Hugo Oconór	Juan Maria, Baron de Ripperdá	n/a
1770 b	Carlos Francisco de Croix	Hugo Oconór	Juan Maria, Baron de Ripperdá	n/a
1771 a	Antonio María de Bucareli y Ursua	Hugo Oconór	Juan Maria, Baron de Ripperdá	n/a
1771 b	Antonio María de Bucareli y Ursua	Hugo Oconór	Juan Maria, Baron de Ripperdá	n/a
1772 a	Antonio María de Bucareli y Ursua	Hugo Oconór	Juan Maria, Baron de Ripperdá	n/a
1772 b	Antonio María de Bucareli y Ursua	Hugo Oconór	Juan Maria, Baron de Ripperdá	n/a
1773	Antonio María de Bucareli y Ursua	Hugo Oconór	Juan Maria, Baron de Ripperdá	Antonio Gil Ibarvo

(*continued*)

YEARS	VICEROY	COMMANDANT GENERAL	GOVERNOR	COMMANDANT NACOGDOCHES
1774	Antonio María de Bucareli y Ursua	Hugo Oconór	Juan Maria, Baron de Ripperdá	Antonio Gil Ibarvo
1775	Antonio María de Bucareli y Ursua	Hugo Oconór	Juan Maria, Baron de Ripperdá	Antonio Gil Ibarvo
1776 a	Antonio María de Bucareli y Ursua	Hugo Oconór	Juan Maria, Baron de Ripperdá	Antonio Gil Ibarvo
1776 b	Antonio María de Bucareli y Ursua	Teodoro de Croix	Juan Maria, Baron de Ripperdá	Antonio Gil Ibarvo
1777 a	Antonio María de Bucareli y Ursua	Teodoro de Croix	Juan Maria, Baron de Ripperdá	Antonio Gil Ibarvo
1777 b	Antonio María de Bucareli y Ursua	Teodoro de Croix	Juan Maria, Baron de Ripperdá	Antonio Gil Ibarvo
1778 a	Antonio María de Bucareli y Ursua	Teodoro de Croix	Juan Maria, Baron de Ripperdá	Antonio Gil Ibarvo
1778 b	Antonio María de Bucareli y Ursua	Teodoro de Croix	Domingo Cabello y Robles	Antonio Gil Ibarvo
1779 a	Antonio María de Bucareli y Ursua	Teodoro de Croix	Domingo Cabello y Robles	Antonio Gil Ibarvo
1779 b	Martin de Mayorga Ferrer	Teodoro de Croix	Domingo Cabello y Robles	Antonio Gil Ibarvo
1779 c	Martin de Mayorga Ferrer	Teodoro de Croix	Domingo Cabello y Robles	Antonio Gil Ibarvo

(*continued*)

YEARS	VICEROY	COMMANDANT GENERAL	GOVERNOR	COMMANDANT NACOGDOCHES
1779	Martin de Mayorga Ferrer	Teodoro de Croix	Domingo Cabello y Robles	Antonio Gil Ibarvo
1780	Martin de Mayorga Ferrer	Teodoro de Croix	Domingo Cabello y Robles	Antonio Gil Ibarvo
1781a	Martin de Mayorga Ferrer	Teodoro de Croix	Domingo Cabello y Robles	Antonio Gil Ibarvo
1781 b	Martin de Mayorga Ferrer	Teodoro de Croix	Domingo Cabello y Robles	Antonio Gil Ibarvo
1782	Martin de Mayorga Ferrer	Teodoro de Croix	Domingo Cabello y Robles	Antonio Gil Ibarvo
1783 a	Martin de Mayorga Ferrer	Teodoro de Croix	Domingo Cabello y Robles	Antonio Gil Ibarvo
1783 b	Matias de Galvez y Gallardo	Felipe de Neve	Domingo Cabello y Robles	Antonio Gil Ibarvo
1784 a	Matias de Galvez y Gallardo	Felipe de Neve	Domingo Cabello y Robles	Antonio Gil Ibarvo
1784 b	Matias de Galvez y Gallardo	Jose Antonio Renjel	Domingo Cabello y Robles	Antonio Gil Ibarvo
1785	Bernardo de Gálvez	Jose Antonio Renjel	Domingo Cabello y Robles	Antonio Gil Ibarvo
1786 a	Bernardo de Gálvez	Jose Antonio Renjel	Domingo Cabello y Robles	Antonio Gil Ibarvo

(*continued*)

YEARS	VICEROY	COMMANDANT GENERAL	GOVERNOR	COMMANDANT NACOGDOCHES
1786 b	Bernardo de Gálvez	Jose Antonio Renjel	Domingo Cabello y Robles	Antonio Gil Ibarvo
1787 a	Alonso Nunez de Haro y Peralto	Juan de Ugalde	Rafael Martinez Pacheco	Antonio Gil Ibarvo
1787 b	Manuel Antonio Flórez Maldonado	Juan de Ugalde	Rafael Martinez Pacheco	Antonio Gil Ibarvo
1788 a	Manuel Antonio Flórez Maldonado	Juan de Ugalde	Rafael Martinez Pacheco	Antonio Gil Ibarvo
1788 b	Manuel Antonio Flórez Maldonado	Juan de Ugalde	Rafael Martinez Pacheco	Antonio Gil Ibarvo
1789 a	Manuel Antonio Flórez Maldonado	Juan de Ugalde	Rafael Martinez Pacheco	Antonio Gil Ibarvo
1789 b	Conde de Revilla Gigedo II	Juan de Ugalde	Rafael Martinez Pacheco	Antonio Gil Ibarvo
1790 a	Conde de Revilla Gigedo II	Juan de Ugalde	Rafael Martinez Pacheco	Antonio Gil Ibarvo
1790 b	Conde de Revilla Gigedo II	Pedro de Nava/ Ramón de Castro	Manuel Munoz	Antonio Gil Ibarvo
1791	Conde de Revilla Gigedo II	Pedro de Nava/ Ramón de Castro	Manuel Munoz	Antonio Gil Ibarvo
1792	Conde de Revilla Gigedo II	Pedro de Nava/ Ramón de Castro	Manuel Munoz	Juan Flores

(*continued*)

YEARS	VICEROY	COMMANDANT GENERAL	GOVERNOR	COMMANDANT NACOGDOCHES
1793	Conde de Revilla Gigedo II	Pedro de Nava/ Ramón de Castro	Manuel Munoz	Cristobal Cordova
1794 a	Conde de Revilla Gigedo II	Pedro de Nava	Manuel Munoz	Cristobal Cordova
1794 b	Marqués de Branciforte	Pedro de Nava	Manuel Munoz	Cristobal Cordova
1795	Marqués de Branciforte	Pedro de Nava	Manuel Munoz	Bernardo Fernández
1796 a	Marqués de Branciforte	Pedro de Nava	Manuel Munoz	Bernardo Fernández
1796 b	Marqués de Branciforte	Pedro de Nava	Manuel Munoz	José María Guadiana
1797	Marqués de Branciforte	Pedro de Nava	Manuel Munoz	José María Guadiana
1798 a	Marqués de Branciforte	Pedro de Nava	Manuel Munoz	José María Guadiana
1798 b	Miguel José de Azanza	Pedro de Nava	Manuel Munoz	José María Guadiana
1799 a	Miguel José de Azanza	Pedro de Nava	Manuel Munoz	José María Guadiana
1799 b	Miguel José de Azanza	Pedro de Nava	Juan Bautista de Elguézabal	Miguel del Moral

(*continued*)

YEARS	VICEROY	COMMANDANT GENERAL	GOVERNOR	COMMANDANT NACOGDOCHES
1800 a	Miguel José de Azanza	Pedro de Nava	Juan Bautista de Elguézabal	Miguel del Moral
1800 b	Felix Berenguer de Marquina	Pedro de Nava	Juan Bautista de Elguézabal	Miguel Musquiz
1801	Felix Berenguer de Marquina	Pedro de Nava	Juan Bautista de Elguézabal	Miguel Musquiz
1802 a	Felix Berenguer de Marquina	Pedro de Nava	Juan Bautista de Elguézabal	Miguel Musquiz
1802 b	Felix Berenguer de Marquina	Nemesio de Salcedo y Salcedo	Juan Bautista de Elguézabal	Miguel Musquiz
1803 a	Felix Berenguer de Marquina	Nemesio de Salcedo y Salcedo	Juan Bautista de Elguézabal	Miguel Musquiz
1803 b	José de Iturrigaray	Nemesio de Salcedo y Salcedo	Juan Bautista de Elguézabal	José Joaquín Ugarte
1804	José de Iturrigaray	Nemesio de Salcedo y Salcedo	Juan Bautista de Elguézabal	José Joaquín Ugarte
1805 a	José de Iturrigaray	Nemesio de Salcedo y Salcedo	Juan Bautista de Elguézabal	José Joaquín Ugarte or Dionisio Valle
1805 b	José de Iturrigaray	Nemesio de Salcedo y Salcedo	Antonio Cordero y Bustamante	Sebastian Rodriguez or Dionisio Valle
1806 a	José de Iturrigaray	Nemesio de Salcedo y Salcedo	Antonio Cordero y Bustamante	Dionisio Valle

(*continued*)

YEARS	VICEROY	COMMANDANT GENERAL	GOVERNOR	COMMANDANT NACOGDOCHES
1806 b	José de Iturrigaray	Nemesio de Salcedo y Salcedo	Antonio Cordero y Bustamante	Francisco Viana
1807	José de Iturrigaray	Nemesio de Salcedo y Salcedo	Antonio Cordero y Bustamante	Francisco Viana
1808 a	José de Iturrigaray	Nemesio de Salcedo y Salcedo	Antonio Cordero y Bustamante	Francisco Viana
1808 b	Pedro Garibay	Nemesio de Salcedo y Salcedo	Manuel Maria de Salcedo	Francisco Viana
1809 a	Pedro Garibay	Nemesio de Salcedo y Salcedo	Manuel Maria de Salcedo	Francisco Viana
1809 b	Francisco Javier de Lizana y Beaumont	Nemesio de Salcedo y Salcedo	Manuel Maria de Salcedo	Francisco Viana
1810 a	Francisco Javier de Lizana y Beaumont	Nemesio de Salcedo y Salcedo	Manuel Maria de Salcedo	Francisco Viana
1810 b	Francisco Javier de Venegas	Nemesio de Salcedo y Salcedo	Manuel Maria de Salcedo	Francisco Viana
1811	Francisco Javier de Venegas	Nemesio de Salcedo y Salcedo	Manuel Maria de Salcedo	José María Guadiana
1812 a	Francisco Javier de Venegas	Nemesio de Salcedo y Salcedo	Manuel Maria de Salcedo	Bernardo Montero
1812 b	Francisco Javier de Venegas	Nemesio de Salcedo y Salcedo	Manuel Maria de Salcedo	Cristoval Domìnguez

(*continued*)

YEARS	VICEROY	COMMANDANT GENERAL	GOVERNOR	COMMANDANT NACOGDOCHES
1813 a	Francisco Javier de Venegas	Nemesio de Salcedo y Salcedo	Manuel Maria de Salcedo	Cristoval Domìnguez
1813 b	Francisco Javier de Venegas	Joaquín de Arredondo	Manuel Maria de Salcedo	Cristoval Domìnguez

Sources

Chipman, Donald E. *Spanish Texas, 1519-1821.* Austin: University of Texas Press, 2010. Appendix I is for the Governors of Spanish Texas, 1761–1821. Appendix II includes Commandants General of the Provincias Internas, 1776–1821. Appendix III lists the Viceroys of New Spain, 1535–1821.

Loomis, Noel M. "Commandants-General of the Interior Provinces: A Preliminary List." *Arizona and the West* 11, no. 3 (1969): 261-268.

APPENDIX E

Caddo Periods of History

PERIOD	TIME FRAME
Early Archaic	10,000–8,000 years BP
Middle Archaic	8,000–5,000 years BP
Late Archaic	5,000–2,500 years BP
Woodland	2,500–1,150 years BP
Formative Caddo	1,150–950 years BP
Early Caddo	950–700 years BP
Middle Caddo	700–510 years BP
Late Caddo	510–260 years BP
Historic Caddo	260+ years BP

Sources

Thanks to Tim Perttula. BP stands for Before Present. This has replaced the former usage of BC (Before Christ) and AD (Anno Domini). “Present” time changes, of course, so the convention among archaeologists and others is that January 1, 1950, is defined as “present.”

APPENDIX F

River Names, Now and Then

The names assigned to rivers over the centuries have varied greatly depending on who was doing the naming. In some cases, such as the Alazan or the Ayish, their current names are derivatives of names from the past. In others, such as the Trinity River and Larrison Creek, there is little connection. Many of the names used by the Spanish may have been their interpretations of names by the native tribes. We can be certain that many of those original names are lost to history. Present names listed are those currently used by the US Geological Survey.

PRESENT NAMES	EARLIER NAMES
Alazan Bayou	Alasan, Alasam
Angelina River	Santa Barbara, Río de Angelinas
Attoyac River	Río Atoyaque, Todos Santos
Ayish Bayou	Ais
Bayou La Nana	Lanana Creek, La Nana Bayou
Bayou Loco	La Asunción de Nuestra Señora, Arroyo de la Assumption.
Bedias Creek	San Tomas
Bonita Creek	Banita, Bonito
Caney Creek	Arroyo Los Burros, Boca Chica
Cedar Bayou	San Antonio de Padua
Cummins Creek	Mill Creek, San Bernabe
Elkhart Creek	Santa Efigenia
Hurricane Creek	Arroyo de San Nicolas, Arroyo del Uracan
Larrison Creek	Arroyo San Juan
Mill Creek	Los Terreros, Nuestra Señora de la Asunción Creek
Navasota River	San Buenaventura

(*continued*)

PRESENT NAMES	EARLIER NAMES
Neches River	San Pedro de Navidachos, San Pedro de los Nechas, Rio de Nechas, Rio Mexicano, Nachawi, Bois d'Arc, Mission River, Nabadache, Nuestra Señora de las Nieves
Old River	Santa Barbera
Pool's Creek	Arroyo San Tomás, Scull Creek
Rusk's Brook	Bridget's Branch, Agua Dulce
Sabine River	Rio de Sabinas
San Bernard River	Rio de Zivoras/Cibolas
San Gabriel River	San Xavier
San Jacinto River	Nombre de Dios
Spring Creek	Arroyo de Santa Rosa
Tantabogue Creek	Mustang Creek
Trinity River	Daycao, Rio de la Santisima Trinidad, Rio de los Orcouquisas, Rio de la Trinidad, Rio San Fernando, Rio San Juan Bautista, River of the Canoes, Encarnación de Verbo
Turtle Creek	Arroyo de Santa Rosa Maria
Wright's Creek	Arroyo Viejo, Cosache Bayou, Los Christos
Young's Creek	Nisperos

Sources

"Geographic Names Information System," Board on Geographic Names. US GeologicalSurvey. Accessed July 19, 2022, https://www.usgs.gov/us-board-on-geographicnames/domesticnames.

Gray, Glenn A. *Gazetteer of streams of Texas*. US Geological Survey, Department of the Interior. Washington, DC: Government Printing Office, 1919.

McGraw, A. Joachim, John Wilburn Clark, Elizabeth A. Robbins, and F. Jesus de la Teja. "The Camino Real: Colonial Texas' Lifeline to the World." Essay in *A Texas Legacy, the Old San Antonio Road and the Caminos Reales: A Tricentennial History, 1691–1991, 43–48*. Austin: Texas State Department of Highways and Public Transportation, Highway Design Division, 1991.

Pichardo, Jose Antonio. "El Nuevo Mexico y Tierras Adyacentes Mapa Levantado Para La Demarcacion De Los Limites De Los Dominios Españoles y De Los

Estados Unidos Por El P.d. Jose Pichardo Quien Lo Dedica Al Exmo. Sor. D. Francisco Xavier Venegas Virrey De Esta N.E. Año De 1811." Digital Collection. The Library of Congress. Accessed July 15, 2022. https://www.loc.gov/item/2016588016/.

Ramon, Diego, and Debbie S. Cunningham. "The Domingo Ramon Diary of the 1716 Expedition into the Province of the Tejas Indians: An Annotated Translation." *Southwestern Historical Quarterly* 110, no. 1 (July 2006): 38–67.

Santos, Richard G., and Juan Antonio de la Pena. *Aguayo Expedition into Texas, 1721: An Annotated Translation of the Five Versions of the Diary Kept by Br. Juan Antonio De La Peña*. Austin, TX: Jenkins Publishing Co., 1981.

Simek, Peter. "Is It Time to Change the Name of the Trinity River Back to the Arkikosa River?" *D Magazine,* May 20, 2019. https://www.dmagazine.com/frontburner/2019/05/is-it-time-to-change-the-name-of-the-trinity-river-back-to-the-arkikosa-river/.

Sjoberg, Andrée F. "The Bidai Indians of Southeastern Texas." *Southwestern Journal of Anthropology* 7, no. 4 (1951): 391–400. https://doi.org/10.1086/soutjanth.7.4.3628513.

"Texas GLO Map Store." The Texas General Land Office. Accessed June 26, 2022. https:// s3.glo.texas.gov/ glo/ history/ archives/ map-store/#search.

Weddle, Robert S. "Spanish Exploration of the Texas Coast, 1519-1800." *Bulletin of the Texas Archaeological Society* 63 (1992): 99–122.

APPENDIX G

Monetary Units

There were variations on this structure of currency, but for the period covered by this work, the following monetary units are the best equivalencies to consider.

peso (piastre)	1 peso = $1.45. This peso conversion is from the period around 1808, cited in Haggard. A Spanish coin of one ounce of silver and monetary unit that, between 1777 and 1811, was equivalent to 8 reales.
reale	1 reale = about 18 cents. A Spanish coin and monetary unit that, between 1777 and 1811, consisted of a little more than 11 granos, or the eighth part of a peso. In plural, this was also used to mean cash, as in "paid in reales."
grano	The smallest denomination of Spanish currency—96 granos equaled 1 gold peso, or 1/12 reale.

Sources

"Bexar Archives (1717–1836)." Bexar Archives Online. Dolph Briscoe Center for American History. Accessed June 24, 2022. https://briscoecenter.org/projects/bexar-archives-online/.

Haggard, J. Villasana. "House of Barr and Davenport," *Southwestern Historical Quarterly* 49, no. 1 (July 1945): 66-88, https://doi.org/https://www.jstor.org/stable/30240618.

Marquez, Ophelia, and Lillian Ramos Navarro Wold. *Compilation of Colonial Spanish Terms and Document Related Phrases*. Midway City, CA: SHHAR Press, 1998.

McGraw, A. Joachim, John Wilburn Clark, Elizabeth A. Robbins, and F. Jesus de la Teja. "The Camino Real: Colonial Texas' Lifeline to the World." Essay in *A Texas Legacy, the Old San Antonio Road and the Caminos Reales: A Tricentennial History, 1691-1991*. 43–48. Austin, TX: Texas State Department of Highways and Public Transportation, Highway Design Division, 1991.

GLOSSARY

The authors found this to be a helpful guide to gaining familiarity with Spanish words and phrases. Sources for the definitions are included at the end of the glossary.

abajo: Lower.
aburrado: A mare mule destined for breeding.
acequia: Irrigation ditch.
adelea: Loose cigarettes as change in a transaction.
adobe: Mud brick.
agraciados: Individuals who received special favors in return for services rendered to the king.
agua: Water.
agua negro: Contaminated water or sewage.
aguaje: A watering place.
aguardiente: Brandy, whiskey, liquor; literally, "fire water."
alcabala: An excise tax of a certain percentage of the price of certain goods paid by the buyer, or in some cases by the seller. Sales tax.
alcalde: Mayor of a town, or chairman of a town council; a justice of the peace. The *alcalde mayor* is one of two alcaldes sharing administrative duties in a larger villa; the chief of two municipal officials.
alcalde mayor: District magistrate.
alcanzado (adj.): In debt, needy, short of money.
alférez: A military rank approximately equal to a modern lieutenant or second lieutenant.
almacenes generals: General warehouses for storing tobacco and paper.
almud: A measure for land and grain—in some places one-twelfth of a fanega; in others, half a fanega. About one and one-quarter bushels of grain.
alto: Tall or high; can also mean stop.
andullo: Tobacco twist.
Apacheria: Land of the Apache Indians.
aparejo: A packsaddle made from two pieces of leather sewed at their edges. Draped over the back of pack animals, it offered little padding at the spine but, on each side, provided a large pouch, stuffed with straw, to protect the beast's vulnerable ribs.
apostada militar: Military post.
arancel: Schedule of fees, duties, or tariffs; book of rates.
armas: Large rawhide saddle covers used for riding in thorny brush.

arriba: Upper.
arrieria: Mule-train transport.
arriero: Muleteer, teamster.
arrieros: Muleteers.
arroba: Spanish weight of about twenty-five pounds, or about eleven and one-half kilos; also, a liquid measure of about three to four gallons.
arroyo: Creek.
asesor: Assessor, a lawyer appointed to assist the ordinary judge by giving advice in a legal process. Legal advisor to a government agency.
atadera: Halter ring or hook.
atascoso (adj.): Boggy or sandy.
audiencia: An administrative and judicial tribunal serving as a consultative council; it was the highest royal court of appeal in a given district; high court of justice. Also translated as court hearing. It is also a court of first instance in certain cases (*casos de corte*), usually involving higher officials. It was divided into two chambers, one for criminal cases (*sola del crimen*).
auto: Judicial decree or sentence; in plural, the proceedings of a trial or related action. Decree or edict. Legal documents that could be a judicial sentence in secondary matters that ordinarily did not demand a sentence or a decree of the *audiencia*.
ayuntamiento: A municipal council, also known as *cabildo*, consisting of several *regidores*, the number of which depended on the size and organization of the municipality. The senior regidor, or *regidor de cano*, was the equivalent of a mayor, while the others corresponded to aldermen.
azadón: Pickaxe or hoe.

bahia: Bay.
balas: Ammunition.
bando: Proclamation, including an official proclamation read aloud publicly at a specified location, such as a town square.
barriles: Barrels.
bastimentos: Provisions, supplies.
bayeta: Baize, thick flannel, woolen cloth.
bestia de carga: Pack mules or burros.
bestia de silla: Riding animals collectively; either riding mules or a mixed group of riding mules and horses (see *caballada*).
bosque: Woods or forest.
bousillage (French): Bousillage is made by mixing clay and water with straw, Spanish moss, or another binder, and occasionally with lime. It is used as an infill between posts in French timber-frame building construction. The moist *bousillage* was draped over slats and smoothed to fill the spaces between the timbers. It could also be used as chinking between closely spaced boards in horizontal board construction.
Brazos de Dios: The arms of God; the Brazos River.

caballada: Properly, a group of horses; often a herd of horses and mules.
caballada de cria: Herd of broodmares.
caballerango: Groom, stableman.
caballero: A knight, the lowest ranking of nobility. A gentleman or horseman.
cabeza: Head.
cabildo: Municipal corporation, consisting of a *justicia* (judiciary) and *regimiento* (body of aldermen, or regidores). See also *ayuntamiento*. Town council.
cabo distinguido: A corporal of noble birth, accorded certain distinctions and privileges because of his lineage. See also *soldado distinguido*.
cabras: Goats.
cacique: A Native American leader, chief, or noble.
caja matriz: Central treasury.
cajones: Large packing crates or chests for packets and cartons of cigars and cigarettes.
camino: A road or the way to go.
camino real: Royal highway; a government road patrolled by the military and serving as the principal mail route. A principal road or trail for mounted travelers or pack trains.
caminos reales: Royal highways.
canbalache: Barter; trade.
canoa: A dugout canoe large enough to carry men and supplies in the gulf.
capitán de indios: Indian chief.
carga: Maximum load that could legally be carried by Indian bearers, about fifty pounds. A load, generally of two *fanegas*, or about two hundred pounds. Unit of dry measure equaling from 300 to 330 pounds.
carretas: Wooden carts drawn by oxen or mules.
carrizo: Cane.
casa: House.
casas de vecindad: Colonial apartment house; multiple family dwelling.
castizos: The offspring of one white parent and one mestizo parent.
cédula: Order, bill, decree at law; patented royal letter.
cerrero: An adjective referring to wild or undomesticated stock, especially horses and mules.
cerrito: A hill.
cerro: A high hill or mountain.
chapa: Flat board or shingle.
charco: Pool or pond of water.
cíbolo: Bison, buffalo.
ciudad: Settlement with royally granted privileges. In New Spain, such municipalities were authorized by twelve councilmen and two magistrates.
cochina: Sow.
cojinillos: Saddlebags, which in Spanish Texas looked more like little leather boxes.
color quebrado: Of broken color; a person of mixed blood showing definite color; mulatto.

Comancheria: Land of the Comanche.
comandante: Commander.
comiso: Confiscation of contraband.
compañía volante: A "flying company," or cavalry troop frequently on the move to pursue hostile tribes and protect frontier settlements; unit detached from the main garrison. A quick-response military group.
congregacion: The grouping together of Native Americans into permanent villages; an Indian settlement, as in a mission.
contador interventor: Auditor.
coraza: Breastplate, cuirass, armor.
corregidor: Magistrate who exercised royal jurisdiction in his territory with single or joint authority, hearing private and governmental cases, and punishing offenders. Also, an *alcalde* named by the king to preside over an *ayuntamiento* and exercise some governmental functions.
cortada: A patrol meant to cut off an enemy.
coureurs de bois (French): French itinerant traders.
Créole (French): Nonindigenous person born in the colonies. After the 1760s, the term was used to distinguish the French-speaking population from the English and American settlers who were entering the Louisiana colony in increasing numbers.
criollo: A native of the Americas, born of European parents. Used an adjective, it means an American, native, or domestic.
cuadro: A square; town measurement of four square leagues.
cuartillo: One-fourth, especially of *almud* or *real*.
cuera: A heavy leather jacket worn by presidial soldiers.
cuero: Hide, animal skin, leather coat of armor.
cuervo: Crow.
cueva: Cave or rock shelter.
cueva de otero: Course or route of an expedition or journey.

dados: Dice.
decima: Songs in a Spanish form with five verses.
delitos: Crimes.
derecho indiano: Law of the Indies, or law of the New World.
derrotero: Diary or description of a journey of exploration.
desterrado: Banished, exiled.
diario: Diary or journal.
dictamen: Recommendations.

ell (French): A unit of length of cloth equivalent to forty-five inches or 1.25 yards.
embargo (law): Seized; attachment.
embriaguez: Intoxication; drunkenness.
empresario: One who has a concession from the government to introduce colonists to an area.
encinal: Oak grove.

encino: A live oak.
encomienda: A royal grant giving of a group of Native Americans to a colonist.
entrada: The entrance or first exploration of a particular territory.
escondido: Hidden.
escopeta: Firelock or gun.
escribano: Notary.
escribiente: Scribes.
escrito (law): Petition.
espada: Sword.
Espiritu Santo (religious): Holy Spirit.
estanco: Government supervised store with exclusive rights to the sale of certain merchandise; the merchandise purchased from such stores. Estanquillo is an alternative term for the same type of state store, with possible specific reference to tobacco.
estero: Marsh or inlet.
expediente: A file of papers or collected record of legal proceedings in a particular case. See also *auto*.

fanega: A dry measure, varying from one and one-half to three bushels. Measurement of 1.6 bushels. Measurement of grain and seed, usually equal to about two and one-half bushels, but the amount varied according to locale.
fardo: Bale, bundle.
fiel: Public inspector; inspector of weights and measures. A *fielato* is the office of such an inspector. Usually, the merchant managing the *estanco*.
fiesta: Festival; communal celebration.
filiación (military): Regimental register; service record; personal description of a soldier (height, age, physical characteristics), his period of enlistment, etc.
fiscal: The minister appointed to represent the king in civil suits in which he has an interest and to prosecute in criminal cases. Attorney for the crown or city. In civil cases he represented the royal interests and in criminal cases was prosecutor.
fiscal de lo civil: Prosecuting attorney in civil cases.
fiscal de real hacienda: Crown attorney.
flotistas: Import merchants.
foja úti: Page in an official or legal document upon which writing appears, as opposed to a blank page.
foja, *foxa*: A page in an official document.
Fondo de Mesteños: Mustang Fund. A permit requiring a payment of two *reales* per captured horses. All proceeds from this tax went into the Fondo de Mesteños.
forasteros: Migrants.
fornituras (military): Cartridge belts.
Fray (religious): Title of men in certain religious orders; brother; friar.
frazadas: Blankets.
fuero: Privilege or exemption extended to a province, city, or individual, or to a jurisdiction, such as military or ecclesiastical. Legal privileges granted to certain groups, usually such corporations as the church and the military.

fusiles: Guns; muskets.
fuste: In general, a pole or shaft; in saddlery, the bows of a saddletree.

gachupín: Derogatory term for Peninsular Spaniards.
galleria: A narrow bank of trees and dense vegetation along streams.
gamuza: Chamois; deer.
ganado: Livestock.
ganado alzado: Half-wild to wild stray cattle.
ganado caballar: Horses.
ganado de cerda: Hogs.
ganado de pelo: Goats.
ganado mayor: Large livestock such as horses, cattle, oxen, etc.
ganado menor: Small stock such as sheep and goats.
ganado vacuno: Cattle.
ganan: Peon.
generos: Commercial goods.
gente de razón: Well-born people of Spanish descent. Not meaning *peninsulares*, but just generally Hispanic people and non-Indians. Literally, "people of reason."
grano: A Spanish weight, monetary unit, and after 1750, coin equal to one-twelfth of a real. The par value in 1936 US currency was $0.019.
gritones: Callers or shouters.
guajolote: The Hispanicized Nahuatl word for turkey.
guía: The everyday use is as a guide, like a Native American guide. A second use is as a queue or line formation.

habilitación: Equipment; equipping, fitting out, supplying; financing; (military) paymaster. Also *abilitaciíon*, *habilitación*. In the military, the office and bureau of a paymaster, or *habilitado*.
habilitado: An officer in every Spanish regiment charged with the agency of his regiment; a paymaster. Also *abilitado*, *abilittado*, *havilitado*.
hachuela: Beads.
hondo: Deep; a river with high banks.

Indies: The Spanish colonies in America.
Indigenes: People native, or indigenous, to an area.
Indios, Yndios: Indians.
inundar: To inundate or flood.
itinerario: Itinerary, or list of localities on a route.

jacal: Hut with a straw roof; improvised structure covered with branches.
junta: A gathering, committee, government board.
Junta de Ministros: A special interministerial committee, the purpose of which was to propose policies designed to increase revenues from the Spanish American colonies.

junta de real hacienda: Chief financial committee of the viceroyalty.
junta superior de real hacienda: Chief finance committee after the creation of the intendencias. It had its origin in the Americas after 1786 under the reign of Carlos III.
justicia mayor: Chief justice.
justicias ordinaries: Magistrates.

labor: A tract of land or field under cultivation, approximately 175 acres.
labradores: Farmers and farmhands.
laguna: Lake.
lagunillas: Small lakes or large ponds.
legua: A distance measure of about 2.6 miles, or an area of about 4,428 acres.
limosnas: Alms.
línea: Loosely, a "line," one-twelfth of an inch (*pulgada*).
loma: Hill.
lomeria: Range of hills.
lomita: Small hill, knoll.

machorraje: In cattle, a condition of barrenness. Also, a fee for removing old, barren cows from a herd.
manada: Herd, drove.
manadero: Herdsman, shepherd; lead animal.
manojo: Small budle of leaf tobacco.
mayordomo: An overseer.
mediación: Measurement or halfway point.
mercador: Merchant.
mestenada: A herd of wild large stock such as cattle or horses.
Mesteñas Fund: A fund resulting from a tax of two *reales* per head for wild, unbranded stock rounded up in the Interior Provinces of New Spain.
mesteño, -a: Wild, unowned horses or cattle; mustang; a horse of the half-wild breed common to the plains of northern Mexico and the southwestern United States. In Texas, the feminine form *mesteiias*, also *mesteiiada*, are generally used and applied also to bovine stock. Used as an adjective and noun.
mestizacion: Racial amalgamation or crossbreeding.
mestizo, -a: In Spanish racial terminology, the offspring of a European man and an indigenous woman, or vice versa. In general, a cultural or racial mixture. Used as a noun and adjective.
mojonera: A boundary marker, usually a cairn or stone monument.
molinos: Mills.
montaña: Mountain.
monte: Wilderness; woods, brushland, thicket, an uninhabited place.
moradores: Residents.
mostrenco: Having no known owner and therefore belonging to the crown or state, as, for example, orejano cattle.

mulada: Mule herd.
murmuraciones: Gossip; grumbling.

naipes: Playing cards.
naquisa: Red cape two varas long worn by Indians.
negociante: Trader; merchant.
nogal: Walnut.
notas de medias: Field notes
Nuestra Señora (religious): Our Lady.

obligacion: Obligation, duty, contract.
obsequiar: Gift, present.
octava: Eighth part, as in the eighth part of a *grano*.
oficial de libros: Bookkeeper.
ojo de agua: A spring, or eye, of water.
ordenanzas: Ordinances.
orejano, -a: Ownerless, unbranded, or wild head of cattle; offspring of such cattle found on public or royal land. Used as an adjective or noun.

padre (religious): Priest; also used as a title, Father, with the priest's surname or with another title. The *padre ministro* of a mission was the priest who administered the affairs of the mission in addition to his ecclesiastical duties. *Padre conductor* was a general term for the presidente, or president, of the missions. The *padre lector* was an instructor in theology, the Gospel, and the catechism. The *padre guardián* was the head of a Franciscan convent. The *padre predicador* was a preacher of sermons, theory, or doctrine. A *padre doctrinero* was a priest in charge of an Indian parish, or doctrina.
paño: Cloth, material, fabric; flannel, woolen cloth.
paraje: A stopping or camping place used on a regular basis; place, residence; see *punto*. A stopping or camping place with water and pasturage sufficient to support the *caballada* of a party for the length of its stay.
parrita, *parras*: Grapevine.
partida que reconoce: Reconnoitering party.
partidas: Certificate of birth, marriage, etc.
paso: A crossing, but more properly a ford of a river or creek.
peones: Peasants or laborers.
permutar: Barter.
peso: A Spanish coin of one ounce of silver and monetary unit which, between 1777 and 1811, was equivalent to eight *reales*. The par value in 1936 US currency was $1.7151.
picardias: Malicious, offensive comments.
piquete: Picket.
pirogue (French): Dug-out canoe.

población: A settlement of any kind. Unchartered frontier village of Spanish-speaking people.
poblador: Spanish settler or founder of a community. A first settler who often claimed credit for opening and developing an area. One who inhabits a place; a colonist.
polvo: Finely powdered tobacco.
polvora: Gunpowder.
pot (French): A liquid measure equal to about one-half gallon.
poteaux-en-terre (French): French building technique in which wall posts or square timbers were set vertically into the ground and the tops joined to a plate, forming the top of the walls. The areas between the post could be filled with bousillage. An example of this type of construction is the Badin Roque House along Cane River near Melrose in Natchitoches Parish.
pregonero: Town crier and auctioneer.
presidio: Fort.
prest: Soldier's wages.
procurador: Solicitor.
propietario: Owner
Provincias Internas: The Interior Provinces were a jurisdiction set up apart from the viceregal regime to handle problems on the northern borderlands of New Spain. The region of northern Mexico that included the states of Durango, Coahuila, Chihuahua, Sonora, and Texas, particularly in the eighteenth century.
proximo: Last.
pueblo: Native American town; lowest level of municipal administration. Unchartered frontier village or town under direct royal control and administration; an established community of sedentary Indians.
puesto: A military post, usually of small size.
pulperia: General store.
pulque: Alcoholic drink made from the juice of the maguey plant.
pulqueria: Tavern, bar.
punto: Point (as a geographical place); see *paraje*.
Purisima Concepcion (religious): The Virgin Conception.
rancheria: Small Indian settlement or campsite; a temporary habitation. A cluster of huts; hamlet; horde; camp.

ranchero: One who ranches or raises stock.
rancho: In Mexico, a stock farm, small farm, or ranch. A non-Indian ranch. Small estate, small village of farmers. It can also mean mess, as in meals for workers or soldiers.
rayadillo: Striped cotton ducking.
real: A Spanish coin and monetary unit which, between 1777 and 1811, consisted of a little more than eleven granos, or the eighth part of a peso. The par value in 1936 US currency was $0.2131. In plural, also used to mean cash, as in "paid in *reales*."

reglamento: Rules that govern agency conduct.
remuda de caballos: A relay or string of horses.
reo: Defendant; culprit; offender; runaway slave.
resaca: Oxbow lake or old river channel.
residencia: Review of a governor's administration.
rio: River.
roble: A deciduous oak tree.

Su Magestad: Your Majesty. Also written as "S. M."
sabinas: Cypress trees.
salado: Salty or brackish.
salinas: Salt pits. A salt pan, a natural surface deposit of salt in an inlet from the sea; salt pit.
santisima: Most holy.
sartas: Bundles of tobacco leaves.
señor: Mister, sir.
sin novedad: Without unusual incident.
sitio: A square league, or 4,338 acres, with a plot for a house and garden. A Spanish square league of land that can vary in size according to use, with water and grazing potential.
soldado: Soldier.
suertes: Farmlands.
sumaria: Preliminary proceedings in a trial; indictment.

tama (Caddo): Indian captain.
Tejano: native born Hispanic Texan.
teligencia: For your information.
teniente: Lieutenant, or the officer second in command of a military unit.
teniente de justicia: Assistant justice or magistrate.
testament: Will, or a document in which one declares his last will and in which he disposes of his property and makes other arrangements for after his death.
testimonio: In Spanish law, an official copy of a deed or proceedings made by a notary and given to an interested party as evidence of his title, with the original remaining in the archives. Certificate, testimony, affidavit.
tortuga: Turtle.
traficar: To traffic, trade; travel, roam.
Trinidad (religious): The Holy Trinity in the Christian belief.

vuesamerced or *vuestra merced*: You, sir; your worship, your honor; usually abbreviated as Vm. or Vmd.
vuesefioria or *vuestra sefioria*: Your lordship; your grace; usually abbreviated as Vs.
vara: Unit of measure, about thirty-three inches.
vecindario: Community; neighborhood.

villa: A town that enjoyed special privileges by charter. Village.
visita: General or specific investigation of governmental operation and abuses.

yegua: Mare
yegua de cria: Brood mare.
yeoman: A small independent farmer.

Sources

Byrd, Kathleen M. *Colonial Natchitoches: Outpost of Empires*. Philadelphia: Xlibris, 2008.

Bexar Archives Online. "Bexar Archives (1717-1836)." Dolph Briscoe Center for American History. Accessed June 24, 2022, https://briscoecenter.org/projects/bexar-archives-online/.

Deans-Smith, Susan. *Bureaucrats, Planters, and Workers the Making of the Tobacco Monopoly in Bourbon Mexico*. Austin: University of Texas Press, 2010.

Galán, Francis X. *Los Adaes: The First Capital of Spanish Texas*, College Station: Texas A&M University Press, 2020.

Gerona, Carla. "With a Song in Their Hands: Incendiary Décimas from the Texas and Louisiana Borderlands during a Revolutionary Age." *Early American Studies: An Interdisciplinary Journal* 12, no. 1 (2014): 93–142. https://doi.org/10.1353/eam.2014.0002.

Marquez, Ophelia, and Lillian Ramos Navarro Wold. *Compilation of Colonial Spanish Terms and Document Related Phrases*. Midway City, CA: SHHAR Press, 1998.

Robbins, Elizabeth A., John Wilburn Clark, and A. Joachim McGraw, eds. *A Texas Legacy: the Old San Antonio Road and the Camino Reales; a Tricentennial History, 1691-1991*. Austin: Texas State Department of Highways and Public Transportation, 1991.

NOTES

Epigraph

i. "Why History Matters," Stephen L. Hardin, PhD, the Texan's Historian, website, accessed August 7, 2024, https://stephenlhardin.com/668-2/.

Introduction

1. Tom Middlebrook of Nacogdoches, of Nacogdoches, led the author and members of the Texas Archaeological Stewardships Network to conduct a follow-up survey and excavation at Monk's Cave in January and February 2022. Detailed digital imaging by archaeologist Mark Willis produced 3D imaging of the cave and the petroglyphs. See also Henry F. Ball, "Rock Art at Monk's Cave (41RK84), Rusk County Texas," *Bulletin of the Texas Archeological Society* 55 (1984): 153–169, University of North Texas Libraries, The Portal to Texas History, https://texashistory.unt.edu/ark:/67531/metapth1013889, accessed June 22, 2022.

2. The Gault School of Archaeological Research is a heavily researched site that has revealed Paleoindian artifacts from over thirteen thousand years ago. See Gault School of Archaeological Research (website), accessed June 22, 2022. https://www.gaultschool.org. See Mary S. Black, *Secrets in the Dirt: Uncovering the Ancient People of Gault* (College Station: Texas A&M University Press, 2019). It is an excellent resource.

3. The Caddo Mounds State Historic Site is part of the Texas Historical Commission. For more about Caddo Mounds, see Caddo Mounds State Historic Site (website), Texas Historical Commission, accessed June 22, 2022, https://www.thc.texas.gov/historic-sites/caddo-mounds-state-historic-site.

4. Gary L. Pinkerton, *Trammel's Trace: The First Road to Texas from the North* (College Station: Texas A&M University Press, 2016).

5. The math done on the language was Spanish: 1836 – 1542 = 294 years; English 2022 – 1836 = 186 years.

6. Bruce Clavey, *To the Republic* (Austin, TX: self-pub., 2020).

7. Gregory Curtis, "The Reasonable Cannibals," *Texas Monthly*, October 1988, 5–6.

8. John Spong, "Confessions of a Seventh-Grade History Teacher," *Texas Monthly*, September 2012.

9. Stephen Harrigan, *Big Wonderful Thing: A History of Texas* (Austin: University of Texas Press, 2019).

10. "The Alamo Official Trailer #1 – John Wayne Movie (1960) HD." The scene is

at 1:52. In it, John Wayne, playing the role of David Crockett, explains the difference between right and wrong. https://www.youtube.com/watch?v=QYtguIsp2B8, accessed June 22, 2022.

11. The dedication plaque on the Bucareli rifle reads, "In Memory of GEORGE MONROE BARNES, Aug. 29, 1941 – Mar 22, 1980, By His Family."

12. A card inside a library display case at Blanche K. Werner Library in Trinity, Texas.

13. See Bo Nelson and Timothy K. Perttula, "The Looting of Prehistoric Caddo Indian Cemeteries in Northeast Texas," *Texas Forum on Civil Liberties and Civil Rights* 4, no. 1 (1998): 77–86.

See also Robert Cast and Timothy K. Perttula, "The Long-Term Looting of Caddo Indian Sites on Federal Property in Northeastern Texas," *Cultural Resource Management* 25, no. 2 (2002): 26–28, http://npshistory.com/newsletters/crm/crm-v25n2.pdf.

14. Evidence of a borrow pit for the dirt used to construct the mounds was still identifiable by that time, but it had become filled by trees that had grown, matured, died, and rotted over the centuries. When members of the Caddo nation came to Nacogdoches to claim the remains of three of their ancestors and sixty vessels excavated in the 1970s, they found a single remaining mound, only a bump, in the front yard of one of the fashionable houses on Mound Street. Nacogdoches residents had leveled the other mounds in the name of progress years before. No doubt, more of their ancestors were accidentally caught in the discarded fill. See James E. Corbin and John P. Hart, "The Washington Square Mound Site: A Middle Caddo Mound Complex in South Central East Texas," *Bulletin of the Texas Archaeological Society* 69 (1998): 47–78. See also, John P. Hart and Timothy K Perttula, "The Washington Square Mound Site and a Southeastern Ceremonial Complex Style Zone among the Caddo of Northeastern Texas," *Midcontinental Journal of Archaeology* 35, no. 2 (2020), 199–228. For further insight, see Donna McCollum, "Caddo Nation Come for Remains of Their Ancestors," *KTRE* (ABC channel 9, Lufkin, TX), October 23, 2008, https://www.ktre.com/story/9230799/caddo-nation-come-for-remains-of-their-ancestors.

15. "The Old Stone Fort, It Has Been Entirely Obliterated, But the Stones Remain," *Brownsville Herald*, April 21, 1902, 1. Image from: Lois Foster Blount, "Last of Stone Fort (1902)," East Texas Digital Archives at Stephen F. Austin State University, https://digital.sfasu.edu/digital/collection/eastTexRC/id/14181/rec/9, accessed June 22, 2022.

16. "In Old Nacogdoches Town, A Little Place That Has a Stirring History," *Houston Post*, December 13, 1896, 38.

17. Perkins Brothers, "For Sale, Old Stone Fort," *Houston Post*, December 3, 1901, 9.

18. "Nacogdoches, News Item," *Shreveport Times*, March 23, 1917, 5. Excavations beneath some of the present buildings at the edges of the former plaza have unearthed some of these artifacts, and archaeologists diligently recorded them for history's sake. Archaeologist George Avery has carried on the work of James Corbin at Stephen F. Austin State University, and Texas Historical Commission archaeological stewards Morris K. Jackson and Tom Middlebrook have masterfully illuminated the long history of previous habitation of Nacogdoches and the use of spaces around the plaza.

See Morris K. Jackson et al., *Trade and Cultural Interaction along El Camino Real de los Tejas: During the Spanish Colonial and Republic Periods in Nacogdoches County, Texas*, vol. 1, "Nacogdoches, TX: Nine Flags Museum, 2012).

19. "Skulls and Bones, Unearthed on Nacogdoches Court House Site," *Houston Post*, October 10, 1911, 3; "Nacogdoches, Bids for Old Courthouse Rejected, Old Cemetery of Century Ago," *Shreveport Times*, October 10, 1911, 10; "Ashes of Pioneer Texas Disturbed, Burying Ground Discovered Under Old Court House at Nacogdoches," *Tyler Courier-Times*, October 21, 1911, 4.

20. William C. Foster, *Spanish Expeditions into Texas: 1689-1768* (Austin: University of Texas Press, 1995), 131.

21. The edge of a prairie along a forest tree line is an example of an ecotone. The easiest place to see this illustrated in stark contrast is the dividing line between a mowed highway right-of-way and wooded land beyond. In those mechanically created ecotones, the undergrowth at the edge is thick and sometimes impenetrable, but it transitions cleanly and opens up beyond a few feet. Redbud trees that fail to prosper in the understory of a darkened forest peek out for light at the edges of the ecotone.

22. Andrée F. Sjoberg, "The Bidai Indians of Southeastern Texas," *Southwestern Journal of Anthropology* 7, no. 4 (1951), 393: https://doi.org/10.1086/soutjanth.7.4.3628513.

23. "Translation of proceedings in the case against Juan Cortés, Sergeant Treviño, and others, charged with smuggling," Bexar Archives, 1792-06-16, e_bx_009847.

The Bexar Archives are a digital collection of the Briscoe Center for American History in Austin. Documents can be located using the "e_bx" number provided when using the search tools at https://briscoecenter.org/projects/Bexar-archives-online/.

Chapter 1

1. Ben Logan and Curt Meine, *The Land Remembers: The Story of a Farm and Its People* (Madison: The University of Wisconsin Press, 2017).

2. "Seeing What the Land Remembers: Geography, Ecology, and the History of Place," The San Francisco Estuary Institute, 2005), accessed December 23, 2022, https://www.sfei.org/projects/seeing-what-land-remembers-geography-ecology-and-history-place.

3. Joe C. Truett and Daniel W. Lay, *Land of Bears and Honey: A Natural History of East Texas* (Austin: University of Texas Press, 1994), 12.

4. Del Weniger, *The Explorer's Texas* (Austin, TX: Eakin Press, 1984), vii. When this quote was shared with Weniger's son, Andrew, his reply was that his "father constantly looked at the world this way. And his world view also brought him love, affection and admiration." Andrew Weniger, email message to author, November 11, 2020.

5. Zack Sharf, "Peter Jackson Restored and Colorized 100 Hours of World War I Footage, and the Final Results Are Remarkable — Watch," *IndieWire*, October 10, 2018, https://www.indiewire.com/2018/10/peter-jackson-world-war-one-footage-restored-colorized-1202010938/.

6. Francis X. Galan, "Between Imperial Warfare: Crossing of the Smuggling Frontier and Transatlantic Commerce on the Louisiana-Texas Borderlands, 1754-1785,"

in *Texans and War New Interpretations of the State's Military History*, eds. Alexander Mendoza and Charles David Grear (College Station: Texas A&M University Press, 2012), 159.

7. Velicia R. Hubbard and David H. Jurney, "Reconstruction of the Past Vegetation on the Headwaters of Piney Creek Watershed in Houston and Trinity Counties, Texas," *Journal of Northeast Texas Archaeology* 11 (1998): 59.

8. Hubbard and Jurney, "Reconstruction of the Past Vegetation," 56.

9. David H. Jurney, John Ippolito, and Velicia Bergstrom, "The Frequency of Fire in East Texas Forests," *Index of Texas Archaeology* 13 (2000): 40. https://doi.org/10.21112/.ita.2000.1.21, accessed June 22, 2022.

10. José Antonio Chireno land grant, Nacogdoches County, Abstract 17, File SC 000111:5, Texas General Land Office. December 27, 1833. The Texas General Land office surveys are a digital collection of the Original Texas Land Surveys. Documents can be located using the county name and abstract number provided when searching at https://s3.glo.texas.gov/glo/history/archives/land-grants/index.cfm.

11. Foster, *Spanish Expeditions*, 193.

12. "Report of Captain Pedro Lopez Prieto, Commandant of Trinidad de Salcedo to Lieutenant-Colonel Manuel De Salcedo, Governor of Texas [Béxar], May 21, 1810." Texas General Land Office, Spanish Collection, Box 129, Folder 21, 197–198. Translation corrected and annotated by Bob D. Skiles, Dec 2014.

13. James V. Sciscenti, *Environmental and Cultural Resources Within the Trinity River Basin* (Corps of Engineers, Fort Worth District, 1971): 108.

14. Mary Sherwood Helm, *Scraps of Early Texas History* (Austin, TX: Self-published by Helm, 1884), 154. The quote is attributed to her former husband, Eli Wightman, who made a trip through the region in 1828.

15. William C. Foster and Jack Jackson, eds., "The 1693 Expedition of Gregorio De Salinas Varona to Sustain the Missionaries Among the Tejas Indians," trans. Ned F. Brierley, *Southwestern Historical Quarterly* XCVII, no. 4 (April 1994): 265–311.

16. Michael H. MacRoberts and Barbara R. MacRoberts, "The Big Thicket: Typical or Atypical?" *East Texas Historical Journal* 42, no. 1 (2004): 42–51.

17. MacRoberts and MacRoberts, 43. According to Kress, Zocosote, or Xoconoclvtli, is a species of cactus or tuna plant. It is an indigenous word, and is also spelled socosote, soscosote, soconosles, and sensoncles.

18. Foster, *Spanish Expeditions*, 296.

19. Foster, *Spanish Expeditions*, 155, 226.

20. Riverbanks designated as right and left are oriented as for a boatsman going downstream.

21. Juan Antonio de la Pena and Richard G. Santos, *Aguayo Expedition into Texas, 1721: An Annotated Translation of the Five Versions of the Diary Kept by Br. Juan Antonio De La Peña* (Austin, TX: Jenkins Publishing Co., 1981) 51-54.

22. Diego Ramon and Debbie S. Cunningham. "Of the 1716 Expedition into the Province of the Tejas Indians: An Annotated Translation." *Southwestern Historical Quarterly* 110, no. 1 (July 2006): 38–67.

23. Frederic Benjamin Page, *Prairiedom: Rambles and Scrambles in Texas or New Estrémadura* (New York: Paine and Burgess, 1845) 70.

24. This location was Robbins Ferry where in 1828, Nicholas Trammell was living with his family on land owned by Ignacio Sertuche.

25. Ramon and Cunningham, "The Domingo Ramon Diary," 63.

26. Jose Maria Sanchez, "A Trip to Texas in 1828," trans. Carlos E. Castañeda, *Southwestern Historical Quarterly* XXIX, no. 4 (April 1926): 249.

27. Adolphus Sterne, "Diary of Adolphus Sterne, XI," ed. Harriet Smither, *Southwestern Historical Quarterly* XXXII, no. 4 (April 1929): 351.

28. Truett and Lay, *Land of Bears and Honey*, 78. For more information about historic wildlife and pigeon roosts, see Steve Nelle, "Historic Wildlife of Texas, In Numbers, Numberless," Texas Wildlife Association, accessed June 22, 2022, https://www.texas-wildlife.org/resources/publications/historic-wildlife-of-texas.

29. Page, *Prairiedom*, 70.

30. Cruger & Moore. *Telegraph and Texas Register*, Vol. 2, No. 32, Ed. 1, Tuesday, August 22, 1837, 2. https://texashistory.unt.edu/ark:/67531/metapth47945/, accessed June 22, 2022.

31. Much of this information comes from the excellent scientists at the US Geologic Survey. "Watersheds and Drainage Basins," US Geological Survey, June 8, 2019, https://www.usgs.gov/special-topics/water-science-school/science/watersheds-and-drainage-basins, accessed June 22, 2022.

32. Bonita Creek, with an "o," is west of downtown Nacogdoches, and Banita Creek, with an "a" enters Bayou La Nana north of the city. It is Bonita Creek that is part of this history.

33. Jackson et al., *Trade and Cultural Interaction*.

34. Monsieur de Pagès, *Travels Round the World: In the Years 1767, 1768, 1769, 1770, 1771* (London: Printed for J. Murray, 1791) 77.

35. Margaret Kenney Kress, Gaspar Jose de Solís, and Mattie Austin Hatcher, "Diary of a Visit of Inspection of the Texas Missions Made by Fray Gaspar José De Solís in the Year 1767-68," *Southwestern Historical Quarterly* 35, no. 1 (July 1931): 71-72.

36. De Pagès, *Travels*, 62.

37. Truett and Lay, *Land of Bears and Honey*, 7.

38. Page, *Prairiedom*, 141.

39. Kress, "Solís Diary," 64.

40. Colin Brummitt Goodykoontz. "Spanish Exploration of Louisiana and the Adjacent Borders of New Spain, 1762-1800." (master's thesis, University of California, 1914), 190–193.

41. Three Spanish scholars were independently asked to weigh in on the definition, and all three suggested the gall definition and application. Thanks to Bruce Clavey, Bob Skiles, and Brian Stauffer.

42. Sergio A. Iruegas et al., *Lobanillo Swales, National Register of Historic Places Registration Form*, (National Park Service, US Department of the Interior, 2015) sec. 7, p. 9.

43. GPS coordinates 31.480980483954735, −93.94938987571315.

44. Iruegas, *Lobanillo Swales,* 19.

45. Iruegas, *Lobanillo Swales,* 7.

46. Carlos E Castañeda, *Our Catholic Heritage in Texas* (Austin, TX: Von Boeckman-Jones Company, 1936), vol. 5, 161. Castañeda's work is comprised of seven volumes.

47. Page, *Prairiedom*, 41.

48. Karle Wilson Baker, "Nacogdoches: I. The Indian and Spanish Town," *Southwest Review* 21, no. 1 (October 1935): p. 14, https://www.jstor.org/stable/43462215, accessed June 22, 2022.

Chapter 2

1. Map from Tim Seiter in "The Karankawa-Spanish War from 1778 to 1789: Attempted Genocide and Karankawa Power," *Southwestern Historical Quarterly* 124, no. 4 (April 2021): 379, https://doi.org/10.1353/swh.2021.0026. See also "Indian Tribes Reported on Spanish Expeditions into Texas, 1689-1768," found in the appendix of William C. Foster and Jack Jackson, eds., "The 1693 Expedition of Gregorio De Salinas Varona to Sustain the Missionaries Among the Tejas Indians," trans. Ned F. Brierley, *Southwestern Historical Quarterly* XCVII, no. 4 (April 1994): 265-311, 265-289.

2. Iris H. W. Engstrand, "How Cruel Were the Spaniards?" *Organization of American Historians Magazine of History* 14, no. 4 (2000): 14. https://doi.org/10.1093/maghis/14.4.12, accessed June 23, 2022. The quote is from historian Phillip Wayne Lowell, whose work has been demonstrated to be culturally biased.

3. Light T. Cummins, email message to author, March 26, 2021.

4. Juliana Barr, "Geographies of Power: Mapping Indian Borders in the 'Borderlands' of the Early Southwest," *The William and Mary Quarterly* 68, no. 1 (January 2011): 6, https://www.jstor.org/stable/10.5309/willmaryquar.68.1.0005, accessed June 23, 2022.

5. Pekka Hämäläinen, "Into the Mainstream: The Emergence of a New Texas Indian History," in *Beyond Texas through Time Breaking Away from Past Interpretations*, ed. Walter L. Buenger and Arnaldo de León (College Station: Texas A&M University Press, 2011) 50-84.

6. Elizabeth A. John, *Storms Brewed in Other Men's Worlds the Confrontation of Indians, Spanish, and French in the Southwest, 1540–1795* (Norman: University of Oklahoma Press, 1996).

7. Pekka Hämäläinen, *The Comanche Empire* (New Haven, CT: Yale University Press, 2009).

8. Juliana Barr, *Peace Came in the Form of a Woman: Indians and Spaniards in the Texas Borderlands* (Chapel Hill: The University of North Carolina Press, 2009).

9. Parul Sehgal, "'Lakota America' Puts the Tribe of Sitting Bull and Crazy Horse Front and Center," *The New York Times*, October 22, 2019, sec. Books of the Times. https://www.nytimes.com/2019/10/22/books/review-lakota-america-pekka-hamalainen.html, accessed June 23, 2022.

10. Barr, *Peace Came*, 3. Quoting from Nicolás de Lafora, the diarist of Marqués de Rubí's expedition in 1767.

11. As of December 7, 2020, the number of Archaeological Site Forms logged in the THC Atlas by county: Nacogdoches 452; Angelina 302; Rusk 816; San Augustine 399; Walker 261; Houston398; Trinity 154; Cherokee 539. The precise location of archaeological sites is not available to the public so that they can be preserved for everyone. Landowners who have questions about possible archaeological sites on their land can reference the Texas Historical Commission's "Property Owner's Guide to Archaeological Sites," https://www.thc.texas.gov/public/upload/archeology-property-owners-guide.pdf.

12. Appendix F of this book is a reference used by archaeologists to define periods of history.

13. Jack Jackson, Manuel de Mier y Terán, Scooter Cheatham, and Lynn Marshall. *Texas by Terán: The Diary Kept by General Manuel De Mier y Terán on His 1828 Inspection of Texas.*
(Austin: University of Texas Press, 2000), 80.

14. For more about the Caddo Nation, see "Caddo Nation" (website), https://mycaddonation.com/, accessed June 23, 2022.

15. Barr, "Geographies of Power," 21.

16. Edward B. Jelks and Timothy K. Perttula, "The Caddo," *Journal of Northeast Texas Archaeology* 16 (2002): p. 2.

17. Chester P. Walker and Timothy K. Perttula, "Archaeogeophysical Investigations at an Eighteenth-Century Caddo Site in Nacogdoches County, East Texas," *Southeastern Archaeology* 29, no. 2 (November 25, 2010): p 311-312. https://doi.org/10.1179/sea.2010.29.2.007, accessed June 23, 2022.

18. Jack Jackson and William C. Foster, *Imaginary Kingdom: Texas as Seen by the Rivera and Rubí Military Expeditions, 1727 and 1767* (Austin: Texas State Historical Association, 1995), 126. An example of a Caddo grass house can be seen at the Caddo Mounds State Historic Site near Alto, Texas.

19. Kress, "Solís Diary," 70-71.

20. Jackson and Foster, *Imaginary Kingdom*, 126.

21. George Howden, "The expedition of Father Gaspar Jose de Solis into Texas, 1767–1768 translation of sources, introduction and Notes." (Master's thesis, University of California, 1915) 78.

22. John Reed Swanton, *The Indian Tribes of North America* (Washington, DC: United States Government Printing Office, 1953), 308.

See also, Henry Ker, *Travels through the Western Interior of the United States, from the Year 1808 up to the Year 1816: With a Particular Description of a Great Part of Mexico, or New-Spain: Containing a Particular Account of Thirteen Different Tribes of Indians* (Elizabethtown, NJ: Printed for Ker, 1816), 122.

23. Marvin C. Burch, "The Indigenous Indians of the Lower Trinity Area of Texas," *Southwestern Historical Quarterly* 60, no. 1 (July 1956): 48.

24. Lawrence E. Aten, "Indians of the Upper Texas Coast: Ethnohistoric and Archeological Frameworks" (PhD dissertation, University of Texas, 1979), University Microfilms International, 1981, 75.

25. Céliz Francisco, *Diary of the Alarcón Expedition into Texas, 1718-1719* (Los Angeles: The Quivira Society, 1967), 78.

26. Communication with Bob Skiles has contributed much to the understanding of the Bidai. See also James Woodrick, *The Bidai, a Tribe of Native Americans in Texas* (Austin, TX: self-pub., 2018), 5. Chief Tomás was also head of a village at the head of Spring Creek, near Waller.

27. Sjoberg, "The Bidai Indians," 398.

28. Herbert E. Bolton, "The Native Tribes about the East Texas Missions," *The Quarterly of the Texas State Historical Association* 11, no. 4 (April 1908): 249-276, https://www.jstor.org/stable/30242560.

29. Herbert Eugene Bolton and Athanase de Mézières, *Athanase De Mézières and the Louisiana-Texas Frontier 1768-1780: Documents Published for the First Time, from the Original Spanish and French Manuscripts, Chiefly in the Archives of Mexico and Spain*, vol. 2 (Cleveland, OH: A.H. Clark, 1914), 189. Bolton cites a letter from de Mézières to Croix of March 18, 1778.

30. Frederick Webb Hodge, ed., *Handbook of American Indians North of Mexico, in Two Parts*, vol. 1 (Washington, DC: Government Printing Office, 1907), 145.

31. James L. McCorkle Jr., "Los Adaes and the Borderlands Origins of East Texas," *East Texas Historical Journal* 22, no. 2 (1984): 8.

32. Herbert E. Bolton, "The Spanish Abandonment and Reoccupation of East Texas, 1773-1779," *The Quarterly of the Texas State Historical Association* 9, no. 2 (October 1905): 105.

33. "Córdova to Muñoz, acknowledging instructions of Muñoz to maintain enmity between Apaches and other tribes," Bexar Archives, 1793-04-27, e_bx_019461.

34. Aten, "Indians of the Upper Texas Coast," 59.

35. Aten, "Indians of the Upper Texas Coast," 58.

36. Mark Allan Goldberg, *Conquering Sickness: Race, Health, and Colonization in the Texas Borderlands* (Lincoln: University of Nebraska Press, 2017), 56.

37. Illustrated panel from the Florentine Codex (1540–85.) Thanks to Dan Worrall for calling attention to this image. See Dan M. Worrall, *A Prehistory of Houston and Southeast Texas: Landscape and Culture* (Fulshear, TX: Concertina Press, 2021), 115.

38. Kress, "Solís Diary," 70.

39. John, *Storms Brewed*, 505, 510.

40. John, *Storms Brewed*, 2.

41. John Reed Swanton, Source Material on the History and Ethnology of the Caddo Indians (Washington, D.C.: United States Government Printing Office, 1942), p. 219.

42. Sjoberg, "The Bidai Indians," 399. Sparkleberry is *Vaccinium arboreum*.

43. Aten, "Indians of the Upper Texas Coast," 109–110.

44. John, *Storms Brewed*, 499, 523.

45. Worrall, *A Prehistory*, 95.

46. Shawna Chen and Russell Contreras, "Native American Vaccination Rates Skyrocket as Tribes Help Others despite Internet Challenges," *Axios*, March 11, 2021, https://www.axios.com/2021/03/11/covid-vaccine-native-americans-internet-access.

47. A generation is generally considered to be thirty-three years.

48. Barr, *Peace Came*, 288.

49. Foster, *Spanish Expeditions*, 231.

50. The text in the Declaration of Independence is: "He [the King] has excited domestic Insurrections amongst us and has endeavored to bring on the Inhabitants of our Frontiers, the merciless Indian Savages, whose known Rule of Warfare, is an undistinguished Destruction, of all Ages, Sexes and Conditions."

51. Erik Wemple, "CNN Stays Silent on Rick Santorum's Comments about Native American Culture," *The Washington Post*, April 27, 2021, https://www.washingtonpost.com/opinions/2021/04/27/cnn-stays-silent-rick-santorums-comments-about-native-american-culture/.

52. "Correspondence between Muñoz and Ibarvo, concerning traders among Taguayases," Bexar Archives, 1794-01-04, e_bx_019884.

Chapter 3

1. Letter from Diego Ramón to Francisco Hidalgo, July 22, 1714, in the Catholic Archives of Texas, as cited in Donald E. Chipman and Harriett Denise Joseph, *Notable Men and Women of Spanish Texas* (Austin: University of Texas Press, 2015), 53.

2. Stephen Harrigan, *They Came from the Sky: The Spanish Arrive in Texas* (Austin: University of Texas Press, 2017), p45.

3. "Texas History Timeline," Bullock Texas State History Museum, https://www.thestoryoftexas.com/discover/texas-history-timeline, accessed June 23, 2022.

4. H. Sophie Burton, "Vagabonds along the Spanish Louisiana-Texas Frontier, 1769-1803: 'Men Who Are Evil, Lazy, Gluttonous, Drunken, Libertinous, Dishonest, Mutinous, Etc. Etc. Etc—and Those Are Their Virtues,'" *Southwestern Historical Quarterly* 113, no. 4 (April 2010): 438-467, https://doi.org/10.1353/swh.2010.0083.

5. Herbert E. Bolton, "Spanish Activities on the Lower Trinity River, 1746-1771," *Southwestern Historical Quarterly* 16, no. 4 (April 1913): 339.

6. Scott Sosebee, email message to author, July 25, 2020.

7. Full-text PDFs of the work are fully searchable through "HathiTrust Digital Library," https://www.hathitrust.org/.

8. Castañeda, *Our Catholic Heritage*, 919–920.

9. Donald E. Chipman and Harriett Denise Joseph, *Spanish Texas, 1519-1821* (Austin: University of Texas Press, 2010).

10. Foster, *Spanish Expeditions*.

11. A. Joachim McGraw and James E. Corbin, "A Review Essay of 'Spanish Expeditions into Texas," by William C. Foster (1995)," *Bulletin of the Texas Archaeological Survey* 70 (1999): 439-456.

12. Barr, "Geographies of Power," 21-24.

13. San Pedro Creek enters the Neches River about six and one-half miles upstream from where the river crosses Texas State Highway 21 west of Caddo Mounds State Historic Site and forms part of the boundary of Mission Tejas State Park to its south. For more about the possible location of the mission, see Robert S. Weddle, Donald E. Chipman, and Carol A. Lipscomb. "The Misplacement of Mission San Francisco De Los Tejas in Eastern Texas and Its Actual Location at San Pedro De Los

Nabedaches." *Southwestern Historical Quarterly* 120, no. 1 (July 2016): 75–84. https://doi.org/10.1353/swh.2016.0044.

14. Robert S. Weddle, "Archival and Archeological Research: Camino Real De Los Tejas and Texas State Parks," University of North Texas Libraries, The Portal to Texas History, August 2012. https://texashistory.unt.edu/ark:/67531/metapth638748/citation/?q=%22san+francisco%22#top, accessed June 23, 2022.

15. Ramon and Cunningham, "The Domingo Ramon Diary," 41.

16. Castañeda, *Our Catholic Heritage*, Vol 2, 42.

17. Barr, "Geographies of Power," 12.

18. Light T. Cummins, email message to author, March, 10, 2021.

19. Jackson et al, *Trade and Cultural Interaction*, 133. See also Dr. Tom Middlebrook, "Finding Tejas: The Archaeology of the First Location of Mission Concepción and its Associated Sites." Online report for the Texas Historical Commission. https://www.youtube.com/watch?v=hvzgIpHHtXU&t=3s. Accessed June 23, 2022.

20. Ramón and Cunningham, "The Domingo Ramon Diary," 65.

21. Jackson et al., *Trade and Cultural Interaction*, 131.

22. Timothy K. Perttula, "Diversity in Ancestral Caddo Vessel Forms in East Texas Archaeological Sites," *Journal of Northeast Texas Archaeology* 56 (2015): 1–18.

23. The mission site is on private land and not accessible to the public. However, the author was able to visit the site in late 2020 escorted by Tom Middlebrook and found a firsthand experience of the site brought life to the description of it from 1716. This is definitely one of the sites in East Texas where the history of a place can be felt—a place where the land remembers.

24. It is commonly believed that the mission was located between Bayou La Nana and Bonita Creek on the same hill where the primary village of the Nacodoche tribe of the Hasinai Caddo confederacy was found. The location is presumed to be the site where the current county courthouse is located at the intersection of Main and North streets. That would be correct for the reconstruction of the church in 1804 as Misíon Nuestra Señora del Pilár, but there are several indications that the earlier church may have been south of the hill.

The late James Corbin, an archaeologist at Stephen F. Austin State University, noted that names applied to Bonita Creek west of downtown as Arroyo de la Misíon did not appear until after the 1804 church was formed. Additionally, Corbin called attention to documentation that the original chapel was "notably distant from the dwellings" where the town of Nacogdoches ultimately grew. He wondered if the original location for Mission Guadalupe was in fact well south of the plaza near where Bonita Creek joins Bayou La Nana. This would place it on more level ground above the flood plain and taking advantage of the fertile creek bottom. It is an intriguing possibility that does not appear to have been fully explored archaeologically. See James E. Corbin, "Retracing the Camino De Los Tejas from the Trinity River to *Los Adaes*: New Insights into East Texas History," in *A Texas Legacy: the Old San Antonio Road and the Camino Reales; a Tricentennial History, 1691–1991* (Austin: Texas State Department of Highways and Public Transportation, 1991), 191–219.

25. Lawrence Kinnaird and Nicolas de Lafora, *The Frontiers of New Spain: Nicolas De Lafora's Description, 1766-1768* (Berkeley, CA: The Quivira Society, 1958), 168.

26. Bolton, "The Native Tribes about the East Texas Missions," 270.

27. Ramón and Cunningham, "The Domingo Ramon Diary," 24.

28. Robert Bruce Blake, "Locations of the Early Spanish Missions and Presidio in Nacogdoches County," *Southwestern Historical Quarterly* 41, no. 3 (January 1938): 222. https://www.jstor.org/stable/30235774, accessed June 23, 2022.

29. Timothy K Perttula, Bill Young, and P. Shawn Marceaux, "Caddo Ceramics from an Early 18th Century Spanish Mission in East Texas: Mission San Jose De Los Nasonis (41RK200)," *Journal of Northeast Texas Archaeology* 29 (2009): p. 84. Mission San José de los Nasonis is documented as site 41RK200 by the Texas Historical Commission. Two other related sites of the Nasoni Caddo are 41RK191 and 41RK197.

30. Perttula, Diversity in Ancestral Caddo Vessel Forms," 1–18. See also Marceaux, dissertation.

31. More information about these sites is found in the Appendix.

32. Francis X. Galan, *Los Adaes: The First Capital of Spanish Texas* (College Station: Texas A&M University Press, 2020).

33. Jack Jackson, Robert S. Weddle, and Winston De Ville, *Mapping Texas and the Gulf Coast the Contributions of Saint-Denis, Olivan, and Le Maire* (College Station: Texas A & M University Press, 2008), 8, 15.

34. Jackson, *Mapping Texas*, 512–13.

35. Robert S. Weddle, "Chicken War," *Handbook of Texas*, Texas State Historical Association, accessed December 19, 2020, https://www.tshaonline.org/handbook/entries/chicken-war.

For a short essay about the Chicken War by the venerable Archie P. McDonald see, Archie P. McDonald, "The Chicken War," *Texas Escapes*, March 26, 2007, http://www.texasescapes.com/AllThingsHistorical/Chicken-War-AM307.htm.

36. Eleanor Claire Buckley, "The Aguayo Expedition into Texas and Louisiana, 1719-1722," *The Quarterly of the Texas State Historical Association* 15, no. 1 (July 1911): 1-65.

37. Buckley, "The Aguayo Expedition," 2.

38. Margil Antonio de Jesús, *Nothingness Itself: Selected Writings of Ven. Fr. Antonio Margil 1690-1724* (Chicago, IL: Franciscan Herald Press, 1976), 24.

39. Buckley, "The Aguyao Expedition," 7.

40. Bachelor Pedro Fuentes's letter certifying mission books of Nacogdoches, December 7, 1773, found in Robert Bruce Blake, "Robert Bruce Blake Research Collection," FamilySearch (Salt Lake City, UT: The Church of Jesus Christ of Latter-Day Saints, 2009), "Volume 40," 357.

Online access to the collection is through Family Search at https://www.familysearch.org/search/catalog/1622062, and at https://www.familysearch.org/search/catalog/1622067 for the supplement volumes.

Print versions of the Blake Collection can be found at the East Texas Research Center in Nacogdoches, and the Clayton Library Center for Genealogical Research in Houston.

41. Buckley, "The Aguyao Expedition," 24.
42. Buckley, "The Aguyao Expedition," 24.
43. Edward W. Heusinger, *Early Explorations and Mission Establishments in Texas* (San Antonio, TX: Naylor Co., 1936), 98-99.
44. De la Pena and Santos, *Aguayo Expedition*, 55-56.
45. Buckley, "The Aguayo Expedition," 54.
46. Jackson and Foster, *Imaginary Kingdom*, 9.
47. Jackson and Foster, *Imaginary Kingdom*, 12.
48. Bolton, "Spanish Abandonment," 73.
49. Jackson and Foster, *Imaginary Kingdom*, 62.
50. Castañeda, *Our Catholic Heritage*, vol. 4, 32–34.
51. Kress, "Solís Diary," 69. See also, Castañeda, *Our Catholic Heritage*, vol. 4, 33.
52. Chipman and Joseph, *Notable Men and Women*, 183–184.
53. "Croix to Oconór, forbidding the entry of settlement of foreigners in Texas," Bexar Archives, 1768-07-31, e_bx_000321 and e_bx_002218.

Chapter 4

1. Howden, "The expedition of Father Gaspar Jose de Solis," 96.
2. Buckley, "The Aguyao Expedition," 34.
3. In more current times, there has been a movement to change the name of the upper Trinity River back to its Caddo name, Arkikosa, acknowledging the homelands of its native people. See, Peter Simek, "Is It Time to Change the Name of the Trinity River Back to the Arkikosa River?," *D Magazine*, May 20, 2019, https://www.dmagazine.com/frontburner/2019/05/is-it-time-to-change-the-name-of-the-trinity-river-back-to-the-arkikosa-river/.
4. Charles D. Fisher et al., *A Survey of the Environmental and Cultural Resources of the Trinity River* (Nacogdoches, TX: Stephen F. Austin State University, for the U.S. Army Corps of Engineers, 1972), 2.
5. De Pagès, *Travels*, p. 81.
6. Foster and Jackson, "The 1693 Expedition of Gregorio De Salinas Varona, » 301.
7. Mattie Austin Hatcher, *The Expedition of Don Domingo Terán De Los Rios into Texas*. (Austin: Texas Knights of Columbus Historical Commission, 1932), 41–42.
8. Foster and Jackson, "The 1693 Expedition of Gregorio De Salinas Varona," 134.
9. Foster and Jackson, "The 1693 Expedition of Gregorio De Salinas Varona," 134.
10. Thanks to Bob Skiles for noticing this connection. A map with that name for the stream was found at "*America Septentrional: Parte del Golfo Mejicano que comprehende Nuevo Santander, Tejas y Floridas*." Numero 114. His research found that the placename "Quitacalzon" applied to numerous streams and villages in Costa Rica, Argentina, and other Central and South American Hispanic countries.
11. De la Pena and Santos, *Aguayo Expedition*, 55–56.
12. De la Pena and Santos, *Aguayo Expedition*, 51–54.
13. Fisher, *A Survey*, 235.

14. William M. Sorrow, *Investigations into the Location of Nuestra Senora Del Pilar De Bucareli*, (Austin: Texas Archaeological Salvage Project, University of Texas, 1972).

15. Donahoe Shoals was on a 1921 list of proposed locations for one of the locks and dams on the Trinity River, indicating the substrata were deemed favorable for that purpose. Its location is marked on the 1962 Weyser Bottom topographic map near the mouth of Graveyard Creek. See: "Report on Reexamination of Project for the Improvement of Trinity River, Tex.," Vol. 19 Report on Reexamination of Project for the Improvement of Trinity River, Tex. (1921), 77. https://www.govinfo.gov/app/details/SERIALSET-08580_00_00/summary, accessed June 24, 2022. Historic topographic maps can be viewed using "Historic Topographic Map Overlays," topoView (US Geological Survey), https://ngmdb.usgs.gov/topoview/, accessed June 24, 2022.

16. E. T. Dumble, *The Geology of East Texas* (Austin: University of Texas, 1918) 160.

17. Morris K. Jackson and Peggy A. Jasso, "El Salto, East Texas Rancho of Mission Guadalupe, Historical Marker Application," Texas Historical Commission, 2021.

18. David Mitchell, "The Trinity River Project, 1852-1922," *East Texas Historical Journal* 28, no. 2 (1990): 39-45, https://scholarworks.sfasu.edu/ethj/vol28/iss2/9/, accessed June 24, 2022. For a 1913 photo of the construction see, "Trinity River: Lock and Dam at W.R.S. (1913 Photo)," University of North Texas Libraries, The Portal to Texas History, July 26, 2005, https://texashistory.unt.edu/ark:/67531/metapth4060/m1/1/, accessed June 24, 2022.

19. For current views of Bedias Creek and the shoals upstream from the mouth at the Trinity, see these YouTube videos. "Bedias Creek White Bass Run 2017," produced by Russell Almond, March 23, 2017, https://www.youtube.com/watch?v=U4wIggbhCXA; and "Fish Tales: New Water-Bedias Creek," produced by William B. Tedrick, Mary 7, 2022, https://www.youtube.com/watch?v=s48CewsGa_A. Both accessed on June 24, 2022.

20. Chief Tomás was known to have led the Bidai in 1754–55. Herbert Eugene Bolton and Athanase de Mézières, *Athanase De Mézières and the Louisiana-Texas Frontier 1768–1780: Documents Published for the First Time, from the Original Spanish and French Manuscripts, Chiefly in the Archives of Mexico and Spain, Vol 2.* (Cleveland, OH: A.H. Clark, 1914), 74, 260.

21. "Croix to Cabello, requesting opinion as to the location of Bucareli at *Paso Tomás*," Bexar Archives, 1778-07-30, e_bx_002725.

22. Given the focus of this book, the details that led to these conclusions will not be addressed in depth.

23. Bolton, "Spanish Abandonment," 99.

24. Bob Skiles, email message to author, June 21, 2021.

25. Castañeda, *Our Catholic Heritage*, vol. 4, 229.

26. A lengthy survey of the commercial and strategic value of the nation's rivers by the secretary of war's chief of engineers included details of work done on the Trinity River to improve navigation. Although there were many shoals identified and documented as having a base of rock suitable for constructing locks and dams for navigation, there were only a handful listed as most notable in the report. See "Trinity River,

Sheet 15," Records of the Office of the Chief off Engineers, 1789–1999. (Fort Worth, TX: National Archives and Records Administration 1940) https://catalog.archives.gov/id/148373298, accessed Jun 25, 2022.

27. Helm, *Scraps*, 157.

28. "Report of the Secretary of War: Being Part of the Message and Documents Transmitted to the Two Houses of Congress at the Beginning of the 43 Congress, vol. 2," (Washington, D.C.: Government Printing Office, 1873). Page 288 of the report reads, "The most noted of these shoals are: Haygood's, 600 feet in length, with 1.9-foot fall; Kickapoo, 1,600 feet in length, with 1.6-foot fall; Beavers, 3,000 feet in length, with 9.9-foot fall; Bedis [Bedias], 50 feet in length, with 2.3-foot fall; White Rock, 1,400 feet in length, with 3.6-foot fall; Carolina, 100 feet in length, with 2.0-foot fall; Duncan, 1,300 feet in length, with 1.5-foot fall; Cannon-Ball, 100 feet in length, with 0.9-foot fall."

29. Dumble, *The Geology of East Texas*, 156-157.

30. Page, *Prairiedom*, 80.

31. A well-rounded group of scholars aided in this part of the research. They are Bob Skiles, former archaeologist with the Texas General Land Office, Dr. Jim Tiller, professor of Geography at Sam Houston State University (retired), and David Hoffpauir, GIS expert formerly with Sam Houston State University.

Chapter 5

1. Prieto's report can be found at the Texas General Land Office, "Report of Captain Pedro Lopez Prieto, Commandant of Trinidad de Salcedo to Lt.-Colonel Manuel De Salcedo, Governor of Texas [Bexar], 21 May 1810," Spanish Collection, Box 129, Folder 21, pp. 197-198. Robert Moor, *On Trails: An Exploration* (New York: Simon and Shuster, 2016) 14.

2. Lawrence E. L'Herisson. "The Evolution of the Texas Road and the Subsequential Settlement Occupancy of the Adjacent Strip of Northwestern Louisiana, 1528-1824." (Master's thesis, Louisiana State University,1981) 149, 152.

3. "Corridor: Interstate 69 (I-69) Texas to Michigan," Corridors of the Future. US Department of Transportation, Federal Highway Administration, https://www.fhwa.dot.gov/pressroom/fsi69.cfm, accessed June 25, 2022.

4. Jason Barrett, archaeologist formerly with the Texas Department of Transportation, compiled this map while working on the Dimond Knoll project. To view his presentation on the project, see Jason W. Barrett, "The Dimond Knoll Project in Perspective: A New Path for Southeast Texas Prehistory." Report presented to Houston Archaeological Society, March 18, 2021. https://www.youtube.com/watch?v=4KQuS5MNQ68.

5. Tim Perttula, "Texas in the Year 1000," *Journal of Northeast Texas Archaeology* 15, no. 15, (2001): 30.

6. Lisa Miesch, "Discoveries from the Andy Kyle Archeological Collection at the Sam Houston Center," *Out of the Stacks* (blog), Texas State Library and Archives Com-

mission, November 4, 2020, https://www.tsl.texas.gov/outofthestacks/discoveries-from-the-andy-kyle-archeological-collection-at-the-sam-houston-center.

7. Wilson "Dub" Crook, "Liberty County: A Major Trade Entrepot for Southeast Texas." Report presented to Houston Archaeological Society, September 20, 2020. https://www.youtube.com/watch?v=lcfIUFZqm9Y, accessed June 25, 2022.

8. Jeffrey M. Williams, *GIS Aided Archaeological Research of El Camino Real de los Tejas with Focus on the Landscape and River Crossings along El Camino Carretera* (Nacogdoches, TX: Arthur Temple College of Forestry and Agriculture, 2007), 175.

9. Mattie Austin Hatcher, *The Expedition of Don Domingo Terán De Los Rios into Texas* (Austin: Texas Knights of Columbus Historical Commission, 1932), 22.

10. Foster, *Spanish Expeditions*, 148.

11. Bob Skiles, email message to author, April 15, 2020.

12. Donald E. Chipman, "In Search of Cabeza De Vaca's Route Across Texas: An Historiographical Survey," *Southwestern Historical Quarterly* 91, no. 2 (October 1987): 127–148, https://www.jstor.org/stable/30240015.

13. "Texas General Land Office Land Grant Search," The Texas General Land Office, https://s3.glo.texas.gov/glo/history/archives/land-grants/index.cfm, accessed June 25, 2022.

14. The McCall Family Cemetery honors family members dating back to the 1870s. It is located on private land and is not accessible to the public.

15. For a summary of the history of US Highway 59, see "US Highway 59," Highway Designation File, Texas Department of Transportation, March 1, 1935, http://www.dot.state.tx.us/tpp/hwy/us/us0059.htm, accessed June 25, 2022.

16. Nelson and Perttula, "The Looting of Prehistoric Caddo Indian Cemeteries," 77–85.

17. A. Joachim McGraw et al., "The Camino Real: Colonial Texas's Lifeline to the World," in *A Texas Legacy, the Old San Antonio Road and the Caminos Reales: A Tricentennial History, 1691-1991* (Austin: Texas State Department of Highways and Public Transportation, Highway Design Division, 1991) 43-48.

18. "El Camino Real de los Tejas National Historic Trail, Maps," National Parks Service, US Department of the Interior, https://www.nps.gov/elte/planyourvisit/maps.htm, accessed June 25, 2022.

19. Jackson and Foster, *Imaginary Kingdom*, 205.

20. James L. McCorkle, Jr., "Los Adaes and the Borderlands Origins of East Texas," *East Texas Historical Journal* 22, no. 2 (September 1984): 3–12. Closer to Nacogdoches and after 1832, a middle route came in to use. The lower road west from Nacogdoches was sometimes called the Barr Road, based on land that the traders Barr & Davenport owned at the Angelina River. The road later split, creating a middle route known in Nacogdoches as the John Durst Road.

21. Spaniards associated the trails with the Bidai, but multiple related tribes all used the trails. Akokisas, Cocos, Mayeyes, Tonkawas, and Karankawas lived along them, but the Bidai were more closely aligned with the long-term use.

22. McGraw and Corbin, "A Review Essay."

23. Robert Bruce Blake, "Bedias Road," *Handbook of Texas*, Texas State Historical Association, accessed June 19, 2021. https://www.tshaonline.org/handbook/entries/bedias-road.

24. Herbert E. Bolton, *Map of Texas and Adjacent Regions in the Eighteenth Century (1915)*. Texas Maps Collection. Texas State Library & Archives Collection. Originally published by the University of California Press, 1915. Accessed June 26, 2022.

25. Bolton, "Spanish Activities," 341.

26. Castañeda, *Our Catholic Heritage*, vol. 4, 47.

27. "Proceedings concerning Orobio y Bazterra's order for investigation of French settlements in Texas," Bexar Archives, 1745-10-01, e_bx_001976.

28. "Proceedings concerning Orobio y Bazterra's order," Bexar Archives.

29. Archaeological studies suggest the locations for these villages are a bit north of McCullom Park in Chambers County, just east of Lake Miller and Lake Charlotte not far off the Interstate 10 bridge at the Trinity River. This archaeological site is 41CH275 identified by the Texas Historical Commission. See W. L. Atwood, "Texas Collection," *Southwestern Historical Quarterly* 56, no. 4 (April 1953): 560–561, https://texashistory.unt.edu/ark:/67531/metapth101145.

30. "Proceedings Concerning Orobio," Bexar Archives. Orobio was told he could not travel that direction due to "woods, the deep miry places, and the difficult terrain intervening."

31. Bolton, "Spanish Activities," 341.

32. More information about historical markers is found in the Appendix.

33. Woodrick, *The Bidai*, 6. Woodrick suggests the location of Santa Rosa de Viterbo was near Livingston, at the Coushatta village known as Long King's, and that Chief Tomás's village mentioned was near the head of Spring Creek in 1755, though these assertions are disputed by Gann's research.

34. Robert S. Weddle, "Spanish Exploration of the Texas Coast, 1519-1800," *Bulletin of the Texas Archaeological Society* 63 (1992): 99–122.

35. There are differences in the spelling of the first name of Bellisle, with some spellings as Simard. The spelling used here is the convention established by the Texas State Historical Association. See Robert S. Weddle, "Bellisle, Francois Simars de," *Handbook of Texas*, Texas State Historical Association, accessed June 26, 2022, https://www.tshaonline.org/handbook/entries/bellisle-francois-simars-de.

36. Upon his arrival with the Hasinai, Bellisle told of a native woman who spoke Spanish welcoming him to a village. That woman was Angelina, the Indian matron who lived near the site of where Mission Concepción had been placed west of Nacogdoches. Bellisle did not mention a Spanish mission so he may have gone all the way to the Tejas village on the Neches.

37. Donald E. Chipman, "Rubí, Marqués de," *Handbook of Texas*, Texas State Historical Association, accessed February 1, 2021. https://www.tshaonline.org/handbook/entries/rubi-marques-de.

38. Kinnaird and De Lafora, *The Frontiers of New Spain*.

39. Foster, *Spanish Expeditions*, 188. The palm fiber could have been from the palmettos that grow profusely in the river bottoms.

40. Gann and the author visited this location in January 2022 and observed the hills described. An archaeological study done near here (41AG8) found eleven pottery sherds.

41. For more about the Nacogdoches Road, see Howard N. Martin, "Liberty-Nacogdoches Road," *Handbook of Texas*, Texas State Historical Association, https://www.tshaonline.org/handbook/entries/liberty-nacogdoches-road, and for more on Fort Terán see, Howard N. Martin, "Fort Teran," *Handbook of Texas*, Texas State Historical Association, https://www.tshaonline.org/handbook/entries/fort-teran.

42. Worrall, *A Prehistory*, 56.

43. Guillaume de L'Isle, *Carte De La Louisiane Et Du Cours Du Mississipi. Dressee Sur Un Grand Nombre De Memoires Entr'autres Sur Ceux De Mr. Le Maire. Par Guillme. De L'Isle De L'Academie Rle. Des Sciences. A Amsterdam, Chez Jean Covens Et Corneille Mortier, Geographes. (1742).* David Rumsey Historical Map Collection, https://www.davidrumsey.com/luna/servlet/s/u208ul, accessed June 26, 2022.

From this map it appears that the Neches River flows into the Trinity, shown at the point where the Cenis (Tejas) mission was established and where multiple roads converge. This point of confluence is incorrect. However, at that point is a stream flowing into the Trinity from the west at a location noted as Bidai villages. The confluence shown on the map is correct even if the stream incorrectly appears to be the Neches. This confluence matches the point where White Rock Creek, on the east (left bank) side of the Trinity, and Harmon Creek from the west (right bank) merge with the Trinity River.

44. There is further support for this eastern-trending route in the orientation of a later road tracking to the northeast from the Upper Coushatta Village toward this Bidai trail and near a known archaeological site identified as a possible village. Given that Orobio, acting on the advice of the Hasinai chief, would have avoided the flooded, miry edges of the Trinity River for as long as possible, it makes sense that this due south route could have been an early Bidai trail.

45. Aten, "Indians of the Upper Texas Coast," 116–117.

46. Antonio Leal to Governor Manuel Muñoz, July 10, 1794. Blake Collection Supplement, "Volume 3," 136.

47. Elizabeth A. H. John, "Walker, Juan Pedro," *Handbook of Texas*, Texas State Historical Association, accessed April 19, 2021, https://www.tshaonline.org/handbook/entries/walker-juan-pedro.

48. Juan Pedro Walker and Jean Louis Berlandier, "Voyage Au Mexique: Itineraires, Ports, Cotes, Baies, Etc. De La Republique Mexicaine, Par Jn. Louis Berlandier," Yale University, Beinecke Rare Book and Manuscript Library, WA MSS S-300. https://collections.library.yale.edu/catalog/2020047, accessed June 26, 2022.

49. Edward Blount, "Location of the Old Contraband Trace in Nacogdoches County," *Junior Historian* (December 1945): 7-11. See also "El Camino del Caballo," *Handbook of Texas*, Texas State Historical Association, accessed April 19, 2021, https://www.tshaonline.org/handbook/entries/el-camino-del-caballo.

50. Other modern interpretations of this route exist. See Harry Pettey. *Map of Smuggler's Road Drawn by Harry Pettey*, Date Unknown; https://texashistory.unt.edu/ark:/67531/metapth493167/ : University of North Texas Libraries, The Portal to Texas History, accessed February 2, 2021.

51. For a look at Shawnee Landing and some of the road leading to it see, see Shane Gordon, *Shawnee Landing / Hand Launch on Angelina River*, S G Outdoors, February 7, 2021, https://www.youtube.com/watch?v=NrsdRHX96H8, accessed 4/20/2021.

52. Gunnar M. Brune, *Springs of Texas* (College Station: Texas A&M University Press, 2002), 342.

53. Morris K. Jackson and Peggy A. Jasso, "The Mansola Road of Nacogdoches, Historical Marker Application," Historical Marker Application, Texas Historical Commission, 2021.

54. Jackson and Jasso, "The Mansola Road."

55. J. H. Colton, *History of Texas from Its First Settlement in 1685 to Its Annexation to the United States in 1846, Map of Spanish-Texas*, University of North Texas Libraries, The Portal to Texas History, https://texashistory.unt.edu/ark:/67531/metapth20778/, accessed June 26, 2022.

56. Bob Skiles is a bit more generous with Yoakum. In an email to the author on June 23, 2021, he said, "I found Yoakum to be the most accurate of all the OG (Old Guard) Texas historians, especially as related to TDS location (note he has it accurately located/depicted on this map), and the roads . . . including depicting the 'contraband trail' (although his crossing of Trinity is questionable, likely erroneous, showing it crossing above TDS, but he did know that the eastern destination was the Ais mission. . . . Most of the route of the 'contraband road' that crossed the southern part of Nacogdoches County, was one-and-the-same as the route of the 'old road' the road from Béxar to Los Adaes, but which could just-as-aptly be called the road from La Bahía to the Ais mission."

57. Kress, "Solís Diary," 62-63.

58. Bolton, De Mézières, *Athanase De Mézières*, vol. 1, 74. Gorgoritos followed Chief Tomás who led the Bidai in 1754–55 and again in later years. Gorgoritos was mentioned in Spanish documents between 1767 and 1777.

59. Both of these important leaders died in 1777 in an epidemic among the Hainai in East Texas. See P. Shawn Marceaux and Timothy K. Perttula, "Negotiating Borders: The Southern Caddo and Their Relationships with Colonial Governments in East Texas," in *American Indians and the Market Economy, 1775-1850*, eds. Lance Greene and Mark R. Plane (Tuscaloosa, AL: University of Alabama Press, 2010), 80-97.

60. "Proceedings carried out by Martos y Navarrete concerning the apprehension of certain contraband goods coming from Natchitoches," Bexar Archives, 1766-11-19, e_bx_002179.

61. "Manuel de Leon placed under arrest, Ugarte to Elguézabal," Bexar Archives, 1804-05-06, e_bx_020049.

62. De la Pena and Santos, *Aguayo Expedition*, 50–51.

63. Stephen F. Austin, *Mapa Topográfico De La Provincia De Texas (1822)*, Geography and Map Division, The Library of Congress, Washington, DC, https://www.loc.gov/item/98687158/, accessed June 26, 2022.

64. *A Map of Austin's Colony and adjacent Country in Texas drawn principally from actual Survey by Stephen F. Austin, circa 1820–1829*, Cumings Family Papers, 1824–1926, Col 8978, The Daughters of the Republic of Texas Collection, Texas A&M University-San Antonio.

The Texas General Land Office version is Map no. 93353 found at https://s3.glo.texas.gov/glo/history/archives/map-store/index.cfm#item/93353, accessed June 27, 2022.

65. Although an image of this map is available on the Texas General Land Office website, it is not at a level of resolution that allows detailed research. The Daughters of the Republic of Texas at Texas A&M-San Antonio in San Antonio is the keeper of the map. A digital file available only from them is what allowed this level of research scrutiny.

66. Howard N. Martin, "Long King's Village," *Handbook of Texas*, Texas State Historical Association, accessed March 12, 2022, https://www.tshaonline.org/handbook/entries/long-kings-village.

67. "Report of Captain Pedro Lopez Prieto, Commandant of Trinidad de Salcedo to Lieutenant-Colonel Manuel De Salcedo, Governor of Texas [Béxar], May 21, 1810." Texas General Land Office, Spanish Collection, Box 129, Folder 21, 197–198. Translation corrected and annotated by Bob D. Skiles, December 2014.

Skiles notes there were many shoals and falls between Trinidad and the bay, but Prieto would only have personal knowledge of those nearer to Trinidad. One of those falls at Nelson Creek was commonly referred to as El Salto, Spanish for the falls. Skiles, email message to author, January 11, 2022.

68. Skiles, email message to author, March 25, 2021.

69. It is interesting to note that Morris Jackson, an archaeological steward and historian, states that "present generations of Spanish and Mexican settlers do not recognize the term Don Joaquín crossing but know the crossing as the Procella Crossing or the Michell or Micheli Crossing." See Jackson and Jasso, "Mansola Road, Historical Marker Application."

70. "Records from the Texas Historical Commission's Protected Site Atlas," Texas Historical Commission. Sites 41AG3 and 41AG4 are extensive villages and earthworks; 41AG7 is a series of earth mounds; 41AG8 is a possible Bidai farmstead; 41AG9 found potsherds and bone fragments, possibly human, suggesting a village; 41AG10 is another possible village; 41AG16 is village site and small mound; 41AG22 is a village and burial site, small mounds.

71. *Angelina County Nacogdoches District*, Map 3234, 1882, Texas General Land Office, General Map Collection, https://historictexasmaps.com/collection/search-results/3234-angelina-county-nacogdoches-district-general-map-collection, accessed June 26, 2022.

72. Starnes, H. L. "The John D. Gann House", photograph, 1936; University of North Texas Libraries, The Portal to Texas History, https://texashistory.unt.edu/ark:/67531/metadc1755523/, accessed June 20, 2021.

73. Dumble, *The Geology of East Texas* 313.

74. David Hoffpauir, email message to author, July 16, 2021.

75. "Title of Possession of Two Leagues of Land in favor of Citizen José Antonio Sepulveda, situated on Cochino Creek in the proximity of the Neches River." Texas General Land Office. Trinity County, A-40, Translation 3547. https://s3.glo.texas.gov/glo/history/archives/land-grants/landgrants.cfm?intID=45905, accessed June 27, 2022.

76. "Francisco Perez land grant," Houston County A-63, Texas General Land

Office, https://s3.glo.texas.gov/glo/history/archives/land-grants/landgrants.cfm?intID=22992, accessed June 27, 2022. See the English field notes.

Chapter 6

1. "Certified copy of Fray José Francisco Mariano de la Garza's affidavit as to Ibarvo's character and services," Bexar Archives, 1787-11-14, e_bx_008021. See also in Blake Collection Supplement, "Volume 2," 208.

2. George Avery, "Archival Investigations of the People of Los Adaes," *Southern Studies* 7, no. 1 (1996): 66.

3. Galan, *Los Adaes*, 115.

4. Avery, "Archival Investigations," 68, Appendix.

5. "Winthuysen reporting condition of presidios and missions in Texas and recommending removal of capital from Los Adaes to Béxar," Bexar Archives, 1744-08-19, e_bx_001967. Includes brief descriptions of topography, climate, construction, crops, and reduction of Indians. Tomás Felipe de Winthuysen was the governor of the Province of Texas from 1741–43. He was a civilian, not a soldier, and did not engage in or allow illicit trade.

6. Jackson and Foster, *Imaginary Kingdom*, 129.

7. Elizabeth Howard West and Marques de Altamira, "Bonilla's Brief Compendium of the History of Texas, 1772 (An Annotated Translation)," *The Quarterly of the Texas State Historical Association* 8, no. 1 (July 1904): 70, https://www.jstor.org/stable/30242842.

8. West and de Altamira, "Bonilla's Brief Compendium," 61.

9. "Los Adaes, Spanish Capital Through Time (a Timeline)," Texas Beyond History, Texas Archeological Research Laboratory, https://texasbeyondhistory.net/adaes/time.html, accessed June 27, 2022.

10. Castañeda, *Our Catholic Heritage*, vol. 4., 295–99.

11. Avery, "Archival Investigations," 79. The three Frenchmen were Nicolás Beausolille, Carlos Grande, and Ramón Terio.

12. Galan, *Los Adaes*, 2.

13. Galan, *Los Adaes*, 146.

14. Jackson and Jasso, "El Salto Historical Marker Application."

15. Castañeda, *Our Catholic Heritage*, vol. 4, 300.

16. Herbert Eugene Bolton. *Texas in the Middle Eighteenth Century: Studies in Spanish Colonial History and Administration*. (Berkeley: University of California Press, 1915, and Forgotten Books, 2018) 391. See also Gene A. Smith, *Nexus of Empire: Negotiating Loyalty and Identity in the Revolutionary Borderlands, 1760s-1820s*. (Gainesville: University Press of Florida, 2011) 166, 169.

17. Bolton, *Texas in the Middle Eighteenth Century*, 393.

18. Heusinger, *Early Explorations*, 106.

19. Bolton, *Texas in the Middle Eighteenth Century*, 391.

20. Smith, *Nexus of Empire*, 170.

21. Bolton, *Texas in the Middle Eighteenth Century*, 401.

22. “Certified copy of Fray José Francisco Mariano de la Garza’s affidavit as to Ibarvo’s character and services,” Bexar Archives, 1787-11-14, e_bx_008021. See also in Blake Supplement, “Volume 2,” 212.

23. José Zepeda signed on behalf of those absent or who could not write well enough to sign their name.

24. Blake Collection, “Volume 40,” 333. “Acts that have been introduced for the Citizens of the Presidio of Los Adaes, concerning that it was permitted to them to settle in that of the Mission of Ais, and establishment of the Village of Our Lady of the Pilar of Bucareli,” October 4, 1773.

25. Blake Collection, “Volume 40,” 333.

26. Blake Collection, “Volume 40,” 346.

27. Blake Collection, “Volume 40”, 346. Ripperdá to Bucareli y Ursua. Bigotes, who wished to join their march to San Antonio de Béxar and convince the governor to allow their return with a Franciscan missionary. See page 359 for Oconór’s letter on this.

28. Bolton, *Texas in the Middle Eighteenth Century*, 392.

29. “Certified copy of Fray José Francisco Mariano de la Garza’s affidavit as to Ibarvo’s character and services,” Bexar Archives, 1787-11-14, e_bx_008021. See also in Blake Supplement, “Volume 2,” 5.

30. Bolton, *Texas in the Middle Eighteenth Century*, 403.

31. “Bucarely y Ursua to Ripperdá, prohibiting citizens of *Los Adaes* to settle in Natchitoches,” Bexar Archives, 1774-05-17, e_bx_002422.

32. Blake Collection, “Volume 44,” 52, 54. Juan María Baron de Ripperdá to Antonio María Bucareli y Ursua, Permission for Ibarvo to settle on the Trinity, May 17, 1774.

Chapter 7

1. Castañeda, vol 4, p 315, citing a letter from Hugo Oconór to the Viceroy on December 31, 1775.

2. This was also the later location for Calhoun’s Ferry.

3. Blake Collection, “Volume 63,” 390, “Antonio Gil Ibarvo, Founder of Modern Nacogdoches.”

4. John, *Storms Brewed*, 339.

5. Jami Horne, “Cincinnati, Texas,” East Texas History, https://easttexashistory.org/items/show/238, accessed June 27, 2022.

6. “Croix to Cabello, requesting opinion as to the location of Bucareli at *Paso Tomás*,” Bexar Archives, 1778-07-30, e_bx_002725.

7. Cabello’s official title was “Don Domingo Cabello, Colonel in the Royal Armies, Governor and Commandant of Arms of the Province of Texas, its Missions, Conquests, and Frontiers, Captain of the Cavalry Company of the Royal Presidio of San Antonio de Béxar, and Inspector General of the Militia Corps and Presidial Troops of the said Province by Commission Conferred by the Lord Commandant General of the Interior Provinces of this Kingdom of New Spain; at this Royal Presidio of San Antonio de Béxar and villa of San Fernando.”

8. "Croix to Cabello, requesting opinion as to the location of Bucareli at Paso Tomás," Bexar Archives, 1779-03-31, e_bx_002880.

9. Castañeda, *Our Catholic Heritage*, vol. 4, 312.

10. "Translation of proceedings concerning copy of Navarro's opinion on the abandonment of *Los Adaes*, settlement and abandonment of Bucareli, removal of settlers at Nacogdoches and selection of another settlement of the Trinity, San Marcos or some other suitable spot," Bexar Archives, 1780-01-18, e_bx_003199.

11. Blake Collection, "Volume 44," 103. Father Pedro Ramírez de Arellano to Sir Caballero de Croix, in "Expediente Concerning that the Citizenship of the Village of Nuestra Senora del Pilar de Bucareli has designated to them A Priest for the Account of The Royal Treasury.

12. Robert Bruce Blake, "Tomas, Chief," *Handbook of Texas*, Texas State Historical Association, accessed March 19, 2020, http://www.tshaonline.org/handbook/online/articles/ft015.

13. Bob Skiles, "Location of the Bedias Indian village on Bedias Creek, ca. 1828." Unpublished typescript, 2010. With support from Elias R. Wightman's 1828 account in Helm, Bob Skiles analyzed and mapped the likely location of likely nearby Bidai villages.

14. Castañeda, *Our Catholic Heritage*, vol. 4, 313.

15. Sorrow, *Investigations*, 6. These two villages were found by Athanase de Mézières.

16. Castañeda, *Our Catholic Heritage*, vol. 4, 314.

17. Bolton, "Spanish Abandonment," 108.

18. "Croix to Cabello, requesting opinion as to the location of Bucareli at Paso Tomás," Bexar Archives, 1778-07-30, e_bx_002725.

19. Castañeda, *Our Catholic Heritage*, vol. 4, 315. Citing a letter from Oconór to the Viceroy on December 31, 1775.

20. Helm, *Scraps*, 155.

21. Certified copy of Navarro's decree, included in "Translation of proceedings concerning copy of Navarro's opinion on the abandonment of *Los Adaes*, settlement and abandonment of Bucareli, removal of settlers at Nacogdoches and selection of another settlement of the Trinity, San Marcos or some other suitable spot," Bexar Archives, 1780-01-18, e_bx_003199.

22. James M. McReynolds, "Family Life in a Borderland Community: Nacogdoches, Texas, 1779-1861" (PhD dissertation, Texas Tech University, 1978). See also, Joe S. Graham, "Texas-Mexican Vernacular Architecture," *Handbook of Texas*, Texas State Historical Association, accessed April 6, 20202. http://www.tshaonline.org/handbook/online/articles/cbtut. See also "Mission Dolores, Simulating Mission Dolores Today." Texas Beyond History, https://texasbeyondhistory.net/dolores/today.html, accessed June 27, 2022. See also *Handbook of Hispanic Culture-Anthropology*. (Houston: Arte Publico Press, 1994). https://www.google.com/books/edition/_/7hMsnIMQxN8C?hl=en, accessed June 27, 2022.

23. McReynolds, *Family Life*, 48.

24. McReynolds, *Family Life*, 49.

25. De Pagès, *Travels Round the World*, 53.

26. Sorrow, *Investigations*, 8.

27. Axel I. Mundigo and Dora P. Crouch, "The City Planning Ordinances of the Laws of the Indies Revisited: Part I: Their Philosophy and Implications," *Town Planning Review* 48, no. 3 (1977): 249. https://www.jstor.org/stable/40103542, accessed June 27, 2022.

28. Bolton, *Texas in the Middle Eighteenth Century*, 414.

29. Castañeda, *Our Catholic Heritage*, vol. 4, 315.

30. Castañeda, *Our Catholic Heritage*, vol. 4, 317.

31. Blake Collection, "Volume 44," 83, 263, Ripperdá to Bucareli y Ursua, April 9, 1776.

32. Bolton, "Spanish Abandonment," 112. His footnote cites Letter of May 15, 1775, in Quaderno que Corresponde, 38 as his source of concerns about "liberty of conscience."

33. "Bucarely y Ursua to Ripperdá, discussing the appointment of priest for Bucareli," Bexar Archives, 1776-08-21, e_bx_002513.

34. Bucarely y Ursua to Ripperdá, discussing the appointment of priest for Bucareli," Bexar Archives, 1776-08-21, e_bx_002513. The president of the missions was Father Pedro Ramírez de Arrellano.

35. "Antonio Gil Ibarvo, Founder of Modern Nacogdoches," Blake Collection, "Volume 63," 390.

36. Bolton, "Spanish Abandonment," 108.

37. "Proceedings carried out by Martos y Navarrete concerning the apprehension of certain contraband goods coming from Natchitoches," Bexar Archives, 1766-11-19, e_bx_002179, p. 14. The proceeding cites "the punishment provided by Law seven, book nine, title twenty-seven, and Law eight, book third, title thirteen."

38. Jack Jackson, *Los Mesteños: Spanish Ranching in Texas, 1721–1821* (College Station: Texas A&M University Press, 2006), 121.

39. "Cabello to Croix, discussing settlement of Bucareli at *Paso Tomás*," Bexar Archives, 1779-03-31, e_bx_02880.

40. Bob Skiles, email message to author, May 2020.

41. Blake, "Volume 44," 100. Areche to Oconór regarding appointment of Béxar priest for Bucareli.

42. Oconór's letter is mentioned in: Bucarely y Ursua to Ripperdá, concerning order to report to Oconór all matters pertaining to the resettlement of people of Los Adaes," Bexar Archives, 1775-02-28, e_bx_002459.

43. Bucarely y Ursua to Ripperdá, Bexar Archives.

44. "Judicial proceedings conducted against Don Marcos Vidal for smuggling," 1775-09-13, Bexar Archives, e_bx_002402.

45. Athanase de Mézières arrested Vidal for an earlier incident after he entered Louisiana "without passport, with eight servants, money, a drove of mules, baggage, and equipment." Vidal said he was there only to pay for goods he had bought from three people in Natchitoches. Vidal's claim hardly seemed credible considering the size of his entourage, so De Mézières imprisoned Vidal and his servants and sold his

belongings at auction "as a warning to others who might plan similar enterprises." See De Mézières to Amézaga (The governor of Louisiana) in Herbert Eugene Bolton and Athanase de Mézières, *Athanase De Mézières and the Louisiana-Texas Frontier 1768-1780: Documents Published for the First Time, from the Original Spanish and French Manuscripts, Chiefly in the Archives of Mexico and Spain*, (Cleveland, OH: A.H. Clark, 1914), Volume 2, 108.

46. Trevor Denning, *The Playing-Cards of Spain: A Guide for Historians and Collectors* (London: Cygnus Arts, 1996), 142.

47. Herbert Eugene Bolton, *Guide to Materials for the History of the United States in the Principal Archives of Mexico* (New York: HardPress Publishing, 2012), 98.

48. "Judicial proceedings conducted against Don Marcos Vidal for smuggling," Bexar Archives, 1775-09-13, e_bx_002402.

49. "Bucarely y Ursua to Ripperdá, repeating orders to cease correspondence with De Mézières," Bexar Archives, 1775-02-15, e_bx-002454.

50. "Certified copy of proceedings, Ripperdá vs. Juan Antonio Díaz and José Manuel Díaz, accused of contraband," Bexar Archives, 1775-02-04, e_bx_002440.

51. "Ripperdá vs. Jacinto de Mora and Marcos Hernández, charged with contraband," Bexar Archives, 1775-04-09, e_bx_002465.

52. "Ripperdá vs. Jacinto de Mora and Marcos Hernández, charged with contraband," Bexar Archives, 1775-04-09, e_bx_002465. Hernandez was much better off. He had a shotgun with a case; a lance and shield, from his days as a soldier; a bed with linens, a quilt, and a pillow; a *comal*; a *metate*; a plow and ax, seven mules and five horses; and the house where he lived. He also had a pregnant slave with a child at her feet.

53. "Report of French tobacco at Bucareli, Luis Cazorla to Bucareli y Ursua," Blake Collection, "Volume 44," 58, 62.

54. "Reports made by the Governor of Texas, and the Captain of La Bahía concerning the settlement that he established on the Trinity River, Oconór to Bucareli y Ursua," December 31, 1775, Blake Collection, "Volume 44," 65.

55. Blake Collection, "Volume 44," 65.

56. "Blake Collection, "Volume 44," 77–86. Regarding village of Nuestra Señora del Pilár, Ripperdá to Bucareli y Ursua.

57. Robert S. Weddle, "Croix, Teodoro De," *Handbook of Texas*, Texas State Historical Association, accessed June 27, 2022, http://www.tshaonline.org/handbook/online/articles/fcr26, accessed.

58. Bolton, *Athanase De Mézières, Volume 2*, 122–129.

59. Bolton, *Athanase De Mézières, Volume 2*, 133–134.

60. Bolton, *Athanase De Mézières Volume 2*, 135–136. Letter From Governor Ripperdá to Croix, October 28, 1777.

61. "Certified copy of proceedings concerning Gil Ibarvo's appointment as captain of Bucareli," Croix to Ripperdá, Bexar Archives, 1778-01-12, e_bx_002655.

62. Bolton, *Athanase De Mézières Volume 2*, 187–192. Letter from de Mézières to Croix, March 18, 1778.

63. Certified copy of Navarro's decree, included in "Translation of proceedings concerning copy of Navarro's opinion on the abandonment of *Los Adaes*, settlement and abandonment of Bucareli, removal of settlers at Nacogdoches and selection of another settlement of the Trinity, San Marcos or some other suitable spot," Bexar Archives, 1780-01-18, e_bx_003199.

64. Bolton, "Spanish Abandonment," 110.

65. Sharon M. Derrick and Diane E. Wilson, "The Effects of Epidemic Disease on Caddo Demographic Structure," *Bulletin of the Texas Archaeological Society* 72 (2001): 91–103, 94. The symptoms described lead some historians to suggest it was one of the three types of plague contracted from rats in the hull of a French vessel sunk on the coast.

66. John, *Storms Brewed*, 499, 523. Also see Jackson and Foster, *Imaginary Kingdom*, xvi.

67. Paul Shawn Joseph Marceaux, "The Archaeology and Ethnohistory of the Hasinai Caddo: Material Culture and the Course of European Contact" (PhD dissertation, University of Texas, 2011).

68. Bolton, *Athanase De Mézières Volume 2*, 270.

69. Bolton, *Athanase De Mézières Volume 2*, 112.

70. Certified copy of Unzaga y Amezaga's letter to De Mézières, repeating ban on trade with New Spain," Bexar Archives, 1775-03-13, e_bx_002462.

71. Blake Collection, "Volume 44," 84. Ripperdá to Bucareli y Ursua, April 9, 1776.

72. Blake Collection, "Volume 44," 190–193. Ibarvo to Ripperdá, level of Construction in Bucareli. June 30, 1777.

73. Bolton, *Athanase De Mézières Volume 2*, 190–192. Citing letter from de Mézières to Croix dated March 23, 1778.

74. Bolton had identified this as *Echium vulgare*, which is also called viper's bugloss. Viper's grass was identified in *The Family Herbal*, an 1812 compendium by John Hill, but that was a different plant, *Scorzonera hispanica*. Both seemed to have indications for helping with fevers and headaches. See "Viper's Grass," Henriette's Herbal Homepage. Henrietta Kress. https://www.henriettes-herb.com/eclectic/hill/vipers-grass.html, accessed June 27, 2022.

75. Bolton, *Athanase De Mézières Volume 2*, 193–196. Citing De Mézières to Croix, April 5, 1778.

76. Bolton, *Athanase De Mézières Volume 2*, 197–199. Letter from de Mézières to Croix, April 8, 1778.

77. "Croix to Cabello, requesting opinion as to the location of Bucareli at *Paso Tomás*," Bexar Archives, 1778-07-30, e_bx_002725.

78. "Conditions at Bucareli, Father Juan García Botello to Cabello," Blake Collection, "Volume 44," 210–213, 226. Even Bolton said he could not quite determine what Botello's exact role was with regard to Bucareli, but it appears he had served there at one time prior to Father Garza's appointment.

79. Bolton, *Athanase De Mézières Volume 2*, 231.

80. Bolton, *Athanase De Mézières Volume 1*, 84.

81. Blake Collection, "Volume 44," 216–20. Discussing conditions at Bucareli, Father José Francisco maria de la Garza to Cabello, January 8, 1779.

82. Blake Collection, "Volume 63," 384–98. Ibarvo biography.

83. Chipman, *Spanish Texas*, 199.

84. Blake Collection, "Volume 44," 214. Letter from de Mézières to Croix, November 15, 1778.

85. Bolton, *Athanase De Mézières Volume 2*, 289. Letter from de Mézières to Croix, September 30, 1779.

86. Blake, "Supplement 1," 299. Letter from Cabello to Croix, August 31, 1779,

87. Blake, "Supplement 1," 279.

88. "Cabello to Croix, reporting Comanche depredations at Bucareli," Bexar Archives, 1779-02-09, e_bx_002833.

89. Blake Collection, "Volume 44," 217. Discussing conditions at Bucareli, Father José Francisco maria de la Garza to Cabello, January 8, 1779.

90. Chipman and Joseph, *Notable Men and Women*, 208–09.

91. "Gil Ibarvo to Ripperdá, requesting relief of duty," Bexar Archives, 1778-09-22, e_bx_002754.

92. Blake Collection, "Volume 44," 216–20. Letter from Botello to Cabello, January 8, 1779.

93. Blake Collection, "Volume 44," p. 221–23. Letter from Ibarvo to Cabello, January 12, 1779.

94. Blake Collection, "Volume 44," 250. Letter from Ibarvo to Croix, May 13, 1779.

95. Blake Collection, "Volume 44," 226–37. Letter from Cabello to Croix, February 2, 1779.

96. "Cabello to Croix, reporting abandonment of Bucareli," Bexar Archives, 1779-02-11, e_bx_000931.

97. Sorrow, *Investigations*, 10.

98. Juan Agustín Morfi, *Provincias Internas: Antología*, ed. Guadalupe Curiel (Mexico: Universidad Nacional Autonoma de México, 2003). From: R. P. Fr. Juan Agustin Morfi, *Memorias Paras la Historia de la Provincia de Texas*. Thanks to Bob Skiles for this source and his translation.

99. Morfi, *Provincias Internas*.

100. Blake Collection, "Volume 44," 254–57. Letter from José Francisco Mariano de la Garza to Caballero de Croix, April 30, 1779.

101. Blake Collection, "Volume 44," 51. Letter from Ibarvo to Croix, May 13, 1779.

102. "Cabello to Croix, reporting results of Nicolás La Mathe's visit to various Indian tribes," Bexar Archives, 1779-08-30, e_bx_003043.

103. Blake Collection, "Volume 63," 393. Road from Bucareli to Nacogdoches.

104. Bolton, *Athanase De Mézières Volume 2*, 269–71.

105. "Cabello to Croix, reporting abandonment of Bucareli," Bexar Archives, 1779-02-11, e_bx_000931.

106. "Ripperdá to Croix, discussing Gil Ibarvo's resignation from Bucareli," Bexar Archives, 1778-10-31, e_bx_002775.

Chapter 8

1. "Expediente, Government vs Antonio Gil Ibarvo," Bexar Archives, 1790-12-10 to 1795-10-01, in Blake, Volume 67, pp. 125-131. This is Verazadi's secret report on Ibarvo.

2. Karle Wilson Baker, "Nacogdoches: I. The Indian and Spanish Town," *Southwest Review* 21, no. 1 (October 1935): 6.

3. Bolton, *Athanase De Mézières Volume 2*, 309.

4. "Proceedings concerning copy of Navarro's opinion on the abandonment of *Los Adaes*, settlement and abandonment of Bucareli, removal of settlers at Nacogdoches, and selection of another settlement of the Trinity, San Marcos or some other suitable spot," Bexar Archives, 1780-01-18, e_bx_003199.

5. Bolton, *Athanase De Mézières Volume 2*, 309.

6. "Proceedings concerning copy of Navarro's opinion on the abandonment of Los Adaes." Bexar Archives, 1780-01-18, e_bx_003199.

7. Castañeda, *Our Catholic Heritage*, vol. 4, 336.

8. "Inventory of effects belonging to Los Adaes chapel," Bexar Archives, 1779-04-12, e_bx_002894. A chasuble is the sleeveless outer tunic worn by a Catholic priest during Mass. Even in the frontier, they would have been decoratively ornate, but with a simple design. See also, "Croix to Cabello, giving instructions for the retention of effects belonging to chapel of the abandoned presidio of *Los Adaes* until selection of site for Bucareli's new settlement," Bexar Archives, 1780-01-05, e_bx_003179.

9. "Croix to Cabello, requesting opinion as to the location of Bucareli at Paso Tomás," Bexar Archives, 1778-07-30, e_bx_002725.

10. "Cabello to Croix, discussing settlement of Bucareli at Paso Tomás," Bexar Archives, 1779-03-31, e_bx_002880.

11. "Croix to Cabello, discussing plans for improving conditions at Bucareli," Bexar Archives, 1779-05-14, e_bx_002906.

12. "Certified copy of contract between Antonio Gil Ibarvo and Juan Ignacio Guerrero concerning management of ranch near Atoyac," Bexar Archives, 1779-04-06, e_bx_002889.

13. Bolton, *Athanase De Mézières Volume 2*, 291–298.

14. "Letter from Croix to de Mézières, Bexar Archives, September 10, 1778. 214–217.

15. Bolton, *Athanase De Mézières Volume 2*, 306–311.

16. "Cabello's letter to Croix, requesting instructions concerning Indian presents brought by De Mézières and listed in the enclosed documents," Bexar Archives, 1779-10-12, e_bx_003097.

17. "Croix to Cabello, giving instructions for payment of money to De Mézières upon arrival in Texas," Bexar Archives1779-10-09, e_bx_003095.

18. Bolton, *Athanase De Mézières Volume 1*, 121.

19. "Cabello's notification to Gil Ibarvo concerning salary assigned to the said Gil Ibarvo," Bexar Archives 1780-03-11, e_bx_003260.

20. Bolton, "Spanish Abandonment," 133.

21. "Proceedings concerning copy of Navarro's opinion on the abandonment of Los

Adaes, settlement and abandonment of Bucareli, removal of settlers at Nacogdoches, and selection of another settlement of the Trinity, San Marcos or some other suitable spot," Bexar Archives 1780-01-18, e_bx_003199.

22. "Cabello to Croix, acknowledging receipt of documents ordering survey of land for the new town of Bucareli," Bexar Archives 1780-04-01, e_bx_003295.

23. "Cabello to Croix, acknowledging receipt of documents ordering survey of land for the new town of Bucareli, Bexar Archives, 1780-04-01, e_bx_003295.

24. "Croix to Cabello, discussing survey of area for new town of Bucareli," Bexar Archives, 1780-06-19, e_bx_003388.

25. "Cabello to Croix, reporting on contraband cases," Bexar Archivess,1780-10-09, e_bx_003482.

26. Bolton, "Spanish Abandonment," 136.

27. Bolton, "Spanish Abandonment," 107, footnote 1.

28. Mario Marcel Salas and John Reynolds, "Social Caste in Early Béxar," *ArcGIS StoryMaps* (ESRI), Accessed April 28, 2021, https://storymaps.arcgis.com/stories/7114300813eb4db6892d477882233f1e.

29. "Census report of Nacogdoches," Bexar Archives, 1793-00-00, e_bx_019827.

30. McReynolds, *Family Life*, 121.

31. Matthew Babcock, "Roots of Independence: Transcultural Trade in the Texas-Louisiana Borderlands," *Ethnohistory* 60, 2 (Spring 2013): 248.

32. McReynolds, *Family Life*, 119.

33. "Census report of Nacogdoches," Bexar Archives, 1793-00-00, e_bx_019827.

34. McReynolds, *Family Life*, 81. Part of a report by Father Solís in 1767.

35. "Certified copy of Fray José Francisco Mariano de la Garza's affidavit as to Ibarvo's character and services," Bexar Archives, 1787-11-14, e_bx_008021.

36. "Certified copy of Fray José Francisco Mariano de la Garza's affidavit as to Ibarvo's character and services," Bexar Archives, 1787-11-14, e_bx_008021.

Chapter 9

1. "Proceedings conducted by Antonio Gil Ibarvo against Joaquín de Córdoba, charged with contraband, Bexar Archives, 1790-09-22, e_bx_009014.

2. David L. La Vere, "Barr, Davenport, Murphy and Smith: Traders on the Louisiana-Texas Frontier." (Master's Thesis, Northwestern State University, 1989), 111.

3. "Documents concerning confiscation and custody of goods belonging to Marcos Vidal," Bexar Archives, 1778-10-31, e_bx_002778.

4. Clinton McKenzie, Lindy Martinez, and Raymond Mauldin, "Archaeological Monitoring and Test Excavations at the 1722 Presidio San Antonio de Béxar (Plaza De Armas Buildings), Appendix D - Catalog of the Effects of Col Don Diego Ortiz Parilla at San Antonio in 1760." Texas Antiquities Permit No. 6526, (San Antonio: Center for Archaeological Research, University of Texas at San Antonio, 2016) 195–204. https://www.sanantonio.gov/Portals/0/Files/HistoricPreservation/arc_reports/ArchaeologicalMonitoringTestExcavations.pdf, Accessed July 4, 2022.

5. "Proceedings in the case against Juan Cortés, Sergeant Treviño, and others, charged with smuggling," Bexar Archives, 1792-06-16, e_bx_009847.

6. Brian Stauffer, email message to author, February 3, 2022.

7. Jesse Levis Cromwell, "Covert Commerce: A Social History of Contraband Trade in Venezuela, 1701–1789" (PhD dissertation, University of Texas, 2012), 5.

8. Marion Lowrie Haskell, "Rubí's inspection of the frontier presidios of New Spain, 1766–1768: Translation of sources, introduction and Notes." (Master's thesis, University of California, 1917), 2.

9. McGraw, "The Camino Real," 44.

10. Gabrielle Banks and St. John Barned-Smith, "Inside the Lucrative Smuggling Operation That Sees Millions of Chinese Cigarettes Pass through Texas," *Houston Chronicle*, June 29, 2021, Local edition, sec. Crime. https://www.houstonchronicle.com/news/houston-texas/crime/article/china-cigarettes-tobacco-trafficking-tx-16281704.php.

11. George T. Diaz and David-James Gonzalez, "Interview with George T. Diaz, 'Border Contraband: A History of Smuggling across the Rio Grande,'" People and Places. New Books Network, November 8, 2016, https://newbooksnetwork.com/george-t-diaz-border-contraband-a-history-of-smuggling-across-the-rio-grande-u-of-texas-press-2015/, accessed July 4, 2022. Based on George t. Diaz, *Border Contraband: A History of Smuggling across the Rio Grande* (Austin: University of Texas Press, 2015).

12. Cromwell, "Covert Commerce," 61. See also, Casey Schimtt, Review of "The Smuggler's World: Illicit Trade and Atlantic Communities in Eighteenth-Century Venezuela," H-LatAm, *H-Net Reviews*, May 2019.

13. Cromwell, "Covert Commerce," 18.

14. Bob Skiles, email message to author, May 9, 2020.

15. H. Sophie Burton and F. Todd Smith, *Colonial Natchitoches: A Creole Community on the Louisiana-Texas Frontier* (College Station: Texas A&M University Press, 2008), 110.

16. Elizabeth Howard West and Marques de Altamira, "Bonilla's Brief Compendium of the History of Texas, 1772 (An Annotated Translation)," *The Quarterly of the Texas State Historical Association* 8, no. 1 (July 1904): 70, http://www.jstor.org/stable/30242842, accessed February 5, 2022.

17. See "Governor Manuel de Salcedo to Second Commanding General, Brigadier Bernardo Bonavia, 24 April 1809," in *Documentos de la Independencia*, Tomo I, Col. de documentos del Museo Nacional de Arqueología, Historia y Etnografía, Vol. IV, 1928, 333–35. This source was shared by Bob Skiles, a version that he transcribed and translated to English in April 2010, from an original dated Béxar April 24, 1809.

18. J. Edward Townes, "Invisible Lines: The Life and Death of a Borderland" (PhD dissertation, Texas Christian University, 2008), 62.

19. Bolton, "Spanish Abandonment," 133.

20. Bolton, *Texas in the Middle Eighteenth Century*, 445.

21. "Report of salaries paid to soldiers of squad organized at Nacogdoches with

soldiers and citizens from the abandoned town of Bucareli," Bexar Archives, 1779-08-31, e_bx_003045.

22. "Certified copy of proceedings concerning Gil Ibarvo's commission as judge in contraband cases," Bexar Archives, 1780-04-20, e_bx_003317.

23. "Cabello to Croix, requesting instructions for the disposal of contraband goods confiscated by Gil Ibarvo and Amangual," Bexar Archives, 1780-03-18, e_bx_003277. Ibarvo was not the only one working on improving his standing with Croix. In a letter reporting his own confiscation of contraband in Béxar, Cabello advocated for his own questioning of the suspects by availing himself of "subtleties which expert criminalists recommend for justices to use." See "Cabello to Croix, reporting seizure of contraband goods introduced from Louisiana," Bexar Archives, 1780-05-09, e_bx_003327.

24. "Cabello to Ugarte y Loyola, reporting that Ibarvo expelled Frenchmen from the Neches River," Bexar Archives,1786-09-10, e_bx_007628.

25. "Martínez Pacheco to Ugalde, transmitting Ibarvo's explanations for allowing French to introduce goods in Texas," Bexar Archives, 1788-05-29, e_bx_008277.

26. "Gil Ibarvo to [Martínez] Pacheco, reporting the presence of traders from Natchitoches among the Indians with large stores of merchandise, and asking for instructions on how to proceed in the matter," Bexar Archives, 1789-09-06, e_bx_008737.

27. Thomas Frank Schilz and Donald E. Worcester, "The Spread of Firearms among the Indian Tribes on the Northern Frontier of New Spain," *American Indian Quarterly* 11, no. 1 (1987): 5, https://doi.org/10.2307/1183724, accessed February 5, 2022.

28. Schilz and Worcester, "The Spread of Firearms," 6.

29. "Cabello to Croix, transmitting Ibarvo and Arman's letters on the pacification of Northern Indians," Bexar Archives, 1780-09-17, e_bx_003451.

30. "Cabello to Croix," Bexar Archives.

31. "Value of Trade Goods Expressed in Deerskins, 1782," a table by Hiram M. (Pete) Gregory et al. in, "Los Adaes Legacy," Texas Beyond History (website). https://www.texasbeyondhistory.net/adaes/legacy.html, accessed November 11, 2021.

Sources for this table are George E. Avery, *1997 Annual Report for the Los Adaes Station Archaeology Program* (Natchitoches, LA: Department of Social Sciences, Northwestern State University, 1996), 75. Adapted from Dedra S. McDonald and Kinga Perzynska, *Guide to the Spanish and Mexican Manuscript Collection at the Catholic Archives of Texas* (Austin: Catholic Archives of Texas, 1994), 29.7b:664-665.

32. Pinkerton, *Trammel's Trace*, 94.

33. Jackson, *Texas by Terán*, 101.

34. Kress, "Solís Diary," 63.

35. "A Criminal Code Published in Nacogdoches in 1783," Blake Collection, "Volume 45," 244–55.

36. "List of criminal cases at Nacogdoches from 1779 to 1796," Bexar Archives, 1796-02-25, e_bx_011436. Translations in Bexar Archives "Volume 214," 96.

37. David La Vere, Katia Campbell, and Francois Grappe, "An Expedition to the Kichai: The Journal of François Grappe, September 24, 1783," *Southwestern Historical Quarterly* 98, no. 1 (July 1994): 58–78, https://www.jstor.org/stable/30238961, accessed August 25, 2021.

38. David La Vere, email message to author, August 27, 2021.

39. La Vere, "An Expedition to the Kichai," 6–67. In the article, La Vere and his co-authors wonder how Ibarvo was able to get a detachment of French soldiers. They speculate that the commandant at Natchitoches and an ally of Ibarvo, Estevan Vaugine, and Ibarvo hoped to intrude on the trade relationship that De Blanc had established with the Kichai. Ibarvo hoped that Vaugine would partner with him and Joseph Marie Armand, the designated Indian trader connected to Ibarvo

40. La Vere, "An Expedition to the Kichai," 74–75.

41. La Vere, "An Expedition to the Kichai," 75.

42. "Certified copy of Fray José Francisco Mariano de la Garza's affidavit as to Ibarvo's character and services," Bexar Archives, 1787-11-14, e_bx_008021.

43. John, *Storms Brewed*, 638.

44. John, *Storms Brewed*, 639.

45. "Certified copy of Fray José Francisco Mariano de la Garza's affidavit as to Ibarvo's character and services," Bexar Archives, 1787-11-14, e_bx_008021.

46. "Nicolás La Mathe vs. Antonio Gil Ibarvo, demanding settlement of accounts," Bexar Archives, 1782-06-26, e_bx_003572, p. 50.

47. "Cabello to Neve, explaining mistake made in sending gunpowder to New Orleans, and discussing relations between La Mathe and Ibarvo," Bexar Archives, 1784-06-09, e_bx_006975.

48. Tim Seiter, "The Karankawa-Spanish War from 1778 to 1789: Attempted Genocide and Karankawa Power," *Southwestern Historical Quarterly* 124, no. 4 (April 2021): 402, https://doi.org/10.1353/swh.2021.0026, accessed May 20, 2021.

49. Tim Seiter, email message to author.

50. "Proceedings resulting from Nicolás Lamatte's case against Antonio Gil Ibarvo," Bexar Archives, 1790-01-11, e_bx_008839.

51. "Certified copy of Fray José Francisco Mariano de la Garza's affidavit as to Ibarvo's character and services," Bexar Archives, 1787-11-14, e_bx_008021.

52. "Certified copy of Fray José Francisco Mariano de la Garza's affidavit as to Ibarvo's character and services," Bexar Archives, 1787-11-14, e_bx_008021, p. 7.

53. "Certified copy of Fray José Francisco Mariano de la Garza's affidavit as to Ibarvo's character and services," Bexar Archives, 1787-11-14, e_bx_008021, p. 9.

54. "Certified copy of certificate of award to Ibarvo for good work," Bexar Archives, 1786-10-31, e_bx_0077672.

55. "Certified copy of certificate of award to Ibarvo for good work," Bexar Archives, 1786-10-31, e_bx_0077672.

56. "Drafts of letters from the Governor of Texas to Ibarvo," Bexar Archives, 1790-08-16, e_bx_008983. See letter dated February 10, 1791.

57. "Drafts of letters from the Governor of Texas to Ibarvo," Bexar Archives, 1790-08-16, e_bx_008983. See letter dated February 10, 1791.

58. "Drafts of letters from the Governor of Texas to Ibarvo," Bexar Archives, 1790-08-16, e_bx_008983. See letter dated February 10, 1791.

Chapter 10

1. "Ibarvo to Muñoz, asking him to intercede in his favor with the Commandant General," Bexar Archives, 1791-10-19, e_bx_009550.

2. Ugalde's opinion is restated in a letter dated December 10, 1790, from Revilla Gigedo to Cortès when appointing him to investigate Ibarvo. The translation says 1778 instead of 1788, but this appears to be a typo since Ugalde did not assume the post until 1787. See Bexar Archives, Volume 210, p 198.

3. "Superior Board of Royal Treasury," April 21, 1789. Blake Collection, "Volume 45," 118. Blake's source for this translation is cited as A. G .M. Historia, University of Texas Archives, v. 100, p. 144.

4. Blake Collection, "Volume 45," 118.

5. Muñoz's service was from August 14, 1790, through December 31, 1793.

6. Castañeda, *Our Catholic Heritage*, vol. 5, 174.

7. Bexar Archives, volume 210, 198.

8. "Census report of Nacogdoches Mission," Bexar Archives, 1790, e_bx_009181.

9. "Ibarvo to Muñoz, reporting plans to build a new church," Bexar Archives, 1791-02-03, e_bx_009225.

10. "Ibarvo to the Viceroy, asking to be retired on half pay," Bexar Archives, 1791-03-22, e_bx_009301.

11. "Correspondence between Ibarvo and Muñoz, concerning documents for the Viceroy, requesting retirement from service," Bexar Archives, 1791-03-22, e_bx_009299.

12. "Ibarvo to the Viceroy, asking to be retired on half pay," Bexar Archives, 1791-03-22, e_bx_009301.

13. "Correspondence between Ibarvo and Muñoz, concerning documents for the Viceroy, requesting retirement from service," Bexar Archives, 1791-03-22, e_bx_009299.

14.In record searches, Verazadi's last name is also seen as Verazady, Verasadi, Berazadi, Berasadi, and Berazady.

15. "Census of Béxar" Bexar Archives, 1793-12-31, e_bx_019826. Little more is known about Verazadi. Dr. Frank de la Teja reports that he was in sacramental records as a godfather for a 1794 baptism and as a sponsor of a wedding in 1798. De la Teja, email message to author, October 21, 2021.

16. "Muñoz to Ibarvo, concerning Apache attempts to obtain the alliance of Bidais, to fight the Tonkawas," Bexar Archives, 1791-05-14, e_bx_009362. There was indication that Verazadi may have tried to provide letters to smugglers that excused them from searches on his authority, even though they did not have passports. There is also mention of communication between Ibarvo and Verazadi before the investigation. Ibarvo had sent Muñoz a letter on April 26, 1791, about an Apache chief going to the Caddo village with some Bidai Indians to talk about making war on the Tonkawa. They would "go live on the shores of the Trinity River."

17. Frank de la Teja, email message to author, October 22, 2021.

18. Archive General de Mexico, Briscoe Center for American History, University of Texas, 2q186 Historia, v 100, 1791-03-10.

19. Archive General de Mexico, Briscoe Center, 1791-03-10.

20. Revilla Gigedo reminded Muñoz of this in a letter on July 20, 1791. Archive General de Mexico. Briscoe Center for American History, University of Texas, 2q186 Historia, v 100. See also Jose Manuel Serrano Alvarez, "Ramón De Castro" Real Academia de la Historia (website), https://dbe.rah.es/biografias/39235/ramon-de-castro, accessed February 14, 2022.

21. "Ibarvo to Muñoz, giving evidence of publication of orders introducing Castro as Commandant General," Bexar Archives, 1791-06-12, e_bx_009385.

22. This material draws heavily on the "Expediente Advanced on account of the Captain Don Antonio Gil Ibarbo [Ibarvo] Demanding the Accusations Against his Conduct for Explanation of the Charges That Were Rendered by Them Against Him," Blake Collection, "Supplement 3," 236–52. These documents are dated from December 10, 1790, to October 1, 1795.

23. McGraw, "The Camino Real," 45.

24. "A Criminal Code Published in Nacogdoches in 1783," Blake Collection, "Volume 45," 250.

25. La Vere, "An Expedition to the Kichai."

26. "Proceedings concerning case of Gaspar Higaldo vs. Antonio Gil Ibarvo," Bexar Archives, 1789-12-01, e_bx_008800.

27. "Proceedings concerning payment of salaries and cost of construction of city hall buildings at San Antonio, Bexar Archives, 1793-04-11, e_bx_019434.

28. "Martínez Pacheco to Ugalde, transmitting testimony in the case of Gaspar Hidalgo vs. Antonio Gil Ibarvo," Bexar Archives, 1788-05-26, e_bx_008274.

29. "Proceedings concerning case of Gaspar Hidalgo vs. Antonio Ibarvo," Bexar Archives, 1790-12-01, e_bx_008800.

30. Bexar Archives, 1790-12-01, e_bx_008800.

31. John Wheat, email message to author, October 22, 2021.

32. Ramón de Castro to Viceroy; August 23, 1791, Blake Collection, "Volume 45," 125. This is Blake's translation from the A. G. M. Historia (Archivo General de México), Volume 100, p. 95; Briscoe Center for American History, University of Texas. See also, Viceroy to Ramón de Castro, July 20, 1791, Blake Collection, "Volume 45," 122. See also, The Governor of Texas, Don Manuel Muñoz from Castro. Archive General de Mexico, Briscoe Center, University of Texas, 2q186 Historia, v 100, 1791/06/16.

33. "Ibarvo to Muñoz, giving a brief history of his services to Texas," Bexar Archives, 1791-10-19, e_bx_009549.

34. "See also Ibarvo to Muñoz, asking him to intercede in his favor with the Commandant," Bexar Archives, 1791-10-19, e_bx_009550.

35. Blake Collection, "Volume 45," 126–27. Castro to Viceroy, December 4, 1791. See also, Blake Collection, "Supplement 3," 1, Viceroy of Mexico to Governor of Texas, January 2, 1792.

36. "Castro to Muñoz, requesting a copy of letter sent to Revilla Gigedo concerning proceedings against Ibarvo," Bexar Archives, 1792-01-03, e_bx_009660.

37. "Order to bring Ibarvo to Béxar, Ramón de Castro to Viceroy, December 4, 1791," Blake Collection, Volume 45, 126. See also, "Castro to Muñoz, ordering the arrest of Ibarvo and to start proceedings against him," Bexar Archives, 1791-12-27, e_bx_009640.

38. "Revilla Gigedo to Sierra Gorda, concerning census of foreigners," Bexar Archives, 1792-05-23, e_bx_009826.

39. "Muñoz to Ibarvo, requesting information on foreigners residing in Nacogdoches," Bexar Archives, 1792-03-10, e_bx_009800.

40. "Castro to Muñoz, ordering the arrest of Ibarvo and to start proceedings against him," Bexar Archives, 1791-12-27, e_bx_009640.

41. "Revilla Gigedo to Governor of Texas, concerning arrest of Ibarvo by Ramón de Castro, Bexar Archives, 1792-01-31, e_bx_009683.

42. "Castro to Cortes, January 10, 1792, Expediente Concerning Gil Ibarbo [Ibarvo]," Blake Collection, "Supplement 3," 237.

43. "Castro to Cortes," January 10, 1792, Blake Collection, "Volume 45," 131.

44. "Castro to Cortes, January 10, 1792, Expediente Concerning Gil Ibarbo [Ibarvo]," Blake Collection, "Supplement 3," 241.

45. Blake Collection, "Supplement 3," 241.

46. "Muñoz to Ibarvo, requesting information on foreigners residing in Nacogdoches, Bexar Archives, 1792-03-10, e_bx_009800.

47. Bexar Archives, 1792-03-10, e_bx_009800.

48. "Proceedings in the case against Juan Cortés, Sergeant Treviño, and others, charged with smuggling," Bexar Archives, 1792-06-16, e_bx_09847.

49. The interim governor was Manuel Ignacio de Escandon, known as the second Conde de Sierra Gorda. He served as governor of Nuevo Santander from 1790 to 1800. He was the son of Jose de Escandon.

50. "Proceedings in the case of Ibarvo vs. Barrera, to recover some mules," Bexar Archives, 1793-02-19, e_bx_010163.

51. "Proceedings in the case against Juan Cortés, Sergeant Treviño, and others, charged with smuggling," Bexar Archives, 1792-06-16, e_bx_09847.

52. "Correspondence between Castro and Sierra Gorda, concerning case against Juan Cortés," Bexar Archives, 1792-07-14, e_bx_009879.

53. Bexar Archives, 1792-07-14, e_bx_009879.

54. "Cortés to Muñoz, asking him to write the Commandant General on his behalf, requesting license to go to Santa Rosa for treatment of injured left arm," Bexar Archives, 1793-02-04, e_bx_019374.

55. "Proceedings in the case against Juan Cortés, Sergeant Treviño, and others, charged with smuggling," Bexar Archives, 1792-06-16, e_bx_09847.

56. "Revilla Gigedo to Muñoz, concerning contraband trade of Juan Cortés," Bexar Archives, 1792-09-26, e_bx_009959.

57. "Proceedings and document of the auction of contraband items introduced by Cortés," Bexar Archives, 1792-10-26 to 1792-11-19, e_bx_010003.

58. "Case against Toribio Durán for contraband trade from Nacogdoches," Bexar Archives, 1792-10-19 to 1794-02-22, e_bx_009991.

59. "Ibarvo to Muñoz, denouncing illicit introduction of merchandise from Nacogdoches," Bexar Archives, 1792-12-18, e_bx_10059.

60. "Cortés and Muñoz, forwarding a report on the case of the citizens of Nacogdoches," Bexar Archives, 1793-01-11, e_bx_019351 (e_bx_010120).

61. "Proceedings concerning confiscated good from three people from Nacogdoches," Bexar Archives, 1792-12-27, e_bx_010072.

62. Bexar Archives, 1792-12-27, e_bx_010072. Pages include the *guías* issued to each and the goods they carried.

63. "Cortés and Muñoz, forwarding a report on the case of the citizens of Nacogdoches," Bexar Archives, 1793-01-11, e_bx_019351 (e_bx_010120).

64. "Muñoz to Cortés, concerning articles that should have been seized from the goods introduced to La Bahía by Father Garza and other citizens of Nacogdoches," Bexar Archives, 1793-01-18, e_bx_019362 (e_bx_010131).

65. "Correspondence between Cortés and Muñoz, concerning orders on admission of goods from Nacogdoches," Bexar Archives, 1793-12-06, e_bx_019785 (e_bx_010554).

66. "Correspondence between Cortés and Muñoz, concerning report on trade introduced from Nacogdoches, Bexar Archives, 1793-12-15, e_bx_019795.

Chapter 11

1. "Ibarvo complains of mistreatment, Ibarvo to de Nava, July 12, 1797," Bexar Archives Translations, Volume 223, 92–93.

2. "Fernández to Muñoz, forwarding correspondence and news from Béxar," Bexar Archives, 1793-03-17, e_bx_019415.

3. Governor Manuel Muñoz to Don Pedro de Nava, July 29, 1793, Blake Collection, "Supplement 3," 78.

4. Blake Collection, "Supplement 3," 90.

5. Blake Collection, "Supplement 3," 80.

6. Blake Collection, "Supplement 3," 97.

7. Blake Collection, "Supplement 3," 81.

8. Blake Collection, "Supplement 3," 156.

9. "Muñoz to de Nava, reporting de Cordova took command of Nacogdoches on February 21, 1795," Bexar Archives Translations, Volume 206, letter of March 21, 1795, 68.

10. "Three books containing case against Ibarvo, Muñoz to de Nava," Bexar Archives 1793-12-22, Bexar Archives Translations, Volume 188, 195.

11. "Nava to Governor of Texas, returning documents concerning case of Antonio Gil Ibarvo," Bexar Archives, 1795-03-19, e_bx_011047. English translation in Bexar Archives Translations, Volume 188, 113.

12. "Nava to Governor of Texas, reporting desire of Antonio Gil Ibarvo to settle his case," Bexar Archives, 1795-01-15, e_bx_010984. English translation in Blake Collection, "Supplement 3," 164.

13. "Report on Petition of Don Antonio Gil Ybarbo [Ibarvo], Muñoz to de Nava, February 4, 1795," Bexar Archives Translations, Volume 206, 41–44.

14. Bexar Archives Translations, Volume 206, 41–44.

15. Bexar Archives Translations, Volume 206, 41–44.

16. "Nava to Governor of Texas, urging expediency to end the case against Antonio Gil Ibarvo," Bexar Archives, 1795-03-19, e_bx_011048. English translation in Bexar Archives Translations, Volume 207, 113.

17. "Ibarvo's urging for completion of his case, Muñoz to de Nava, March 15, 1795," Blake Collection, "Supplement 3," 196–97.

18. Examination of seven witnesses in Ibarvo matter, Muñoz to de Nava, May 11, 1795, Bexar Archives Translations, Volume 206, pp. 82-83.

19. "Nava to Governor of Texas, urging him to complete Ibarvo's case and to remit it to Chihuahua for sentence, Bexar Archives, 1795-07-15, e_bx_011164. English translation found in Bexar Archives Translations, Volume 209, 106.

20. "Expediente brought by Captain Don Antonio Gil Ybarvo [Ibarvo] requesting the reports issued against his conduct, in order to respond to the charges that resulted from them," 1795-09-30, Bexar Archives Translations, Volume 210, 192–202.

21. "Letter from Nava to Muñoz, ordering him to finalize Ibarvo's case as soon as possible," 1795-12-29, Bexar Archives Translations, Volume 212, 90.

22. "Correspondence between Córdoba and Muñoz, concerning death of María Padilla, wife of Antonio Gil Ibarvo, and discussing settlement of estate," Bexar Archies, 1794-09-24, e_bx_010927. English translation in Bexar Archives Translations, Volume 204, 76–77. Ibarvo's wife died the previous January. Whether the governor knew of the passing of Ibarvo's wife prior to Córdoba's letter is not known.

23. "Nava to Governor of Texas, granting permission for marriage of Antonio Gil Ibarvo to María Guadalupe de Herrera," Bexar Archives, 1796-01-25, e_bx_001408. English translation in Bexar Archives Translations, Volume 214, 45. Ibarvo was notified of Nava's approval by letter dated February 20, 1796.

24. "Proceedings in the case brought against Don Antonio Gil Ybarbo [Ibarvo], Muñoz and Amador to de Nava," 1796-03-14, Béxar Archives Translations, Volume 213, Part 1, 83–84.

25. "Nava to Muñoz, and Amador, announcing that proceedings in Antonio Gil Ibarvo's case have been forwarded to Assessor General," Bexar Archives, 1796-04-04, e_bx _011473. English translation found in Bexar Archives Translations, Volume 215, 46.

26. "Proceedings concerning Nava's decision in the Gil Ibarvo case, Bexar Archives, 1796-09-15, e_bx_011624. English translation is found in Béxar Archives Translations, Volume 218, 19–20. Somewhat strangely, there is a letter from Nava to Muñoz dated September 4 where Nava again urged Muñoz to speed up the proceedings, even though the onus was on Nava to make a final decision. Letter is found in Bexar Archives Translations, Volume 218, 4.

27. Per John Wheat, translator for the Béxar Archives, the phrase in Spanish is *fenecida governativamente. Fenecida* means concluded; *governativamente* means governmentally, which he opted to translate as administratively.

28. "Nava to Governor of Texas, retiring Antonio Gil Ibarvo from military service,"

Bexar Archive, 1796-09-15, e_bx_011625. English translation in Bexar Archives Translations, Volume 218, 4.

29. H. Sophie Burton, "'To Establish a Stock Farm for the Raising of Mules, Horses, Horned Cattle, Sheep, and Hogs': The Role of Spanish Bourbon Louisiana in the Establishment of Vacheries along the Louisiana-Texas Borderland, 1766–1803," *The Southwestern Historical Quarterly* 109, no. 1 (July 2005): 128.

30. "Nava to Governor of Texas, acknowledging receipt of José María Guadiana's dossier and promotion request," Bexar Archives, 1796-05-16, _bx_011516. English translation found in Béxar Archives Translations, Volume 216, Nava to Muñoz, 13. See also, "Muñoz to Fernández, instructing him to give the command of Nacogdoches to Guadiana and to move to Béxar," Bexar Archives 1796-09-25, e_bx_011637. English translation in Bexar Archives Translations, Volume 218, 44.

31. "Guadiana charged with command of Nacogdoches, Muñoz to de Nava, November 21, 1796," Blake Collection, Supplement 3, 311–12. Blake cites "Governor's Letter Book" from January 4, 1796, to July 10, 1799.

32. "Inventory of articles turned over to Guadiana by Fernández," Bexar Archives, 1796-10-15, e_bx-011654. English translations in Bexar Archives Translations, Volume 218, 67–70.

33. "Guadiana to Muñoz, reporting that Antonio Gil Ibarvo will be returned his property," Bexar Archives, 1796-11-23, e_bx_011698. English translation found in Bexar Archives Translations, Volume 218, 135.

34. "Proceedings concerning Antonio Gil Ibarvo's request for recovering forfeited property," Bexar Archives, 1796-11-15, e_bx_011682. English translation in Bexar Archives Translations, Volume 218, "Muñoz to Cortes," pdf 138–39.

35. "Proceedings brought by Don Antonio Gil Ybarvo [Ibarvo] regarding receipt of the property held in the possession of Captain Don Juan Cortés as a result of the seizure that he made of it in Nacogdoches," 1796-12-02, Béxar Archives Translations, Volume 218, 110–16.

36. Bexar Archives Translations, Volume 218, 113.

37. "Ibarvo not to reside again in Nacogdoches, Muñoz to de Nava, November 29, 1796," Bexar Archives Translations, Volume 218, 140.

38. Bexar Archives Translations, Volume 218, 140.

39. "Don Antt[oni]o Gil Ybarbo, Spanish, age 64 years, married to Guadalupe de Herrera, Spanish, age 34 years. He has a son of 12 years. He has 7 slaves, including two females, the 1 of 40 years, the 2nd of 30, the 3rd of 19, the 4th of 9, the 5th [female] of 60, [MS: no entry for 6th] and the 7th [female] of 2 months. He has 8 servants, 7 single, M, aged 70, 50, 40, 30, 34, 29, and 28 years, another married to Rosa Lara, [both] coyotes, the 1 of 32 years and the 2 [female] of 27, with a son of 12 years." See "1797 census report by families," Bexar Archives, 1797-12-31, e_bx_012198. English translation in Bexar Archives Translations, Volume 228, 93–115.

40. Lyle N. McAlister, *The "Fuero Militar" in New Spain: 1764–1800* (Gainesville: University of Florida Press, 2012), 9.

41. "Ibarvo complains of mistreatment, Ibarvo to de Nava, July 12, 1797," Bexar Archives Translations, Volume 223, 92–93.

42. "Repeated orders that Ibarvo receive his assets, de Nava to Muñoz, August 8, 1798," Bexar Archives Translations, Volume, 224, 61.

43. "Nava to Muñoz, ordering him not to prevent Antonio Gil Ibarvo from leaving the province," Bexar Archives, 1798-10-17, e_bx_012276. English translation in Bexar Archives Translations, Volume 213, part 1, 252.

44. "Gil Ibarvo to Commandant General, asking permission to go to Nacogdoches to collect his property," Bexar Archives, 1798-08-22, e_bx_012378. English translation in Bexar Archives Translations, Volume 213, 41.

45. "Nava to Governor of Texas, forwarding Antonio Gil Ibarvo's petition requesting license to go to Nacogdoches to attend personal business," Bexar Archives, 1798-09-18, e_bx_012408. English translation in Bexar Archives Translations, Volume 231, 90.

46. Permission for Ibarvo to collect property, de Nava to Muñoz, June 12, 1799. English translation in Béxar Archives Translations, Volume 213, part 1, 291.

47. "Nava to Muñoz, ordering him not to prevent Antonio Gil Ibarvo from leaving the province," Bexar Archives, 1798-04-17, e_bx_012276. English translation in Béxar Archives Translations, Volume 229, 128.

48. "Muñoz to Cordero, discussing impossibility of restraining Indian hostilities," Bexar Archives, 1798-05-29, e_bx_012315. English translation in Bexar Archives Translation, Volume 230, 44–45.

49. "Nava to Governor of Texas, asking if his health forbids the prompt performance of his job," Bexar Archives, 1796-11-01, e_bx_011673. English translation in Bexar Archives Translations, Volume 218, 98.

50. "Nava to Muñoz, reporting plans to relieve Muñoz of part of his duties which are to be assumed by Elguézabal," Bexar Archives, 1798-08-17, e_bx_012373. English translation in Béxar Archives Translations, Volume 231, 33.

51. "Muñoz thanks de Nava for his retirement, Muñoz to de Nava, January 30, 1797," English translation in Bexar Archives Translations, Volume, 213, Part 1, 152–54.

52. "Governor explains the reasons he had not to allow Ibarvo to leave Béxar, Muñoz to de Nava," Bexar Archives Translations, Volume 213, part 1, 218–22. The following details are from this lengthy letter.

53. "Actions and unrest in Nacogdoches caused by Ibarvo kin, Muñoz to de Nava, November 27, 1796," Bexar Archives Translations, Volume 213, part 1, 261–62. See also, "Muñoz to de Nava, January 22, 1799," 1799-01-22, Munoz to Nava, Béxar Archives Translations, Volume 213, part 1, 269–71.

54. Carla Gerona, "With a Song in Their Hands: Incendiary Décimas from the Texas and Louisiana Borderlands during a Revolutionary Age." *Early American Studies: An Interdisciplinary Journal* 12, no. 1 (2014): 93–142. https://doi.org/10.1353/eam.2014.0002.

55. "Retirement granted to Captain Don Juan Cortès, Cortès to de Nava, June 13, 1798," Bexar Archives Translations, Volume 213, part 1, 224.

56. "Mismanagement of funds at La Bahía, Arispe to Muñoz, February 27, 1797," Bexar Archives Translations, Volume 220, 1–2.

57. "Mismanagement of funds at La Bahía, de Nava to Cortès, February 17, 1797" Bexar Archives Translations, Volume 220, 15.

58. "Mismanagement of funds at La Bahía, De Nava to Elguezabal, April 5, 1797," Bexar Archives Translations, Volume 221, p. 12.

59. Bexar Archives Translations, Volume 222, June 13, 1797

60. "Mismanagement of funds at La Bahía, Elguézabal to de Nava, June 25, 1797," Bexar Archives Translations, Volume 221, 33–4. The goods to be returned for auction also included a watch belonging to Espadas that Cortès had in his possession.

61. "Report of the removal from active duty of Captain Cortès, Elguézabal to de Nava, June 13, 1797," Bexar Archives Translations, Volume 221, 50.

62. "Request to retire in Nacogdoches, Cortès to Elguézabal, June 5, 1798," Bexar Archives Translations, Volume 221, 51.

63. "Cortès prevented from retiring in Nacogdoches, de Nava to Elguezabal, July 20, 1798," Bexar Archives Translations, Volume 230, 101.

64. Bexar Archives Translations, Volume 230, 101.

65. "Lack of horses, Cortes to Munoz, April 7, 1797," Bexar Archives Translations, Volume 221, 16.

66. "Cortes departs La Bahía, Captain on assignment in La Bahía," Bexar Archives Translations, Volume 221, 32.

Chapter 12

1. "Guadiana to Muñoz, reporting that all is quiet in Nacogdoches," Bexar Archives, 1796-12-25, e_bx_011721. English translation in Bexar Archives Translations, Volume 219, 30.

2. Castañeda, *Our Catholic Heritage*, vol. 5, 205.

3. "Nava to Governor of Texas, refusing to permit Nolan to introduce goods into Texas," Bexar Archives, 1798-03-20, e_bx_012253. English translation in Bexar Archives Translations, Bexar Archives, Volume 229, 84.

4. "Guadiana to Muñoz, discussing the case of Gil Ibarvo's property, in which Capurán, Belanger and Barr are involved, and other details," Bexar Archives, 1799-04-10, e_bx_012600. English translation in Bexar Archives Translations, Volume 234, 13–14.

5. "Nava to Governor of Texas, insisting on having Moral as commandant of Nacogdoches at this time, and Muñoz" proposal letter," Bexar Archives, 1799-05-14, e_bx _012625. English translation in Bexar Archives Translations, Volume 234, 48.

6. McReynolds, *Family Life*, 14.

7. Vallejo was appointed priest in the town of Nuestra Señora del Pilar de Nacogdoches and went on to become president of the Zacatecan missions.

8. "Father Vallejo to Guadiana, complains about unfaithful, February 20, 1797," Bexar Archives Translations, Volume 220, 17.

9. Bexar Archives Translations, Volume 220, 17.

10. "Guadiana to Father Vallejo, February 26, 1792," Béxar Archives Translations, Volume 220, 29.

11. "Answer to doubts regarding the limits of Texas and Louisiana, Muñoz to Guadiana, March 25, 1797," Béxar Archives Translations, Volume 220, 31.

12. Galan, *Los Adaes*, 212.

13. University of North Texas Libraries, The Portal to Texas History, "Description of Nacogdoches District, from August 1, 1804," *San Antonio Texan*, July 5, 1855, 1. https://texashistory.unt.edu/ark:/67531/metapth232656/m1/1/zoom/?q=atoyaque&resolution=2&lat=4335.27166498l508&lon=2976.176241359014. See also Matthew Babcock, "Nacogdoches Census Report Project," Center for Regional Heritage Research (website), Stephen F. Austin State University, accessed July 15, 2022, https://www.sfasu.edu/heritagecenter/100.asp.

14. "Fernández report of Frenchmen residing in Nacogdoches," Bexar Archives, 1796-06-30, e_bx_011547. English translation in Blake Collection, Volume 18, 322–24.

15. Mattie Austin Hatcher, "Conditions in Texas Affecting the Colonization Problem, 1795–1801." *Southwestern Historical Quarterly* 25, no. 2 (October 1921): 90–2. https://doi.org/https://www.jstor.org/stable/30234823.

16. Hatcher, "Conditions in Texas," 93.

17. Gustine Courson Weaver. "My Philip Nolan Scrapbook," University of North Texas Libraries, The Portal to Texas History, crediting UNT Libraries Special Collections, https://texashistory.unt.edu/ark:/67531/metadc304851/m1/1/, accessed December 15, 202.1

18. Castañeda, *Our Catholic Heritage*, vol. 5, 227.

19. "Nava to Governor of Texas, ordering the arrest of Felipe Nolan," Bexar Archives, 1800-08-08, e_bx_013006. English translation in Bexar Archives Translations, Volume 240, 15–16.

20. "Certified copy of proceedings concerning registration of Guillermo Barr's iron brand," Bexar Archives, 1798-09-03, e_bx_012393. English Translation in Bexar Archives Translation, Volume 231, 71. See also, "Permission for Barr to export mules, October 30, 1799," Bexar Archives Translations, Volume 235, 62.

21. For more about Barr & Davenport see La Vere, "Barr, Davenport, Murphy and Smith," and Hatcher, "Conditions in Texas," 95–97. See also J. Villasana Haggard, "House of Barr and Davenport," *Southwestern Historical Quarterly* 49, no. 1 (July 1945): 66–88. https://doi.org/https://www.jstor.org/stable/30240618.

22. Haggard, "House of Barr," 71–72.

23. Haggard, "House of Barr," 75.

24. Gerona, "With a Song in Their Hands," 96.

25. "Auction of Ibarvo's slaves and livestock to Micheli, June 14, 1796," Bexar Archives Translations, Volume 210, 24–31.

26. "Micheli loans money for troops to Guadiana, April 3, 1798," Bexar Archives Translations, Volume 229, 114.

27. "Proceedings concerning Vicente Micheli's proposal to use cotton gin at Béxar," Bexar Archives, 1801-04-17, e_bx_013219. English translation in Bexar Archives Translations, Volume 242, 106–07.

28. Castañeda, *Our Catholic Heritage*, vol. 5, 221.

29. Castañeda, *Our Catholic Heritage*, vol. 5, 208.

30. "Proclamation of the Agents of the King of Spain for Surrendering Louisiana to Frances, Dated New Orlans, May 18th, 1803," *Cobbett's Weekly Political Register*,

November 5, 1803, Volume IV edition, sec. No. 18, 664–66. Many thanks to Bob Skiles for this source.

31. Thomas Maitland Marshall, *A History of the Western Boundary of the Louisiana Purchase, 1819–1841* (Berkeley: University of California Press, 1914), 10.

32. Elizabeth A. H. John, "The Riddle of Mapmaker Juan Pedro Walker," in *Essays on the History of North American Discovery and Exploration*, eds. Stanley H. Palmer and Dennis Reinhartz (College Station: Texas A&M University Press, 1988), 113.

33. For more about Trinidad de Salcedo, see Bradley Folsom, "Trinidad De Salcedo: A Forgotten Villa in Colonial Texas, 1806-1813," *East Texas Historical Journal* 52, no. 2 (October 2014): 49–78, https://scholarworks.sfasu.edu/ethj/vol52/iss2/9/; Castañeda, *Our Catholic Heritage*, vol. 5. Many thanks to Bob Skiles for his extensive personal research into Trinidad.

34. "The Governor of the province of Texas sets forth his opinion and the ideas that occur to him touching the establishment of settlements and the construction of the fort proposed by Captain Ugarte," Juan Bautista Elguazabal to commandant general, January 18, 1804, Blake Collections, "Supplement 4," 249–52. Blake cites the Bexar Archives, "Draft in Letter Book," January 4, 1804, to December 19, 1804.

35. Castañeda, *Our Catholic Heritage*, vol. 5, 253.

36. Folsom, "Trinidad De Salcedo," 52.

37. Folsom, "Trinidad De Salcedo," 53.

38. Gerald Eugene Poyo, *Tejano Journey: 1770 1850*. (Austin: University of Texas Press, 1996), 17.

39. Dan L. Flores, Thomas Freeman, and Peter Custis, *Southern Counterpart to Lewis and Clark: The Freeman and Custis Expedition of 1806* (Norman: University of Oklahoma Press, 2002).

40. J. Edward Townes, "Invisible Lines: The Life and Death of a Borderland." (PhD dissertation, Texas Christian University, May 10, 2008). Townes is citing a letter from Turner to Claiborne on November 21, 1804; Territorial Papers, Volume IX, 335–7.

41. Castañeda, *Our Catholic Heritage*, vol. 5, 254.

42. Townes, "Invisible Lines," 149

43. Townes, "Invisible Lines," 150.

44. Ernest Wallace, David M. Vigness, and George B Ward, eds. *Documents of Texas History* (Austin: Texas State Historical Association, 2002). Found on the University of North Texas Libraries, The Portal to Texas History website, https://texashistory.unt.edu/ark:/67531/metapth296840/m1/50/, accessed December 23, 2021. The phrase "inhospitable wilds" has a sonorous elegance that has attracted this author over several years.

45. Betje Klier Black and Pavie Théodore, *Pavie in the Borderlands: The Journey of Théodore Pavie to Louisiana and Texas, 1829-1830, Including Portions of His Souvenirs Atlantiques* (Baton Rouge: Louisiana State University Press, 2000), 28.

46. "Detachment of Nacogdoches, Report showing the number of men in the force of this detachment and the duties in which they have been engaged to date," José Joaquín Ugarte, January 1, 1805, Bexar Archives, non-digitized translation provided by John Wheat, Briscoe Center.

47. "Father Mariano Sosa to Governor Manuel Salcedo, May 26, 1810," Blake Collection, "Supplement 7," 171–77. Blake cites the Bexar Archives.

48. Timothy Seiter, "How Best to Retrieve Stolen Horses: The Transformation of Spanish-Indian Diplomacy in Late Eighteenth-Century Texas," (unpublished manuscript, 2022). See also Sidney B. Brinckerhoff and Odie B. Faulk, *Lancers for the King* (Tucson: Arizona Historical Foundation, 1965), 19.

49. "Father Mariano Sosa to Governor Manuel Salcedo, May 26, 1810", Blake Collection, "Supplement 7," 171–77.

50. "Report of the Jurisdiction of this Village of Nacogdoches directed to the Sir Governor of the Province of Texas José María Guadiana to Governor Manuel Salcedo," July 22, Blake Collection, "Supplement 7," 208–14.

51. "Guadiana to Elguézabal, reporting steps taken to prevent illegal exportation of horses from Texas," Bexar Archives, 1802-02-01, e_bx_013490. English translation in Bexar Archives Translations, Volume 242, 75.

52. Letter from José María Guadiana to Pedro Lopez Prieto, October 21, 1809, Blake Collection, Supplement 7, p. 15.

53. "Letter from José Antonio Cuellar to Pedro López Prieto, January 17, 1810," Blake Collection, "Supplement 7," 25–27.

54. "Letter from Pedro López Prieto to Governor Manuel Salcedo, May 31, 1810," Blake Collection, "Supplement 7," 186–87.

55. Sjoberg, "Bidai Indians of Southeast Texas" (master's thesis, University of Texas, January 1951), 38.

56. F. Todd Smith, *From Dominance to Disappearance: The Indians of Texas and the near Southwest, 1786-1859* (Lincoln: University of Nebraska Press, 2009), 72.

57. Smith, *From Dominance to Disappearance*, 138.

58. Sjoberg, "Bidai," 40.

59. Castañeda, Our Catholic Heritage, vol. 5, 431.

60. Jesús "Frank" de la Teja, "Mexican War of Independence," *Handbook of Texas*, Texas State Historical Association, accessed December 25, 2021, https://www.tshaonline.org/handbook/entries/mexican-war-of-independence.

61. Félix D. Almaráz, *Tragic Cavalier Governor Manuel Salcedo of Texas, 1808-1813*, College Station: Texas A&M University Press, 1991), 124.

62. Ed Bradley, *"We Never Retreat": Filibustering Expeditions into Spanish Texas, 1812–1822.* (College Station: Texas A&M University Press, 2015) xiii.

63. Almaraz, *Tragic Cavalier.* Citations from January 13, 1812 (p. 131); March 4, 1812 (p. 135); March 17, 1812 (p. 138).

64. Bradley, *We Never Retreat*, 40.

65. Jose Antonio Pichardo, *El Nuevo Mexico y Tierras Adyacentes Mapa Levantado Para La Demarcacion De Los Limites De Los Dominios Españoles y De Los Estados Unidos Por El P.d. Jose Pichardo Quien Lo Dedica Al Exmo. Sor. D. Francisco Xavier Venegas Virrey De Esta N.E. &. Año De 1811*, Geography and Map Division, The Library of Congress, Washington, DC, accessed July 15, 2022, https://www.loc.gov/item/2016588016/. More Information about this map and others is found in Jack Jackson, "Father José María De Jesús Puelles and the Maps of Pichardo's Document 74," *Southwestern*

Historical Quarterly 91, no. 3 (January 1988): 317–47, https://doi.org/http://www.jstor.org/stable/30237036.

66. Almaráz, *Tragic Cavalier*, 147.

67. Page, *Prairiedom*, 82.

68. George Avery and Connie Hodges, *Summary Report for Camino Real De Los Tejas Oral History Project from the Sabine River to the Angelina River, Texas, Phase 1: Data Recovery from Elderly Informants*, Center for Regional Heritage Research (Nacogdoches: Stephen F. Austin State University, September 2010), 47. https://www.sfasu.edu/heritagecenter/documents/Oral_History-Phase_I_report_9-2010-all.pdf.

69. Avery and Hodges, *Summary Report*, 48. Mountain Cemetery is at GPS latitude 31.5997030, longitude -94.4192620.

70. Avery and Hodges, *Summary Report*, 48.

71. Samuel Truett, *Fugitive Landscapes: The Forgotten History of the U.S.-Mexico Borderlands* (New Haven, CT: Yale University Press, 2008), 8–9.

72. "Expediente on Plots Against the Government," Declaration of José Miguel Crow, Blake Collection, "Supplement 7," 322–37. Thanks to James Bernsen for bringing this back to present awareness in his presentation for the 2021 Texas State Historical Association.

BIBLIOGRAPHY

Abernethy, Francis E. "Locating the Eyes of Father Margil." *East Texas Historical Journal* 42, no. 1 (March 2004): 3–9.

Abernethy, Francis E. "The Flow of the Neches." *East Texas Historical Journal* 46, no. 1 (March 2008): 3–10.

Adam, Louis A. *Adam's Directory of Points and Landings on Rivers and Bayous: In the States of Alabama, Arkansas, Florida, Georgia, Indiana, Illinois, Kentucky, Iowa, Louisiana, Minnesota, Mississippi, Missouri, Nebraska, Ohio, Tennessee, Texas, and Wisconsin*. New Orleans: W. L. Murray, 1877.

"Alamo Plan." The Alamo. Alamo Trust, Inc.; Texas General Land Office, 2020. https://www.thealamo.org/support/alamo-plan.

Almaráz, Félix D. *Tragic Cavalier Governor Manuel Salcedo of Texas, 1808–1813*. College Station: Texas A&M University Press, 1991.

"Alonso De León's Last Expedition into Texas in 1690." The Portal to Texas History. University of North Texas Libraries. Accessed June 23, 2022. https://texashistory.unt.edu/ark:/67531/metapth493023/citation/#top.

Alvarez, Jose Manuel Serrano. "Ramón De Castro." Real Academia de la Historia. Accessed February 14, 2022. https://dbe.rah.es/biografias/39235/ramon-de-castro.

"Ashes of Pioneer Texas Disturbed, Burying Ground Discovered Under Old Court House at Nacogdoches." *Tyler Courier-Times*, October 21, 1911.

Aten, Lawrence E. *Indians of the Upper Texas Coast*. United Kingdom: Academic Press, 1983.

Atwood, W. L. "Texas Collection." *Southwestern Historical Quarterly* 56, no. 4 (April 1953): 560–61. https://doi.org/https://texashistory.unt.edu/ark:/67531/metapth101145.

Austin, Stephen F. *Mapa Topográfico De La Provincia De Texas (1822)*. Geography and Map Division, The Library of Congress, Washington, DC. Accessed June 26, 2022. https://www.loc.gov/item/98687158/.

Avery, George E. *1997 Annual Report for the Los Adaes Station Archaeology Program*. Natchitoches, LA: Dept. of Social Sciences, Northwestern State University, 1996.

Avery, George, and Connie Hodges. *Summary Report for Camino Real De Los Tejas Oral History Project from the Sabine River to the Angelina River, Texas, Phase 1: Data Recovery from Elderly Informants*. Nacogdoches, TX: Center for Regional Heritage Research, Stephen F. Austin State University, September 2010. https://www.sfasu.edu/heritagecenter/documents/Oral_History-Phase_I_report_9–2010-all.pdf.

Avery, George. "Archival Investigations of the People of Los Adaes." *Southern Studies* 7, no. 1 (1996): 65–88.

Babcock, Matthew. *Nacogdoches Census Report Project*. Nacogdoches, TX: Center for Regional Heritage Research, Stephen F. Austin State University. Accessed July 15, 2022. https://www.sfasu.edu/heritagecenter/100.asp.

Babcock, Matthew. "Rethinking the Establecimientos, Why Apaches Settled on Spanish-Run Reservations, 1786–1793." *New Mexico Historical Review* 84, no. 3 (2009): 363–97.

Badger, J. Ryan. "Texas in the Southwestern Fur Trade, 1718–1840." Master's Thesis. Utah State University, 2018. https://digitalcommons.usu.edu/gradreports/1277/.

Baker, Karle Wilson. "Nacogdoches: I. The Indian and Spanish Town." *Southwest Review* 21, no. 1 (October 1935): 1–14. https://doi.org/https://www.jstor.org/stable/43462215.

Ball, Henry F. "Rock Art at Monk's Cave (41RK84), Rusk County Texas." *Bulletin of the Texas Archeological Society* 55 (1984): 153–69. https://doi.org/https://texashistory.unt.edu/ark:/67531/metapth1013889.

Banks, Gabrielle, and St. John Barned-Smith. "Inside the Lucrative Smuggling Operation That Sees Millions of Chinese Cigarettes Pass through Texas." *Houston Chronicle*, June 29, 2021, Local edition, sec. Crime. https://www.houstonchronicle.com/news/houston-texas/crime/article/china-cigarettes-tobacco-trafficking-tx-16281704.php, accessed June 29, 2022.

Barr, Juliana. "Geographies of Power: Mapping Indian Borders in the 'Borderlands' of the Early Southwest." *The William and Mary Quarterly* 68, no. 1 (January 2011): 5–46. https://doi.org/https://www.jstor.org/stable/10.5309/willmaryquar.68.1.0005.

Barr, Juliana. *Peace Came in the Form of a Woman: Indians and Spaniards in the Texas Borderlands*. Chapel Hill: The University of North Carolina Press, 2009.

Barrera-Enderle, Alberto. "Smuggling across the Border: Clandestine Trade Relations in Northeastern New Spain, 1808–1821." Translated by Bob D. Skiles. *Fronteras d la Historia* 20, no. 1 (2015): 44–69.

Barrett, Jason W. "The Dimond Knoll Project in Perspective: A New Path for Southeast Texas Prehistory." Report presented to Houston Archaeological Society, March 18, 2021. https://www.youtube.com/watch?v=4KQuS5MNQ68.

Benson, Nettie Lee. "A Governor's Report on Texas in 1809." *Southwestern Historical Quarterly* 71, no. 4 (April 1968): 603–15.

Berlandier, Jean Louis, and John C. Ewers. *The Indians of Texas in 1830*. Washington, DC: Smithsonian Institution Press, 1969.

"Bexar Archives (1717–1836)." Bexar Archives Online. Dolph Briscoe Center for American History. Accessed June 24, 2022. https://briscoecenter.org/projects/bexar-archives-online/.

Black, Betje Klier, and Pavie Théodore. *Pavie in the Borderlands: The Journey of Théodore Pavie to Louisiana and Texas, 1829–1830, Including Portions of His Souvenirs Atlantiques*. Baton Rouge: Louisiana State University Press, 2000.

Black, Mary S. *Secrets in the Dirt: Uncovering the Ancient People of Gault*. College Station: Texas A&M University Press, 2019.

Blake, Robert Bruce. "Bedias Road." *Handbook of Texas*. Texas State Historical Association. Accessed June 19, 2021. https://www.tshaonline.org/handbook/entries/bedias-road.

Blake, Robert Bruce. "Locations of the Early Spanish Missions and Presidio in Nacogdoches County." *Southwestern Historical Quarterly* 41, no. 3 (January 1938): 212–24. https://doi.org/https://www.jstor.org/stable/30235774.

Blake, Robert Bruce. "Robert Bruce Blake Research Collection, Supplements." FamilySearch. Salt Lake City, UT: The Church of Jesus Christ of Latter-Day Saints, 2009. https://www.familysearch.org/search/catalog/1622067.

Blake, Robert Bruce. "Robert Bruce Blake Research Collection." FamilySearch. Salt Lake City, UT: The Church of Jesus Christ of Latter-Day Saints, 2009. https://www.familysearch.org/search/catalog/1622062.

Blount, Lois Foster. "Last of Stone Fort (1902)." *East Texas Digital Archives*. Nacogdoches: Stephen F. Austin State University, 1902. https://digital.sfasu.edu/digital/collection/eastTexRC/id/14181/rec/9.

Bobb, Bernard E. "Bucareli and the Interior Provinces." *Hispanic American Historical Review* 34, no. 1 (February 1954): 20–36. https://doi.org/10.1215/00182168-34.1.20.

Bolton, Herbert E. *Map of Texas and Adjacent Regions in the Eighteenth Century (1915)*. Texas Maps Collection. Texas State Library & Archives Collection. Originally published by the University of California Press, 1915. Accessed June 26, 2022. https://www.tsl.texas.gov/apps/arc/maps/maplookup/01440.

Bolton, Herbert E. "Spanish Activities on the Lower Trinity River, 1746–1771." *Southwestern Historical Quarterly* 16, no. 4 (April 1913): 339–37.

Bolton, Herbert E. "The Native Tribes about the East Texas Missions." *The Quarterly of the Texas State Historical Association* 11, no. 4 (April 1908): 249–76. https://doi.org/https://www.jstor.org/stable/30242560.

Bolton, Herbert E. "The Spanish Abandonment and Reoccupation of East Texas, 1773–1779." *The Quarterly of the Texas State Historical Association* 9, no. 2 (October 1905): 67–137.

Bolton, Herbert Eugene, and Athanase de Mézières. *Athanase De Mézières and the Louisiana-Texas Frontier 1768–1780: Documents Published for the First Time, from the Original Spanish and French Manuscripts, Chiefly in the Archives of Mexico and Spain (2 Vols)*. Cleveland, OH: A. H. Clark, 1914.

Bolton, Herbert Eugene. *Guide to Materials for the History of the United States in the Principal Archives of Mexico*. New York: HardPress Publishing, 2012.

Bolton, Herbert Eugene. *Texas in the Middle Eighteenth Century: Studies in Spanish Colonial History and Administration*. Berkeley: University of California Press, 1915.

Bolton, Herbert Eugene. *The Hasinais: Southern Caddoans as Seen by Earliest Europeans*. Norman: University of Oklahoma Press, 2002.

Bonnell, George W. *Topographical Description of Texas: to Which Is Added, an Account of the Indian Tribes*. Austin, TX: Clark, Wing, & Brown, 1840.

Bradley, Ed. *"We Never Retreat": Filibustering Expeditions into Spanish Texas, 1812–1822*. College Station: Texas A&M University Press, 2015.

Brannum, Julianna, Jeffrey Brown, and David Hartstein, producers. *Through the Repellent Fence*. Fence Film, LLC, 2017. https://www.imdb.com/title/tt6524696/ .

Brinckerhoff, Sidney B., and Odie B. Faulk. *Lancers for the King*. Tucson: Arizona Historical Foundation, 1965.

Brooks, Lisa T. *The Common Pot: The Recovery of Native Space in the Northeast*. Minneapolis: University of Minnesota Press, 2008.

Brune, Gunnar M. *Springs of Texas*. College Station: Texas A&M University Press, 2002.

Buckley, Eleanor Claire. "The Aguayo Expedition into Texas and Louisiana, 1719–1722." *The Quarterly of the Texas State Historical Association* 15, no. 1 (July 1911): 1–65.

Buenger, Walter Louis, and León Arnoldo De. *Beyond Texas through Time: Breaking Away from Past Interpretations*. College Station: Texas A&M University Press, 2011.

Bugbee, Lester Gladstone. *The Real Saint-Denis*. Austin: Texas State Historical Association, 1908.

Burch, Marvin C. "The Indigenous Indians of the Lower Trinity Area of Texas." *Southwestern Historical Quarterly* 60, no. 1 (July 1956): 36–52.

Burton, H. Sophie, and F. Todd Smith. *Colonial Natchitoches: A Creole Community on the Louisiana-Texas Frontier*. College Station: Texas A&M University Press, 2008.

Burton, H. Sophie. "Vagabonds along the Spanish Louisiana-Texas Frontier, 1769–1803: 'Men Who Are Evil, Lazy, Gluttonous, Drunken, Libertinous, Dishonest, Mutinous, Etc. Etc. Etc—and Those Are Their Virtues.'" *Southwestern Historical Quarterly* 113, no. 4 (April 2010): 438–67. https://doi.org/10.1353/swh.2010.0083.

Burton, H. Sophie. "'To Establish a Stock Farm for the Raising of Mules, Horses, Horned Cattle, Sheep, and Hogs': The Role of Spanish Bourbon Louisiana in the Establishment of Vacheries along the Louisiana-Texas Borderland, 1766—1803." *Southwestern Historical Quarterly* 109, no. 1 (July 2005): 98–132. https://doi.org/https://www.jstor.org/stable/40495623.

Burton, Helen Sophie. "Databases for 'Family and Economy in Frontier Louisiana: Colonial Natchitoches, 1714–1803." PhD dissertation, Texas Christian University, 2002.

Byrd, Kathleen M. *Colonial Natchitoches: Outpost of Empires*. Philadelphia, PA: Xlibris, 2008.

Caddo Nation. "Caddo Nation." Caddo Nation website. https://mycaddonation.com/. Accessed July 28, 2024.

Cashion, Ty. *Lone Star Mind: Reimagining Texas History*. Norman: University of Oklahoma Press, 2018.

Cast, Robert, and Timothy K. Perttula. "The Long-Term Looting of Caddo Indian Sites on Federal Property in Northeastern Texas." *Cultural Resource Management* 25, no. 2 (2002): 26–28. https://doi.org/http://npshistory.com/newsletters/crm/crm-v25n2.pdf.

Castañeda, Carlos E. *Our Catholic Heritage in Texas, in Seven Volumes, 1519 to 1936*. Edited by Paul J. Foik. Austin, TX: Von Boeckman-Jones Company, 1936.

"The Castillo De San Marcos National Monument Digital Documentation and

Interpretation Program—DHHC: Digital Heritage & Humanities Collections." Digital Heritage and Humanities Collections, University of South Florida. February 17, 2021. https://dhhc.lib.usf.edu/project/the-castillo-de-san-marcos-national-monument-digital-documentation-and-interpretation-program/.

Céliz, Francisco. *Diary of the Alarcón Expedition into Texas, 1718–1719*. Los Angeles: Quivira Society, 1967.

Chardon, Roland. "The Elusive Spanish League: A Problem of Measurement in Sixteenth-Century New Spain." *Hispanic American Historical Review* 60, no. 2 (1980): 294–302. https://doi.org/10.1215/00182168-60.2.294.

Chen, Shawna, and Russell Contreras. "Native American Vaccination Rates Skyrocket as Tribes Help Others despite Internet Challenges." *Axios*, March 11, 2021. https://www.axios.com/2021/03/11/covid-vaccine-native-americans-internet-access.

Chipman, Donald E. "In Search of Cabeza De Vaca's Route Across Texas: An Historiographical Survey." *Southwestern Historical Quarterly* 91, no. 2 (October 1987): 127–48. https://doi.org/https://www.jstor.org/stable/30240015.

Chipman, Donald E. *Spanish Texas, 1519–1821*. Austin: University of Texas Press, 2010.

Chipman, Donald E., and Harriett Denise Joseph. *Notable Men and Women of Spanish Texas*. Austin: University of Texas Press, 2015.

Chipman, Donald Eugene, and Harriet Denise Joseph. *Explorers and Settlers of Spanish Texas*. Austin: University of Texas Press, 2015.

Clark Jr., John W. "Acts of Foundation, Salcedo (Appendix 2)" in *A Texas Legacy: The Old San Antonio Road and the Caminos Reales, A Tricentennial History, 1691–1991*. Edited by A. Joachim McGraw, John W. Clark Jr., and Elizabeth A. H. Robbins. 369–73. Austin: Texas State Department of Highways and Public Transportation, 1991.

Clark, Robert Carlton. *The Beginnings of Texas, 1684–1718. Vol. 98*. Bulletin of the University of Texas. Austin: University of Texas, 1907.

Clavey, Bruce. *To the Republic*. Austin: Bruce Clavey, 2020.

Codinach Guadalupe Jiménez. *The Hispanic World, 1492–1898: A Guide to Photo Reproduced Manuscripts from Spain in the Collections of the United States, Guam and Puerto Rico*. Washington, DC: Library of Congress, 1994.

Colton, J. H. "History of Texas from Its First Settlement in 1685 to Its Annexation to the United States in 1846, Map of Spanish-Texas." The Portal to Texas History. University of North Texas Libraries. Accessed June 26, 2022. https://texashistory.unt.edu/ark:/67531/metapth20778/.

Congressional Serial Set, House Documents, Vol. 19. "Report on Reexamination of Project for the Improvement of Trinity River, Tex." Document No. 989 (1921).

Corbin, James E. "Retracing the Camino De Los Tejas from the Trinity River to Los Adaes: New Insights into East Texas History" in *A Texas Legacy: the Old San Antonio Road and the Camino Reales; a Tricentennial History, 1691–1991*. 191–219. Austin: Texas State Department of Highways and Public Transportation, 1991.

Corbin, James E., Arlan Kalina, and Thomas C. Alex. *Mission Dolores De Los Ais:*

Archaeological Investigations of an Early Spanish Colonial Mission, San Augustine County, Texas. Nacogdoches: Stephen F. Austin State University, 1980.

"Corridor: Interstate 69 (I-69) Texas to Michigan." Corridors of the Future—Fact Sheet. US Department of Transportation, Federal Highway Administration. Accessed June 25, 2022. https://www.fhwa.dot.gov/pressroom/fsi69.cfm.

Cox, Isaac Joslin. *The Louisiana-Texas Frontier.* Austin: Texas State Historical Association, 1906.

Crocket, G. L. *Two Centuries in East Texas*. Dallas: South West Press, 1962.

Cromwell, Jesse Levis. "Covert Commerce: A Social History of Contraband Trade in Venezuela, 1701–1789," PhD dissertation, University of Texas at Austin, 2012.

Cromwell, Jesse. *The Smugglers' World: Illicit Trade and Atlantic Communities in Eighteenth-Century Venezuela*. Williamsburg, VA: Omohundro Institute of Early American History and Culture, 2018.

Crook, Wilson "Dub." "Liberty County: A Major Trade Entrepot for Southeast Texas." Report presented to Houston Archaeological Society, September 20, 2020. https://www.youtube.com/watch?v=lcfIUFZqm9Y.

Crook, Wilson W. *The Peopling of the Americas: A Brief Synopsis on the Status of the Current Debate with a Focus on North America*. Houston: Houston Archeological Society, 2020.

Cubas, Antonio Garcia. *Diccionario geográfico, Historico y Biografico De Los Estados Unidos Mexicanos. 1–5. Vol. 1–5.* Mexico: Antigua Imprenta de Murguia, 1888.

Curtis, Gregory. "The Reasonable Cannibals." *Texas Monthly*, 1988.

de Pagès, Monsieur. *Travels Round the World: In the Years 1767, 1768, 1769, 1770, 1771.* London: Printed for J. Murray, 1791.

Deans-Smith, Susan. *Bureaucrats, Planters, and Workers the Making of the Tobacco Monopoly in Bourbon Mexico.* Austin: University of Texas Press, 2010.

Denning, Trevor. *The Playing-Cards of Spain: A Guide for Historians and Collectors.* London: Cygnus Arts, 1996.

Derbes, Brett, ed. *Handbook of Texas*. Texas State Historical Association. Accessed June 26, 2022. https://www.tshaonline.org/handbook.

Derrick, Sharon M., and Diane E. Wilson. "The Effects of Epidemic Disease on Caddo Demographic Structure." *Bulletin of the Texas Archaeological Society* 72 (2001): 91–103.

Diaz, George T. *Border Contraband: A History of Smuggling across the Rio Grande.* Austin: University of Texas Press, 2015.

Diaz, George T., and David-James Gonzalez. "Interview with George T. Diaz, 'Border Contraband: A History of Smuggling across the Rio Grande.'" People and Places. New Books Network, November 8, 2016. https://newbooksnetwork.com/george-t-diaz-border-contraband-a-history-of-smuggling-across-the-rio-grande-u-of-texas-press-2015/.

Dumble, Edwin T. *Report on the Brown Coal and Lignite of Texas: Character, Formation, Occurrence, and Fuel Uses*. Austin, TX: Ben C. Jones & Co. State Printers, 1892.

Dumble, Edwin T. The *Geology of East Texas*. Austin: University of Texas, 1918.

Dumble, Edwin T., William Kennedy, Theo B. Comstock, and W. H. Von Streeruwitz. *Second Annual Report of the Geological Survey of Texas, 1890*. Austin, TX: Geological Survey of Texas, 1891.

Edward, David B. *The History of Texas, or, the Emigrant's, Farmer's, and Politician's Guide to the Character, Climate, Soil and Productions of That Country*. Cincinnati, OH: J. A. James and Company, 1836.

Comprehensive Management Plan/Environmental Assessment. El Camino Real De Los Tejas National Historic Trail. Santa Fe, NM: National Trails Intermountain Region, National Park Service, 2011.

"El Camino Real De Los Tejas National Historic Trail, Maps." National Parks Service. U. S. Department of the Interior. Accessed June 25, 2022. https://www.nps.gov/elte/planyourvisit/maps.htm.

"Elguezabal, Juan Bautista (1741–1805)." *Handbook of Texas*. Texas State Historical Association, January 1, 1995. https://www.tshaonline.org/handbook/entries/elguezabal-juan-bautista.

Engstrand, Iris H. W. "How Cruel Were the Spaniards?" *Organization of American Historians Magazine of History* 14, no. 4 (2000): 12–15. https://doi.org/10.1093/maghis/14.4.12.

Epperson, Jean L. *Lost Spanish Towns: Atascosito and Trinidad De Salcedo*. Woodville, TX: Dogwood Press, 1997.

Ericson, Carolyn Reeves, and Linda Ericson Devereaux. *Antonio Gil Y'Barbo: Father of Nacogdoches*. Nacogdoches, TX: Carolyn Reeves Ericson, 2015.

Ericson, Carolyn Reeves. *Nacogdoches—Gateway to Texas: A Biographical Directory*. Nacogdoches, TX: Ericson Books, 2003.

"Finding Aid to the Archivo General De Indias Records: Spanish Exploration and Settlement Related Materials, circa 1530-circa 1820." Collection Guide, Collection number: BANC MSS Z-E1. Online Archive of California. Accessed July 17, 2022. https://oac.cdlib.org/findaid/ark:/13030/kt5199s1jg/.

Fisher, Charles D., Darrel D. Hall, Hershel L. Jones, Jack D. McCullough, Archie P. McDonald, Elray S. Nixon, and J. Robert Singer. *A Survey of the Environmental and Cultural Resources of the Trinity River*. Nacogdoches, TX: Stephen F. Austin State University (for the US Army Corps of Engineers), 1972.

Flores, Dan L., Thomas Freeman, and Peter Custis. *Southern Counterpart to Lewis & Clark: The Freeman & Custis Expedition of 1806*. Norman: University of Oklahoma Press, 2002.

Flyingvranch. "Boat Ramp at Wilson Shoals." 2 Cool Fishing Forum. VerticalScope, Inc, January 13, 2017. https://www.2coolfishing.com/threads/boat-ramp-at-wilson-shoals.2164113/.

Foik, Paul J., and Domingo Ramon. *Captain Don Domingo Ramon's Diary of His Expedition into Texas in 1716*. Austin, TX: Texas Catholic Historical Society, 1933.

Folsom, Bradley. "Trinidad De Salcedo: A Forgotten Villa in Colonial Texas, 1806–1813." *East Texas Historical Journal* 52, no. 2 (October 2014): 49–78. https://doi.org/https://scholarworks.sfasu.edu/ethj/vol52/iss2/9/.

"The Formation of the Galveston Bay Ecosystem, the Indigenous People, and the

European Intruders Pre-History to 1800." Texas Commission on Environmental Quality, March 2015. https://www.tceq.texas.gov/assets/public/comm_exec/pubs/gbnep/gbnep-39/gbnep_39_03-15.pdf.

Foster, William C, and Jack Jackson, eds. "The 1693 Expedition of Gregorio De Salinas Varona to Sustain the Missionaries Among the Tejas Indians." Translated by Ned F. Brierley. *Southwestern Historical Quarterly* XCVII, no. 4 (April 1994): 265–311.

Foster, William C. *Spanish Expeditions into Texas: 1689–1768.* Austin: University of Texas Press, 1995.

"From the Spanish Collection: Overlapping Sovereignty and Private Property on the East Texas Frontier." Save Texas History. Texas General Land Office, April 30, 2020. https://medium.com/save-texas-history/from-the-spanish-collection-overlapping-sovereignty-and-private-property-on-the-east-texas-7272dd373b21.

Frost, Harwood. *The Art of Roadmaking: Treating of the Various Problems and Operations in the Construction and Maintenance of Roads, Streets, and Pavements . . . Etc.* New York: Engineering News Publishing Co., 1910.

Fulmore, Zachary Taylor. *The History and Geography of Texas as Told in County Names.* Austin, TX: S. R. Fulmore, 1926.

Galán, Francis X. "Between Imperial Warfare: Crossing of the Smuggling Frontier and Transatlantic Commerce on the Louisiana-Texas Borderlands, 1754–1785." Essay. In *Texans and War New Interpretations of the State's Military History*, edited by Alexander Mendoza and Charles David Grear, 157–77. College Station: Texas A&M University Press, 2012.

Galán, Francis X. "The Chirino Boys: Spanish Soldier-Pioneers from Los Adaes on the Louisiana-Texas Borderlands, 1735–1792." *East Texas Historical Journal* 46, no. 2 (October 2008): 42–58.

Galán, Francis X. *Los Adaes: The First Capital of Spanish Texas.* College Station: Texas A&M University Press, 2020.

Gann, Tom H. "Tom H. Gann Research Collection." Lufkin, Texas. This citation is for the body of research compiled by Tom H. Gann. It is the impetus for this work.

"Geographic Names Information System." Board on Geographic Names, Domestic. US Geological Survey. Accessed July 19, 2022. https://www.usgs.gov/us-board-on-geographic-names/domestic-names.

Gerona, Carla. "With a Song in Their Hands: Incendiary Décimas from the Texas and Louisiana Borderlands during a Revolutionary Age." *Early American Studies: An Interdisciplinary Journal* 12, no. 1 (2014): 93–142. https://doi.org/10.1353/eam.2014.0002.

Giraud, Marcel. *A History of French Louisiana (in 5 Volumes).* Translated by Brian Pearce and Joseph C. Lambert. Baton Rouge: Louisiana State University Press, 1987.

"GLO GIS Viewer." ArcGIS web application. Texas General Land Office. https://gisweb.glo.texas.gov/glomapjs/index.html, Accessed June 22, 2022.

Goldberg, Mark Allan. *Conquering Sickness: Race, Health, and Colonization in the Texas Borderlands*. Lincoln: University of Nebraska Press, 2017.

Goodykoontz, Colin Brummitt. "Spanish Exploration of Louisiana and the Adjacent Borders of New Spain, 1762–1800." Master's thesis, University of California, 1914.

Gordon, Shane. "Shawnee Landing / Hand Launch on Angelina River." S G Outdoors. YouTube, February 7, 2021. https://www.youtube.com/watch?v=NrsdRHX96H8.

Gow, James E. "An Ecological Study of the Sabine and Neches Valleys, Texas." *Proceedings of the Iowa Academy of Sciences for 1904* 12 (1905): 39–50.

Gray, Glenn A. *Gazetteer of Streams of Texas*. US Geological Survey, Department of the Interior. Washington, DC: Government Printing Office, 1919.

Gregory, Hiram M. (Pete), George Avery, Francis X. Galán, and Steve Black. "Los Adaes Legacy." Los Adaes. Texas Beyond History. Accessed November 11, 2021. https://www.texasbeyondhistory.net/adaes/legacy.html.

Haggard, J. Villasana. "House of Barr and Davenport." *Southwestern Historical Quarterly* 49, no. 1 (July 1945): 66–88. https://doi.org/https://www.jstor.org/stable/30240618.

Haltom, Richard W. *History and Description off Nacogdoches County, Texas*. Austin, TX: Pemberton Press, 1880.

Hamilton, Peter Joseph. *History of North America. Volume III: The Colonization of the South*. Philadelphia, PA: George Barrie's Sons, 1904.

Harby, Lee C. "The Old Stone Fort of Nacogdoches." *The American Magazine* 7, no. New Series, Volume 2, 1887.

Harby, Mrs. Lee C. "The Tejas: Their Habits, Government, and Superstitions." *Annual Report of the American Historical Association, 1895*. 63–82.

Hargraves, Abbott. Ms. "Search for King's Highway Location. Lufkin, TX, 2015." Unpublished research in the Tom H. Gann Collection. It is a review of individual property deeds from south of Nacogdoches to the Neches River in Angelina County.

Harrigan, Stephen. *Big Wonderful Thing: A History of Texas*. Austin: University of Texas Press, 2019.

Harrigan, Stephen. *They Came from the Sky: The Spanish Arrive in Texas*. Austin: University of Texas Press, 2017.

Harrison, James. "The Failure of Spain in East Texas: The Occupation and Abandonment of Nacogdoches, 1779–1821," PhD dissertation, University of Nebraska,1980.

Hart, John P., and Timothy K Perttula. "The Washington Square Mound Site and a Southeastern Ceremonial Complex Style Zone among the Caddo of Northeastern Texas." *Midcontinental Journal of Archaeology* 35, no. 2 (2020): 199–228.

Haskell, Marion Lowrie. "Rubí's Inspection of the Frontier Presidios of New Spain, 1766–1768: Translation of Sources, Introduction and Notes." Master's thesis, University of California, 1917.

Hatcher, Mattie Austin. "Conditions in Texas Affecting the Colonization Problem, 1795–1801." *Southwestern Historical Quarterly* 25, no. 2 (October 1921): 81–97. https://doi.org/https://www.jstor.org/stable/30234823.

Hatcher, Mattie Austin. *The Expedition of Don Domingo Terán De Los Rios into Texas*. Austin: Texas Knights of Columbus Historical Commission, 1932.

Hatcher, Mattie Austin. "The Opening of Texas to Foreign Settlement, 1801–1821." *University of Texas Bulletin* 2714 (April 8, 1927): 7–368.

HathiTrust Digital Library. Accessed June 23, 2022. https://www.hathitrust.org/.

Hämäläinen, Pekka. "Into the Mainstream: The Emergence of a New Texas Indian History." Essay. In *Beyond Texas through Time Breaking Away from Past Interpretations*, edited by Walter L. Buenger and León De Arnoldo, 50–84. College Station: Texas A&M University Press, 2011.

Hämäläinen, Pekka. *The Comanche Empire*. New Haven, CT: Yale University Press, 2009.

Helm, Mary Sherwood. *Scraps of Early Texas History*. Austin, TX: Published by the Author, 1884.

Heusinger, Edward W. *Early Explorations and Mission Establishments in Texas*. San Antonio, TX: Naylor Co., 1936.

"Historic Topographic Map Overlays." topoView. US Geological Survey. Accessed June 24, 2022. https://ngmdb.usgs.gov/topoview/.

Hodge, Frederick Webb, ed. *Handbook of American Indians North of Mexico, in Two Parts*. Washington, DC: Government Printing Office, 1907.

Hoffmann, Fritz Leo, and Francisco Celiz. *Diary of the Alarcon Expedition into Texas: 1718–1719*. Los Angeles, CA: Quivira Society, 1935.

Horne, Jami. "Cincinnati, Texas." East Texas History (website). Accessed June 27, 2022. https://easttexashistory.org/items/show/238.

"How to Fire a Cannon." Fort Matanzas National Monument. National Park Service. Accessed June 27, 2022. https://www.nps.gov/foma/learn/education/upload/Cannon-Equipment.pdf.

Howden, George. "The Expedition of Father Gaspar Jose De Solis into Texas, 1767–1768 Translation of Sources, Introduction and Notes." Master's thesis, University of California, 1915. http://hdl.handle.net/2027/uc1.b5298999.

Hubbard, Velicia R., and David H. Jurney. "Reconstruction of the Past Vegetation on the Headwaters of Piney Creek Watershed in Houston and Trinity Counties, Texas." *Journal of Northeast Texas Archaeology* 11 (1998): 55–65.

Hudson, Wilson M. *The Story of Champ DAsile*. Austin: Steck-Vaughn Co., 1969.

Hyatt, Emily, and Jonathan Gerland. "Finding Angelina: The Search for East Texas' Little Angel." *The Pine Bough*, December 2012, 12–21.

"In Old Nacogdoches Town, A Little Place That Has a Stirring History." *Houston Post*. December 13, 1896.

Jackson, Jack, and William C. Foster. *Imaginary Kingdom: Texas as Seen by the Rivera and Rubí Military Expeditions, 1727 and 1767*. Austin: Texas State Historical Association, 1995.

Jackson, Jack, Manuel de Mier y Teran, Scooter Cheatham, and Lynn Marshall.

Texas by Terán: The Diary Kept by General Manuel De Mier y Terán on His 1828 Inspection of Texas. Austin: University of Texas Press, 2000.

Jackson, Jack, Robert S. Weddle, and Winston De Ville. *Mapping Texas and the Gulf Coast the Contributions of Saint-Denis, Olivan, and Le Maire.* College Station: Texas A&M University Press, 2008.

Jackson, Jack. "Father José María De Jesús Puelles and the Maps of Pichardo's Document 74." *Southwestern Historical Quarterly* 91, no. 3 (January 1988): 317–47. https://doi.org/http://www.jstor.org/stable/30237036.

Jackson, Jack. *Los Mesteños: Spanish Ranching in Texas, 1721–1821.* Texas A&M University Press, 2006.

Jackson, Jack, and William C. Foster. *Imaginary Kingdom: Texas as Seen by the Rivera and Rubí Military Expeditions, 1727 and 1767.* Austin: Texas State Historical Association, 1995.

Jackson, John Brinckerhoff. *The Necessity for Ruins.* Amherst: University of Massachusetts Press, 1980.

Jackson, Morris K., and Peggy A. Jasso. "El Salto, East Texas Rancho of Mission Guadalupe, Historical Marker Application." Texas Historical Commission, 2021.

Jackson, Morris K., and Peggy A. Jasso. "The Mansola Road of Nacogdoches, Historical Marker Application." Texas Historical Commission, 2021.

Jackson, Morris K., Tom Middlebrook, George E. Avery, Harry J. Shafer, and Barbara Meissner. *Trade and Cultural Interaction along El Camino Real De Los Tejas: During the Spanish Colonial and Republic Periods in Nacogdoches County, Texas. Vol. 1.* Nacogdoches, TX: Nine Flags Museum, 2012.

Jelks, Edward B., and Timothy K. Perttula. "The Caddo." *Journal of Northeast Texas Archaeology* 16 (2002): 1–28.

John, Elizabeth A. H. *Storms Brewed in Other Men's Worlds: The Confrontation of Indians, Spanish, and French in the Southwest, 1540–1795.* Norman: University of Oklahoma Press, 1996.

John, Elizabeth A. H. "The Riddle of Mapmaker Juan Pedro Walkeeer." Essay in *Essays on the History of North American Discovery and Exploration*, edited by Stanley H. Palmer and Dennis Reinhartz. College Station: Texas A&M University, 1988.

John, Elizabeth A. H., Adan Benavides, Jr., Pedro Vial, and Francisco Xavier Chaves. "Inside the Comanchería, 1785: The Diary of Pedro Vial and Francisco Xavier Chaves." *Southwestern Historical Quarterly* 98, no. 1 (July 1994): 26–56.

John, Elizabeth A. H., and John Wheat. "Governing Texas, 1779: The Karankawa Aspect." *Southwestern Historical Quarterly* 104, no. 4 (April 2001): 560–76.

Jones, C. Allan. *Texas Roots: Agriculture and Rural Life Before the Civil War.* College Station: Texas A&M University Press, 2005.

Jones, Martha Tannery, and Donna Loughran. *The Mystery of YBarbos Tunnel.* Dallas: Hendrick-Long Pub. Co., 1991.

Joseph, Harriett Denise, and Donald E. Chipman. *Notable Men and Women of Spanish Texas.* Austin: University of Texas Press, 2015.

Joutel, Henri. *Joutel's Journal of La Salle's Last Voyage: A Reprint (Page for Page and*

Line for Line) of the First English Translation, London 1714: With the Map of the Original French Edition, Paris, 1713, in Facsimile; and Notes by Melville B. Anderson. Chicago: Caxton Club, 1896.

Judkins, Jennifer. "On Things That Are Not There Anymore." *Journal of Aesthetics and Art Criticism* 72, no. 4 (2014): 441–45.

Jurney, David H., John Ippolito, and Velicia Bergstrom. "The Frequency of Fire in East Texas Forests." *Index of Texas Archaeology* 13 (2000): 40–49. https://doi.org/10.21112/.ita.2000.1.21.

Kennedy, William. *Texas, Its Geography, Natural History and Topography.* New York: Benjamin and Young, 1844.

Ker, Henry. *Travels through the Western Interior of the United States, from the Year 1808 up to the Year 1816: With a Particular Description of a Great Part of Mexico, or New-Spain: Containing a Particular Account of Thirteen Different Tribes of Indians.* Elizabethtown, NJ: Printed for the author, 1816.

King, Nyal C. "Captain Antonio Gil Y'Barbo—Founder of the Modern Nacogdoches, 1729–1809." PhD dissertation, Stephen F. Austin State Teachers College, 1949.

Kinnaird, Lawrence, and Nicolas de LaFora. *The Frontiers of New Spain: Nicolas De Lafora's Description, 1766–1768.* Berkeley, CA: The Quivira Society, 1958.

Klier, Betje Black, and Pavie Théodore. *Pavie in the Borderlands: The Journey of Théodore Pavie to Louisiana and Texas, 1829–1830, Including Portions of His Souvenirs Atlantiques.* Baton Rouge: Louisiana State University Press, 2000.

Korsmeyer, Carolyn. *Things: In Touch with the Past.* New York: Oxford University Press US, 2022.

Kress, Margaret Kenney, Gaspar Jose de Solis, and Mattie Austin Hatcher. "Diary of a Visit of Inspection of the Texas Missions Made by Fray Gaspar José De Solís in the Year 1767–68." *Southwestern Historical Quarterly* 35, no. 1 (July 1931): 28–76.

La Vere, David L. "Barr, Davenport, Murphy and Smith: Traders on the Louisiana-Texas Frontier." Master's thesis, Northwestern State University, 1989.

La Vere, David, Katia Campbell, and Francois Grappe. "An Expedition to the Kichai: The Journal of François Grappe, September 24, 1783." *Southwestern Historical Quarterly* 98, no. 1 (July 1994): 58–78. https://doi.org/https://www.jstor.org/stable/30238961.

La Vere, David. "Between Kinship and Capitalism: French and Spanish Rivalry in the Colonial Louisiana-Texas Indian Trade." *The Journal of Southern History* 64, no. 2 (May 1998): 197–218. https://doi.org/https://www.jstor.org/stable/2587944.

Lamar, Mirabeau Buonaparte. "Mirabeau B. Lamar Travel Journal, 1835 [Digital Version]." Rice Scholarship Home. Rice University, 1835. http://scholarship.rice.edu/jsp/xml/1911/21658/1/aa00359.tei.html.

Leggett, Mike. "8 Arrested In Fish Sting, 11-Month Investigation Targeted Black Market Seafood Industry." *Austin American-Statesman.* February 10, 1995.

León, Alonso de. *General Alonso De León's Expeditions into Texas, 1686–1690.* Edited by Lola Orellano Norris. College Station: Texas A&M University Press, 2017.

León, Nicholas. *Las Castas Del México Colonial o Nueva España: Noticias Etno-Antropológicas*. Madrid, Spain: Historia y Etnografía, 1924.

Leutenegger, Benedict, Marion A. Habig, and Jose Maria de Jesus Puelles. "Puelles' Report of 1827 on the Texas-Louisiana Boundary." *Louisiana History: The Journal of the Louisiana Historical Association* 19, no. 2 (1978): 133–81.

Leutenegger, Benedict. *Apostle of America, Fray Antonio Margil*. Chicago: Franciscan Herald Press, 1956.

Levi, Daniel J. "Does History Matter? Perceptions and Attitudes Toward Fake Historic Architecture and Historic Preservation." *Journal of Architectural and Planning Research* 22, no. 2 (2005): 148–59.

Leysath, Maggie, and Rachel Galan. "Shahó and the Power of Place." *Teaching Artist Journal* 19, no. 1–2 (2021): 1–13. https://doi.org/10.1080/15411796.2021.1925555.

Lieber, Dave. "For Decades, a Comic Book Showing Texas History in the Most Racist Ways Was Given to Texas Students." *Dallas Morning News*, December 17, 2021.

Linn, Brianna. "Lasting Legacy: 4 Beloved Storytellers Have Statue Dedicated in Their Honor." https://www.ktre.com. KTRE (ABC, channel 9, Lufkin), July 23, 2021. https://www.ktre.com/2021/07/23/longlasting-legacy-four-beloved-storytellers-have-statue-dedicated-their-honor/.

L'isle, Guillaume de. *Carte De La Louisiane Et Du Cours Du Mississipi I.e. Mississippi: Dressée Sur Un Grand Nombre De Mémoires Entrautres Sur Ceux De Mr. Le Maire*. Geography and Map Division, The Library of Congress, Washington, DC. Paris: Chez l'auteur le Sr. Delisle sur le quay de l'horloge avec privilege du roy, 1718. Map. https://www.loc.gov/item/2001624908/.

"Lobanillo Swales." National Parks Service. US Department of the Interior. https://www.nps.gov/places/lobanillo-swales.htm. Accessed July 29, 2024.

Logan, Ben, and Curt Meine. *The Land Remembers: The Story of a Farm and Its People*. Madison: The University of Wisconsin Press, 2017.

Loomis, Noel M. "Commandants-General of the Interior Provinces: A Preliminary List." *Arizona and the West* 11, no. 3 (1969): 261–68.

"Los Adaes, Spanish Capital Through Time (a Timeline)." Texas Beyond History. Texas Archeological Research Laboratory (TARL). Accessed June 27, 2022. https://texasbeyondhistory.net/adaes/time.html.

MacRoberts, Michael H., and Barbara R. MacRoberts. "The Big Thicket: Typical or Atypical?" *East Texas Historical Journal* 42, no. 1 (2004): 42–51.

"Mapping Emigrant Trails Manual, Fifth Edition." Preservation training, Official OCTA Training Briefings. Oregon-California Trails Association (OCTA), June 2014. https://octa-trails.org/preservation-training/.

Marceaux, P. Shawn, and Timothy K. Perttula. "Negotiating Borders: The Southern Caddo and Their Relationships with Colonial Governments in East Texas." Essay in *American Indians and the Market Economy, 1775–1850*. Edited by Lance Greene and Mark R. Plane, 80–97. Tuscaloosa: University of Alabama Press, 2010.

Marceaux, Paul Shawn Joseph. "The Archaeology and Ethnohistory of the Hasinai

Caddo: Material Culture and the Course of European Contact." PhD dissertation, University of Texas, 2011.

Margil Antonio de Jesús. *Nothingness Itself: Selected Writings of Ven. Fr. Antonio Margil 1690–1724*. Chicago: Franciscan Herald Press, 1976.

Marquez, Ophelia, and Lillian Ramos Navarro Wold. *Compilation of Colonial Spanish Terms and Document Related Phrases*. Midway City, CA: SHHAR Press, 1998.

Marriott, Paul Daniel. *Saving Historic Roads: Design and Policy Guidelines*. Washington, DC: Preservation Press, 1998.

Marshall, Thomas Maitland. *A History of the Western Boundary of the Louisiana Purchase, 1819–1841*. Berkeley: University of California Press, 1914.

Martin, Howard N. *Myths & Folktales of the Alabama-Coushatta Indians of Texas*. Austin, TX: Encino Press, 1977.

Matz, Maria Rosario. "Spanish Indian Policy in the Internal Provinces, 1765–1786." Master's thesis, Texas Tech University, 1998.

McAlister, Lyle N. *The "Fuero Militar" in New Spain: 1764–1800*. Gainesville: University of Florida Press, 2012.

McClain, S. *A Taint on Texas: An Untold Chapter in the Fight for an Independent Texas*. Bloomington, IN: AuthorHouse LLC, 2013.

McCollum, Donna. "Caddo Nation Come for Remains of Their Ancestors." https://www.ktre.com. KTRE (ABC channel 9, Lufkin), October 23, 2008. https://www.ktre.com/story/9230799/caddo-nation-come-for-remains-of-their-ancestors/.

McCorkle, Jr., James L. "Los Adaes and the Borderlands Origins of East Texas." *East Texas Historical Journal* 22, no. 2 (1984): 3–12.

McDonald, Archie P. "The Chicken War." All Things Historical. Texas Escapes, March 26, 2007. http://www.texasescapes.com/AllThingsHistorical/Chicken-War-AM307.htm.

McDonald, Dedra S., and Kinga Perzynska. *Guide to the Spanish and Mexican Manuscript Collection at the Catholic Archives of Texas*. Austin: Catholic Archives of Texas, 1994.

McGraw, A. Joachim, and James E. Corbin. "A Review Essay of 'Spanish Expeditions into Texas," by William C. Foster (1995)." *Bulletin of the Texas Archaeological Survey* 70 (1999): 439–56.

McGraw, A. Joachim, John Wilburn Clark, Elizabeth A. Robbins, and F. Jesus de la Teja. "The Camino Real: Colonial Texas' Lifeline to the World." Essay in *A Texas Legacy, the Old San Antonio Road and the Caminos Reales: A Tricentennial History, 1691–1991*. 43–48. Austin: Texas State Department of Highways and Public Transportation, Highway Design Division, 1991.

McKenzie, Clinton, Lindy Martinez, and Raymond Mauldin. "Archaeological Monitoring and Test Excavations at the 1722 Presidio San Antonio De Bexar (Plaza De Armas Buildings), San Antonio, Bexar County, Texas." Texas Antiquities Permit No. 6526. Center for Archaeological Research, University of Texas at San Antonio, 2016. https://www.sanantonio.gov/Portals/0/Files/HistoricPreservation/arc_reports/ArchaeologicalMonitoringTestExcavations.pdf.

McReynolds, James M. "Family Life in a Borderland Community: Nacogdoches, Texas, 1779–1861," PhD dissertation, Texas Tech University, 1978.

Mitchell, David. "The Trinity River Project, 1852–1922." *East Texas Historical Journal* 28, no. 2 (1990): 39–45. https://doi.org/https://scholarworks.sfasu.edu/ethj/vol28/iss2/9/.

"The Modern Gazetteer: Being a Copious Geographical Dictionary of All the Nations, Empires, Kingdoms, Republics, States, Departments, Provinces, Counties, Cities, Towns, Forts, Oceans, Seas, Rivers, Lakes, Canals, Harbours, Hills, Mountains, &c. in the World . . . Brought down to the Present Time and Illustrated with Thirty-Two New and Correct Maps. 2 vols." Edinburgh, Scotland, 1810.

Montigny, Dumont de. *The Memoir of Lieutenant Dumont 1715–1747: A Sojourner in the French Atlantic.* Edited by Carla Zecher. Translated by Gordon M. Sayre. Chapel Hill: University of North Carolina Press, 2012.

Moor, Robert. *On Trails—an Exploration.* New York: Simon & Shuster, 2016.

Morfi, Juan Agustín. *Provincias Internas: Antología.* Edited by Guadalupe Curiel. Mexico: Universidad Nacional Autonoma de México, 2003.

Mundigo, Axel I., and Dora P. Crouch. "The City Planning Ordinances of the Laws of the Indies Revisited: Part I: Their Philosophy and Implications." *Town Planning Review* 48, no. 3 (1977): 247–68. https://doi.org/https://www.jstor.org/stable/40103542.

"Nacogdoches, Bids for Old Courthouse Rejected, Old Cemetery of Century Ago." *Shreveport Times.* October 10, 1911.

"Nacogdoches, News Item." *Shreveport Times.* March 23, 1917.

"Nacogdoches, News." *The Galveston Daily News.* July 20, 1882.

"Nacogdoches, News." *The Galveston Daily News.* July 31, 1883.

"Nacogdoches, News." *The Galveston Daily News.* October 21, 1884.

The National Map—Advanced Viewer. US Geological Survey (USGS). Accessed June 24, 2022. https://apps.nationalmap.gov/viewer/.

National Park Service. "Lobanillo Swales, National Register of Historic Places Registration Form." Submitted by Sergio A. Iruegas, Melinda T. Iruegas, Michel Romero Taylor, and Angelica Sanchez-Clark, 2015). Accessed July 28, 2024.

Neuman, Henry. *New Dictionary of the Spanish and English Languages: Wherein the Words Are Correctly Explained, Agreeably to Their Different Meanings, and a Great Variety of Terms, Relating to the Arts, Sciences, Navigation, & Trade, Elucidated. / Compiled from the Most Valuable Words of English and Foreign Lexicographers.* London: W. Wilson, 1809.

Newcomb, Jr., William W. "A Reappraisal of the 'Cultural Sink' of Texas." *Southwestern Journal of Anthropology* 12, no. 2 (1956): 145–53. https://doi.org/10.1086/soutjanth.12.2.3629110.

Newcomb, W. W. *The Indians of Texas: From Prehistoric to Modern Times.* Austin: University of Texas Press, 1961.

Nielson, R. LaRell, Mike Read, Mindy Faulkner, Hannah C. Chambers, and

Jessica O'Neal. "Geology of Nacogdoches Texas." *Texas Academy of Science* 19 (March 2020): 1–46. https://scholarworks.sfasu.edu/geology/19.

Nomikos, Ariane. "Place Matters." *The Journal of Aesthetics and Art Criticism* 76, no. 4 (2018): 453–62. https://doi.org/10.1111/jaac.12598.

Norvell, Helen P. *King's Highway, the Great Strategic Military Highway of America, El Camino Real, the Old San Antonio Road.* Austin, TX: Firm Foundation Pub. House, 1945.

Oak, Henry Lebbeus. *Annals of the Spanish Northwest: North Mexican States 1531–1800.* San Francisco, CA: Bancroft, 1884.

The Old San Antonio Road Association. "State Memorial Dedication: Honoring the First Provincial Governor of Texas, Don Domingo Teran de los Rios, and his Blazing 1691 of El Camino Real by Orders of the King of Spain." May 25, 1939.

"The Old Stone Fort, It Has Been Entirely Obliterated, But the Stones Remain." *Brownsville Herald.* April 21, 1902.

"The Old Stone Fort, Many Relic Hunters Are Exploring the Ruins." *Houston Post.* March 15, 1902.

Onellion, Jr., Willard Mills. "Roads and Travel in Louisiana, 1803–1860." Master's Thesis, Northwestern State University of Louisiana. 1986.

Page, Frederic Benjamin. *Prairiedom: Rambles and Scrambles in Texas or New Estrémadura.* New York: Paine & Burgess, 1845.

Pagès, Pierre Marie Francois. *Travels Round the World: In the Years 1767, 1768, 1769, 1770, 1771.* London, England: Printed for J. Murray, 1791.

Palacios, Antonio. "Trans-Texas Corridor." Public Roads—Vol. 69, No. 1, Publication No. FHWA-HRT-05–006. US Department of Transportation, Federal Highway Administration, 2005. https://highways.dot.gov/public-roads/julyaugust-2005/trans-texas-corridor.

Perales, Monica, and Raĺul A. Ramos. *Recovering the Hispanic History of Texas.* Houston: Arte Publico Press, 2010.

Perkins Brothers. "For Sale, Old Stone Fort." *Houston Post.* December 3, 1901.

Persat, Maurice, and Schlumberger Gustave Léon. *Mémoires Du Commandant Persat, 1806 à 1844.* Paris, France: Plon-Nourrit & Co., 1910.

Perttula, Timothy K, Bill Young, and P. Shawn Marceaux. "Caddo Ceramics from an Early 18th Century Spanish Mission in East Texas: Mission San Jose De Los Nasonis (41RK200)." *Journal of Northeast Texas Archaeology* 29 (2009): 81–88.

Perttula, Timothy K., Bo Nelson, LeeAnna Schniebs, and Mark Walters. "The Caddo Archaeology of the San Pedro Creek Valley, Houston County, in East Texas" *Index of Texas Archaeology* (2016): 1–72. https://scholarworks.sfasu.edu/cgi/viewcontent.cgi?article=1907&context=ita, Accessed July 28, 2024.

Perttula, Timothy K. *Caddo Landscapes in the East Texas Forests.* Oxford: Oxbow Books, 2017.

Perttula, Timothy K. "Texas in the Year 1000: What It Was Like Then in East Texas." *Journal of Northeast Texas Archaeology* 15 (2001): 29–36.

Perttula, Timothy K. *The Caddo Nation: Archaeological and Ethnohistoric Perspectives.* Austin: University of Texas Press, 1997.

Perttula, Timothy K., and Bo Nelson. "The Looting of Prehistoric Caddo Indian Cemeteries in Northeast Texas." *Texas Forum on Civil Liberties & Civil Rights* 4, no. 1 (1998): 77–86.

Perttula, Timothy K., and Tom Middlebrook. "The Historic Caddo Archaeological Record in East Texas." *Journal of Northeast Texas Archaeology Special Publication* no. 56 (2020).

Pichardo, Jose Antonio. *El Nuevo Mexico y Tierras Adyacentes Mapa Levantado Para La Demarcacion De Los Limites De Los Dominios Españoles y De Los Estados Unidos Por El P.d. Jose Pichardo Quien Lo Dedica Al Exmo. Sor. D. Francisco Xavier Venegas Virrey De Esta N. E. &. Año De 1811.* Geography and Map Division, The Library of Congress, Washington, DC. Accessed July 15, 2022. https://www.loc.gov/item/2016588016/.

Pinkerton, Gary L. *Trammel's Trace: The First Road to Texas from the North.* College Station: Texas A&M University Press, 2016.

Pitblado, Bonnie L. "On Rehumanizing Pleistocene People of the Western Hemisphere." *American Antiquity* 87 (2) (2022): 217–35.

"Plano Del Presidio De Nuestra Señora De Los Dolores, En La Provincia De Tejas, Erigido y Delineado Por El Marqués De San Miguel De Aguayo." Portal de Archivos Espanoles (PARES). Gobierno de Espana, Ministerio de Cultura y Deporte, June 13, 1722. http://pares.mcu.es/ParesBusquedas20/catalogo/description/20939?nm.

Pleasant, Darryl, and Randall Pleasant. "The Village of Adaes: A Nineteenth Century Refugee Settlement in Natchitoches Parish Louisiana." Academia.edu, February 18, 2020. https://www.academia.edu/42011085/The_Village_of_Adaes_A_Nineteenth_Century_Refugee_Settlement_in_Natchitoches_Parish_Louisiana.

Pleasant, Darryl. "The Ranchos of Los Adaes: Spanish Geography and American Land Claims in Western Louisiana." *Caddo Archaeology Journal* 23 (2013): 117–38.

Poyo, Gerald E., and Gilberto M. Hinojosa. "Spanish Texas and Borderlands Historiography in Transition: Implications for United States History." *The Journal of American History* 75, no. 2 (September 1988): 393–416. https://doi.org/10.230/1887864.

Poyo, Gerald Eugene. *Tejano Journey: 1770–1850.* Austin: University of Texas Press, 1996.

Pratz, Le Page du. *The History of Louisiana; Translated from the French of M. Le Page Du Pratz.* Edited by Joseph G. Tregle, Jr. Baton Rouge: Louisiana State University Press, 1975.

Priestly, Herbert Ingram. "Spanish Colonial Municipalities." *Louisiana Historical Quarterly*, April 1922.

"Proclamation of the Agents of the King of Spain for Surrendering Louisiana to Frances, Dated New Orlans, May 18th, 1803." *Cobbett's Weekly Political Register.* November 5, 1803, Volume IV edition, sec. No. 18.

Ramon, Diego, and Debbie S. Cunningham. "The Domingo Ramon Diary of the

1716 Expedition into the Province of the Tejas Indians: An Annotated Translation." *Southwestern Historical Quarterly* 110, no. 1 (July 2006): 38–67.

Rebolledo, Juan de Olivan. *Mapa De La Costa Del Golfo De México y Del Interior De Las Provincias De Tejas, Nuevo México y Nueva Galicia, Hecho Por Juan De Oliván Rebolledo.* Portal de Archivos Espanoles (PARES). Gobierno de Espana, Ministerio de Cultura y Deporte, December 18, 1717. http://pares.mcu.es/ParesBusquedas20/catalogo/description/20936.

Red Shirt, Delphine. "Lakota America Review." *Lakota Times*, January 2, 2020. https://www.lakotatimes.com/articles/lakota-america-review/.

Reeves, Walter. "Oak—Gall on Trunk." Walter Reeves (website). June 20, 2020. https://www.walterreeves.com/landscaping/oak-gall-on-trunk/.

"Report of the Secretary of War: Being Part of the Message and Documents Transmitted to the Two Houses of Congress at the Beginning of the 43rd Congress. 2. Vol. 2." Washington, DC: Government Printing Office, 1873.

Riddell, John Leonard. *A Synopsis of the Flora of the Western States.* Cincinnati, OH: E. Deming, 1835.

Robbins, Elizabeth A., John Wilburn Clark, and A. Joachim McGraw, eds. *A Texas Legacy: the Old San Antonio Road and the Camino Reales; a Tricentennial History, 1691–1991.* Austin: Texas State Department of Highways and Public Transportation, 1991.

Roberts, Oran Milo. *A Description of Texas, Its Advantages and Resources: With Some Account of Their Development, Past, Present, and Future.* St. Louis, MO: Gilbert Book Co., 1881.

Robinson, Jenefer. *Deeper than Reason: Emotion and Its Role in Literature, Music and Art.* Oxford: Clarendon Press, 2005.

Robinson, Willard B. "Colonial Ranch Architecture in the Spanish-Mexican Tradition." *Southwestern Historical Quarterly*, 83, no. 2 (October 1979): 123–50.

Ryder-Taylor, Henry, and Charles H. Stanford. *History of the Alamo and of the Local Franciscan Missions. 6th ed.* San Antonio, TX: N. Tengg, 1908.

Salas, Mario Marcel, and John Reynolds. "Social Caste in Early Béxar." ArcGIS StoryMaps. ESRI, April 28, 2021. https://storymaps.arcgis.com/stories/7114300813eb4db6892d477882233f1e.

"Sam Houston Regional Library and Research Center." Texas State Library and Archives Commission. Accessed June 25, 2022. https://www.tsl.texas.gov/shc/index.html.

Sanchez, Jose Maria. "A Trip to Texas in 1828." Translated by Carlos E. Castaneda. *Southwestern Historical Quarterly* XXIX, no. 4 (April 1926).

Santos, Richard G., and Juan Antonio de la Pena. *Aguayo Expedition into Texas, 1721: An Annotated Translation of the Five Versions of the Diary Kept by Br. Juan Antonio De La Peña.* Austin, TX: Jenkins Publishing Co., 1981.

Schilz, Thomas Frank, and Donald E. Worcester. "The Spread of Firearms among the Indian Tribes on the Northern Frontier of New Spain." *American Indian Quarterly* 11, no. 1 (1987): 1–10. https://doi.org/10.2307/1183724.

Schimtt, Casey. "Review of The Smugglers' World: Illicit Trade and Atlantic

Communities in Eighteenth-Century Venezuela." H-LatAm, H-Net Reviews, May 2019.

Sciscenti, James V. ed., "Environmental and Cultural Resources Within the Trinity River Basin." Report submitted to the Corps of Engineers, Fort Worth District, 1971. https://apps.dtic.mil/sti/tr/pdf/ADA096191.pdf

Sehgal, Parul. "'Lakota America' Puts the Tribe of Sitting Bull and Crazy Horse Front and Center." *New York Times*. October 22, 2019. Books of the Times section.

Seiter, Timothy. "How Best to Retrieve Stolen Horses: The Transformation of Spanish-Indian Diplomacy in Late Eighteenth-Century Texas." Unpublished manuscript, 2022.

Seiter, Timothy. "The Karankawa-Spanish War from 1778 to 1789: Attempted Genocide and Karankawa Power." *Southwestern Historical Quarterly* 124, no. 4 (April 2021): 375–410. https://doi.org/doi:10.1353/swh.2021.0026.

Sharf, Zack. "Peter Jackson Restored and Colorized 100 Hours of World War I Footage, and the Final Results Are Remarkable—Watch." *IndieWire*. October 10, 2018. https://www.indiewire.com/2018/10/peter-jackson-world-war-one-footage-restored-colorized-1202010938/.

Sibley, John W. *A Report from Natchitoches in 1807*. Edited by Annie Heloise Abel. New York: Museum of the American Indian, Heye Foundation, 1922.

Sibley, Marilyn McAdams. *Travelers in Texas, 1761–1860*. Austin: University of Texas Press, 2012.

Sibly, Marilyn McAdams. "Across Texas in 1767: The Travels of Captain Pagès." *Southwestern Historical Quarterly* 70, no. 4 (April 1967): 593–622.

Simek, Peter. "Is It Time to Change the Name of the Trinity River Back to the Arkikosa River?" *D Magazine*, May 20, 2019. https://www.dmagazine.com/frontburner/2019/05/is-it-time-to-change-the-name-of-the-trinity-river-back-to-the-arkikosa-river/.

Sjoberg, Andrée F. "The Bidai Indians of Southeastern Texas." *Southwestern Journal of Anthropology* 7, no. 4 (1951): 391–400. https://doi.org/10.1086/soutjanth.7.4.3628513.

Skiles, Bob D. "Documents Relating to Location and Juxtaposition of the Villa Trinidad De Salcedo and Barr Rancho, in 1812, on Trinity River, Texas." ResearchGate, March 2016. https://www.researchgate.net/publication/299467010_Documents_relating_to_location_and_juxtaposition_of_the_Villa_Trinidad_de_Salcedo_and_Barr_Rancho_in_1812_on_Trinity_River_Texas.

Skiles, Bob D. *Taking the Road to Trinidad*. Unpublished manuscript. 2009.

"Skulls and Bones, Unearthed on Nacogdoches Court House Site." *Houston Post*. October 10, 1911.

Smith, F. Todd. "A Native Response to the Transfer of Louisiana: The Red River Caddos and Spain, 1762–1803." *Louisiana History* 37, no. 2 (1996): 163–85.

Smith, F. Todd. *From Dominance to Disappearance: The Indians of Texas and the Near Southwest, 1786–1859*. Lincoln: University of Nebraska Press, 2009.

Smith, F. Todd. *The Caddo Indians: Tribes at the Convergence of Empires, 1542–1854*. College Station: Texas A&M University Press, 1995.

Smith, Gene A. *Nexus of Empire: Negotiating Loyalty and Identity in the Revolutionary Borderlands, 1760s–1820s*. Gainesville: University Press of Florida, 2011.

Smith, Ralph A. "Account of the Journey of Bénard De La Harpe: Discovery Made by Him of Several Nations Situated in the West." *Southwestern Historical Quarterly* 62, no. 3 (January 1959): 371–85. https://doi.org/https://www.jstor.org/stable/30235704.

"Soil Map, Nacogdoches County Texas (1925); United States Bureau of Chemistry and Soils." The Portal to Texas History. University of North Texas Libraries, September 7, 2012. https://texashistory.unt.edu/ark:/67531/metapth252103/.

Sorrow, William M. *Investigations into the Location of Nuestra Senora Del Pilar De Bucareli*. Austin: Texas Archaeological Salvage Project, University of Texas, 1972.

Spaight, A. W. *The Resources, Soil and Climate of Texas*. Galveston, TX: A. H. Belo & Co., 1882.

"Spanish Florida—Culture—Weights and Measures—Quick Conversions." Faculty homepage: Dr. John E. Worth (website). University of Western Florida. Accessed July 13, 2022. https://pages.uwf.edu/jworth/jw_spanfla_measures_conversions.html#Spanish_Varas.

Spong, John. "Confessions of a Seventh-Grade History Teacher." *Texas Monthly*, September 2012.

Sterne, Adolphus. "Diary of Adolphus Sterne, XI." Edited by Harriet Smither. *Southwestern Historical Quarterly* XXXII, no. 4 (April 1929): 344–51.

Swanton, John Reed. *Source Material on the History and Ethnology of the Caddo Indians*. Washington, DC: United States Government Printing Office, 1942.

Swanton, John Reed. *The Indian Tribes of North America*. Washington, DC: United States Government Printing Office, 1953.

Teutsch, Delbert. *Excavation of Town Plaza for Post Office*. Photograph. Nacogdoches, TX, 1917. East Texas Research Center. http://archives.sfasu.edu/repositories/2/resources/274.

"Texas & Tribes, Shared Traditions." Beyond the Road. Texas Department of Transportation. Accessed July 17, 2022. https://ftp.txdot.gov/pub/txdot-info/env/beyond-the-road/shared%20traditions.pdf.

"US Highway 59." Highway Designation File. Texas Department of Transportation, March 1, 1935. http://www.dot.state.tx.us/tpp/hwy/us/us0059.htm.

"Texas General Land Office Land Grant Search." The Texas General Land Office. Accessed June 25, 2022. https://s3.glo.texas.gov/glo/history/archives/land-grants/index.cfm.

"Texas GLO Map Store." The Texas General Land Office. Accessed June 26, 2022. https://s3.glo.texas.gov/glo/history/archives/map-store/#search.

"Texas History Timeline." Bullock Texas State History Museum, https://www.thestoryoftexas.com/discover/texas-history-timeline. Accessed July 29, 2024.

Townes, J. Edward. "Invisible Lines: The Life and Death of a Borderland." PhD dissertation, Texas Christian University, 2008.

"TPWD Cracks down on Illegal Fishing." *Marshall News-Messenger*. August 13, 1995.

"Trinity River, Sheet 15." Records of the Office of the Chief off Engineers, 1789–1999. National Archives and Records Administration, 1940. https://catalog.archives.gov/id/148373298.

"Trinity River: Lock and Dam at W. R. S. (1913 Photo)." The Portal to Texas History. University of North Texas Libraries, July 26, 2005. https://texashistory.unt.edu/ark:/67531/metapth4060/m1/1/.

Truett, Joe C., and Daniel W. Lay. *Land of Bears and Honey: A Natural History of East Texas*. Austin: University of Texas Press, 1994.

Truett, Samuel. *Fugitive Landscapes: The Forgotten History of the U.S.-Mexico Borderlands*. New Haven: Yale University Press, 2008.

US Department of War, "Report of the Secretary of War: being part of the message and documents transmitted to the two houses of Congress at the beginning of the 43rd Congress, Vol II, 1873." "Report of the Chief of Engineers." Washington, DC: Government Printing Office, 1873.

"Understanding Site Formation Processes: The Construction and Burning of a Jacal." Center for Archaeological Research. University of Texas-San Antonio. Accessed June 27, 2022. https://car.utsa.edu/CARResearch/SiteFormation.html.

Underwood, Ammon. "Journal of Ammon Underwood, 1834–1838." Edited by James K. Greer. *Southwestern Historical Quarterly* 32 (1928): 124–51.

"Upper Neches Basin Highlights Report 2019." Clean Waters Report. Angelina & Neches River Authority, 2019. https://www.anra.org/divisions/water_quality/crp/pdfs/reports/Highlights_Reports/2021_Upper_Neches_Basin_Highlights_Report.pdf.

Vallejo, Francisco Antonio. "Antonio Maria De Bucareli y Ursua." Oil on canvas painting. 36.2 inches by 28.7 inches. Wikipedia Commons, 1772. https://common.wikimedia.org/wiki/File:AntonioMariadeBucareliyUrsua.jpg

A Visit to Texas: Being the Journal of a Traveler through Those Parts Most Interesting to American Settlers with Descriptions of Scenery, Habits, &c. New York: Goodrich & Wiley, 1834.

Walker, Chester P., and Timothy K. Perttula. "Archaeogeophysical Investigations at an Eighteenth-Century Caddo Site in Nacogdoches County, East Texas." *Southeastern Archaeology* 29, no. 2 (November 25, 2010): 310–22. https://doi.org/10.1179/sea.2010.29.2.007.

Walker, Juan Pedro, and Jean Louis Berlandier. "Voyage Au Mexique: Itineraires, Ports, Cotes, Baies, Etc. De La Republique Mexicaine, Par Jn. Louis Berlandier." Beinecke Rare Book and Manuscript Library, WA MSS S-300. Yale University, 1806. https://collections.library.yale.edu/catalog/2020047.

Walker, Juan Pedro. *Texas, Route De Nacogdoches Au Rio Trinidad, J. P. W (1806).* From the exhibit "Imagining Texas: An Historical Journey with Maps." Diboll, TX: The History Center, 1806. https://www.thehistorycenteronline.com/exhibits/imagining-texas-an-historical-journey-with-maps.

"Watersheds and Drainage Basins." Water Science School, US Geological Survey, June 8, 2019. https://www.usgs.gov/special-topics/water-science-school/science/watersheds-and-drainage-basins.

Weaver, Gustine Courson. "My Philip Nolan Scrapbook." Portal to Texas History. University of North Texas Libraries, 1942. https://texashistory.unt.edu/ark:/67531/metadc304851/.

Weber, David J. *Barbaros: Spaniards and Their Savages in the Age of Enlightenment*. New Haven, CT: Yale University Press, 2006.

Weddle, Robert S. "Archival and Archeological Research: Camino Real De Los Tejas and Texas State Parks." The Portal to Texas History. University of North Texas Libraries, August 2012. https://texashistory.unt.edu/ark:/67531/metapth638748/citation/?q=%22san+francisco%22#top.

Weddle, Robert S. "Cross and Crown: The Spanish Missions in Texas." Essay in *Hispanic Texas: A Historical Guide*. Edited by Helen Simmons and Cathryn A. Hoyt, 25–36. Austin: University of Texas Press, 1992.

Weddle, Robert S. "Spanish Exploration of the Texas Coast, 1519–1800." *Bulletin of the Texas Archaeological Society* 63 (1992): 99–122.

Weddle, Robert S. *The French Thorn: Rival Explorers in the Spanish Sea, 1682–1762*. College Station: Texas A&M University Press, 1991.

Weddle, Robert S., Donald E. Chipman, and Carol A. Lipscomb. "The Misplacement of Mission San Francisco De Los Tejas in Eastern Texas and Its Actual Location at San Pedro De Los Nabedaches." *Southwestern Historical Quarterly* 120, no. 1 (July 2016): 75–84. https://doi.org/10.1353/swh.2016.0044.

Wemple, Erik. "CNN Stays Silent on Rick Santorum's Comments about Native American Culture." Opinion. *The Washington Post*, April 27, 2021. https://www.washingtonpost.com/opinions/2021/04/27/cnn-stays-silent-rick-santorums-comments-about-native-american-culture/.

Wendels, Maria Anna. "French Interest in and Activities on the Spanish Border of Louisiana, 1717–1753." Master's thesis, University of California, 1914.

Weniger, Del. *The Explorer's Texas*. Austin, TX: Eakin Press, 1984.

West, Elizabeth Howard, and Marques de Altamira. "Bonilla's Brief Compendium of the History of Texas, 1772 (An Annotated Translation)." *The Quarterly of the Texas State Historical Association* 8, no. 1 (July 1904): 3–78. https://doi.org/http://www.jstor.org/stable/30242842.

Williams, Jeffrey M. *GIS Aided Archaeological Research of El Camino Real De Los Tejas with Focus on the Landscape and River Crossings along El Camino Carretera*. Nacogdoches, TX: Arthur Temple College of Forestry and Agriculture, 2007.

Woodrick, James V. "Chronology of Travels in Spanish and Mexican Texas, With a Brief Description and Reference to the Primary Sources." Unpublished manuscript, 2019.

Woodrick, James. *The Bidai, a Tribe of Native Americans in Texas*. Austin, TX: Self-published by author, 2018.

Worrall, Dan M. *A Prehistory of Houston and Southeast Texas: Landscape and Culture*. Fulshear, TX: Concertina Press, 2021.

Wright, Mrs. S. J., and J. M. Longmire. *San Antonio De Bexar: Historical, Traditional, Legendary*. Austin, TX: Morgan Printing, 1916.

INDEX

OTHER TITLES IN THE RED RIVER BOOKS SERIES

Beyond Redemption: Texas Democrats after Reconstruction
Patrick G. Williams

Planting the Union Flag in Texas: The Campaigns of Major General Nathaniel P. Banks in the West
Stephen A. Dupree

The Ahern Home of Texarkana
Doris Douglas Davis

The Great Southwest Railroad Strike and Free Labor
Theresa A. Case

The Red River Bridge War: A Texas-Oklahoma Border Battle
Rusty Williams

Trammel's Trace: The First Road to Texas from the North
Gary L. Pinkerton